WELLINGTON STUDIES V

WELLINGTON STUDIES V

EDITED BY

C.M.WOOLGAR

UNIVERSITY OF SOUTHAMPTON

2013

ISBN 978 085432 957 1

Contents

Preface

Wellington Studies V brings together eleven essays about the first Duke of Wellington, the wider context in which he served and of his life and times generally. Ten of the papers have their origins in the Fourth Wellington Congress, held at the University of Southampton in July 2010; the eleventh paper, by Clive Willis, is based on one given at the Portuguese embassy in London in 2008, to mark the bicentenary of the first stages of the Peninsular War — and other contributors have written their essays against the background of the commemorations that have taken place in England and on the Continent to mark the principal events of that conflict.

The Fourth Wellington Congress was attended by more than 100 delegates over a four-day period. Some 45 papers were given, with keynote lectures by Professor Alan Forrest of the University of York, on 'The Peninsular War: a French perspective'; Professor Bruce Collins of Sheffield Hallam University, on 'The wars of 1793–1815 and British militarism'; and Professor Chris Woolgar on 'Military communication and the Peninsular War'. There were outings to Stratfield Saye House and Portsmouth Dockyard, a reading of *The uniform of Marshal Wellington*, a one act comedy by August Friedrich Ferdinand von Kotzebue, and a concert by The Madding Crowd, specialists in the church and secular music of the English village bands and choirs of the eighteenth and nineteenth centuries.

This volume comes to fruition just as the next in the series of Wellington Congresses is about to take place, in April 2013, and plans are already in place for a further event in April 2015. It is a great encouragement to any conference organiser to have not only enthusiastic presenters of papers, and equally enthusiastic participants.

In producing this volume, I have incurred many debts. My first is to the contributors, who have written thoughtfully and engagingly about the first Duke from a broad range of perspectives. It is very pleasing to see Wellington's papers at Southampton — and related material in many repositories elsewhere — utilised to such good effect. The University of Southampton is grateful to the Marquess of Douro for his encouragement for work on the Wellington Papers, and for kindly allowing the Congress delegates to visit his home at Stratfield Saye. Many people have helped promote the Congresses, and I am grateful to my immediate colleagues Karen Robson, Sarah Maspero and Pearl Romans for assistance during the event, and to Dr Mark Brown, the University Librarian, for his support and encouragement.

Christopher M. Woolgar
Southampton
January 2013

Abbreviations

AW   Arthur Wellesley, first Duke of Wellington

BL   British Library

Bodl.   Bodleian Library, University of Oxford

NLS   National Library of Scotland

ODNB   Oxford Dictionary of National Biography ed. H.C.G.Matthew and B.Harrison (61 vols., Oxford, 2004)

RO   Record Office

SD   *Supplementary despatches and memoranda of Field Marshal Arthur Duke of Wellington, KG* ed. A.R.Wellesley, second Duke of Wellington (15 vols., London, 1858–72)

TNA   The National Archives, Kew

WD   *The dispatches of Field Marshal the Duke of Wellington, KG, during his various campaigns ... from 1799 to 1818* ed. J.Gurwood (new edition, 13 vols., London, 1837–9)

WP   University of Southampton Library, MS 61, Wellington Papers

CHAPTER 1

Britain and the wars of 1793–1815
Bruce Collins

I

How effective was Britain as a war-fighting power in the long struggle against France from 1793 to 1815? This obvious question has been answered in the recent literature from a variety of angles. We have learned a great deal about the strength of mobilisation and the power of British identity, perhaps stimulated by cultural affirmations of Britishness. We have seen how the religious differentiation of Britain from France added a deep ideological underpinning to long-standing resistance to the Catholic enemy across the Channel. We have been reminded of the importance of British economic and financial resilience and the vital importance of effective and high taxation to sustaining the war effort. We have been made aware of the determined conduct of the long wars by politicians who stuck to their commitments and the testing task they set themselves of resisting France. We have been guided to a proper appreciation of the scale and effectiveness of the administrative machinery and managerial skills dedicated to the war effort. And we now know how much the long wars were commented on, celebrated and commemorated in the visual arts, including the flour-ishing production of prints from the 1770s, in the theatre, in the production of artefacts, in imaginative literature, and, from the 1820s, in memoirs and histories.[1]

Assessing military efficiency is made difficult for the period 1793–1815 by three factors. First, there is a tendency to focus on French models and practices as the measure of military modernity. Jeremy Black has argued that the dominance of the French paradigm has distorted the assessment of other countries' divergent paths of military development in this period, paths which might have been more suitable ones for them to follow.[2] But even strong cases against the extent and depth of French military exceptionalism, as argued, for example by Paddy Griffith in 1998,[3] require the re-examination of continental methods of waging war, not a review of British military competence, which was never challenged by French mass invasion and a face-to-face struggle for national defence. The second factor, again stressed by Black, was the failure to articulate the particular requirements of British warfare in this period. As Black noted,

> Had the British armed forces in 1793–1815 been expected simply to maintain internal order, to preserve the integrity of the British Isles, defeat the French at sea, and conquer the French colonies, then … success would have been more rapidly achieved.[4]

But the British opted to work towards the containment and eventual overthrow of France as a great continental power and also engaged in extensive diplomacy and warfare in India.

This, in turn, relates to the third difficulty impeding analysis, the long-running debate over whether or not Britain's primary focus was on the continental commitment or its global interests. The debate concerns four alternatives: global/colonial interests as primary; global/colonial competition as a way of weakening France in Europe; the continental balance of power as primary; and the exercise of power on or over the European continent by pressing in upon its peripheries rather than by direct land assault. The last approach was given edge by the insistence in the 1930s that campaigning upon the periphery of continental Europe more accurately reflected British war-making capability than efforts to raise and deploy large armies for European continental fighting. One repost, elegantly sustained by Michael Howard, was that the ultimate strategic objective was always the European continental balance of power, and that only direct and large-scale intervention on the continent achieved British objectives.[5]

In the fullest recent development of the continental commitment argument for the Napoleonic wars Christopher Hall starts with the eighteenth century: 'Whatever the scale of the colonial conquests ... a very large proportion of Britain's military means was invariably tied down in European operations.' When war recommenced against France in 1803, 'the bankruptcy of the colonial strategy that had been part of policy in 1793–8' led governments to prioritise European expeditions, with 'British planners frequently being prepared to accept what amounted to a live-and-let live strategy with their enemies in colonial regions'. According to this interpretation, both the Caribbean and India remained secondary, with such local conquests being undertaken by troops already stationed in those regions, while naval forces and plans for power projection focused on the Low Countries and the Scheldt estuary, the Mediterranean and the Baltic. When the opportunity for British intervention in the Peninsula occurred, it offered numerous advantages: Spanish sea power was neutralised, French forces were tied down, British trade with the continent was re-opened, commercial opportunities in the Portuguese and Spanish empires became available, and British commitment to the war was demonstrated to continental allies.[6] Although the British sought to open up Latin American colonial trade, 'One striking feature of strategy in 1803–15 was that there was little emphasis on extending Britain's imperial position.' Much was done to defend the empire and its trade, but Napoleon's moves shaped British actions and those moves hinged on Europe.[7]

There are two dilemmas in this approach. One is the argument that any expeditions which were mounted outside Europe were manned by troops who were already in theatre, and were thus quite unlike eighteenth-century expeditions which were launched from Britain and on a far larger scale. This emphasis disguises the extent of colonial and Indian garrisoning. For example, in 1810

Lord Liverpool, as the responsible minister, is quoted as insisting that 10,000 troops would be the maximum assigned to the Leeward and Windward Islands. Yet in August 1813 there were over 15,000 troops there. Of course, war with the USA had broken out in 1812 and colonial defences had to be strengthened, but the strategic need for substantial colonial defences was neither limited nor inconstant.[8] In 1813 there were over 28,000 UK forces in India, Ceylon, Mauritius and the Cape of Good Hope. The Caribbean, the Bahamas and Bermuda absorbed 21,000, while nearly 18,000 troops were in the colonies which later became Canada. These colonial forces exceeded the total commitment of UK troops to the Peninsula of 60,000, and even that figure had only been attained relatively recently. The second contradiction is that the relative unimportance of colonial campaigning flowed from success in re-taking the colonies ceded back to the French and other powers at Amiens in 1802. The Cape was secured once more. Caribbean islands were invaded with, for example, the expedition to Martinique in 1809 absorbing 12,000 troops. In 1810, some 7,800 men were assembled from Halifax, Nova Scotia, from Barbados and other Caribbean islands, and from Portsmouth in order to attack Guadeloupe. In the same year, French islands in the Indian Ocean were seized, with the force sent to Rodriguez reaching 10,000 troops and about 70 ships, including transports. Using Indian sepoys as well as British troops based in India, some 12,000 troops, and 25 warships, were assembled at Malacca in June 1811 for an expedition to Java.[9] More extensively, Canada was defended in 1812–14 from American attacks. By March 1813, nearly as many general officers on active duty were assigned to the New World as to the Peninsular War: 40 to 49 out of a total of 204 generals on active service.[10] Moreover, Britain's greatest losses of manpower throughout 1793–1815 occurred in the Caribbean. Roger Norman Buckley has suggested a grand total of 100,000 deaths among British forces in the West Indies for the entire period 1793–1815, including 24,000 deaths among the seamen of Royal Navy and transport ships. The justification for this expenditure of manpower was that it both denied France its major source of overseas trade and added to Britain's commercial prosperity, which in turn assisted the British in raising loans with which to finance their own and their allies' war efforts.[11] But imperial activity during 1806–11 involved expeditions to the Cape, Buenos Aires, Montevideo, Egypt, Madeira and Senegal, as well an array of conquests in the Caribbean, the Indian Ocean and East Indies.[12]

Beyond these contradictions, there is ambiguity, if not confusion, over the definition of strategy. The word itself became current only in about 1800 and the formal and modern concept was quite alien to thinking and planning in this period.[13] A fundamental objective of British policy was the promotion and protection of trade and the sea routes essential to commerce. Much of the British distribution of military and especially naval forces was directed to the protection of trade and denial of French access to the Near East and to Mediterranean trade.[14] Thus in 1813, Hall shows that about 22,500 British troops were stationed at Gibraltar, Malta, Sicily, the Ionian Islands and through the Mediterranean.[15] The large garrison in Sicily was tasked with defending the island against French invasion, but also with guaranteeing that food produced in Sicily was available for Malta, which was critical as a naval base in the central Mediterranean. Holding the Ionian Islands enabled the British to prevent the French from advancing out of the Adriatic littoral into the eastern Mediterranean. The commitment to holding islands and bases in the Mediterranean was independent of British policy in the Peninsula. It flowed from the protection of British commercial interests in the Mediterranean and from a desire to contain French expansion in the eastern Mediterranean which had implications in the 1790s, at least in some British ministerial assessments, for the British position in India. In that sense the policy of containment had as much to do with trade and empire as with a continental commitment.

The argument against the primacy of the continental

commitment depends upon the seriousness of intent behind British global expansionism. Alan Frost has argued for the beginnings in this period of genuinely global thinking about British interests. The practical demonstration of this outreach came with the securing of key trading routes, protected by their attendant bases, to eastern Australia, via Penang on the northern routes and the Bass Straits, newly explored, along the southern route, as well as the quest for a north-west passage around northern Canada.[16] Such global activism, according to Christopher Bayly, went beyond the quest for commercial advantage. The period 1780–1820 became the decisive age of globalisation, with change driven by states and their greatly enhanced military and financial power:

> The slowly emerging patriotic and information-rich state… was quite suddenly inflated to a massive degree. It grew gargantuan in its ideological ambitions, its global reach, and its demands for military and civilian labour. Its appetites stretched across the continents. Before the impact of the steam engine or the electric telegraph had been registered, the European state, its soldiers and bureaucrats, became hyperactive in what was an 'axial age' for world history.[17]

This conclusion rests upon the degree of intent behind British expansionism.

Intent was certainly demonstrated in India, where the renewal of European warfare in 1803 coincided with an acceleration of war-making. The campaigning of 1803–5 and 1817–19 against the Marathas saw the British co-ordinate the operations of 100,000 troops across territories more extensive than those over which they operated in the Peninsula. The invasion of Nepal in 1815 involved 49,000 troops and an estimated 56,000 camp followers, in terrain which was highly challenging and where the British had not marched before. The forces under British command in India numbered 194,000 by 1814 and they were supplemented by troops supplied by allies. The Anglo-Portuguese army, the comparable force in the Peninsula, was about half the size of the armies directly controlled by the British in India. Moreover, the armies in the east continued to grow after 1815, unlike the British regular army. By the end of the campaigns against the Marathas and Pindari bands in 1816–19, the forces in India totalled 207,571. Of these, only 30,253 were Europeans, while 152,585 were Indian regulars and 24,741 were Indian irregular troops.[18] This steady increment of force had been applied to the subjugation of the Maratha princes and the substantial extension of British suzerainty over central India. Assessing British military achievements during the long wars against France makes no sense without reference to those extensive Indian conquests.

But that expansionism went beyond simply campaigning. Any continental commitment involved the concentration of strategic and therefore political and diplomatic calculation and negotiation upon Europe. Clearly foreign policy, as conducted by the Foreign Office, was dominated by Europe. But the Foreign Office, whose scope may be indicated by its operating 29 overseas missions in the late 1820s,[19] did not control or shape Indian policy. The governors general in Bengal managed a quite separate international relations system through residents or agents at the courts of Indian princes. The number of representatives grew rapidly after 1800, to over 30 by the late 1820s and a maximum of 47, some of them admittedly assigned to minor princes, in 1840.[20] Britain operated two foreign policy systems, with some residents in the Indian subcontinent by the 1800s becoming as important as ambassadors to European courts other than those accredited to Vienna, St Petersburg and perhaps Berlin.

II

The first, and easily overlooked, measure of British wartime effectiveness was home defence. This in turn depended upon a prosperous and growing economy whose most dynamic sector in the 1790s and 1800s was not manufacturing or commerce but, unsurprisingly in wartime, government spending.[21] Steady economic growth was sustained by a dynamic internal market. Although London-based pressure groups and ministers, perhaps influenced by the size and transparent presence of the Customs revenues, focused heavily on overseas trade, only about 10–15% of GNP was attributable to the external market, and only part of that market was European. Economic growth naturally made military recruitment difficult in a relatively high-wage economy. But manpower could be mobilised in times of threatened invasion. It was estimated in 1805 that the UK population included 3,750,000 men aged 17 to 55. Of these 386,621 were in the army and navy, a proportion higher than in the regular forces of France, Russia and Austria. But a further 415,151 men belonged to the volunteers and the sea fencibles. Thus, when fears of invasion peaked, some 22% of adult men served in some way in the army or navy, the vast majority being assigned to defensive duties.[22]

It would be wrong, however, to see militia duties and volunteering as devoid of challenge, given the Royal Navy's dominance of home waters. Part of the successful defence of the homeland involved maintaining a grip on Ireland, where rebellion was a recurrent possibility and became a ferocious reality in 1798. By the end of the year, the British deployed 100,000 troops in Ireland, including militia from Britain and volunteers raised within Ireland, in the largest concentration in the field of simply *British* soldiers — as distinct from sepoys in India or Portuguese and Spanish troops in the Peninsular War — anywhere during the long wars of 1793–1815. Although operations were essentially directed against civilians, the conflict was locally intense. In one year perhaps as many Irish people died violently as Americans died as a direct result of their revolution throughout 1775–82. Crushing an insurgency was scarcely the stuff of heroic military dreams, and almost anything the British have done in Ireland has become since the 1960s almost a matter of embarrassment to most British historians. But continental armies, including the French revolutionary armies in the bloodbath of the Vendée, were tasked with suppressing rebellions, and the rising in Ireland, supported (if feebly and fleetingly) by the French, challenged, or appeared to challenge, the very foundations of the British state.[23]

This challenge was not confined to the rebellion of 1798. Concerns for the security of Ireland recurred throughout the long wars. An extensive mobilisation of volunteers occurred in 1803, in response to fears of French invasion on the renewal of war. In 1807 there were occasional scares of a possible French invasion.[24] Sir Arthur Wellesley, as Chief Secretary for Ireland, argued for the establishment of a permanent naval station at Bantry Bay, for the construction of fortified depots for munitions and stores at strategic points in the country, for the strengthening of Dublin's defences, and for the maintenance of, and preferably an increase in, the existing level of regular troops in Ireland. He insisted that a French invasion would spark a general uprising and that '... Ireland, in a view of military operations, must be considered as an enemy country'. A French invasion, in Wellesley's judgement, was not prevented by British command of the seas — this was after Trafalgar — but by the condition of French naval resources, which might still enable France to land a force capable of pinning down 'a very large proportion of our army'.[25] Detailed plans were drawn up in late 1807 and early 1808 to establish procedures for mobilising volunteers in case of invasion.[26] Continuing resources were applied to maintaining or extending the Irish military establishment. In his review of Ireland's defences of May 1807, Wellesley had stressed the inadequacies of the army barracks. Some £274,000 was spent on barracks in Ireland in the four years 1809–12 inclusive, to accommodate 5,750 officers and men, with the capacity to add nearly 4,000 more in wartime. In total, some 103 permanent barracks and 213 temporary facilities were maintained in Ireland in May 1813. Ten of the permanent barracks could each accommodate at least 1,000 men and six of the temporary ones could house 500 men or more. But the majority of these 319 establishments took 50 or fewer men, an indication of the widespread police presence seen to be required.[27]

Even though it did not appear clear cut to Wellington in 1807–8, a French invasion of Ireland was prevented and the defence of the kingdom was maintained by the Royal Navy. A balance sheet of British effectiveness in war-making therefore gives pride of place to the Royal Navy and particularly to the first few years of the war. Much of the challenge flowed from the nature of the war itself. When hostilities started, Sir Charles Middleton, a former Comptroller of the Navy, predicted that the conflict would be 'a war against trade' because the French lacked the ships of the line they would need to launch great fleets against the British. Instead, they would organise numerous and active squadrons, 'keeping to their ports in readiness to attack British merchant ships at sea'. He there-fore urged the need for frigates and smaller warships to engage the French in the Channel and the North Sea. Noting that French attacks on British trade would encourage complaints from merchants and give ammunition to opponents of the war, Middle-ton stressed that the Admiralty would have to manage this threat.[28] Combating such a threat through blockade and frigate warfare shaped the professional thinking and practice of a generation of naval officers. Frigate victories in 1793 were thus vigorously celebrated and the first five years of the long wars saw the Royal Navy winning a decisive advantage. The French lost 125 warships of 22 guns or more in 1793–7, as against British losses of 38 similar sized warships. Among ships of the line, the French lost 35 against British losses of only 11, and these mostly to fire, accident and storms at sea rather than to enemy action. The British capture of Toulon and the destruction of so many French warships at their principal Mediterranean port was a stunning victory by any previous measure. The fact that the evacuation from Toulon has been criticised for making the triumph incomplete serves as a fine example of how the historiography of British warfare can qualify success by setting impossibly high expectations. These initial gains were further reinforced by the destruction of the French squadron at Aboukir Bay in 1798. By 1801, the British had also humiliated the Danish, Dutch and Spanish fleets.[29]

Naval power was instrumental in seizing many of the French West Indian colonies, although a good deal of unglamorous fighting on land had also to be done. The achievement was qualified by two factors. In terms of documenting purely British success, the most damaging French loss in the Caribbean was the collapse of its colony of Saint Domingue, and that was essentially brought about by the most successful slave rebellion in the era of New World slavery. The other qualification was the appalling death-rate among British soldiers sent to the West Indies in 1793–6. Yet, despite the loss of perhaps 38,000 men to disease, the British achieved what they had failed to secure in 130 years of recurrent warfare in the Caribbean.[30] The French empire there was overthrown and the principal source of French external trade was cut off, an achievement equalling or exceeding any contributions to victory made by West Indian expeditions launched by Britain earlier in the century.

Table 1. Ships of the line captured

	British taken by French	French and Spanish taken by British
War of the Austrian Succession, 1740–8	1	16
Seven Years War, 1756–63	1	27
Wars of the American Revolution, 1778–83	1	23 (including Dutch)

Naval success, however, was anticipated. The naval achievement in previous conflicts is set out in Table 1. This superiority was confirmed in 1793–4 when no fewer than 33 French ships of the line were taken, destroyed, scuttled, or lost, a blow exceeding the loss of nine ships of the line at Trafalgar.[31] By 1796–7 there was an assumption that the British would win naval victories against numerical odds. In August 1796, when he contemplated the prospect of a battle between Sir John Jervis' Mediterranean fleet of 22 ships of the line (in which he served) and a combined Franco-Spanish fleet of 35 ships of the line, Nelson wrote: 'I will venture my life Sir John Jervis defeats them; I do not mean by a regular battle, but by the skill of our admiral, and the activity and spirit of our officers and seamen.'[32] In 1797 Admiral Adam Duncan led 11 ships of the line out of Great Yarmouth as soon as he received news that the Dutch fleet had put to sea from the Texel, even cutting short the provisioning of his warships in the process. On the dark morning of 11 October, the British sighted 16 Dutch line and immediately gave chase. Following orders to make more sail, Duncan instructed his ships to pass through the enemy line, with each ship attacking its opponent and with the British van starting with the enemy rear. The action was intense, with Duncan reporting two days later, 'The carnage on board the two ships that bore the Admiral's flags has been beyond all description.'[33] In May 1799, in reviewing operations conducted by Admiral Lord Bridport, a member of the Admiralty Board noted that George III was 'perfectly convinced that 16 British ships were quite sufficient to beat 25 French'.[34] On 13 July 1799, off Majorca, Lord Keith confided to his sister that, with 31 ships of the line against the Franco-Spanish fleet's 43, he would be blamed by his friends if he failed to prevail in battle: 'If we meet, I do not think they will stand 20 minutes ...'[35] Again, in August 1799 when Vice-Admiral Andrew Mitchell attacked the French squadron at the Texel, he instructed his captains 'to attack the enemy as you arrive up', ignoring 'all etiquette of seniority'.[36] In August 1804, the King enthusiastically responded to intelligence that the French fleet might sail from Brest by expressing his confidence that Admiral William Cornwallis would 'cripple if not take possession of most of them'.[37] The Royal Navy was not only rampant, it was expected to be crushingly successful.

This effectiveness was achieved in fighting between small ships as well as in fleet actions. The opening four and a half years of the revolutionary wars witnessed 183 separate British naval actions at which enemy losses were inflicted. Those engagements resulted in 177 French ships being taken and 35 being destroyed, driven ashore or otherwise incapacitated. The British suffered losses of ships in only 22 of those encounters.[38] This imbalance in outcomes reflected the French navy's severe deficiencies in leadership, manpower, gunnery and time spent at sea. From June 1793 to January 1797, British warships captured or drove to destruction no fewer than 64 enemy frigates (nearly all French) in small-scale engagements. In contrast, they had taken or despatched only 23 French frigates in small-scale actions in the entire period 1778–83 (and only six Spanish frigates in the years 1779–82 in head-to-head engagements).[39] The widespread use of smaller warships meant that naval presence measured by the concentration of vessels of the line in particular fleets gives a misleading impression of naval commitments. Thus in 1809, the expedition to Martinique involved only six ships of the line, but nine frigates, 22 ships of 14 to 20 guns, and five smaller warships brought the naval contingent to 42 ships. The flotilla sent to Rodriguez in 1810 contained 70 ships, including transports, but only one ship of the line; the naval punch came principally from 11 frigates. In 1811, only four ships of the line sailed to attack Java, but 14 frigates and seven 18-gun ships sailed with them.[40]

Small squadrons could face hard fighting and challenging sailing. For example, an engagement between the *Boston* and the French *Embuscade* off the New Jersey coast lasting 100 minutes led to Captain G.W.A. Courtney and one lieutenant being killed, another lieutenant sustaining serious wounds, and the last remaining lieutenant, who had already been wounded, having to return to the upper deck to assume command.[41] During the operations upon Martinique in 1809, a squadron of five British ships of the line sought to prevent three French ships of the line and two frigates

from relieving that island. The French escaped from the adjacent
Saints islands by dividing their force and sailing in opposite
directions at 9.00 p.m. on 14 April, thereby taking advantage of
darkness. The French, who demonstrated excellent sailing skills,
were chased for 32 hours and one of their ships of the line was
closely engaged by a British ship of the line for over an hour, by the
end of which both ships were 'complete wrecks in their rigging and
sails'; while the British ship had become nearly 'unmanageable',
the French one was 'entirely so'.[42] This episode, relatively minor
in itself, indicated the extent of the challenges involved in uphold-
ing naval supremacy.

    Fighting spirit in the navy was fuelled by many induce-
ments, including prize money, professional pride and promotion.
As the wife of Captain Fremantle noted while on board her
husband's ship, reports of nearby Spanish ships led to officers
'building castles in the air' over the 'expectation of getting immense
riches'.[43] The value of captured ships to the officers and men of the
Royal Navy totalled about £30 million from 1793 to 1815, a sum
which might be compared with the £65 million granted in subsidies
to continental governments during that period.[44] Professional emulation and competiveness were fostered through the flourishing print
culture of the late eighteenth century. For example, the annual *Royal
Kalendar* (a generalist almanac) listed all Royal Navy officers with
their dates of first commission.[45] By the 1770s, all holders of
senior rank could be identified by seniority. From 1790 a private
publisher in London produced frequently and regularly updated
navy lists. These were pocket-sized and contained lists by seniority
of all officers, as well as lists of all Royal Navy ships including
their commanders' names if they were in commission. This
publication helped spur emulation, by disseminating information
about decisions made by the Admiralty courts on prize cases and
providing blank boxes to indicate French/Spanish/Dutch and British
ships lost, taken or destroyed since the book's publication.[46] During
the 1790s, more extensive attention was given in print to the

celebration of naval service and exemplary heroism. John Charnock published six volumes of *Biographia navalis*, whose entries offered extensive essays, sometimes of up to 10 pages, on their subjects. Descriptions of actions emphasised individual officers' daring and initiative. Of Lord Rodney, it was said,

> Even his most violent opponents must admit, that no commander ever yet lived who had the good fortune to achieve so many notable services or reduce and destroy, by the fleet under his immediate command, so great a number of his enemy's ships.

The entry on Lord St Vincent concluded that, if his blockading of a superior Spanish force in Cadiz had occurred centuries ago, any contemporary historian would stretch credulity 'to procure belief'. Sir Hyde Parker (whom Nelson overshadowed at Copenhagen) won praise for his exemplary gallantry.[47] Entries in such periodicals as the *Annual Register* and the *Gentleman's Magazine* added further to this cultural environment of emulative action and initiative. Public discourse did not invariably emphasise aggressive leadership: for example, a letter from Nelson's father to another clergyman found its way into the provincial press in early 1799 and described Horatio as having entered the wider world 'without fortune, but with a heart replete with every moral and religious virtue'. Despite all his physical injuries and continuing pain, he remained 'cheerful, generous and good', thereby exemplifying not merely professional competencies but desirable personal virtues.[48] While its timing proved unfortunate — within a year Nelson's affair with Emma Hamilton had exposed him to national lampooning — this characterisation illustrated an emphasis on the moral roots of military and naval success.

With renewed war against France from 1803, the Royal Navy maintained its superiority. By 1814 it had destroyed the medium-rank naval powers of Denmark, Holland and Spain, and hemmed in the French fleet. Success depended on vigorous administration. Following savage cutbacks in naval spending in

1801–4, a decisive contribution to naval achievement in 1805 was the work of the Admiralty in 1804–5 in applying new techniques to speed ship repairs. These measures, and closer co-operation with contractors, yielded an additional 20 ships of the line available for deployment in October 1805, when the total of these ships reached 103.[49] Success in fighting also resulted from superior gunnery. Although figures from French and Spanish ships are not available for comparison, the evidence from the *Victory* at Trafalgar points to more rapid British naval gunfire.[50]

Yet even the staggering victory at Trafalgar could not be decisive in the traditional military sense of that term.[51] It has long been stressed that the naval/strategic situation in the Mediterranean remained challenging long after Trafalgar, with the British Mediterranean fleet absorbed by the need to contain French naval activity from Toulon.[52] Moreover, the shipping lanes so vital to British commerce still needed assiduous protection. When the Île de France (later Mauritius) fell to the British, *The Times* claimed that the capture of 'this nest of pirates and piratical enemies' which 'so long permitted to send forth its swarms of cruisers to prey on our commerce' marked the end of the war at sea. Napoleon, it asserted, 'neither dares to send out a ship, nor, if he dared, has he a single port in the world to send it to'.[53] Yet such claims to overwhelming naval superiority do not sit readily with the need for Britain at the end of the long wars to deploy 140,000 seamen and marines to sustain 713 ships in commission.[54] Of the total expenditure on the army, navy and ordnance between 1793 and 1816 amounting to £830 million, perhaps £334 million went on the navy.[55] Those expenditures were evenly spread, with the Royal Navy reaching its peak size well after Trafalgar.

III

While British naval success during the French revolutionary wars was stunning, military effectiveness seemed dire, particularly with the military failure in the Low Countries, both in the intervention of 1793–5 and in the aborted expedition of 1799. The failure to break the French armies in 1793 and the retreat to Bremerleche during the winter of 1794–5 have been written off as symptomatic of British military incompetence. Yet the shortcomings of 1793 resulted partly from an indecisive allied high command, undermining operations which the British, contributing limited numbers to the allied armies, could support but not shape. The retreat in 1794 occurred because the German powers fielded 80,000 troops rather the 190,000 promised. It became something of a debacle because the British lost access to Antwerp and their re-supply routes, encountered a viciously cold winter and withdrew into areas of the Netherlands which were opposed to the House of Orange, in whose cause the British were fighting. Even so, the retreat between April 1794 and 14 January 1795 involved 3,300 operational casualties, 940 of them suffered at the fighting at Turcoing on 16–18 May; 434 of them, including many prisoners, fell to the French when a single regiment was trapped on the River Waal on 20 October. Holding together an army in retreat in severe winter conditions was never easy: an appreciation of the relative inefficiency or otherwise of the British forces in the Netherlands would benefit from more detailed comparisons with forces under similar pressures elsewhere. Ultimately an army can only seek to fulfil the tasks given it by the government. The British force despatched to the near Continent in 1793 was intended to be a minor addition to a concerted effort by the Austrians and the Prussians, backed by other German allies, to pummel the French revolutionary armies. Vienna and Berlin, distracted by partitioning Poland, failed to assign the requisite numbers to their western front.[56]

Despite the setbacks in the Low Countries, the British achieved major military successes in India during the 1790s. The British launched invasions of the state of Mysore in southern India in 1790–2 and 1799. They proved successful in 1792 and especially in 1799 when the well fortified and heavily defended city of

Seringapatam was stormed and taken and the regime of Tipu Sultan overthrown. This victory ended a sequence of dramatic British defeats, since the early 1780s had seen Mysore, the leading military power in India, attack British territories and defeat or constrain British armies. If most of the troops deployed were raised in India, some of the troops involved were from the regular British army, and much of the planning and leadership was provided by regulars.[57]

Of course, the Peninsular commitment from 1808–9 expanded Britain's contribution to the overall war effort. Hall makes an excellent case for the relative efficiency of the Peninsular campaign, stressing the sheer volume of its logistical underpinnings, the accessibility of Portugal and Spain to British shipping, and the availability of transport animals within Spain.[58] But the British breakthrough in Spain came when French forces there were depleted for the campaign against Russia; when they could not be reinforced after the heavy losses suffered in Russia; and the need, in 1813, for new conscripts to be assigned to defending the French position in central Europe against a revived coalition. As Rory Muir has stressed, however, if Napoleon had won in Russia in 1812, he would have had the resources to reinvigorate his armies in Spain.[59]

The long wars refined British fighting techniques. For example, the army gained considerable experience of campaigning, which was demonstrated by the senior battalion officers at Waterloo. Of 77 lieutenant-colonels and majors fighting with their regiments, some 39 had served in the Peninsula and a further seven had been overseas but not to the Peninsula. Just over 20% had served overseas in the 1790s or in Egypt in 1801. At least 15 had been in battle — and details of officers' service records are incomplete.[60] Joining with the navy, the army developed an impressive capacity to project power overseas. Take two examples of largely forgotten expeditions in 1810, one against Guadeloupe and the other against the Île de France in the Indian Ocean. About

6,500 troops were landed on Guadeloupe on 28 January. They had been shipped only a short distance from their forward base at Dominica; they were well supported with provisions and other supplies by the Royal Navy and by a leading merchant, who organised over 50 hired ships to convey the troops and their stores. The French capitulated within eight days, their 3,500 men depleted by the defection of local levies and by the loss of perhaps 600 sick and wounded. There was some sharp fighting, particularly where the Royal York Rangers lost 10% of their force in casualties in a flanking manoeuvre to turn a French defensive position. If the overall casualties were under 5%, they occurred in a very short campaign and before sickness and disease had a chance to kick in. The innovative features of this campaign, refined since the early 1790s, were the widespread use of light infantry troops, including the deployment of flank companies from a number of regiments, and the use of Africans from four West Indian regiments, who made up about one-quarter of the soldiers sent.[61]

The seizure of the Île de France in December 1810 depended more on naval competence. The forward base was at the island of Rodriguez, some 350 miles from the objective. Contrary winds prolonged the sailing time to six days. Reefs surrounding the island inhibited landing: 'every part of the leeward side of the island was minutely examined and sounded' before a protected stretch of the coast was identified. As at Guadeloupe, the landing was unopposed, and one might speculate whether the presence offshore of naval guns deterred enemy opposition. Captain Beaver was commended in his commanding admiral's public despatch for superintending 'the disposition and debarkation of the army'; he was qualified by previous experience for such work. The army commander added his praise for Beaver, while also noting the widespread admiration within the army for the way in which the seamen had brought forward the guns in very difficult country. Following limited resistance to the British advance, the French capitulated on relatively generous terms. At the cost of 166 casualties, the British had taken a strategically important island together with 269 ordnance, a 51-gun ship, five frigates, and 33 other ships, including gunboats and captured East India Company vessels being used as prison ships.[62] Isolated French island garrisons were no doubt soft targets by 1810, but the ease with which the British forced them to surrender also testified to the British mastery of the skills necessary for effective power projection. At the Île de France, both Vice-Admiral Albemarle Bertie and Major General John Abercromby made much in their official despatches of the close and effective co-operation between the army and navy. It may not have been entirely coincidental that Abercromby's father had in 1801 commanded the landing in Egypt and set a high standard of preparation for landings in enemy country and for inter-service collaboration. The experience of conflict bears out Mackesy's conclusion that while British amphibious operations in Europe failed, seaborne power succeeded outside Europe because enemy forces were denied supplies and reinforcements.[63] But it also demonstrates the effectiveness of inter-service co-operation.

IV

We have illuminated a number of contradictions concerning Britain's effectiveness in making war in 1793–1815. Security at home and in Ireland came at a high cost in military preparedness, in fighting in 1798 and in naval defence, while power was effectively projected in colonial campaigns and in India. But naval strength could not defeat France and success in the Peninsula in 1813–14 flowed in large part from severe reductions in the French armies in that theatre. The central limitations on British effectiveness against France were its failure to secure militarily significant or committed allies and its own restless ambitions as a global power.

The greatest inhibitor of British military efficacy abroad was the lack of reliable or enduring alliances. The military failures created by the alliance with Austria in 1793–4 have already been noted. Problems in working within any grand alliance, where allies' intentions and adhesion to a medium-term strategy remained doubtful, persisted throughout the period. When Wellington considered British strategic options in November 1812, he argued that the British would not drive the French from Spain, but that Napoleon would eventually 'give up Spain'. The British should then, he urged, advance into southern France rather than shift their forces to northern Europe. The British army would be too small in that theatre to operate on its own while the northern powers would use British resources and military assets for their own purposes and share only in 'their distresses'.[64] The challenge to British operations on the continent of Europe was therefore to find sustainable territorial bases which would be accessible from the sea, amenable to British political influence, open to the recruitment of local troops, defensible and easy to evacuate. Among numerous attempts made to secure alliances, it might be worth considering the difficulties faced in southern Europe, where the quest for continental springboards took its most dramatic and persistent form in Corsica in 1794–7, in Naples in 1798–9, in Portugal in 1808–14 and in Sicily in 1810–14. The tone was set by Corsica, of which Nelson complained in November 1796:

> Its situation was most desirable for us, but the generality of its inhabitants are so greedy of wealth, and so jealous of each other, that it would require the patience of Job, and the riches of Croesus to satisfy them. They say themselves they are only to be ruled by the ruling power shooting all its enemies and bribing all its friends.[65]

British efforts to establish firm alliances with and bases in Naples, Portugal and Sicily demonstrated the frustrating quest for sustainable collaboration with strategically usable and reliable European states.

One test of coherence in policy-making as well as courage in political action was British involvement in the Mediterranean. The British decision in late 1796 to withdraw from the

Mediterranean, precipitated by Spain's entry into the war on the French side, was unsuccessfully resisted by Henry Dundas, who argued for three quite distinct applications of British power. First, he insisted that the Mediterranean fleet of 30 ships of the line was quite strong enough to keep 40 French and Spanish ships of the line in their ports; if they put to sea, no one in Britain 'would entertain a moment's anxiety as to the result'. Second, he asserted that, by holding Gibraltar and getting access to the ports of Naples, the fleet could operate in the Mediterranean. Naples' significance as a source of supply increased with the closure to the British, under occupation by the French from June 1796, of Leghorn (Livorno), Tuscany's principal port and one with which British merchants had developed considerable trade in the eighteenth century. Naples thus became a substitute supply base. Thirdly, Dundas hoped that the eventual return of peace would encourage the Italian states to form

> some efficient confederacy for their general safety against that destruction in detail which the present war with France has brought upon them. If such a confederacy is possible to be formed, it can only be on the confidence that a British fleet in the Mediterranean would be the keystone of the whole.

This bold strategy fell down with Spencer's insistence that 30 ships were insufficient for the task if supplies could not be obtained from Naples, whose government was bound by a recent treaty with France to exclude British warships from its ports.[66]

In 1798–1800 Nelson made an alliance with the kingdom of Naples his regional priority. He had earlier indicated his views about an admiral's conduct in diplomacy when he informed his wife: 'Political courage in an officer abroad is as highly necessary as military courage.'[67] Nelson followed British government policy in using his victory at the Nile to encourage Naples and Austria into offensive operations against France in Italy. Yet Nelson's own drive became a substitute for the lack of energy at the Neapolitan court and in Vienna, as he admitted before he became too deeply entangled with the Neapolitan court: 'What precious moments the two courts are losing: three months would liberate Italy; this court is so enervated that the happy moment will be lost.'[68] When the government of Naples then undertook the campaign Nelson so desired, Sir William Hamilton, the minister to Naples, after praising Nelson's 'vigour and activity', informed the Foreign Secretary:

> When the particulars of what has passed rapidly in the last month in the kingdom of Naples, and in Tuscany, and when the real numbers of the enemy and of the troops that were, or might have been opposed to them, shall have been ascertain'd, it must astonish all Europe, but what is to be done when treachery, corruption and cowardice have infected the whole of His Sicilian Majesty's army and navy.[69]

The deficiencies of Naples, the kingdom of the Two Sicilies, as an ally were well known. The country chronically lacked resources. In October 1796, Jervis as Commander-in-Chief, Mediterranean, had noted that Naples suffered from the 'worst of exertion in the executive government, the delays occasioned by forms, and the miserable poverty of the country'.[70] Politically, ministers hoped that Naples would draw Austria back into the war, its influence, or supposed influence, over Vienna giving it, in Spencer's words, 'a rather higher rank in the scale of politics than on a superficial view might at first appear'.[71]

With Austria's entry into the war and with Austro-Russian military successes in northern Italy by May 1799, the British strategic need for Naples disappeared. St Vincent wrote in March 1799: 'no reliance whatever can be placed on Neapolitan officers, seamen, or soldiers; and the island of Sicily can only be preserved by British ships and troops.'[72] In mid-April, 1799, his second-in-command, Lord Keith, privately summarised reports he had received from Sicily: 'the king despised and insulted by the people, squeezing money off the public to hoard up and carry off to Trieste'

— presumably to finance possible exile within the Austrian empire.[73] The restoration of the Bourbons to their mainland possessions in the summer of 1799 brought no regeneration. As 1800 opened, the election of a new pope gave Sir William Hamilton an insight into Austrian policy. The Austrians wanted a new pope whose 'reliance should always be the protection of the court of Vienna'. They regarded Naples as too weak and too influenced by Britain to safeguard the papacy and fanned discontent in Rome against the Neapolitan government.[74] By May, the Neapolitan prime minister was reportedly concerned at the Austrian ministry's 'projects of aggrandisement' in Italy. The Queen of Naples, Maria Carolina, a Habsburg by birth, became so anxious about what the British minister described as the 'extremely unfriendly' court of Vienna that she visited the city of her childhood to counter the view held there that Naples was 'weak and defence-less'.[75] The mission seemed to fly in the face of the realities of Neapolitan government. The new British minister, Arthur Paget, noted in March 1800 that there appeared to be 'no shadow of any thing like order or regularity' in any department of state and that all ranks in the army were of poor calibre; indeed the officers were 'a most despicable set'. Some of the provinces were in 'a state of licentiousness and anarchy which will require time and rigour to compress'.[76] Another diplomat reported to Keith in May, 1800: 'The wretched state of the provinces is inconceivable.'[77]

Given Naples' deficiencies and the fast-moving shifts in the fortunes of war in 1799–1800, the British looked to other strategic bases in the Mediterranean, notably Minorca and Malta. Minorca became the centrepiece of British Mediterranean plans once it had been retaken from the Spanish in November 1798. The island's geographical position gave access to both Spanish and French coast-lines and their principal Mediterranean naval ports of Cartagena and Toulon. Its climate was healthy and its farms yielded plentiful vegetables. (It was also, one might add, not too large to control.) Port Mahon, famously taken by the British earlier in the century, stood on an exceptionally well protected and very long deep-water inlet. The large naval hospital, once it had been cleaned up by the British in 1798–9, provided 'altogether the completest thing of its kind in Europe'.[78] Lord St Vincent, as Commander-in-Chief in the Mediterranean, reassured Lord Spencer on 1 January, 1799: '… every nerve shall be stretched to maintain the island, which really is of infinitely greater importance than at any period of our naval history.'[79] By July, Lord Keith, as acting Commander-in-Chief in the Mediterranean, had brushed Naples aside,[80] whereas Nelson, locked into the strategic mindset prevalent nine or ten months earlier, insisted that Minorca was of secondary value to the kingdom of the Two Sicilies.[81]

The disputed significance of Minorca reflected the fluid conditions in which it was expected to be used as a platform for the projection of British power. When Keith returned to the Mediterranean in December, 1799, as Commander-in-Chief in succession to St Vincent, his main focus was on northern Italy and southern France. Immediate attention fell on Genoa and Masséna's besieged army there. Keith enforced a tight blockade, in co-operation with the Austrian land forces, to squeeze Masséna into the capitulation which occurred on 4 June 1800. The Admiralty also instructed Keith to pay 'strict attention' to the French Mediterranean naval port of Toulon.[82] For these operations Minorca proved invaluable as a base, but it also came into its own for use by the army. In May, when Henry Dundas, as Secretary of State for War and the Colonies, outlined campaigning options, he envisaged establishing 'a light moveable force' of 3,500–4,000 troops on Minorca. Acting with 'a superior fleet', this force could be deployed against the French in northern Italy and Piedmont or to assist the allegedly numerous royalists of southern France. It would be up to 'the professional judgement and military spirit' of army and navy commanders to decide how to act depending on 'local information, the wishes and conduct of the allies and the state of affairs upon the spot'.[83] If such planning collapsed with the Austro-Russian forces' defeat at

Marengo on 14 June 1800, the strategic momentum until that battle lay in northern Italy and, in part, depended on holding and using Minorca as a strategically positioned base. Confusion in defining the mission and priorities for the navy and army thus followed the sudden shifts in the continental alliance system and the inter-related fortunes of war. By the end of 1800, Austria was suing for peace with France and Russia was in the process of switching sides and joining France against Britain. Whereas the Austro-Russian coalition threatened in 1799 to re-take Italy, by October 1801 France had secured Russian acceptance for its expansionism in Italy and had forced Naples into becoming a subordinate ally.[84]

The third territorial base of significance was the Iberian Peninsula. Britain's problems with Spain have been well studied. Wellington was exceptionally critical of the capacity of the Cortes and its appointed government to co-ordinate any nationwide war effort, and equally sceptical about the regional authorities' ability to seize military opportunities and raise and maintain armies. His criticisms could be dismissed as the result of political prejudice against the liberal Cortes and a desire to shift responsibility for any failures in the conduct of his own campaign upon his allies. He certainly made no analytical allowance for the extent of social and governmental turmoil occasioned by the collapse of Charles III's enlightened absolutism in the 1790s and the upheavals of 1808. The church, the country's largest landowner, was assailed by land sequestration, the army was undermined by political crises, and the ruling elites were divided between at least four competing approaches to governance represented by Godoy and Charles IV, Ferdinand VII, the *afrancesados*, and liberal nationalists.

But there was something more serious to his critique than prejudiced self-interest. In reflecting during December 1810 on 18 months of campaigning, Wellington argued that 'defects in the national character' and 'the false principles' in managing the country's affairs meant that the Spanish had no army and no means of maintaining one even if they raised one. The real fight in Spain was conducted by guerrillas, and the British task was to tie down as much of the French army as possible to enable guerrilla operations to proceed behind the military frontline. Such an analysis helped to justify Wellington in not planning an advance into Spain; he claimed that an offensive might, for example, draw French forces out of Andalucia, but this would gain relatively little since the Spanish would not raise and deploy any new army from that province once it was evacuated by the French. Tying down French forces in Portugal during the winter of 1810–11 did as much good for the allied cause as an offensive into Spain would have achieved.[85] Wellington repeatedly complained of Spanish passivity and the lack of 'a vigorous system of government'.[86] This had two inter-related consequences, which he spelled out in May 1811 to the Secretary of State for War and the Colonies. First, sea power, apart from being a means of conveying the British and their equipment and food to the theatre of war and guaranteeing a means of evacuation from it if necessary, offered no opportunities to change the strategic balance in Spain. Any British landing on the coast of Spain would simply lead, in Wellington's view, to the Spanish locally demanding from the British money, arms, ammunition, clothing, food, forage, horsesand the means of transport. Moreover, they would not consult much with a British commander in the operations they might undertake. It therefore followed, secondly, that Portugal 'should be the foundation of all your operations in the Peninsula'. Controlling a secure base area and a Portuguese army of 30,000 paid for by a British subsidy provided the sort of co-ordinated approach so lacking in Spain.[87]

There were, however, severe problems in the relationship with Portugal. During the crisis provoked by Masséna's invasion in the winter of 1810–11, Wellington complained repeatedly about the lack of system within the Portuguese administration and the failure of the Portuguese authorities to co-operate with the British. Particular concerns affected the lack of billeting for British soldiers in Lisbon; extreme delays in paying the Portuguese army even when the British subsidy had been despatched; the failure of food supplies to reach the capital, despite good harvest yields; the incompleteness of evacuation measures in the face of the French advance into Portugal; and the failure to assemble more than 800, and sometimes more than 200, workers for the construction of defensive works around the capital, even though 4,000 men were needed and the funds were available from the British — at a time when Lisbon suffered from food shortages and a lack of jobs.[88] If such shortcomings scarcely amounted to fundamental flaws, cumulatively they persuaded Wellington that the Portuguese government needed to act on 'a more vigorous system' and that 'the war cannot be carried on as long as things remain as they are'.[89] Not only did the lack of pay, supplies and medical support for the Portuguese troops throw additional burdens upon the British, they provoked very high levels of desertion, thereby corroding one of benefits derived from Portugal. Wellington attributed these problems to three socio-political causes. He claimed that 'an unconquerable love of their ease' weakened the Portuguese population's commitment to the war effort.[90] This was accentuated, secondly, by the commercial profits made in Lisbon and Oporto as a result of the war and the 'scandalous' failure of the mercantile classes to pay more than trivial amounts of tax. Only 'a more equal and just collection of the income tax on the commercial property', especially in 'those large and rich cities' of Lisbon and Oporto, would furnish the government with sufficient revenues.[91] But the third problem was the absence of government will to reform and to energise the population: 'The magistrate will not force the inhabitants to adopt a measure, however beneficial to the state and himself, which will disturb his old habits; and the government will not force the magistrate to do that which will be disagreeable to him and to the people: thus we shall go on to the end of time.'[92] These concerns continued, with Wellington in November 1812 admonishing the principal minister with whom he dealt, Dom Miguel Forjaz, over delays in payments from the Portuguese government for troops and for transport, despite the payment of the British subsidy.[93]

The issues of effective government raised by Wellington were similar in outline to those raised by critics of the kingdom of Naples in the late 1790s. Wellington went further in identifying tax avoidance as a problem, reminding us that exceptionally high and efficient taxation provided one of the foundations of British success in these long wars.[94] But the key problems obviously concerned the sense of purpose and direction of the government and the ability of the government to mobilise and sustain an army. He insisted that the Portuguese needed to attend far more assiduously to the public good: '... the higher classes of society ... must be forced to perform their duty'.[95] Wellington made little effort to understand the pervasive sense of contingency which afflicted the Portuguese regime, the result of the French occupation of 1808, the threat of renewed occupation, and the exile of the royal family and court to Brazil. But the failed politics which he described was surely an important reality, even if he approached it with a stern indifference to its roots.

The fourth case of struggling alliances concerned Sicily. The British under Lord William Bentinck tried to tackle the underlying lack of political responsibility and responsiveness which had been associated with the Neapolitan regime. Bentinck went far beyond Wellington in establishing a constitution, as well as raising an army, but his experiment crumbled when he left for campaigning in eastern Spain in May–October 1813 and ended in 1814 after Bentinck had fallen back on pro-consular authority. But Bentinck also envisaged a nationalist upsurge on the Italian mainland, directing his attention to central Italy, Genoa and the north while trying to bring Murat's kingdom of Naples into diplomatic play. He argued from 1811 for British intervention in Italy and even led a small expeditionary force, quite against instructions from London, in early 1814.[96] Such strategic visions were dismissed by Wellington when he considered the idea of British involvement in

Italy: '… I have never seen any ground on which I would venture even to think of a military operation in that country.'[97] Collingwood, as Commander-in-Chief of the Mediterranean fleet, had come to the same conclusion about a general Italian rising in the autumn of 1808: 'there is no stuff to work upon there — the people are licentious, the nobles unprincipled. … It is a superior army alone that can effect any change, or maintain it. … They have not the Spanish spirit.' This verdict was delivered after a lively debate had occurred in London over the merits of an Italian or Spanish strategy, with some Whigs confident in July that the Spanish would win their freedom 'by their own energy' and that an Italian rising deserved British aid.[98] There was also the drawback that Austria had long opposed any expansion of British influence at the important port of Genoa or from there into northern Italy.[99] Few ministers in London had condoned the Italian opening in 1812 and Castlereagh saw national uprisings as adjuncts to formal military power, which should be exercised by properly constituted rulers.[100]

Although British critiques of the governments of Naples, Spain and Portugal may have been in part self-serving and aimed at directing blame for military shortcomings to allied governments, the British also confronted allies' defects in governance which gravely impeded coherent or long-term military and naval planning. Britain lacked the ability to mount effective campaigns on the Continent not because its military were incompetent or inefficient, but because the major continental powers proved incapable of either adhering to agreed objectives and or delivering armies to beat the French. Forced to rely for alliances upon minor powers, the British had to work with allies they did not trust and whose political and governmental systems were fractured or broken by the upheaval in international relations, turmoil in domestic politics and uncertainty, if not unrest, in society which the French Revolution and Napoleonic expansionism unleashed upon much of Europe. If British foreign policy in the 1790s especially, but also in the 1800s, launched too many initiatives which proved to be unsustainable, that failure of consistency and continuity mirrored the major European powers' rapidly shifting priorities and alignments. If military interventions in Europe proved so frequently inglorious, they did so because they were not underpinned by committed allies' full co-operation and sustained support.

V

For proponents of the continental commitment, it could be stressed that Britain in 1794 devoted 200,000 men to the navy and to the army in Europe.[101] But the role of the bulk of those men, in the Royal Navy, was to defend Britain itself and her international trade. At no time during the long wars did a British government despatch a large proportion of its land forces to fight on the Continent. British military effort, if not British diplomacy or British naval blockading, concentrated on home defence, the colonial empire, protecting bases along commercial routes and expansion in India. The army's task in Europe was to assist continental allies and find ways of affecting the balance of military power in operations largely planned and executed by allies. In the Peninsula, the British military presence depended upon the recruitment of the Anglo-Portuguese army and the continued attrition of French manpower through Spanish armed resistance. At Waterloo, Napoleon aimed to crush the allied flank by defeating the British; the only reason for Wellington's stand at Waterloo was the agreed arrival of the Prussian army. Of the grand total of £65,830,000 in continental European subsidies granted from 1793 to 1815, about £20 million were voted in 1814–15 in the final allied push of those long wars, and nearly half came in the last five years of the conflict.[102] At the level of grand strategy, one of the persistent contradictions in British practice has been the tension between the concentration on Europe in terms of great fleet operations and diplomacy, and the engagement of much of the frigate navy and a large portion of the army in the wider world.

Strategic decision-making of this period was shaped by three factors. First, the continental powers interacted in fluid and dynamic ways, seeking to protect or advance their interests in many different parts of the Continent. This made it extremely difficult for the British to establish firm and enduring alliances. After 1795, there was so little trust between Britain and the principal German powers, Austria and Prussia, that alliances were dependent on contracts underwritten more by cash than by shared and durable diplomatic objectives. The three allies which were secured over time — Naples with its island of Sicily, Portugal and Spain — were Catholic absolutisms with few cultural or political sympathies with Britain. In the Spanish case, there was a fractured polity desperate for external support, but unwilling to accede to the military requirements of its external supporter. Portugal and Spain also had colonial commercial interests at odds with British international trading objectives. Second, British behaviour typically combined a defence of British possessions and interests, and a denial of French access to overseas assets: containment rather than overthrow was the watch-word. Third, British projection of power on land depended on having secure enclaves. Sea power gave the British great flexibility, but could not be translated into victory on land without a considerable military presence and secure access to extensive areas under British or allied control, to ensure supplies of food, forage, and manpower.

An answer to the question of whether or not Britain was an effective power lies not in a debate between continentalism and the globalists, but in an acknowledgement of their inter-relationship. One of the principles guiding the Addington ministry in 1802 was the overwhelming desire to create stability in Europe, to which end colonies acquired since 1793 were surrendered at Amiens. In 1814–15 no such placatory self-denial was necessary and colonial conquests were retained. In 1802, British India had just subjugated Mysore, but embarked on an intense and unpredictable struggle with the great Maratha princes. By 1815, the empire from the

Cape of Good Hope eastwards was transformed and central India subordinated to British control. Beyond continental Europe, Britain was a restless power, not an adherent of the status quo or of balance. At the heart of Britain's international position was the contradiction that its own restlessness and interventionism overseas contributed to a dispersal of both naval and military resources which incapacitated it from concentrating enough power in Europe to challenge the French on land. On the one hand, the wildly fluctuating policies and alliances pursued by the continental powers made it impossible for Britain to apply consistent and major support to war on the Continent until 1812–15. On the other, Britain suffered not from a lack of military efficiency, but from a dispersed and growing appetite for trade, influence and power, which could only be sustained through war and the bases and resources afforded by territorial, if extra-European, conquest.

References

[1] A selection of the leading works on these topics would include: Linda Colley *Britons: Forging the nation, 1707–1837* (London, 1994); J.E.Cookson *The British armed nation, 1793–1815* (Oxford, 1997); N.A.M Rodger *The command of the ocean: a naval history of Britain, 1649–1815* (London, 2004) pp. 575–83; John Ehrman *The younger Pitt: the consuming struggle* (London, 1996); Rory Muir *Britain and the defeat of Napoleon 1807–1815* (New Haven, 1996); Martin Daunton, 'The fiscal-military state and the Napoleonic wars: Britain and France compared' in *Trafalgar in history. A battle and its aftermath* ed. D. Cannadine (Basingstoke, 2006) pp. 18–43; Roger Knight and Martin Wilcox *Sustaining the fleet 1793–1815. War, the British navy and the contractor state* (Woodbridge, 2010); Marianne Czisnik *Horatio Nelson. A controversial hero* (London, 2005); Holger Hoock *Empires of the imagination. Politics, war and the arts in the British world, 1750–1850* (London, 2010).

[2] J.M.Black, 'Wellington in the context of long-term military history' in *Wellington Studies II* ed. C.M.Woolgar (Southampton, 1999) pp. 26–47.

[3] Paddy Griffith *The art of war of Revolutionary France 1789–1802* (London, 1998) pp. 172–4, 199–205, 230–4, 237–8, 278–84. An excellent discussion is T.C.W.Blanning *The French Revolutionary Wars 1787–1802* (London, 1996) pp. 116–28.

[4] Black, 'Wellington', p. 30.

[5] Michael Howard *The continental commitment* (London, 1972).

[6] Christopher Hall *British strategy in the Napoleonic war, 1803–15* (Manchester, 1992) pp. 77–9, 81, 83–6, 90–5.

[7] Hall, *British strategy*, pp. 79–80, 95, 97–8.

[8] Hall, *British strategy*, pp. 77–8, 185–6, 189–90, 212.

[9] Hall, *British strategy*, p. 212; William Laird Clowes *The Royal Navy: a history* (7 vols., London, 1897–1903) v, pp. 283, 294, 298.

[10] Bruce Collins *War and empire. The expansion of Britain 1790–1830* (Harlow, 2010) p. 472.

[11] Roger Norman Buckley *The British army in the West Indies. Society and the military in the Revolutionary age* (Gainesville, 1998) pp. 271, 276–8.

[12] A list is in Rodger, *Command of the ocean*, pp. 602–4.

[13] N.A.M.Rodger, 'Sea-power and empire' in *The Oxford history of the British empire. Vol. 2, The eighteenth century* ed. P.J.Marshall (Oxford, 1998) pp. 169–83, especially p. 171.

[14] P.Mackesy *The war in the Mediterranean, 1803–1810* (London, 1957) pp. 391, 395.

[15] Hall, *British strategy*, p. 212.

[16] Alan Frost *The global reach of empire. Britain's maritime expansion in the Indian and Pacific Oceans 1764–1815* (Carlton, 2003) pp. 235–67, 313–14.

[17] C.A.Bayly *The birth of the modern world 1780–1914* (Oxford, 2004) p. 83.

[18] *Parliamentary Papers*, House of Commons, 1819 (184).

[19] Peter Jupp *British politics on the eve of reform: the Duke of Wellington's administration 1828–30* (Basingstoke, 1998) p. 111.

[20] Michael H. Fisher, 'Indirect rule in the British empire: the foundations of the residency system in India (1764–1858)', *Modern Asian Studies* 18 (1984) pp. 393–428, especially pp. 400–2.

[21] N.F.R.Crafts *British economic growth during the Industrial Revolution* (Oxford, 1985); Francois Crouzet, 'The British economy at the time of Trafalgar: strengths and weaknesses', in *Trafalgar in history*, ed. Cannadine, pp. 7–17.

[22] J.E.Cookson *The British nation armed 1793–1815* (Oxford, 1997) p. 95.

[23] Collins, *War and empire*, pp. 109–34.

[24] AW to Lord Hawkesbury, 23 Apr 1807, WP1/167/18.

[25] AW to Lord Hawkesbury, 7 May 1807, WP1/167/45.

[26] AW to Lord Hawkesbury, 9 Nov 1807, WP1/178/16; Lord Castlereagh to AW, 28 Dec 1807, WP1/179/132; Duke of Richmond to AW, 5 Jan 1808, WP1/187/34; AW to Lt. Col. Gordon, 19 Feb WP1/192/76.

[27] 'Accounts relating to Barracks in Ireland', *Parliamentary Papers*, House of Commons 1812–13 (237), 710–19.

[28] 'Memorandum, 1793' in *Letters and papers of Charles, Lord Barham* ed. Sir John Knox Laughton (3 vols., London, 1907–11) ii, pp. 365–7.

[29] Clowes, *Royal Navy*, iv, pp. 548–58.

[30] The classic account is Michael Duffy *Soldiers, sugar, and seapower: British expeditions to the West Indies and the war against Revolutionary France* (Oxford, 1987).

[31] Clowes, *Royal Navy*, iv, pp. 114–15.

[32] *The dispatches and letters of Vice Admiral Lord Viscount Nelson* ed. Nicholas Harris Nicholas (7 vols., London, 1997), ii, p. 246.

[33] Earl of Camperdown *Admiral Duncan* (London, 1898) pp. 199, 201–6, 217.

[34] *Private papers of George, second Earl Spencer, First Lord of the Admiralty, 1794–1801* ed. Julian S.Corbett and H.W.Richmond (4 vols., London, 1913–24) iii, pp. 73–4.

[35] Keith to Mary Elphinstone, 13 Jul 1799, *The Keith papers: selected from the papers of Admiral Lord Keith* ed. W.G.Perrin and Christopher Lloyd (3 vols., London, 1927–55) ii, p. 40.

[36] Duncan to Spencer, 28 Aug 1799, *Private papers of... Earl Spencer*, iii, pp. 179–80.

[37] *The later correspondence of George III* ed. A.Aspinall (5 vols., Cambridge, 1968) iv, p. 223.

[38] Clowes, *Royal Navy*, iv, pp. 548–62.

[39] Clowes, *Royal Navy*, iv, pp. 552–60.

[40] Clowes, *Royal Navy*, v pp. 283, 294, 298.

[41] William James *A naval history of Britain* (6 vols., London, 1847) i, pp. 99–102.

[42] *The Times*, 24 May 1809.

[43] *The Wynne diaries. The adventures of two sisters in Napoleonic Europe* ed. Anne Fremantle (Oxford, 1982) pp. 271–2.

[44] Richard Hill *The prizes of war. The naval prize system in the Napoleonic Wars, 1793–1815* (Stroud, 1998) p. 246; J.M.Sherwig *Guineas and gunpowder: British foreign aid in the wars with France, 1793–1815* (Cambridge, MA, 1969) p. 345.

[45] *The Royal Kalendar... for the year 1775* (London, n.d.) pp. 145–58.

[46] For example, *Steel's original and correct list of the Royal Navy February 1801* (London, 1801) pp. 42–5.

[47] John Charnock *Biographia navalis or impartial memoirs of the lives and characters of the officers of the navy of Great Britain from the year 1660 to the present time* (6 vols., London, 1794–8), v, p. 228; vi, pp. 415–16, 523–6. Some 135 biographies, mostly hagiographic, of British naval men were published in Britain in 1830–1914; the Christian theme was important until the 1850s, while toughness and the will to succeed figured prominently in the late nineteenth century. C.I.Hamilton, 'Naval hagiography and the Victorian hero' *Historical Journal* 23 (1980) pp. 381–98.

[48] *The Idris or the Sheffield Advertiser for the Northern Counties*, 21 Mar 1799.

[49] Roger Knight, 'The fleets at Trafalgar: the margin of superiority', in *Trafalgar*

in history, ed. Cannadine, pp. 61–77.

[50] Knight, 'Fleets at Trafalgar', pp. 66–7.

[51] There is an excellent brief discussion by N.A.M. Rodger, 'The significance of Trafalgar: sea power and land power in the Anglo-French wars', in *Trafalgar in history*, ed. Cannadine, pp. 78–89.

[52] Mackesy, *War in the Mediterranean*, pp. 16, 297–9, 359, 379.

[53] *The Times*, 14 Feb 1811.

[54] Michael Lewis *The navy in transition 1814–64: a social history* (London, 1965) pp. 66, 69.

[55] Sherwig, *Guineas and gunpowder*, p. 354; Hill, *Prizes of war*, p. 246.

[56] Collins, *War and empire*, pp. 72–9.

[57] Collins, *War and empire*, pp. 155–92.

[58] Howard, *Continental commitment*; Hall, *British strategy*, pp. 32–6.

[59] Muir, *Britain and the defeat of Napoleon*, p. 216.

[60] The names and career information are drawn from the regimental lists which comprise Charles Dalton *The Waterloo roll call* (London, 1971).

[61] *The Times*, 17 Mar 1810, p. 3.

[62] *The Times*, 13 Feb 1811, p.1; 16 Feb 1811, p. 2.

[63] Mackesy, *War in the Mediterranean*, pp. 385–9.

[64] AW to Bathurst, 7 Nov 1812,*WD*, ix, p. 542.

[65] Vincent, *Nelson*, p. 174

[66] Dundas to Spencer ?, 31 Oct 1796; Spencer to Dundas, 31 Oct 1796; *Private papers of... Earl Spencer*, i, pp. 321–33.

[67] Nelson to Mrs Nelson, 24 Jul 1795; *Dispatches and letters*, ed. Nicholas, ii, p. 59.

[68] Edgar Vincent *Nelson. Love and fame* (New Haven, 2003) p. 299.

[69] Hamilton to Grenville, 7 Jan 1799, TNA FO 70/12.

[70] Edward Brenton *The life and correspondence of John, Earl of St Vincent* (2 vols., London, 1838) i, pp. 254, 498.

[71] Vincent, *Nelson*, p. 300.

[72] Brenton, *Life and correspondence of ... St Vincent*, i, p. 498.

[73] Keith to Mary Elphinstone, 19 Apr 1799, *Keith papers*, ii, p. 37.

[74] Hamilton to Grenville, 16 Jan 1800, TNA FO 70/13.

[75] Paget to Grenville, 12 May 1800, TNA FO 70/14.

[76] Paget to Grenville, 25 Mar and 12 May 1800, TNA FO 70/14.

[77] Lock to Keith, 30 May 1800, *Keith papers*, ii, pp. 172–3.

[78] Brenton, *Life and correspondence of ... St Vincent*, i, p. 485.

[79] St Vincent to Spencer, 1 Jan 1799, *Private papers of... Earl Spencer*, iv, p. 35.

[80] Keith to Nelson, 15, 16, 24 July 1799, *Keith papers*, ii, pp. 50–4.

[81] *Private papers of... Earl Spencer*, iii, p. 91.

[82] *Keith papers*, ii, pp. 59–60. The challenges for allied co-operation are well

illustrated in Kevin D.McCranie *Admiral Lord Keith and the naval war against Napoleon* (Gainesville, 2006) pp. 80–92.

[83] *Keith papers*, ii, pp. 87–9.

[84] Paul W.Schroeder *The transformation of European politics 1763–1848* (Oxford, 1994) pp. 210–22.

[85] AW to Liverpool, 21 Dec 1810, *WD*, vii, pp. 56–60 .

[86] AW to Henry Wellesley, 23 Dec 1810, *WD*, vii, pp. 66–7.

[87] AW to Liverpool, 7 May 1811, *WD*, vii, pp. 524–5.

[88] AW to the Prince Regent of Portugal, 30 Nov 1810; AW to Charles Stuart, 22 Dec 1810, 31 Dec 1810, 8 Jan 1811, 13 Jan 1811, 9 May 1811; AW to Liverpool, 8 May 1810 (two letters); *WD*, vii, pp. 6–17, 62–3, 91–3, 122,140, 535–40.

[89] AW to Charles Stuart, 22 Dec 1810, 27 Dec 1810, *WD*, vii, pp. 63, 79.

[90] AW to Charles Stuart, 3 Jan 1811, *WD*, vii, p. 102.

[91] AW to Charles Stuart, 6 May 1812, *WD*, ix, p. 123.

[92] AW to Charles Stuart, 3 Jan 1811, *WD*, vii, pp. 102–3.

[93] AW to Dom Miguel Forjaz, 14 Nov 1812, *WD*, ix, pp. 552–5.

[94] Daunton, 'The fiscal-military state', pp. 18–43.

[95] AW to Charles Stuart, 11 May 1810, *WD*, vi, p. 103.

[96] John Rosselli *Lord William Bentinck. The making of a liberal imperialist 1774–1839* (Berkeley, 1974) pp. 147–53, 160, 167–77.

[97] AW to Bathurst, 7 Nov 1812, *WD*, ix, p. 543.

[98] E.A.Smith *Lord Grey 1764–1845* (Oxford, 1990) p. 169; Mackesy, *War in the Mediterranean*, pp. 286, 288.

[99] Piers Mackesy *War without victory: the downfall of Pitt, 1799–1802* (Oxford, 1984) p. 115.

[100] Rosselli, *Lord William Bentinck*, p. 169.

[101] Sherwig, *Guineas and gunpowder*, p. 347.

[102] Sherwig, *Guineas and gunpowder*, pp. 345, 354.

CHAPTER 2

Sir Arthur Wellesley as a 'special adviser': politics and strategic planning, 1806–8
Martin Robson

The aim of this paper is to delve into Sir Arthur Wellesley's 'bridging' period between his successful career in India and the decision to commit British troops, initially under his command, to Iberia in June to July 1808. When dealing with these years, the orthodox Wellington biographies recount that in September 1805 Wellesley arrived back in England, had a brief meeting with Nelson, before commanding a brigade in an abortive British expedition to northern Germany. In January 1806 he dabbled in politics in defence of his elder brother, the Marquess Wellesley, and became MP for Rye, then Mitchell in Cornwall, and then, in 1807, for Newport on the Isle of Wight. In April 1806 he married Kitty Packenham. In April 1807 he became Chief Secretary for Ireland under the Portland ministry and played a significant role in the 1807 expedition to Copenhagen. Then, in the summer of 1808, Sir Arthur was engaged in preparing an expedition at Cork to sail for Venezuela or Mexico, to fulfil the misguided and 'hare-brained' schemes of politicians who did not know their business.[1]

When the 'hare-brained' South American schemes put forward by politicians are assessed by historians it is usually to prove that Wellesley brought some common sense to strategic planning. For example, Longford argues that 'Canning had a scheme for bringing in the New World to defeat the tyrant of the Old. Luckily, Wellesley was brought in. He was required to co-operate with the emissary of Venezuelan revolutionaries, General Miranda, in planning an insurrection in his native Spanish America against Napoleon's ally, Spain. Wellesley at once pointed out some of the project's more disastrous flaws.'[2] With regard to inspiring South America to rise up against the Spanish yoke, Ward noted that 'it was Wellesley who pointed out the dangerous implications of such a policy, and quietly demolished a crack-brained scheme to attack Central America simultaneously from Ireland and Madras.'[3] For Corrigan, Wellesley 'turned down the proposed command of an expedition to Mexico, via Singapore, a somewhat far-fetched whimsy that never actually happened'.[4] Holmes even raises a discussion between Pitt and Wellesley in late 1805 in which Sir Arthur 'argued against one especially hare-brained scheme for mounting a two-pronged attack on the Spanish colony of Mexico, with one expedition striking out from Jamaica and the other moving from Madras by way of the Philippines and Australia'.[5] For Fortescue, one plan from early 1807 and 'written before the British troops had left Rio de la Plata, is a scheme for an attack on Mexico which must, I think, have been imposed upon him by the wild brain of William Windham ... In fact these papers of Wellesley's must not all of them be taken too seriously.'[6]

Wellesley's commonsense input into strategic planning is sometimes illustrated by his oft-quoted assertion to Stanhope in 1835 that he 'always had a horror of revolutionising any country for a political object. I always said, if they rise up themselves, well and good, but do not stir them up; it is a fearful responsibility.'[7] Thankfully, so historians would have us believe, all this nonsense from misguided politicians is brought to a halt with the decision to send Sir Arthur to Iberia in June 1808.

In fact, Wellesley had been specifically tasked by the government to inform Miranda that Britain would no longer have anything to do with his plans. So why was Wellesley selected to do that?[8] The problem is that by dismissing those 'hare-brained schemes' many historians have habitually overlooked this important part of Wellesley's career when, during the period 1806–8, he was selected by two successive governments to provide expert advice on a number of military operations, of which plans for British intervention in Spanish America are perhaps the most vexed. Hence, Wellesley, acting at the civil-military interface, played an integral role in the formulation of strategic plans and helped to fuel British interest in South America.

The catalyst

On 12 September despatches from Sir Home Riggs Popham, RN, reached Portsmouth detailing the capture of Buenos Aires. Once ashore, the news was conveyed to London in a carnival procession: eight wagons containing around a million dollars in hard cash (obtained from the Viceroy) were escorted by 30 sailors from HMS *Narcissus*, a Royal Marine band provided suitable martial music and, so no one could miss the spectacle, a salute was fired at every major town on the route.[9] Popham had provided an inkling of what he planned in his despatches from the Cape (and a stop-over at St Helena) which had arrived at the Admiralty on the morning of 24 June,[10] though nobody in government was exactly sure what he was up to.[11]

Spanish America had been on the British political agenda for some time. It was believed by many in Britain that the decrepit, yet wealthy Spanish empire was ripe for commercial exploitation. There had been plans for British attacks against Venezuela, Chile and Buenos Aires itself, alongside more circumspect plans to assist South American patriots to throw off the shackles of Spain, and even plans to ship Spanish dollars to Britain, but nothing material had become of them.[12]

The Ministry of All the Talents had under consideration some vague and ill-defined plans for Spanish America.[13] Now it was different. Arriving at a time of French military dominance on the Continent, with the Austrians, Russians and Prussians defeated in 1805–6 and Napoleon's blockade excluding British goods from Europe, Popham's despatches presented the government with much opportunity. The government response seemingly sent a mixed message: naturally, Popham was recalled to give an account of his actions, yet, on 26 June, it was decided a reinforcement of 2,000 men under Sir Samuel Auchmuty would be sent to Buenos Aires (though their departure was delayed until 12 October), thereby granting official endorsement to British operations in Spanish America.[14]

The question of how to make best use of Popham's initial intervention and the reinforcements destined for the region was already on ministers' minds. On 11 September the Talents' Secretary of State for War and the Colonies, William Windham, wrote to his cousin and the leader of the ministry, Lord Grenville. The object, Windham noted, was not to create a revolution against Spanish rule, but rather to take possession of strategic points in order to establish a British presence leading to 'a mild and gradual' process whereby the entire continent would eventually fall under British influence. Moreover, if the Spanish Americans did turn against the mother country, Britain would be in a position to provide assistance. Finally, but perhaps most importantly, a strong British presence would hopefully prevent the French from establishing themselves in the region.[15]

Definite news of the capture of Buenos Aires by British forces arrived in London on 13 September. Although pointing out the mission had been unauthorised, King George III realised it was 'impossible not to approve of the manner in which it was planned and executed' and hoped 'the acquisition of Buenos Ayres will prove very advantageous to this country'.[16] There were problems, however. Ministers misunderstood the territory Popham had seized: Popham had taken the *city* of Buenos Aires; in London it was believed he had control of the entire *province* of Buenos Aires, in other words, a huge tract of land encompassing territory in the modern states of Argentina, Uruguay, Paraguay and Bolivia. Popham also maintained his forces were well received wherever they went and this, along with his playing up of the value of prospective trade with the specie-rich region, was all too much to think about giving up.[17] Popham had presented the government with a *fait accompli* bringing South America to the forefront of British strategy for the next two years.

Popham's rosy but inaccurate picture gave the impression that Spanish America would welcome British influence with open arms. Grenville for one thought all of Spanish America might fall into British hands 'as it must do in twelve months more of war', thereby preventing the French from gaining access to resources of the region which would aid their war effort against Britain. Spanish America, just like the Mediterranean, West Indies, or India, was another region where Anglo-French rivalry would be played out in a global war.[18]

Although Grenville expressed a 'great reluctance to the embarking in South American proposals because I know it was much easier to get into them than out again', in reality he realised it would be extremely difficult to give up Buenos Aires. His first thoughts were of exchanging conquered Spanish American territory for influence in Europe, for the Talents were engaged in peace talks with France during the summer and autumn of 1806, but Grenville was not hopeful of achieving British aims in Europe through a possible exchange.[19] By 1 October he had made up his mind; military operations would give Britain permanent possession of South America — there would be no handing back of captured territory.[20]

There followed a number of schemes to expand British influence in the region, but with a detachment from reality. Grenville informed his elder brother, the Marquis of Buckingham, that he was 'revolving in my mind a project to attack Mexico on both sides'. 6,000 troops would sail from Europe to the West Indies, freeing up the same number of seasoned troops, to which could be added 2–3,000 black troops to attack the East coast of Mexico. From India, a European regiment and 4,000 sepoys would sail to take Manila, before heading on to seize Acapulco, though Grenville was at least aware such disparate attacks could not be co-ordinated precisely in time.[21] On 15 October Buckingham, admitting he had no documents describing the South American interior, mooted his own idea for an attack on Panama and pressed for a squadron to be based off the coast of Peru to intercept Spanish shipments of specie.[22]

Grenville thought, rather presumptuously, that with 6,000 British troops stationed at Buenos Aires and assuming this force 'will, of course, have taken Monte Video', not more than 3,000 would be necessary to hold the city. There were, therefore, a number of options for the employment of the spare 3,000 men, with the added bonus that the garrison at the Cape of Good Hope was 1,000 men over strength. Grenville noted one option was to send them on, via the Cape, to India, perhaps to replace 4,000 men who would sail from Madras for an attack on the west coast of Spanish America. Another possibility was to send out a further 2,000 European troops to Buenos Aires, along with transports for 7,000 men for more operations in Spanish America. If this force was insufficient, then a further 5,000 Bengal sepoys could provide additional reinforcements from India.[23]

Windham now came up with what Sir John Fortescue called 'one of the most astonishing plans that ever emanated from the brain even of a British Minister of War'.[24] Writing to Brigadier Robert Craufurd on 30 October, Windham noted the success attended on the east coast of South America and surmised news would have spread across the continent of the 'benign protecting government of His Majesty' as opposed to the 'oppressive dominion of Spain'. Craufurd's object, therefore, was to sail with 4,000 men from England to the west coast of South America for 'the capture of the sea ports and fortresses and the reduction of the province of Chili'.[25]

Enter Sir Arthur Wellesley

Perhaps bewildered by his own thoughts and the plans of others and uncertain of the weather and geographical conditions, Grenville sought professional opinion — and at this point turned to Sir Arthur

Wellesley.[26] Such a move was not unusual: Rory Muir and Charles Esdaile have shown that special military advisers were not uncommon.[27] Henry Dundas, while he was Secretary of State for War (1794–1801), had regularly consulted Sir Ralph Abercromby and John and Alexander Hope on military matters, and Windham had already conversed with Craufurd regarding the Talents' plans.[28]

So why did the Talents now turn to Wellesley? He had not even been to South America. Simply put, his political connections placed him in a position to give advice. Arthur's elder brother, Marquis Wellesley, had been at Eton with Grenville. In 1806 Grenville had intended a Cabinet post for Lord Wellesley but the latter had refused following the controversy over his conduct as Governor General of India. Lord Wellesley also acted for Grenville in sounding out Canning to join the Talents as Foreign Secretary after the death of Fox in September 1806. Sir Arthur Wellesley himself had connections to Buckingham, Grenville's brother. In 1787, when Buckingham was Lord Lieutenant of Ireland, Wellesley had been one of his aides-de-camp; Wellesley visited him in late 1805 after returning from India.[29] At this point, Arthur Wellesley had both influence in high political circles and a growing military reputation. He had, so he later stated, gained experience of what not to do in the Low Countries,[30] but more valuable experience of command, planning and logistics came from his time in India where he had prepared expeditions to Manila in 1797 and Mauritius in 1800. Both were eventually aborted, but the strategic planning procedures provided him with experience of drafting, revising and presenting detailed plans for maritime expeditions, including the crucial aspects of sea transport and logistical support. Wellesley had then commanded a brigade in the abortive expedition from Britain to the Rivers Elbe and Weser in September 1805.[31]

Windham had already written to Grenville on 26 May 1806 noting he had hoped to talk to Sir Arthur Wellesley about the possibility of using Indian troops for an attack on Mauritius; Grenville concurred with the idea that Sir Arthur's Indian experience would make him a useful source of expert military advice.[32] Windham had written to Grenville again on 22 September suggesting that Wellesley be appointed to command the expedition destined for South America (that would eventually embark under Craufurd), but with the caveat that 'Sir A.Wellesley will not be popular, though probably really very proper. I am myself very little a judge of his qualifications.' In reply, Grenville stated that with regard to Sir Arthur's participation in operations in South America:

> I have so very high an opinion of his talents and military knowledge, and particularly of his powers of exciting spirit and confidence in his troops, which I have heard so very strongly stated by indifferent persons, that I am very desirous of his being employed there if the scale of our operations be large enough for him.[33]

Clearly, off the record discussions were taking place, for Lord Wellesley wrote to Grenville on 23 September declaring that 'Arthur will be very happy to serve in the regular course of his rank, and that he is extremely anxious for employment.'[34]

Wellesley and the Talents ministry
Wellesley's political connections placed him in a position to give advice; his military experience suggested that would be good, sound advice. According to the memorandum printed in the *Supplementary Despatches* and dated 2 November 1806, Wellesley set aside the plan for a two-pronged attack on Mexico. The plan as envisaged by Grenville was completely impractical. In order to sail from Manila to Spanish America, the attack on Manila had to be made in July, but the weather conditions on the east and west coasts of the continent were completely different. With Manila requiring a garrison of more than the envisaged 1,000 men, Wellesley suggested abandoning that part of the operation for the time being — it was simply too problematic when set against the central object of the plan, the attack on Spanish America. Instead he argued that the occupation of Manila would be a necessary consequence of, not

a precursor to, the possession of New Spain. Here Wellesley identified what was essential to the success of the plan and what was not. With regard to that main object, December and January were the fair season on the east coast of Mexico, but at the same time the west coast would be suffering rains in the most unhealthy season. Hence the two parts of the operation must be considered as just that, 'there could be no concerted co-operation'; instead implementation of the plan 'must be carried into execution by each, independently of the other'. Wellesley realised this posed a grave risk as the defending forces would have the strategic upper hand. Operating on interior lines the Spaniards could concentrate their forces against one of the two British expeditions, crushing it before moving against the other. Instead what Wellesley envisaged was the option of removing all the men for the attack on Mexico, 3,000 from Buenos Aires and the 1,000 destined for India, and basing them at Jamaica, ready for an assault in the proper season. The sepoys from India would land on the west coast only as reinforcements when the season permitted.[35]

In fact Wellesley had produced another memorandum of comments upon the plan of operations as proposed on 2 November, which is not published in the *Supplementary Despatches*. In this he maintained that the plan to use Indian troops for a descent on the west coast of Spanish America, by way of Manila, was practicable with sufficient planning, something at which he of course excelled. In particular he was concerned with sourcing the necessary transport tonnage, whether using China Indiamen or ships from India, but he knew that any quantity could be obtained from Bombay or Calcutta with due notice and could follow on after the expedition to Manila had sailed. Whatever was decided, it might be necessary to order Indian tonnage to go to Prince of Wales Island (modern-day Penang) for the detachment from Buenos Aires. The Indian government should also, Wellesley pointed out, prepare ordnance for the Madras and Buenos Aires detachments, stores for a siege, appropriate pioneers, commissariat and pay department. A second point may relate to Windham's plan for Chile: Wellesley recommended troops from Buenos Aires should not go by way of the Cape, unless to receive provisions, but should go direct to Prince of Wales' Island to join with the Madras detachment.[36]

How did Wellesley know all this? He had already planned for and commenced an ultimately abortive mission from India to Manila in 1797 and had a keen understanding of most things Indian; but what about the climate of Mexico and the different seasons? Charles Frazer was a crucial informant. Not all the correspondence between Wellesley and Frazer is published in the *Supplementary Despatches* and from a reading of that work it is unclear what the connection was. According to Wellesley, Frazer was a commercial trader in the Gulf of Mexico and ports along the Spanish American coastline and had been about to sail for the region when he was 'retained by the service of government'. Wellesley was specifically directed by Grenville to liaise with Frazer regarding the government's plans for Spanish America and Wellesley made extensive use of the information he received. Moreover, thinking he might be useful in implementing government plans in the region itself, Grenville had set aside the considerable sum of £1,000 per annum for him until he could be provided for in the conquered Spanish territories.[37]

Frazer had sent a memorandum on South America to Windham on 22 October and perhaps his engagement was in response to this. In particular Frazer noted a lack of what we would now call cultural understanding or human intelligence, on the part of the British commanders at Buenos Aires. They were 'strangers alike to the country, its inhabitants, and perhaps language' and could have little access to information. Therefore, he argued, it might be sensible to employ a person (i.e. himself) at Buenos Aires to fulfil this role with the ultimate aim of opening and extending intercourse with the interior, including Chile and Peru. Perhaps even 'carrying on a correspondence with influential men of his acquaintance in these kingdoms, [might] make them sensible of the advantages of a change, [and] facilitate the submission of those invaluable countries to His Majesty's Government'.[38]

During October and November Frazer also worked for Wellesley tracking down and interviewing the captains of merchant ships that had recently been in Spanish America, in particular those who had been off the coast of Honduras and from Vera Cruz. Frazer noted they thought the coastline of the former was poorly defended. He also pointed out that as it would take five to six months to get together a force to go out to Buenos Aires, he could, if sent ahead, 'be employed in a manner *productive of incalculable* advantages to government … where in two months I could accomplish all or the greater part of the objects and services' mentioned in his paper to Windham, which had been presented to Grenville. The correspondence also makes it clear that Frazer was preparing for a meeting with Wellesley and Grenville.[39]

Sourcing accurate intelligence on the region was an integral part of Wellesley's role. Obtaining information about the region was something ministers struggled with: in November 1806 Buckingham wrote to Grenville informing him he had just received 'a very valuable and interesting work … a bird's eye view of all the ports, bays, roads, rocks and shoals', by William Hack, covering the whole of the west coast of America from California to the Strait le Maire. Buckingham hoped it might prove useful and was searching for a copy of a book on hydrography by the same author.[40]

In the meantime, on 10 November, the Admiralty ordered Rear Admiral George Murray to escort Craufurd's expedition to Chile, rounding Cape Horn, or by heading east, by way of New South Wales. The unfavourable weather and problems collecting transport tonnage would prevent the expedition sailing until New Year's Eve 1806.[41] This delay allowed for further reflection and the honing of plans. Wellesley's next memorandum (composed after two further meetings with Frazer),[42] of 20 November, provided a lucid explanation of how he thought the expedition should be conducted. After the 'fullest consideration, it appears decided that the principal attack upon New Spain must be made by one corps on its eastern coast; that the operations of this corps should be concentrated as much as possible in the first instance; and that the assistance looked for from the East Indies should be more in the nature of a reinforcement to the troops who should have made the conquest of New Spain, than of a corps to co-operate in the conquest'. To do this he desired a total of 6,000 European infantry, 3,000 black infantry, 2,000 artillerymen, 1,400 cavalry and field and siege guns concentrated at Jamaica. Of these, 3,000 of the European infantry with 400 mules would come from Buenos Aires and sail in September, orders being sent to that effect in late June. Orders for the appropriate logistical support for them, hire of the attendants, hire of transports and procurement of food, should be sent out as early as April. The troops coming from Britain — 3,000 European soldiers, 200 artillery men, 1,400 cavalry, and the 400 horses of the wagon corps, with drivers, ordnance and stores — were to be ready at Falmouth to sail in August. The European infantry and the artillerymen would take the place of seasoned troops in Jamaica, and the last would form the core of the expedition. The idea was to achieve a concentration of force in Jamaica so the expedition could sail for Mexico in November, arriving there in December. 3,000 sepoys and 500 European troops from India would sail in October, to arrive on the west coast of Mexico in February.[43]

This memorandum was followed by a discussion of possible points of attacking Mexico and instructions for the Ordnance, Victualling and Transport Boards, all of which are printed in the *Supplementary Despatches*.[44] What are not printed, and which really do highlight Wellesley's expertise and his attention to detail, were draft orders. One, for the assembly of troops at Falmouth, notes that commanding officers of the regiments should be 'informed that their service will be required in a warm climate and that their men must be furnished with flannel shirts, etc.' and, due to the climate, 'A large medical staff to be furnished and sent to Falmouth to attend these troops'. A draft order to the commander-in-chief of naval forces in the West Indies desires that officer 'to blockade the Havannah and La Vera Cruz closely and to have a good look out kept between Capes Catouche and Antonio, so as if possible to prevent intelligence of the preparations making in Jamaica and the West Indies from reaching the Spanish Main'. In another memorandum, the Governor of Jamaica is to be informed of the mission so he can make suitable preparations, including the raising of 200 black pioneers to be officered by Europeans, the purchase of 400 mules and handlers, and the hire of tonnage suitable for their transport. A memorandum for the Transport Board, and different to that published in the *Supplementary Despatches*, requires the assemblage at Falmouth of tonnage for the troops gathering there. In particular Wellesley wanted to know:

> If the spar decks which were upon the 44 and 50 gun ships in the last war have not been taken off, it would be very desirable if these ships could be used as transports again upon this service. Some time will elapse before it will be possible to remove the fleet from the coast of Mexico, and these ships would add much to its security there from an attack from the enemy.

A final memorandum, this time to the Governor of India, requests that the sepoys to form this part of the operation should be from the presidencies of Bengal and Fort St George. 'As the sepoys must volunteer for this service, it should be desirable that they should be informed that they would serve under my command, as they all know me well.' The sepoys were to be transported to Prince of Wales Island, then to New Holland or an island in the South Seas, where they would be landed and encamped while their transports were watered and cleaned out. Wellesley also ensured their dietary requirements would be met by a couple of supply vessels laden with rice and sheep.[45]

A further memorandum written the same day provides a detailed assessment of the seven possible locations where an attack on the east coast of Mexico could make landfall and any defences that would have to be neutralised. It also considers the value of using the Mexican river system for penetration into the interior of the country. In conclusion Wellesley recommended that he should prefer to make the attack at Vera Cruz for a number of reasons. The forts there were not strong and could be carried by a *coup de main*, with sufficient support from land ordnance in the form of mortars and naval gunfire from small-sized shallow-draughted gun and bomb vessels. Once the expedition was established ashore, there was a practicable road 'through a plentiful country' to Mexico City, 100 leagues distant. If for any reason Vera Cruz was impractical, then it would be best to use one of the Mexican rivers, preferably the Alvarado, hence the transports for the expedition should be small and light, with a shallow draught and plenty of anchors and cables.[46] Another memorandum of the same date requires the raising of a corps of 500–600 free black rangers and 200–300 black pioneers in Honduras, the men to be officered by European and native settlers in Honduras and regular officers drawn from the West Indies. Transports for these men would sail with the Falmouth force, pick the men up from Honduras and rendezvous in theatre at Cape Catoche (at the tip of the Yucatan Peninsula).[47] Of particular note is Wellesley's global strategic planning, his use of imperial resources, his attention to the care of the troops, the importance of secrecy and security of information about the expedition, and his grasp of naval matters.

Again Frazer was the source of much of the intelligence, but Wellesley had been consulting widely. His correspondents between the first memorandum of 2 November and that of 20 November included George Dyer, who provided information regarding the climate of Honduras and a plan from 1804 for an attack on Guatemala which had been forwarded to Mr John Sullivan of the Colonial Department.[48] In the Wellington Papers are a number of letters from Sullivan with a whole host of enclosures detailing correspondence, from earlier in 1806, between Sullivan and

Brigadier General Sir Thomas Hislop, the Governor of Trinidad, regarding the possibilities for a British expedition against the Orinoco River.[49] Another source of note, though perhaps not in direct contact with Wellesley, was the diplomat Sir John Hippisley, who was a good friend of William Windham and it is, perhaps, from that connection that Wellesley gained access to Hippisley's correspondence. Hippisley, it is worth noting, was also a correspondent of Frazer. Hippisley's letters contain details of numerous plans for attacking Spanish America dating back to 1790. Of particular interest is an abstract of a plan for the conquest of Guatemala sent by Colonel William Dalrymple to Dundas, which contains useful information such as equipping the men with light clothes, cotton or flannel shirts and mosquito trousers, the require-ment for light mobile artillery, the logistical support provided by black baggage carriers, the use of seasoned European troops drawn from the West Indies, the requirement to concentrate the expedition at Jamaica and the use of Indian troops.[50] In March 1806, Hippisley had himself sent Windham a long memorandum on Span-ish America, in which he called for an attack on Buenos Aires from the Cape, while a force drawn from India would attack Acapulco and another based in the West Indies could attack the Spanish Main.[51]

On 25 November, Lord Wellesley informed Grenville that Sir Arthur was 'highly pleased with the discussions which have passed between you respecting the proposed expedition … if it should be prosecuted he would prefer that employment to all others.'[52] On this latter point, ministers were certainly impressed with Wellesley's strategic thinking for on 5 December Grenville wrote to Lord Holland:

> I send you for consideration the plan of the Mexican attack, as arranged after much consultation with Sir Arthur Welles-ley, who is to command it. I waited till Windham returned to town in order to shew it to him. He seems well satisfied with it …[53]

On 2 January 1807, however, the difference between planning operations in England and their implementation half a world away was brought home. Just as Murray and Craufurd were finally putting to sea, news arrived in London that the British force at Buenos Aires had been attacked and forced to surrender (12 August 1806).[54] New orders were immediately sent out for Murray to head for either Rio de Janeiro or Buenos Aires, whichever he judged best, and provide assistance to Auchmuty, if he was there. If Auchmuty had been ejected and had retired to the Cape, Murray was to try to retake Buenos Aires if his force was sufficient. If not, he was to wait for reinforcements from the Cape under Lieutenant Colonel Thomas Backhouse.[55] Though the government could not confirm the news until the receipt of more definite intelligence or despatches from Buenos Aires, Grenville for one believed the reports were accurate.[56] All doubts were removed when Popham's account of the capture of the city by the Spaniards arrived in London on 25 January.[57] Having already made a major commitment to attacking Spanish America, the Talents reacted to this unwelcome intelligence by drawing up new plans for the polyglot of forces already on the way to the region. The difficulty of co-ordinating disparate troop and fleet movements thousands of miles away was evident.[58]

Undaunted, Wellesley again raised the question of the Mexican expedition,[59] reminding ministers that, as stated in his memorandum of 20 November 1806, if orders were to go to India they must go by 1 February or the troops would not be ready to sail in October. Wellesley, with his understanding of the vagaries of global strategic planning, noted that orders cancelling the expedition could be sent up to 1 June.[60] Four days later he submitted a confidential memorandum forecasting the likely operations of the various forces in South America, and the possibilities for the recapture of Buenos Aires. He surmised the force under Backhouse would have reached Buenos Aires; he thought Backhouse would not attack Montevideo, but should remain in Maldonado. The combined force, once Auchmuty arrived, would be just over 5,000 men. Wellesley thought Auchmuty would then use the combined force to attack Montevideo. This would be the likely situation Craufurd would find when he arrived with his troops, bringing the army up to 9,500 men. Such a concentration was sufficient to retake Buenos Aires. Once achieved, the force should stay there until further orders arrived from London. Wellesley advised the government to send out two general officers of sufficient rank to assume command. He estimated the Spaniards could muster 18,889 troops to oppose British operations, therefore no less than 5,200 infantry and 2,100 cavalry were needed for the conquest and possession of Buenos Aires, including the town itself, Montevideo, Maldonado and Cordova.[61]

In February Wellesley received a request from Windham to consider the possibility of using the troops eventually destined for Mexico for an attack on Terra Firma (Venezuela, Maracaibo, Cumana, Guiana and St Marguerite), and to produce a memorandum on the subject. Wellesley's response was to estimate the Spanish forces in that region to number a little over 13,000 men, but warned that after the experience of Buenos Aires 'we ought not to rely entirely upon the accounts which we have received of the inefficiency of the Spanish military establishments in America.' Sir Arthur had identified two key problems with the operations of the previous year: a lack of accurate intelligence, and the associated underestimating of the Spanish capacity and willingness to resist British expeditions. An operation against Terra Firma could not be co-ordinated with an attempt on Mexico; and, in any case, Wellesley thought it would require as large a British force to keep the area under British rule as it would for the initial conquest. This convinced him 'the gain which Great Britain will derive from the possession of this colony, under present circumstances, will not compensate for the loss which may be sustained.' The only viable reason to seize territory was to prevent the French claiming it in a peace settlement. Wellesley could only suggest achieving the objective through the establishment of an independent government.[62]

The same month Grenville composed a minute, perhaps for circulation at Cabinet, outlining what the ministry should now try to achieve. A further reinforcement under Lieutenant General John Whitelocke would be sent to the River Plate 'with the utmost practicable expedition'. As was usual in distant operations, Whitelocke was provided with general orders allowing freedom to exercise his judgement. The main object was to seize a strong position as an entrepôt for British goods and from which to spread political influence. If he thought seizing Buenos Aires was possible and that it could be retained by 6,000–7,000 men, he should attack and remain there until receiving further orders. It was up to Whitelocke to decide if, once Buenos Aires had been captured, Montevideo could be destroyed. In essence Whitelocke was only to occupy strategic positions that could be easily captured and garrisoned.[63] After five months of planning and consultation the Talents finally consolidated all the forces in South America, now numbering 11,180 men, under the command of one person: Whitelocke.[64] On 24 February Whitelocke was given the option of despatching a portion of his force for operations in Peru, while Windham considered occupying Panama and establishing communications across the isthmus to the West Indies.[65]

Whitelocke's bungled expedition ended in a disastrous attack on Buenos Aires on 5 July 1807, leading to a humiliating surrender to the Spaniards and the evacuation of the River Plate. He was court-martialled and retired from the service. The Talents' policy, based on misconceptions and the piecemeal application of force, had ended in utter disaster, while the population of Spanish America had been stirred up; they now recognised they possessed the power to fear neither Britain nor their imperial masters in Madrid.[66]

Wellesley and the Portland ministry

The Talents did not have to deal with the consequences of these events. After just over a year in office, the administration collapsed. Taking office in March 1807, it fell to the Portland ministry to deal with the results of the Talents' South American policy. In May 1807, before Whitelocke had even assaulted Buenos Aires, the new Secretary of State for War and the Colonies, Viscount Castlereagh, drafted a detailed memorandum to consider how South America might be handled in future. He recognised the fundamental problem with Popham's expedition was the seizure of Buenos Aires for Britain, thereby prompting an insurrection against not just Spanish, but all imperial control.

With Whitelocke's force on the way to the region, the sensible question for the Cabinet was whether Buenos Aires was actually worth the resources required to hold it. This raised the more fundamental question of British aims in the region and whether there was a way to achieve them by engaging with the Spanish population rather than through military conquest. Events at Buenos Aires had shown the latter might be counterproductive. Castlereagh looked for Britain to approach the region as a trading partner, not as a conqueror. He also recognised the dangers of guaranteeing the independence of the colonies, a volatile process which might remove all government and create a chaotic situation not conducive to British trade — especially at a time when Britain needed to open up new markets to replace those denied in Europe. To provide regional stability, he looked to the creation of strong native forces under British guidance — to dispense with the need to station a British army there. All this might be aided by placing an Anglophile Bourbon prince on a South American throne. In other words, Castlereagh desired the creation of a friendly state in Spanish America, akin to those managed by the British in India, to provide a solid base from which British influence could spread. Finally, Castlereagh noted the Talents had been assembling an expedition of 8,000 men under Wellesley destined for Mexico.[67] George

Canning, at the Foreign Office, responded warmly to Castlereagh's thoughts on 19 May, though doubting the practicalities of placing a Bourbon on a South American throne. What Canning did consider was the possibility of evacuating the bulk of British forces from Spanish America, leaving behind a few military posts and commercial stations, and attempting to negotiate peace terms with Spain. In return Castlereagh raised the idea of an expedition to Mexico and sent General Miranda to the West Indies to procure information.[68]

Events in Europe took centre stage, however, with Wellesley himself playing a high-profile role in the expedition to seize the Danish fleet during July–September 1807. Frustrated at Copenhagen, Napoleon turned his attention south towards Spain and Portugal, which again raised the spectre of him laying claim to all of Portuguese and Spanish America.[69] Again it was bad news from Spanish America which brought the region back onto the strategic agenda. Information regarding Whitelocke's surrender at Buenos Aires arrived in London on 11 September, reinforcing Castlereagh's belief that attempts to conquer the region would be pointless.[70] Instead, he viewed the growing French threat to Portugal as a glorious opportunity to spread British influence throughout South America. If the Portuguese royal family, government infrastructure, fleet and treasury could be plucked from the clutches of France and transported to Brazil, it could 'lay the foundations of a mighty and magnificent empire'. What ministers were thinking of was the possibility of bringing all the population of South America under one government, and one which would be dependent on British maritime power for security.[71] When the Portuguese did indeed flee to Brazil in November 1807, it provided ministers with the glorious opportunity to establish a strong pro-British state in South America. No longer would it be necessary to conquer territory against the will of the indigenous populations. Instead Brazil could serve as an entrepôt for introducing an illicit British trade into the wider region with protection provided by the Royal Navy.[72]

With a maritime commitment to protect British trade and assist with the security of the Portuguese government, the Portland Cabinet, like the Talents before them, did initially reconsider the options for a British military expedition to the region. In essence, Brazil could be utilised as a launch pad for providing direct assistance to the forces of independence in the Spanish colonies. Imperial conquest was not now the British aim, instead the objective was to seize, or gain access to, maritime bases.[73] On 21 December Castlereagh quizzed selected members of the Cabinet about South American strategy. With no plans for offensive operations in Europe and it becoming increasingly clear Spain was subject to French occupation, he looked to British operations in the River Plate. The link between Spanish imperial and domestic issues was obvious, and Castlereagh wanted to pre-empt French plans to utilise her erstwhile ally by examining the possibility of setting aside 8,000 men to seize Montevideo. Alternatively, 5,000 men could be stationed at Buenos Aires to assist the Portuguese in securing their vulnerable southern border and influence any changes in the government of Spanish America.[74]

In this complex strategic situation the Portland Cabinet, like their predecessors, turned to Sir Arthur Wellesley. Not only had Wellesley successfully lobbied Castlereagh for a command in the Copenhagen expedition, their relationship stretched back to 1790, when they served together for a number of years in the Irish Parliament. Castlereagh valued Wellesley's opinion and might even have engineered the famous meeting outside his office between Wellesley and Nelson in September 1805. As leader of the Wellesley clan, Arthur's elder brother Lord Wellesley had strong links to the new government, in particular to Canning — the latter in fact offered to step aside from the Foreign Office if Lord Wellesley wished to take the post, which he did not. Sir Arthur Wellesley's political links were cemented in April 1807, when he became Chief Secretary for Ireland. He joined in government his brothers Henry, the junior Secretary to the Treasury, and William Wellesley-

Pole, who was Secretary to the Admiralty. After the successful completion of the Danish expedition, Sir Arthur Wellesley wasanxious for another active command. He told Canning on 17 October that he was ready to aid the government in any manner they wished and was 'ready to set out for any part of the world at a moment's notice'.[75]

After examining the official papers relating to South America and conversing with Miranda on 8 February 1808, Wellesley submitted a memorandum to the Cabinet. Pointing to the failures of 1806–7, he was convinced that any attempt by Britain to conquer Spanish American territory would fail. That left the option of stirring up the Spanish colonies into a revolt against Spanish rule. It was a common belief that transferring the Portuguese government to South America would encourage the Spanish colonies to fight for independence. Wellesley had not seen any proof in the official papers of the desire of the Spanish colonies to break with Madrid, though he thought it probable some yearned for independence. Therefore, in order to assist those with a revolutionary urge, he recomended:

> ... that the country ... be attacked by such a force as not only will render success nearly certain, but, in the event of success against the troops and establishments of the King of Spain, will enable the person entrusted by government with the management of these transactions to guide the progress of the revolution, and to fix the nature of the government thereafter to be established.

If Britain could apply suitable forces, 'the spirit of revolution will spread over the whole continent of South America'. As a first step he recommended Britain should capture Buenos Aires to enhance Brazilian security, but recognised that it would be difficult to establish a new government there after recent events. Peru and Chile would require a near circumnavigation of the globe and the benefits of seizing them were dubious. That left Mexico and Terra Firma. In the case of the latter, the government had Miranda through whom they could communicate with the population and, upon his judgement, the people were ripe for revolution. With regard to Mexico, there was no sympathetic native to assist the British and the force required would be substantial, around 17,000 men, as with the 1806 plans, to be assembled at Jamaica. Wellesley also pointed out that an independent government, unless assisted by British forces, would be an easy target for an aggressive United States of America. The preferred form of new government would be a monarchy with a representative body. If the British government proceeded on the principle of fostering revolution and then reconstructing the new government in an efficient manner, it would be able to raise indigenous forces in sufficient numbers to remove the need for reinforcements from India.[76] This memorandum sits slightly uneasily with Wellesley's assertion to Stanhope of the 'horror of revolutionising any country for a political object'.[77]

On 2 April 1808 Canning agreed with Castlereagh's earlier assertions that conquest of Spanish America was out of the question. Instead, and perhaps acting on Wellesley's advice, he hoped attention could be moved from South America northward to the province of Mexico where Canning wanted to '*create* a government ... that cannot fail being dependent upon Great Britain'. This would give Britain control of the Mexico trade and pre-empt any ideas the Americans had for promoting Mexican independence in order to control that trade. Securing Mexico, whether by force or by installing an Anglophile Bourbon on the throne, would also help protect British possessions in the West Indies from American encirclement. Canning hoped the 'expedition for Mexico should commence preparation and sail in August'.[78] The object was British commercial dominance, to make:

> ... England the carrier of the commerce of the continent of Europe, as, no other could, under the above circumstances, trade to the West Indies and Spanish America but herself; this would annihilate the marine of all the powers in Europe, as, in a few years for want of employment, it would sink

into insignificance.

In this case 'England would, by adopting these measures with promptitude and vigour, become mistress of the seas'.[79]

With 16,000 men available for some kind of assault on a part of Spanish America,[80] British concerns over French intentions in that region heightened with Napoleon's seizure of Charles IV of Spain. Portland for one expressed his concern to George III on 21 April 1808 that France might lay legitimate claim to Spanish America. Portland, somewhat disingenuously claimed ministers had not previously considered loosening the ties between Spain and her colonies, but with Spanish America potentially open to Napoleon, no time should be lost in enacting swift, pre-emptive action against the Spanish colonies to safeguard them from French attacks.[81] After the tribulations of 1806 and 1807, King George III was understandably cautious and asked for more detailed proposals, recognising the danger of sending forces to South America without clear aims and long-term objects. With the Cabinet desiring troops be withdrawn from the Mediterranean and redeployed in the Baltic, he expressed concerns over the number of men required for the expedition to South America when set against other strategic pressures.[82]

Yet Mexico was still on the agenda. On 1 June, as news filtered through of unrest in Spain, Wellesley noted that troops assembling at Cork under his command, around 8,000 men, could be sent to Iberia first to join with another small British detachment of 5,000 men under General Spencer. If there were no prospect for successful operations, all 13,000 men could then sail onto the West Indies to be ready for an attack on Mexico. A final option was to divide the troops with 5,000 still going to the West Indies and a force of 8,000 heading for the River Plate. As one would by now expect, Wellesley included comprehensive details of the ordnance and stores required, along with thoughts on how to victual the expeditions.[83] Five days later he detailed the naval support each of the potential operations would require.[84]

In another memorandum of June 1808 Wellesley expanded his ideas by pointing out that an attack on Mexico could not commence until December, but it might be possible to attack Caracas in October. This latter plan of action he thought expedient for four reasons. It would be easier to conquer than Mexico, use could be made of Miranda to communicate the objective of the British expedition to the people, operations could commence earlier in the year and success at Caracas would remove difficulties that would be encountered in other areas. In the event of failure, the British force could be withdrawn relatively easily. Therefore, Wellesley again spent some time detailing the troops, stores, victuals and transports required, with a view to sailing on 1 August and commencing the attack in October. Uppermost in his mind was mobility once the army had been landed, and to this effect he directed the purchase of 500 mules in the West Indies with the persons from the commissariat or quartermaster-general's department heading out to the region as soon as possible. Regarding the naval forces, he required a ship of the line, two or three frigates, gun and bomb vessels, and armed launches to protect the troops while landing. As before, he requested troops be sent out in armed 44- or 64-gun ships (troopships), rather than pure transports, not only to provide increased firepower for the expedition, but also because they allowed room for the storage of greater numbers of the flat-bottomed boats essential for landing operations than might be sent in ordinary transports.[85]

Yet again, all the planning came to nothing. On 30 June the Cabinet came to a firm decision: Wellesley's force based at Cork would be sent to assist the Spanish and Portuguese nations 'in throwing off the yoke of France'.[86] Moreover Napoleon could not lay a legitimate claim to Spanish America while the Spaniards rebelled against his rule. Perhaps more importantly, it would be extremely difficult for Britain to justify attacking Spanish possessions while the two countries were fighting a common foe, a point made by Canning in September when he ended any thoughts of further British involvement in Spanish South America.[87]

Conclusion

By the time he set off for Iberia, Wellesley had for two years been at the heart of British strategic planning for Spanish America. He had advised two different administrations on such matters, and he had done this without having first-hand knowledge of much of the region. Instead he had consulted, accumulated and processed a wealth of information about Spanish America — and he used this to identify what was possible and what was not in terms of maritime expeditionary operations and to communicate that to his political masters. One historian has argued that 'Wellesley had been gripped by the general enthusiasm for a South American empire'[88] and it is hard to disagree with this assessment. Certainly there was a degree of self interest in all this: as a professional soldier, Wellesley desired active command and expeditions to Spanish America would have provided him with opportunity for the type of 'independent command' he had been used to in India. He maximised political connections to push his case, but his advice was based on sound military principles, and he displayed his familiar meticulous planning and attention to detail. Muir and Esdaile have argued that the ideal British commander would have displayed:

> ... a readiness to undertake operations; combined with a cool assessment of what was needed and a refusal to ask for more resources than were necessary; someone who would clearly explain the problems he was facing without over-dramatising them or casting aspersions (justified or not) on the ministers; someone who would readily and promptly obey orders except when there was good reason not to do so, and who would then cheerfully act on his own initiative and — to complete the idealised picture — someone who would give generous credit to the ministers for all they did to support his operations, while tactfully passing over any

> governmental shortcomings. Such was the ideal, and it was
> not to be found on earth — or at least not amongst the
> British high command.[89]

This is an exhaustive and taxing list. While no one could fulfil the ideal, Wellesley came as close as anyone. I cannot but beg to differ with Fortescue's remark regarding the memorandum that Wellesley had produced during these years on Spanish America: 'these papers of Wellesley's must not all of them be taken too seriously.'[90] That is unfair to a highly skilled, professional and knowledgeable soldier.

References

[1] See, for example, S.G.P.Ward *Wellington* (London, 1963) pp. 47–56; R.Holmes *Wellington: the Iron Duke* (London, 2003) pp. 91–107; E.Longford, *Wellington: the years of the sword* (London, 1969) pp. 109–39.

[2] Longford, *Wellington: years of the sword*, p. 137. See fn. 12 for more details on Miranda.

[3] Ward, *Wellington*, p. 51.

[4] G.Corrigan *Wellington: a military life* (London, 2001) p. 94.

[5] Holmes, *Wellington*, p. 93.

[6] J.Fortescue *Wellington* (London, 1925) p. 73.

[7] P.H.Stanhope *Notes of conversations with the Duke of Wellington, 1831–1851* (London, 1938) p. 69. Longford, *Wellington: years of the sword*, p. 137, and P.Haythornthwaite *Wellington: the Iron Duke* (Washington, 2007) p. 23, deploy this quote to display Wellesley's good sense.

[8] Stanhope, *Notes of conversations*, p. 69.

[9] The quotation comes from Popham to Marsden, 8 Jul 1806, and the figure of one million from same to same, 12 Jul 1806, *The Royal Navy in the River Plate, 1806–1807* ed. J.D.Grainger (Navy Records Society, 135; 1966) pp. 40, 46. H. Popham *A damned cunning fellow: the eventful life of Rear-Admiral Sir Home Popham 1762–1820* (Tywardreath, 1991) pp. 151–2, states 1.1 million dollars cash. See also Windham to Buckingham, 12 Sep 1806, and T.Grenville to Buckingham, 13 Sep 1806, *Royal Navy in the River Plate*, ed. Grainger, p. 122.

[10] Howick to Grenville, 24 Jun 1806, *Royal Navy in the River Plate*, ed. Grainger, p. 117; Howick to George III, 24 Jun 1806, *The later correspondence of George III* ed. A.A. Aspinall (5 vols., Cambridge, 1962–70) iv, pp. 457–8. Popham's intentions are in Popham to Marsden, 13 Apr 1806, *Royal Navy in the River Plate*, ed. Grainger, p. 19. See also Popham, *Damned cunning fellow*, pp. 144–51. J.W.Fortescue *A history of the British army* (13 vols. in 20, London,

1899–1930) v, p. 318, states late July.

[11] Howick to George III, 24 Jun 1806, *Later correspondence of George III*, ed. Aspinall, iv, pp. 457–8.

[12] As Secretary of State for War, Henry Dundas planned expeditions to Chile in 1796, Venezuela in 1797 and Buenos Aires in 1800. In 1801 Venezuela was considered by the Addington ministry and again in 1804 by Dundas after the war with Spain broke out. Dundas to George III, 23 Jan 1797; George III to Dundas, 24 Jan 1797, *Later correspondence of George III* ed. Aspinall, ii, pp. 537–8; M.Duffy 'World-wide war and British expansion, 1793–1815', in *The Oxford History of the British Empire: volume two. The eighteenth century*, ed. P.J.Marshall (Oxford, 2001) p. 193, provides an overview of the various projects. In 1803 Popham had expressed the need to remove the wealthy Spanish colonies from the influence of European Spain: unsigned memorandum, 26 Nov 1803, TNA, PRO 30/8/345, pp. 83–4 (the author is probably Popham). See also E.Sparrow *Secret service: British agents in France, 1792–1815* (Woodbridge, 1999) p. 315; Popham, *Damned cunning fellow*, pp. 133–4. In 1804 Pitt, uncertain about the future course of the war in Europe as Anglo-Spanish relations deteriorated, was receptive to various schemes for opening the markets of Spanish America. Francisco Miranda, the ex-Spanish Army Officer and perennial Venezuelan patriot, was in London from 1798 until 1804, and Popham, who had met Miranda in 1803, were Pitt's most vociferous and influential advisers on such issues. At a meeting on 14 October 1804, Miranda and Popham presented detailed plans for British intervention in the region to Dundas, now Lord Melville, First Lord of the Admiralty. In November Popham was actually at Spithead expecting Miranda to arrive and, possibly, undertake an operation, but nothing materialised. C.D.Hall *British strategy in the Napoleonic War, 1803–15* (Manchester, 1992) pp. 97, 112–13; W.W.Kaufmann, *British policy and the independence of Latin America, 1804–1828* (Hamden, 1967) pp. 10–13; Popham, *Damned cunning fellow*, pp. 133–4; Fortescue, *History of the British army*, v, p. 312.

[13] Windham to George III, 24 Jun 1806, *Later correspondence of George III*, ed. Aspinall, iv, p. 458. Shortly after taking office Auckland, President of the Board of Trade, was pressing Grenville to encourage trade with Spanish America. Auckland to Grenville, 9 Apr 1806, Historical Manuscripts Commission *The manuscripts of J.B.Fortescue, Esq. preserved at Dropmore* (10 vols., London, 1892–1927), [hereafter *Dropmore*], viii, p. 87. In June, Auckland and Grenville were discussing a project to ship 10 million Spanish dollars from South America in neutral vessels. This scheme had originated with Pitt, to ship quicksilver to Vera Cruz, while the ships returned to British ports laden with dollars, to the account of the Spanish government. Auckland to Grenville, 5 Jun 1806,

Dropmore, viii, p. 178. It seems as if the original plan went ahead, though in October 1806 Grenville was against repeating the venture, possibly due to Popham's exploits in South America. See Auckland to Grenville, 28 Oct 1806; Grenville to Auckland, 28 Oct 1806: *Dropmore*, viii, pp. 405–6.

[14] Cabinet minute, 26 Jun 1806, *Later correspondence of George III*, ed. Aspinall, iv, p. 458; Fortescue, *History of the British army*, v, pp. 366, 372; *Royal Navy in the River Plate*, ed. Grainger, p. 112. In late July the Admiralty decided upon Rear Admiral Stirling as Popham's replacement. Stirling sailed at the end of August. Navy Board to Popham, 28 Jul 1806, *Royal Navy in the River Plate*, ed. Grainger, p. 118.

[15] Windham to Grenville, 11 Sep 1806, *Dropmore*, viii, p. 321.

[16] Windham to George III, 13 Sep 1806, and reply, 14 Sep 1806, *Later correspondence of George III*, ed. Aspinall, iv, pp. 469–70.

[17] *Royal Navy in the River Plate*, ed. Grainger, pp. 111–12. Popham made it clear in his despatch of 12 Jul 1806 that 'Great Britain is now in the possession of the capital of one of the richest provinces of South America': Popham to Marsden, 12 Jul 1806, *Royal Navy in the River Plate*, ed. Grainger, p. 45.

[18] Grenville to Howick, 29 Sep 1806, *Royal Navy in the River Plate*, ed. Grainger, p. 126, and *Dropmore*, viii, pp. 366–8; Hall, *British strategy in the Napoleonic War*, p. 133. Grenville had already considered a South America-Naples exchange on 25 July, *Dropmore*, viii, p. 245.

[19] Grenville to Lauderdale, 22 Sep 1806, *Royal Navy in the River Plate*, ed. Grainger, pp. xi, 123–4; *Dropmore*, viii, p. 352.

[20] Grenville to Lauderdale, 1 Oct 1806, *Royal Navy in the River Plate*, ed. Grainger, pp. 126–7; *Dropmore*, viii, pp. 368–9.

[21] Grenville to Buckingham, 3 Oct 1806, *Royal Navy in the River Plate*, ed. Grainger, pp. 112, 128–9.

[22] Buckingham to Grenville, 15 Oct 1806, *Royal Navy in the River Plate*, ed. Grainger, p. 130; *Dropmore*, viii, pp. 386–7.

[23] Grenville to Buckingham, 31 Oct 1806, *Royal Navy in the River Plate*, ed. Grainger, p. 139; *Dropmore*, viii, pp. 415–6.

[24] Fortescue, *History of the British army*, v, p. 375.

[25] Windham to Craufurd, 30 Oct 1806, *Royal Navy in the River Plate*, ed. Grainger, pp. 136–7. Though by December Windham was having reservations about Grenville's plan, see Windham to T.Grenville, 30 Dec 1806, *Royal Navy in the River Plate*, ed. Grainger, pp. 150–1. Windham to Grenville, 2 Nov 1806, *Royal Navy in the River Plate*, ed. Grainger, p. 140; *Dropmore*, viii, pp. 418–20.

[26] Gurwood to AW, 27 Nov 1836, WP1/165. 'At the end of 1806, Major General Sir Arthur Wellesley was consulted by Lord Grenville as to an attack upon Mexico, New Spain, and Sir Arthur wrote several papers relating exclusively to the professional parts of such an enterprise, in which he entered into the most

extensive and most minute details of necessary preparation and combination.' I am grateful to Professor Chris Woolgar and his excellent staff for their kind help and assistance during my research visits to the Hartley Library.

[27] R.Muir and C.J.Esdaile, 'Strategic planning in a time of small government: the wars against revolutionary France, 1793–1815', in *Wellington Studies I*, ed. C.M.Woolgar (Southampton, 1996) pp. 27–8.

[28] Ward, *Wellington*, p. 51.

[29] Longford, *Wellington: years of the sword*, p. 113.

[30] Stanhope, *Notes of conversations*, p. 182.

[31] Ward, *Wellington*, p. 53.

[32] Windham to Grenville, 25 May 1806; Grenville to Windham, 26 May 1806: *Dropmore*, viii, pp. 156–7, 159.

[33] Windham to Grenville, 22 Sep 1806; Grenville to Windham, 23 Sep1806: *Dropmore*, viii, p. 353.

[34] Marquis Wellesley to Grenville, 23 Sep 1806, *Dropmore*, viii, pp. 353–4.

[35] Windham to Grenville, 2 Nov 1806, *Dropmore*, viii, pp. 418–20; memorandum, 2 Nov 1806, *SD*, vi, pp. 35–8.

[36] 'Memo[randum] upon the plan of operations as proposed Nov 2 1806', WP1/165.

[37] AW to ?, 10 Dec 1806, WP1/165.

[38] Frazer to Windham, London, 22 Oct 1806, WP1/165.

[39] Frazer to AW, n.d., though a few days after 22 Oct 1806, WP1/165.

[40] Buckingham to Grenville, 16 Nov 1806, *Dropmore*, viii, p. 435.

[41] Admiralty to Murray, 10 Nov 1806, *Royal Navy in the River Plate*, ed. Grainger, p. 143.

[42] AW to Grenville, 14 Nov 1806, *Dropmore*, viii, pp. 433–4.

[43] AW to Grenville, 20 Nov 1806, *Dropmore*, viii, pp. 485–7; memorandum, 20 Nov 1806, and memorandum number 4, 20 Nov 1806, *SD*, vi, pp. 40–5, 45–7.

[44] *Dropmore*, viii, pp. 487–93; memorandum, 20 Nov 1806, and memorandum number 4, 20 Nov 1806, *SD*, vi, pp. 40–5, 45–7.

[45] Undated memorandum, Nov 1806 (printed in *SD*, vi, pp. 50–5), with attached memorandum, WP1/165.

[46] Memorandum, 20 Nov 1806, *SD*, vi, pp. 40–4.

[47] Memorandum, 20 Nov 1806, *SD*, vi, pp. 48–9.

[48] George Dyer to AW, 17 Nov 1806, WP1/185.

[49] WP1/185.

[50] 'Abstract of Colonel W.Dalrymple's plan for the conquest of Guatimala by the Gulf of Dolce, given to Mr Secretary Dundas, May 1790', WP1/186.

[51] 'Extract from Hippisley to Windham', 17 March 1806, and Hippisley's notes, WP1/186.

[52] Marquis Wellesley to Grenville, 25 Nov 1806, *Dropmore*, viii, p. 442. In fact it seems as if ministers had decided to give AW the command: see Windham to T.Grenville, 30 Dec 1806, *Royal Navy in the River Plate*, ed. Grainger, pp. 150–1; even Popham had heard rumours to that effect, Popham to Baird, 16 Dec 1806, *Royal Navy in the River Plate*, ed. Grainger, pp. 196–7.

[53] Grenville to Holland, 5 Dec 1806, *Dropmore*, viii, p.459. Interestingly, Holland raised some concerns about the plans, see Holland to Grenville, 7 Dec 1806, *Dropmore*, viii, pp. 460–1.

[54] For details, see Fortescue, *History of the British army*, v, pp. 368–72; Popham, *Damned cunning fellow*, pp. 154–8; *Royal Navy in the River Plate*, ed. Grainger, pp. 10–13. Strangford to Howick, number 49, 20 Dec 1806 (received 2 Jan 1807), TNA FO 63/50.

[55] Admiralty to Murray, 2 Jan 1807, *Royal Navy in the River Plate*, ed. Grainger, p. 153; see also Fortescue, *History of the British army*, v, p. 379.

[56] Grenville to Buckingham, 14 Jan 1807, *Royal Navy in the River Plate*, ed. Grainger, p. 155.

[57] T.Grenville to George III, 25 Jan 1806; Windham to George III, 25 Jan 1806: *Later correspondence of George III*, ed. Aspinall, iv, pp. 507–8; T.Grenville to Collingwood, 27 Jan 1807, *Royal Navy in the River Plate*, ed. Grainger, pp. 155–6.

[58] For example see 'Memorandum on sailing times', *Royal Navy in the River Plate*, ed. Grainger, pp. 156–7.

[59] AW to Grenville, 25 Jan 1807, *Dropmore*, ix, pp. 22–5.

[60] Memorandum, 25 Jan 1807, *SD*, vi, p. 55.

[61] 'Confidential memorandum of Sir Arthur Wellesley in regard to the re-capture of Buenos Ayres', 29 Jan 1807, *Dropmore*, ix, pp. 479–81.

[62] AW to Grenville, 17 Feb 1807, enclosing memorandum, 15 Feb 1807, *Dropmore*, ix, pp. 40–4; *SD*, vi, pp. 56–61. See also *Royal Navy in the River Plate*, ed. Grainger, p. 115.

[63] 'Minute in Lord Grenville's hand': *Royal Navy in the River Plate*, ed. Grainger, p. 157, n.83, dates this to February 1807. With support from the sea such garrisons could also be easily evacuated.

[64] Duffy, 'World-wide war and British expansion', p. 194; see also Hall, *British strategy in the Napoleonic War*, p. 147.

[65] Windham to George III, 8 Mar 1807, *Later correspondence of George III*, ed. Aspinall, iv, p. 523.

[66] Fortescue, *History of the British army*, v, pp. 414–32; Hall, *British strategy in the Napoleonic War*, pp. 147–8; *Royal Navy in the River Plate*, ed. Grainger, pp. 253–8. See also I.Fletcher *The waters of oblivion: the British invasion of the Rio de la Plata, 1806–1807* (Stroud, 2006) chapters 7 and 8; C.J. Esdaile *Napoleon's wars: an international history, 1803–1815* (London, 2008)

pp. 268–9.

[67] Memorandum for the Cabinet, relative to South America, 1 May 1807, in *Memoirs and correspondence of Viscount Castlereagh, second Marquess of Londonderry* ed. C.W.Vane, third Marquis of Londonderry (12 vols., London, 1848–53) [hereafter *Castlereigh papers*], vii, pp. 314–23. Interestingly, in 1806 he had been the recipient of a letter from Popham outlining his actions: see Popham to Castlereagh, 14 Jul 1806, *Royal Navy in the River Plate*, ed. Grainger, p. 47.

[68] Canning to Castlereagh, 19 May 1807, West Yorkshire Archives, Leeds: George Canning Papers 32, by kind permission of the Earl and Countess of Harewood [hereafter HAR GC] see also D.Gray *Spencer Perceval: the evangelical Prime Minister* (Manchester, 1963) p. 161.

[69] Convention of Fontainebleau, 27 Oct 1807, articles 12 and 13, at <http://www.Napoleonseries.org/reference/diplomatic/spain.cfm>, accessed on 31 July 2003; see also F.G.Davenport and C.O.Paullin *European treaties bearing on the history of the United States and its dependencies* (Washington, 1917) p.190; C.Esdaile *The Peninsular War: a new history* (London, 2002) pp. 7, 31–4, and Esdaile, *Napoleon's Wars*, pp. 325–6, 342.

[70] Castlereagh to George III, 11 Sep 1807, *Castlereagh papers*, viii, p. 83.

[71] 'On the transfer of the Portuguese government to the Brazils', *Castlereagh papers*, vi, pp. 357–8.

[72] Pole to Smith, 25 Jan 1808, *The navy and South America, 1807–1823* ed. G.S.Graham and R.A.Humphreys (Navy Records Society, 104; 1962) p. 5. Canning to Strangford, number 1, 17 Apr 1808, TNA FO 63/59, pp. 4–9; number 4, 17 Apr 1808, TNA FO 63/59, pp. 16–21; for the illicit trade, see Canning to Strangford, number 5, 17 Apr 1808, TNA FO 63/59, pp. 32–3.

[73] Marques Antonio Henrique De Oliveira *History of Portugal* (2 vols., New York, 1972) i, p.455.

[74] 'Memorandum for Cabinet: measures suggested respecting South America', 21 Dec 1807; Portland to Castlereagh, 21 Dec 1807; Camden to Castlereagh, 22 Dec 1807, *Castlereagh papers*, viii, pp. 96–101.

[75] AW to Canning, 17 Oct 1807: *SD*, v, p. 139.

[76] Memorandum of 8 Feb 1808; supplementary memorandum to number 4, 8 Feb 1808: *SD*, vi, pp. 61–7.

[77] Stanhope, *Notes of conversations*, p. 69.

[78] Memorandum by Canning, 2 Apr 1808, HAR GC, 46a.

[79] Memorandum by Canning, 2 Apr 1808, HAR GC, 46a.

[80] Castlereagh to George III, 10 Apr 1808, *Later correspondence of George III*, ed. Aspinall, v, pp. 60–2.

[81] Portland to George III, 21 Apr 1808, *Later correspondence of George III*, ed. Aspinall, v, pp. 67–8.

[82] George III to Portland, 22 Apr 1808, *Later correspondence of George III*, ed. Aspinall, v, pp. 68–9.

[83] Memorandum, 1 Jun 1808, *SD*, vi, pp. 68–72.

[84] Memorandum, 6 Jun 1808, *SD*, vi, p.73.

[85] Memorandum, [June] 1808, *SD*, vi, pp. 74–9.

[86] Castlereagh to AW, number 1, 30 Jun 1808, TNA WO 1/228, pp. 5–10; *WD*, iv, pp.16–19; see also R.Muir, *Britain and the defeat of Napoleon, 1807–1815* (New Haven, 1996) pp. 42–3.

[87] Canning to Strangford, number 18, 2 Sep 1808, TNA FO 63/59, pp. 83–4.

[88] L.James, *The Iron Duke: a military biography of Wellington* (London, 1992) p. 106.

[89] Muir and Esdaile, 'Strategic planning in a time of small government', p. 40.

[90] Fortescue, *Wellington*, p. 73.

CHAPTER 3

The first French invasion of Portugal: two rash colonels
Clive Willis

'Gung-ho' is the modern expression that sums it all up. It was first used in 1942 to refer to raids by United States marines. Its origin was Chinese and denoted a team effort. But the practice of the head-long charge against the enemy, either on horseback or on foot, reaches back into the mists of time. Sometimes it met with success; on other occasions the outcome was total disaster. There are many expressions for it: 'to ride (or charge) hell for leather', or 'to go at it full tilt', or, as Lancastrians will have it, 'to go for it, muck or nettles', or, indeed, most memorably from the trenches of World War I, 'to go over the top', alternatively expressed as 'Up, lads, and at 'em'. Undoubtedly the most celebrated and impetuous instance was the 'wild' charge of the Earl of Cardigan's Light Brigade at the battle of Balaclava in 1854, duly immortalised in Alfred Tennyson's rousing poem of the same year.

Too often the charge became an exhilarating form of collective madness, of irrational exuberance, and frequently took hold of the Duke of Wellington's cavalry, much to his exasperation. Such was his reaction, particularly when his order to charge ended with reckless cross-country steeple-chases beyond the point of first encounter and, fatally, into the 'jaws of death' worked by encircling adversaries. In our recognition of the bicentenary of the battle of Talavera in central Spain, fought on 28 July 1809, we need to recall that an infantry charge by foot guards under General Sherbrooke and a cavalry charge by the 23rd Light Dragoons under General

Anson both ran out of control, ended in catastrophe and greatly imperilled Sir Arthur Wellesley's pyrrhic victory. Then there was the wild charge of the heavy cavalry at Waterloo.

In recalling the first of the three French invasions of Portugal and the Anglo-Portuguese victories of August 1808 at Roliça and Vimeiro, there come to mind the respective parts played by two rash lieutenant colonels, the Hon. George Lake of the 29th Foot (the Worcestershire Regiment) and Charles Taylor of the 20th Light Dragoons.

However, the symptom of the rush of blood to the head had already occurred two days prior to the battle of Roliça, namely on 15 August. The Anglo-Portuguese force was commanded by the man whom we must at this stage still refer to as Sir Arthur Wellesley, rather than by his later title of the Duke of Wellington. The opposing French force was under the command of General Henri-François, Comte Delaborde (or Laborde, to give him the sometimes shortened version of his surname). Backing southwards towards Lisbon, Laborde had vacated the historic fortified town of Óbidos on 14 August. Óbidos lies some 45 miles north of the capital. That tactical withdrawal was made specifically in order to prepare, as we shall see, a more advantageous position for the inevitable forthcoming clash of arms. The next day, in order to keep a lookout for Wellesley's approach, he had stationed a group of pickets close to the splendid sixteenth-century aqueduct that lies a few hundred yards to the south-east of Óbidos. This information we owe to Colonel George Landmann of the Royal Engineers, a member of Wellesley's staff. The pickets were spotted by green-jacketed British skirmishers from the Light companies of the 95th Rifles and 60th Rifles, among them the often-cited Rifleman Benjamin Harris of the 95th. There ensued the first encounter of Wellesley's troops with the French in the Peninsular War. The French pickets withdrew, firing as they went, with the four British companies in hot pursuit with fixed bayonets. Landmann tells us that the chase was over 2 miles.[1] The British, commanded by one Major Travers, about whom nothing else is known, led his men into the French rearguard with sickening consequences to themselves: one officer, Lieutenant Ralph Bunbury, was killed; Captain Hercules Pakenham, Wellesley's brother-in-law, was injured, and a further 27 men were killed or wounded. This 'affair of advance posts' (as Wellesley called it) would have ended even more catastrophically had it not been for the swift advance of General Sir Brent Spencer's division in support.[2]

Where exactly did the skirmish end up? Where exactly can we locate the first encounter of the British with the French in the Peninsular War, and what is the name of that place? Writers in English (for example, Oman, Fortescue and Longford) have called it the windmill at 'Brilos'. The Portuguese historian and novelist Raul Brandão called it 'Arrifos'.[3] Recent research by Portuguese historians João Pedro Tormenta and Pedro Fiéis would locate it at the ruined windmill of the Bairro da Luz.[4] That structure stands on a rise to the west of the railtrack, halfway between Óbidos and Caldas da Rainha and therefore to the *north* of Óbidos. They suggest that 'Brilos' ['briluš] was pronounced 'Brailos' ['braıluš], a corruption of Bairro da Luz. However, though not present at the time, General Thiébault, who served on the staff of the French commander-in-chief General Junot, reported that the windmill in question was half a league (or 2 km) forward of, that is, *north* of Roliça,[5] which itself lies 5 km to the *south* of Óbidos. Landmann's 2 miles and Thiébault's half a league fall well short of the Bairro da Luz — unless, of course, the chase was straight through the streets of Óbidos, which it plainly was not.

Nevertheless, the two Portuguese scholars may have unwittingly supplied the answer by telling us that the British riflemen were nicknamed the 'Grilos', the crickets (because of their green uniforms).[6] If that is the case, then we are not dealing with a place-name at all. I suggest that a scribbled, semi-legible version of that word emerged as 'Brilos'. In the handwriting of the time a capital *B* and a capital *G* bore a remarkable similarity. A similar case arises with 'Roliça': quite apart from its anglicisation as 'Rolica' (with stress on the first syllable), it underwent sundry distortions before finally appearing in the *War Office Gazette* as 'Boriça' and amid the battle honours of the 29th Foot as 'Roleia'.[7]

Meanwhile, Brandão's *Arrifos* or *Arrifes* happens to be Portuguese for 'crag' or 'rocky outcrop'. To the west of the village of Dagorda and to the north of the village of Amoreira there stands a ruined windmill. It towers over the River Real. The place-name on the maps of the Instituto Geográfico e Cadastral reads 'Arrifes'. If the chase was indeed over 2 miles (as Landmann says) and ended half a league forward of Roliça (as Thiébault says), then the Arrifes windmill is still a further 2 km away. On the other hand, the Dagorda windmill, which also stands on a rocky outcrop and *is* within the range, could be the better bet. There, without new evidence, we must leave the matter.

The 'gung-ho' folly of Major Travers provides us with a foretaste of the headlong charges of Colonels Lake and Taylor. Before analysing those episodes, we need to set the scene in greater detail.

The first British landings in the Peninsular War had taken place at Lavos, in the first week of August 1808. Lavos is situated just to the south of the Mondego estuary and across the bay from the town of Figueira da Foz, that is to say, some 80 miles north of Lisbon. Well over 13,000 troops had disembarked from the transports. The landings came in answer to the first French invasion of Portugal in the last two months of 1807 and in defence of Britain's oldest ally. The French invasion had been led by General Andoche Junot, the former French ambassador to Lisbon. Junot's total forces numbered some 26,000 and were deployed in Lisbon and certain major towns.

The French, however, did not occupy northern Portugal. In consequence, despite the surrender of the Portuguese forces in Lisbon, a somewhat ragbag Portuguese army had been reconstituted under the command of General Bernardim Freire de Andrade e

Castro — Freire for short. Freire served under the orders of the Bishop of Oporto and notionally protected the unoccupied north from further French incursion. Rather reluctantly, Freire was persuaded by the British to advance south, with 6,000 men, as far as Leiria, a town that lies 25 miles to the south of the British landings at Lavos. There he met Wellesley and, only after hard bargaining, did he agree to release some 1,700 men to Wellesley, of whom some 230 were raw cavalry (including a few dozen mounted Lisbon police). These Portuguese troops were placed under the command of one Lieutenant Colonel Nicholas Trant. Trant was Anglo-Irish, like Wellesley; the latter thought him 'a very good officer, but as drunken a dog as ever lived'.[8] To Trant's Portuguese troops we shall have reason to return, for the very good reason that British accounts of the battles of Roliça and Vimeiro frequently overlook or neglect their presence. In return for the strengthening of his force, Wellesley donated to Freire's remaining forces some 5,000 'Brown Bess' muskets to replace their 'varapaus e fouces', their cudgels and scythes, as Raul Brandão puts it.[9]

Freire lagged behind and would not at first risk venturing south of Leiria, though he gingerly and nervously reached Caldas da Rainha on the day *after* the battle of Roliça, and Óbidos on the day *before* the battle of Vimeiro. Aware of the presence of British forces to the north, the French commander-in-chief, General Junot, had dispatched two armies northwards to intercept and hold up their progress. General Laborde's troops were to block the route close to the coast, while the army of General Louis-Henri Loison stood further inland, close to the Tagus. By this means they guarded the two main northern approaches to the Lisbon peninsula.

Meanwhile, Wellesley's Anglo-Portuguese army was now advancing southwards along the coastal route; this was for ease of contact with the supply ships and transports. Laborde had marched as far north as the town of Alcobaça but, as his numbers were smaller than those at Wellesley's disposal, was now backing away towards Lisbon, with three days' march between his corps and that of the Anglo-Portuguese forces.

From Leiria, Wellesley's march followed the historic trajectory of Batalha, Aljubarrota, Alcobaça and Caldas. A good omen was that the Batalha to Aljubarrota section was completed on 14 August: that date was the 423rd anniversary of the glorious Anglo-Portuguese victory there over the numerically vastly superior forces of Castile in 1385. Major Travers' skirmish at the windmill ensued on the following day, 15 August, and, by the night of the 16th, Wellesley's corps was stationed in and around Óbidos, with many troops bivouacking on the north side.

The Hon. George Lake was born in 1780, the son of Lieutenant Colonel Gerard Lake, who in due course became a full general and Viscount Lake of Delhi. It will be instructive briefly to focus attention on Lake senior. He particularly distinguished himself in the siege of Valenciennes in 1793, when by sheer dogged thrust he led three battalions of foot guards in driving out, at bayonet point, no less than 12 admittedly raw French battalions. In India in 1803, with young George as one of his staff officers, he won a series of conflicts by his bold infantry and cavalry charges, with himself personally and constantly at the head of his men. He believed passionately that the main function of infantry was to charge with fixed bayonets and instilled the same notion into his son. His greatest achievement was his final and resoundingly decisive victory at Laswaree (1803), perhaps the bloodiest battle ever fought by the British in India. Despite heavy losses, his cavalry and infantry charged up a steep slope and overcame the Franco-Indian artillery.

Against superior numbers and no less than 72 guns, General Lake attacked at the head of his 2,500 cavalry and 6,000 infantry, but with his own artillery still far to the rear. The approach to the village of Laswaree was extremely steep and the enemy's entire front was obscured both by high grass and by huge clouds of dust churned up by all the cavalry movements. These were extra advantages to Lake's adversaries. In his eye-witness account Major

William Thorn continues as follows:

> These obstacles, however, which would have deterred an ordinary mind from attempting a desirable object till the prospect of success became more decided, had no other effect on the commander-in-chief than that of leading him to the prompt execution of his *original* plan ...[10]

With his son at his side, General Lake led his cavalry and infantry in charge after charge, intent on over-running and capturing the enemy guns. The two Lakes were constantly in the thick of the fire and unremitting in their daring. Twice Lake senior had his horse killed under him. On the second occasion, his son dismounted and, despite his father's protests, got him to mount his charger. The younger Lake then swung himself into the saddle of a trooper's horse and was immediately severely wounded in the knee by grapeshot. For moments, Lake senior gazed in anguish at his son, then renewed the onslaught at the head of the 76th Foot. Thorn again continues:

> This touching incident had a sympathetic effect upon the minds of all that witnessed it, and diffused an enthusiastic fervour among the troops, who appeared to be inspired by it with more than an ordinary portion of heroic valour.[11]

Despite heavy losses to the 76th Foot (they were reduced from 2,500 to a mere 300),[12] the day was carried, and the enemy utterly devastated.

The junior Lake took command of the Worcestershire Regiment, the 29th Foot, in December 1807. He immediately made a good impression by inviting all his officers to a fine breakfast and giving all his men a substantial meal. On the eve of Roliça, after a drumhead court-martial, he ordered a flogging for two of his men caught drunk in the streets of Óbidos. The flogging took place at once and, as he announced, for two reasons: to deprive the miscreants of the honour of fighting the next day; and to release their erstwhile guards, precisely so that the latter could participate. This decision was most favourably discussed by his men all evening.[13]

On the morning of the next day, 17 August, Wellesley viewed Laborde's disposition at Roliça from a forward position, probably from the Dagorda windmill or from Raposa hill, now identifiable by its triangulation post. He would certainly have seen nothing from the battlements of Óbidos, despite what is usually claimed.[14] He then dispatched Colonel Trant and his Portuguese to the extreme right or west, where in fact they did not participate actively in the conflict. The road from Roliça to Columbeira is now, however, duly named the Rua Nicolau Trante. Major General Sir Ronald Ferguson, with 4,500 men, marched over to the far left or east, in order to seek to block General Loison's expected arrival with the other French army from the direction of Bombarral. Laborde sent three companies to shadow Ferguson's men from a safe distance. The residue was a British main force of 9,000, with 15 guns, against Laborde's force of some 5,000 at the most, along with five guns. The odds against Laborde were, on the face of it, very superior. Indeed, the very size of Laborde's force is contentious. Wellesley at first thought it to be 4,000 and then revised it upwards to 6,000.[15] General Foy, who was not there, calculated that the French numbered 2,500 and Thiébault (likewise absent) thought they were as few as 1,900.[16] Oman's careful researches reveal that Laborde's force was some 5,700 in July but was now depleted to some 4,300.[17] Much of that depletion was due to the constant attrition wrought by the Portuguese guerrilla forces, the *ordenanças*, who were major contributors, like their Spanish counterparts, the *guerrilleros*, to Napoleon's celebrated 'Spanish ulcer'. Even Oman, however, neglects to include the withdrawn garrisons, left behind earlier by General Margaron in July, which now augmented Laborde's corps to around 5,000 as he withdrew south before the British advance.[18]

Laborde, meanwhile, having assessed the size of Wellesley's force, was unwilling to fall an easy victim to a pincer movement. He withdrew his troops in orderly fashion through the villages of Roliça and Columbeira to an obviously pre-established vantage point and what Wellesley described as a 'formidable position' on the heights of Columbeira, half a mile to the rear and which Laborde had had three days to prepare. The hills stand 300 feet above the plain and have an average gradient of one in ten. These heights are approached by several gullies (what Wellesley incongruously calls 'passes').[19] They are uneven, at times tight, overhung with rocks and trees and strewn with boulders. In some places it is possible for only two or three men to stand abreast. Laborde's force of 5,000 now had a truly massive advantage over Wellesley's 9,000.

From the village of Roliça the British centre now advanced in three columns, with General Crauford's brigade on the left, Nightingale's in the middle and Hill's on the right. Lake's 29th Foot formed part of General Nightingale's middle column.

Surgeon Guthrie takes up the story:

Colonel Lake ... now turned round, and called out, 'Gentlemen, display the colours', the colours flew, and shortly afterwards he again turned round and addressed the line thus, 'Soldiers, I shall remain in front of you, and remember that the bayonet is the only weapon for the British soldier!'[20]

Midday came. One officer, Captain Jonathan Leach of the 95th Rifles, reports on the 'intense and suffocating heat' and that to breathe was 'like inhaling air from a bread oven'.[21] Colonel Landmann now continues:

The 29th Regiment was ... coming up with Lieutenant Colonel Lake at their head, the band playing a country dance. Lake was mounted on a complete charger, nearly 17 hands high, with a famous long tail, and was dressed in an entire new suit, even his leathers, boots, hat, feather, epaulettes, sash, etc., being all new, and his hair powdered and queued, his cocked hat placed on his head square to the front, and, in fact, accoutred in the strictest accordance with

King's Regulations. I was so struck with the marked distinction between the 29th Regiment and all others, … that I could not refrain from observing to Lake, 'Well, colonel, you are dressed as if you were going to be received by the King.' Lake smiled and replied with a dignified air, 'Egad, sir, if I am killed today, I mean to die like a gentleman.'[22]

Wellesley was now in grave difficulty. He could not dislodge the French skirmishers, the *tirailleurs*, from the lower slopes, while Laborde's main force had the protection of dry-stone walling and the use of his guns. Viewed either from the base of the hill or from the top, the position is arguably more 'formidable' and apparently more impregnable than many positions in the subsequent Lines of Torres Vedras. Moreover, the Anglo-Portuguese advantage in cannon and cavalry was of little effect in such terrain.

Meanwhile, General Loison's army, numbering some 7,000, was doggedly approaching from the south-east and was only a few hours away. Controversy surrounds the assertion by António Pedro Vicente that a detachment of Freire's forces, led by General Manuel Pinto Bacelar, by advancing from Abrantes on the Tagus, had so manoeuvred as to delay the junction of the two French corps.[23] The addition of Loison's force would almost level the odds numerically and, in view of the territorial advantages, would weigh heavily in the French favour. If and when Loison arrived to bolster Laborde, the best Wellesley could hope for was stalemate, a state of deadlock. He also already knew that the transports were bringing reinforcements and that Sir Hew Dalrymple and Sir Harry Burrard would supersede him within days. Both of them, he knew, were relatively inexperienced, and subsequent events leading to the outrageous Convention of Sintra were to prove them to be incompetent as well. A glorious future career now hung in the balance.

Accordingly, the order came from Wellesley for the infantry to 'make a demonstration' against the gullies and the inevitable cross-firing; it was Wellesley's only hope.[24] The light company of

Lake's 29th, along with two other light companies, was detached with the objective of making a demonstration against a gully to their right. Some of the old grenadiers cried out to Lake, 'We can do it as well as them, colonel!', but he replied 'Never mind, my lads. Let the "light bobs" lather them first, we will shave them afterwards.'[25] Instead of supporting the demonstration against the right-hand gully, Lake now found the right-wing companies of his battalion at the foot of the next gully, which lies further to the left of the Cruz Alta (the High Cross), as Landmann tells us.[26] Disputes rage as to which were the gullies in question. Personally, I believe that they were the two gullies immediately to the right of the former road from Columbeira up to the hilltop village of Azambujeira, a road that is now an overgrown track. The two gullies meet shortly before Lake's Cross.

Just like a chip off the old block, Lake interpreted 'making a demonstration' in the only way that he had ever known, a headlong charge with fixed bayonets, with himself on horseback at the head of his grenadiers. Up they went, under heavy fire, in a column, two or three abreast, slithering, sometimes on all fours.[27] Halfway up, Lake had his horse shot from under him; he had had the foresight to lend his own charger 'Black Jack' to one Major Gregory Way, who now dismounted and gave him back his steed.[28] There was a clear echo of the change of horses at Laswaree. Depleted by very heavy casualties, the grenadiers, led by their inspired and inspiring young colonel, burst their way up and round to an area of cooks, commissars and camp-followers. They also encountered a small group of Swiss, who promptly changed sides.

Lake set about forming his men into a line, fire now coming from General Brenier's battalion, which had to detach itself from the main French force to deal with the problem to its rear. The colonel called out, 'Don't fire, men, don't fire; wait a little, we shall soon charge!' Having supervised the prolongation of his line, he was just shouting the word 'Forward!' when he was hit by skirmisher shots. First, he was struck slightly in the back of the neck, but the ball that killed him passed through from side to side beneath the arms. The now riderless 'Black Jack' galloped into the French lines but was returned to the 29th at the time of the Convention of Sintra, in answer to a plea from Lake's regiment.[29]

The wounded of the 29th were now calling on the surgeons to save their colonel first, but it was already too late. A colour sergeant, who stood astride Lake's corpse, was also killed, only succumbing after being shot nineteen times. Lake's left-wing companies now arrived, accompanied by the 9th Foot, the East Norfolks. In the mêlée, 40 of the 29th were taken prisoner, along with six officers, as a result of the vigorous efforts of General Brenier's troops, but the rest fought on tenaciously against heavy odds.

Grasping the golden opportunity created by the confusion in the French position, Wellesley now sounded a general advance. The remnants of the 29th, plus the 9th, surged backwards and forwards, attacking repeatedly and, in Wellesley's words 'with the utmost impetuosity'.[30] Three times they thrust upwards as columns and then redeployed as lines. Wellesley adds that he 'never saw such fighting as in the pass by the 29th and 9th, or in the three attacks made by the French in the mountains'.[31]

However, Ferguson's brigade, shifting from its intended confrontation with Loison's corps, was now pressing the French right, forcing them from the ridge, and only when General Hill's brigade saw the opportunity created for them to converge on the French left did Laborde sound the retreat. At first it was in orderly fashion but soon became pell-mell to the south, with the abandonment of three of his five guns. It was around 4.30 pm: four hours of daylight remained, and the converging Loison was still three hours or 12 miles away to the south-east (at the village of Cercal).

In his despatch to Viscount Castlereagh, the War Minister, Wellesley simply lamented Lake's loss as of a gallant officer who had 'distinguished himself'.[32] But he recognised his true debt to Lake in a letter which he wrote to the young man's brother-in-law, couched in words that he never equalled, even in writing of the glory of Picton at Waterloo:

> I do not recollect the occasion upon which I have written with more pain to myself than I do at present, to communicate to you the death of your gallant brother-in-law. He fell in the attack of a pass in the mountains, at the head of his regiment, the admiration of the whole army; ... his death ... has deprived the public of the services of an officer who would have been an ornament to his profession, and an honour to his country. ... He deserved and enjoyed the respect and affection of the world at large, and particularly of the profession to which he belonged ... Colonel Lake ... was respected and loved by the whole army, and ... fell, alas!, with many others, in the achievement of one of the most heroic actions that have been performed by the British army.[33]

Roliça was the first battle honour won by the 29th Foot, the Worcesters. A fitting memorial to Lake's heroic impetuosity, a 7-foot high cross and plinth, movingly inscribed by the regiment, and restored for the 2008 bicentenary, stand on the heights of Columbeira at the spot where he fell and was buried. A monument also stands to Lake in the north-west (or belfry) tower of Westminster Abbey. Mementoes in the Worcester City Museum include the now familiar cameo portrait, a belt buckle and the fatal musket ball that was later removed from his skeleton. The regimental archives are located at the nearby Norton Barracks.

Michael Glover called the battle of Roliça 'unnecessary',[34] Sir John Moore and the French thought Wellesley's actions 'rash',[35] Raul Brandão describes both Roliça and Vimeiro as 'meras insignificâncias' (irrelevant trivia),[36] though that is surely special pleading within his view that the French were already virtually defeated by the guerrilla activity of the *ordenanças*. That was certainly true of large areas of Portugal, but the fact remains that only an army, in this instance the Anglo-Portuguese forces, could have prised Junot out of Lisbon. Brandão's study, *El-rei Junot*, nevertheless merits close attention for its impressive documentary evidence on Portuguese resistance to French occupation. Too often British accounts have ignored Portuguese sources. Moore's comment reads ironically when one reflects on the missed chances of his own campaign. In answer to Glover, one should point out that Laborde, by his three to four day wait at Roliça, made the battle very necessary or, at the very least, ensured that sooner or later there had to be a confrontation on terms less favourable to the Anglo-Portuguese forces.

To Wellesley's career Roliça was indeed necessary; yet its outcome he owed to the first hero of his Peninsular War, George Lake, who broke the tactical deadlock at Columbeira and bought Wellesley vital hours. Success at Roliça permitted victory at Vimeiro before the supersession by the two incompetents, Dalrymple and Burrard, could take full effect. As Lady Longford points out, the latest list, posted at Horse Guards, of other generals senior to Wellesley (Moore, Hope, Mackenzie, Fraser and Paget — all bound for Portugal) would have relegated Sir Arthur to eighth in the pecking order.[37] There also existed the absurd view of him as a mere 'sepoy general'. If one recalls that Sir John Moore's subsequent unhappy campaign was a hiccup that removed Wellesley's only competent rival, it becomes clear that Wellesley had been enabled at Roliça to demonstrate that he was the one British general truly capable of defeating Napoleonic armies. That was underlined by his victory at Vimeiro four days later. Lisbon thereafter lay only 30 miles to the south.

Both parties in the conflict had used the intervening days after the battle of Roliça to unite and consolidate their forces. Laborde and Loison fell back towards Lisbon, joining forces with General Junot at Montachique near Torres Vedras. The combined French armies now numbered some 14,000, though reserves still occupied Lisbon. Meanwhile, British reinforcements were arriving by sea: General Anstruther's brigade landed at Paimogo (close to the town of Lourinhã) on the 19th; General Acland's brigade disembarked at Porto Novo, near to the villages of Maceira and Vimeiro, on the following day. With the addition of Anstruther's and Acland's troops, Wellesley had close on 19,000 men. In these circumstances, Junot gambled on a surprise attack from the east, whereas Wellesley had been in readiness for a confrontation from the south. Clouds of early-morning dust revealed Junot's advance, leaving Wellesley's forces a frantic hour in which to re-arrange their position.

Now Sir Arthur was ready with his own surprise: he concealed his troops below the skyline of Vimeiro hill on the celebrated western ridge, thus enabling his lines, directed by Generals Fane and Anstruther, and firing in strict sequence, often at close range, to repel three powerful attacks by French columns, cutting huge swathes through their ranks. Defeat stared Junot in the face. The war of words as to which was more effective, column or line, will no doubt continue for ever, but on this occasion Wellesley's concealed lines had ensured him victory, though all was not yet over.

At this point we come to the role in the battle of Lieutenant Colonel Charles Taylor. Aged 36, he was the son of a physician based in Reading in Berkshire. He had worked hard to reform and discipline his regiment over the previous three years. Wellesley now felt that at long last the time had come for a cavalry charge. Whereas Trant's Portuguese infantry was still held in reserve to the north-west of Vimeiro at a position close to the sea between Ribamar and Marquiteira, the Portuguese cavalry had bivouacked close to the British dragoons at Porto Rio. That spot lies on a bend in the river between the villages of Maceira and Vimeiro, very near to where the Hotel Braga now stands. Sensing victory, Sir Arthur raised his cocked hat, just as later at Waterloo. He shouted to Taylor, 'Now, Twentieth, now is the time!' Taylor's great moment had come: he commanded almost 500 men, his own 20th Light Dragoons plus the rather raw Portuguese cavalry, in virtually equal numbers. Could Taylor emulate Lake? At last the Portuguese, too, had a chance to shine.

Out from behind Vimeiro hill came Taylor's troopers, forming a line, with the British in the centre and the Portuguese on the wings. They charged headlong towards the retreating columns of French grenadiers. However, the columns partly re-formed and fired into the Allied cavalry, causing numerous casualties, including a number of Portuguese. Most of the Portuguese troopers clearly decided that the situation was too dangerous: discretion was the better part of valour. They wheeled and galloped back, taking refuge behind Fane's advancing infantry at the centre of the Allied position on Vimeiro hill. Needless to say, they were loudly jeered by the British infantrymen. Nevertheless, according to one of the Portuguese officers present, Joaquim Pais de Sá, the fatal gallantry of Commandant Elisário of the Lisbon police was noted, and the highest praise was won by one Lieutenant Pinto.[38]

Combining military discipline with tactical folly, Colonel Taylor's dragoons surged on till out of control. They burst through French cavalry which had been sent by General Margaron to protect the retreating French infantry and which was also threatening the flanks of the advancing British foot soldiers. The French infantry again inflicted casualties, including Taylor, who was shot dead through the head. Yet uphill and to the east his cavalry galloped, heading straight for Junot's command post at Esteveiras. They were halted by a dry-stone wall and were then charged by overwhelming numbers from two of Margaron's cavalry regiments, held in reserve. Unbelievably, they were not annihilated, and most of the British cavalry fought their way back to Vimeiro hill. Their losses were 21 killed, 24 wounded and 11 taken prisoner; in all, that was one fifth of their number, not one half, as is sometimes claimed. Dragoon Captain Alexander Eustace was one of the captives: wounded and brought before Junot, he was hugely praised for the valour shown by the British troopers. Rifleman Harris supplies a stirring comment:

I lay where I had fallen for a short time, and watched the

cavalry as they gained the enemy. I observed a fine, gallant
-looking officer leading them on in that charge. He was a
brave fellow, and bore himself like a hero; with his sword
waving in the air, he cheered the men on, as he went
dashing upon the enemy, and hewing and slashing at them
in tremendous style. I watched for him as the dragoons came
off after that charge, *but saw him no more*; he had fallen.
Fine fellow! His conduct indeed made an impression upon
me that I shall never forget, ... I was told afterwards that he
was a brother of Sir John Eustace.[39]

This may be a case of mistaken identity, as Eustace had not fallen,
whereas Taylor had. Released in the exchange of prisoners required
by item nineteen of the Convention of Sintra, Eustace later died of
his wounds in Lisbon in January 1809. Whether Harris had
observed Eustace or Taylor, there is no doubting Taylor's valour,
for all that his achievement did not equal that of Lake. Nor can we
deny the heroic efforts of Pinto, Elisário and Eustace.

Refusing to admit defeat, the French now sought to turn the
allied left flank: their Generals Solignac and Brenier made an
unavailing assault on the eastern ridge, around the hamlets of
Toledo, Ventosa and Fonte de Lima, which lie to the north
of Vimeiro. Again they were repelled, and Brenier was even taken
prisoner. Again, the remnants of the 29th Foot, the Worcesters,
played a prominent role. Junot's cause was lost: the following day
he sent General Kellermann back to the village of Vimeiro to
negotiate an armistice.

Taylor, like Lake, was buried on the site of the battle and
likewise received his due commemoration, in his case at his
Oxford college, Christ Church. There, in the famous cathedral, a
marble plaque proclaims that 'he attacked and defeated a very
superior body of the enemy's cavalry, who were advancing rapidly
against the flanks of the 50th and 52nd regiment of foot. He fell in
the moment of victory.' The 50th Foot formed part of Fane's
brigade, and the 52nd part of Anstruther's brigade; both were

advancing after having already forced the retreat of the French infantry. Their flanks were indeed exposed to Margaron's cavalry, and that threat was defused by Taylor's troopers.

We could debate forever the merits of Portuguese discretion in Taylor's cavalry charge — as against the folly of the British dragoons. We could argue endlessly whether Wellesley was wise to order a charge without imposing limits on its trajectory. But at last he had actively involved the Portuguese. Two years later, at the battle of Buçaco, the Portuguese constituted one half of the allied army and shared evenly in its battle honours. This was the result of the superb training brought about by a remarkable, if not entirely harmonious, team: the outstanding Portuguese War Minister, Dom Miguel Pereira Forjaz, and yet another Anglo-Irishman, Marshal William Carr Beresford. Similarly, we should never forget that the Lines of Torres Vedras were in their origin a Portuguese initiative.[40]

There is a curious postscript: Taylor's son, another Lieutenant Colonel Charles Taylor, was killed in 1846, leading his infantry at the battle of Sobraon, the last battle of the Sikh Wars, sometimes described as the 'Waterloo of India'. It was certainly the crowning victory of British arms in that country. Taylor junior earned his own memorial in Canterbury Cathedral. By an odd coincidence he was leading Lake's regiment, the 29th Foot, the Worcesters, in a headlong bayonet charge against the Sikh ramparts.

References
[1] George Landmann *Recollections of my military life* (2 vols., London, 1854) ii, p. 124.
[2] *WD*, iv, p. 95.
[3] Charles Oman *A history of the Peninsular War* (7 vols., Oxford, 1902–30) i, p. 236; J.W.Fortescue *A history of the British army* (13 vols. in 20, London, 1899–1930) vi, p. 206; Elizabeth Longford *Wellington: the years of the sword* (London, 1971) p. 176; Raul Brandão *El-rei Junot* (Lisbon, 1982) p. 240.
[4] João Pedro Tormenta and Pedro Fiéis *A primeira invasão francesa: as batalhas da Roliça e do Vimeiro* (Caldas da Rainha, 2005) pp. 96–7.
[5] Dieudonné Thiébault *Relation de l'expédition du Portugal* (Paris, 1817) p. 178, 'en avant de Rorissa'.

[6] Tormenta and Fiéis, *A primeira invasão francesa*, pp. 130, 150.

[7] Fortescue, *History of the British army*, vi, pp. 207–8, n. 3.

[8] Longford, *Wellington: years of the sword*, p. 170.

[9] Brandão, *El-rei Junot*, p. 238.

[10] William Thorn *Memoir of the late war in India* (London,1818) p. 213.

[11] Thorn, *Memoir of the late war in India*, p. 220.

[12] Colonel Henry Clinton to his brother, General William Henry Clinton, 3 Nov 1803, Clinton Papers, John Rylands University Library of Manchester.

[13] H.E.E.Everard *History of Thomas Farrington's Regiment* (Worcester, 1891) p. 277.

[14] For example, Longford, *Wellington: years of the sword*, p. 176.

[15] *WD*, iv, pp. 96, 103.

[16] Maximilien Foy *Histoire de la Guerre de la Péninsule sous Napoléon* (5 vols., Paris, 1827) iv, p. 310; Thiébault, *Relation de l'expédition du Portugal*, p. 179.

[17] Oman, *History of the Peninsular War*, i, p. 235, n.1.

[18] Brandão, *El-rei Junot*, p. 229.

[19] *WD*, iv, p. 99.

[20] Everard, *History of Thomas Farrington's Regiment*, p. 278.

[21] Jonathan Leach *Rough sketches from the life of an old soldier* (London, 1831) p.22; the 'suffocating heat' was likewise hampering Loison's advance from the east.

[22] Landmann, *Recollections of my military life*, ii, pp. 137–8.

[23] António Pedro Vicente, 'Um Soldado da Guerra Peninsular — Bernardim Freire de Andrade e Castro' *Boletim do Arquivo Histórico Militar* 40 (1970) pp. 201–576.

[24] Everard, *History of Thomas Farrington's Regiment*, pp. 279, 293.

[25] Everard, *History of Thomas Farrington's Regiment*, p. 279.

[26] Landmann, *Recollections of my military life*, ii, p. 144.

[27] William Warre *Letters from the Peninsula, 1808–12* (London, 1909) p. 25.

[28] Everard, *History of Thomas Farrington's Regiment*, p. 280.

[29] Everard, *History of Thomas Farrington's Regiment*, pp. 280, 289.

[30] *WD*, iv, p. 98.

[31] *SD*, vi, pp.118–19.

[32] *WD*, iv, p. 98.

[33] *WD*, iv, p. 104.

[34] Michael Glover *Britannia sickens...* (London, 1970) p. 83.

[35] *The diary of Sir John Moore*, ed. J.F.Maurice (2 vols., London, 1809) ii, p. 267.

[36] Brandão, *El-rei Junot*, p. 243.

[37] Longford, *Wellington: years of the sword*, p. 171.

[38] René Chartrand *Vimeiro* (Oxford, 2003) p. 76.

[39] *The recollections of Rifleman Harris as told to Henry Curling*, ed. Christopher

Hibbert (Moreton-in-Marsh, 1999) pp. 36–7.

[40] See, for example, Helena Rua *Historical and territorial analysis: a contribution to the study of the defence of the city of Lisbon – the Peninsular Wars* (Lisbon, 2006).

CHAPTER 4

Women in the Peninsular War
Charles Esdaile

It is a curious fact, but, setting aside a handful of senior commanders, the most famous combatant of the Peninsular War is a woman.
I refer, of course, to Agustina Zaragoza Domenech, a young
Catalan girl who in 1808 was, at the age of 22, the wife of a sergeant
in the First Regiment of Artillery named Juan Roca. Stationed at
Barcelona at the outbreak of the Spanish uprising against Napoleon,
like many other soldiers of the garrison, Roca fled the French-
occupied city, and eventually made his way to Zaragoza where he
offered his services to the insurgent garrison commanded by the
famous José Palafoz y Melci. Very soon, however, Roca was sent
out of the city to join a Spanish force that was being organised in
the vicinity of Teruel, and the result was that Agustina, who had
travelled to Zaragoza with her four-year-old son to join her
husband, was on her own in the city when the French closed in on
the defenders and laid siege to the city. Thus was the scene set for
an incident that remains to this day remains absolutely central to
the traditional Spanish view of the Peninsular War. On 2 July 1808
the French launched a massive attack on the defences, and, like
many of the women of Zaragoza, Agustina attempted to assist the
defenders by carrying food and water to the walls and succouring
the wounded. As she was approaching a battery that had been
established at the Portillo gate, however, a shell touched off an
expense magazine, the resulting explosion being so great that most
of the gunners were killed or incapacitated. With the French in the
very act of entering the battery, Agustina seized a linstock and

touched off a canon in their very faces, whereupon the remaining defenders returned to their positions and fought off the enemy.[1]

The story of Agustina Zaragoza, or, as she became known as, Agustina de Aragón, is an important one because it gave rise to one of the two dominant images that we have of women in the Peninsular War. Thus Agustina is the patriotic heroine *par excellence*, the woman who rushes to the barricades to defend hearth and home and king and country and through her sheer frailty encouraged the men around her to regain their courage and fight that much harder, while the fact that Goya immortalised her great feat of arms in the famous *Disasters of war* ensured that its memory would become absorbed by an international audience rather than just a Spanish one — in the engraving entitled 'Que valor!' ('What courage!'), we see the slim figure of Agustina not just standing erect and defiant beside an enormous fieldpiece, but also symbolically shielding the observer from an unseen opponent. Nor, meanwhile, is this the only engraving in the series that projects the idea of the woman as combatant, albeit perhaps as a temporary one who takes up arms only in dire emergency. Thus, in 'Y son fieras' ('And they, too, are furies') a group of women who have obviously been taken by surprise by a party of French troops — one of them is carrying a baby under her arm — are seen fighting desperately to defend themselves with a variety of improvised weapons. Less dramatic, but otherwise rather similar is 'Las mujeres dan valor' ('The women inspire courage') in which we see two women locked in combat with two French soldiers who have evidently been trying to rape them, and 'No quieren' ('They don't love') in which a French soldier grapples with a girl while an old woman — possibly her mother, perhaps — steals up behind him with a knife poised to stab him in the back. However, striking though these four engravings are — engravings which, it should be stressed in no way imply that women were anything other than occasional combatants — on looking at the *Disasters of war* as a whole, we generally see women rather as the helpless victims of man's inhumanity. In 'Tampoco' ('Nor this'), 'Ni por esas' ('Not even for these'), 'Amarga presencia' ('Bitter presence'), 'Ya no hay tiempo' ('There is no longer any time'), women are seen being raped; in 'No se puede mirar' ('One cannot look') they figure in a mass execution; in 'Estragos de la guerra' ('War damage'), they are crushed in the wreckage of a collapsing building; in 'Escapan de las llamas' ('Escaping from the flames'), 'Yo lo vi' ('I saw this') and 'Y esto también' ('And this too'), they become fugitives and refugees; in 'Que alboroto es este?' ('What is all this row'?), they collapse in floods of tears on receiving bad news, possibly, given the context, of the death or execution of a son or husband; and, finally in 'Cruel lástima' ('Cruel misfortune'), 'Caridad de una mujer' ('Charity of a woman'), 'Madre infeliz' ('Unhappy mother'), 'Gracias a la almorta' ('Thanks be to vetch'), 'No llegan a tiempo' ('They did not arrive in time'), 'Sanos y enfermos' ('Healthy and sick'), 'De que sirve una taza?' ('What is the use of a cup?') and 'Si son de otro linaje' ('If they are of other lineage'), they are seen begging in the streets or succumbing to famine and disease. Be it noted that in one or two instances these images of women enduring the utmost misery also show women succouring the poor and starving, but this, of course, merely opens a door on yet another aspect of traditional ideas of how women become engaged with the experience of war.[2]

In the *Disasters of war*, women are either heroines or victims, or, indeed, sometimes both at once, and it is only very rarely that we get a glimpse of a more complicated reality, just about the only example of this being 'Populacho' ('Mob'). In this particular engraving, which is probably a reference to the savage disturbances which gripped Spain in the course of the uprising of May 1808, the inanimate body of a man is being dragged through the streets of some town or village at the end of a rope to the accompaniment of a hail of blows, the point here being that Goya includes a woman among his tormentors and portrays several others watching from the crowd. Exactly what this image is intended to suggest is a complex matter that considerations of length make it impossible to go into here in any detail, but this does not really matter, what should concern us being the fact we have a hint of a more complex reality than the one that we outlined in the previous paragraph.[3] What makes it all the more necessary to address this is the fact that thus far it has been almost entirely absent from the historiography. There is, true, a growing body of material that deals with the subject of women's role in and experience of warfare in what may be defined as the 'horse and musket period' (roughly, 1650–1850), and some of it certainly contains material which is relevant to the Peninsular War: indeed, we even find among it one work that is specifically about the women who accompanied Wellington's army.[4] As yet, however, even in Spanish or Portuguese there is as yet no monograph on the full range of the feminine experience of war in the Peninsula. In fairness, Elena Fernández García has made a major contribution to the literature with an important work that looks at the position of women in Spanish society in 1808, and shows convincingly, first, that women were not entirely absent from the political debates that were unleashed by the uprising of 1808; second, that at least some Spanish women were inspired by patriotic sentiment; and, third, and perhaps most importantly, that the Peninsular War was a moment when the women of Spain first became 'visible' as a separate group in society.[5] Of this last claim, in particular, there is certainly some evidence: anxious to emphasise the general nature of the revolt against Napoleon, chronicler after chronicler realised that it was a useful device to suggest that the determination to resist the French was such that it even spread to the female half of the population — for example, 'As they have done on thousands of other occasions, the very women prepared enormous meals at their own cost, and took them to the troops guarding the walls'[6] — while, in an attempt to play upon gender sensitivities, at least one writer added weight to his plea for greater British involvement in the war by making the women of Spain the mouthpiece for the reproaches he heaped upon

London in respect of its supposed back-sliding and duplicity.[7] When the Spanish struggle was finally accompanied by victory, meanwhile, women, or at least an iconic conception thereof, were sometimes given a central role in proceedings. Here, for example, is Juan Domingo Palomar, a substantial resident of Alcalá de Henares:

> There was dancing in the Plaza Mayor; there were bands of musicians in every street; and there were scenes that is simply impossible to describe without having seen them. In just three hours, too, a cart appeared with a young girl dressed up as Spain; beautifully clothed and armed with a sword in one hand and some broken chains in the other, she represented the freedom of the nation, and was proceeded by a guard of soldiers carrying swords and axes and a choir singing patriotic hymns.[8]

However, all that said, Fernández García's approach does not get us very far: cases of genuinely politicised women are few and far between, and Goya-style representations of women as patriotic furies proof of nothing. Indeed, the general level of the Iberian contribution to the debate has thus far been very disappointing. Thus, the only monograph-length work on the subject known to the author is a collection of essays that takes the reader though a series of women who became famous in the struggle against the French — Agustina Zaragoza; the Condesa de Bureta, another heroine of the siege of the Zaragoza who, as a close relative of José Palafox, threw herself into the task of organising logistical support for the defenders; Manuela Malasaña, a young seamstress who was killed in the Dos de Mayo; and María Bellido, a peasant girl from Bailén who distinguished herself carrying water to the Spanish troops fighting the French.[9] Yet this approach is of even less value than that of Elena Fernández in that the cases that the work concerned discusses are either clearly exceptional — Agustina Zaragoza may have been rewarded for her courage by the ever-demagogic Palafox with a commission in the Spanish army, but she was the only woman to have achieved that honour — or much mythologised: for many years, for example, it was insisted that Manuela Malasaña was killed carrying cartridges to the defenders of the artillery park, whereas she was shot by a firing squad after being searched in the street and found in possession of a pair of scissors; in the first instance, she appears as an ardent patriot, whereas in the second her role is simply that of an innocent bystander who is caught up in the crossfire. Also interesting to note here is that, according to the traditional version of events, she had gone to the artillery park with her father and died acting at his direction, a fact that in effect neutralised any threat that her image might pose to the subordinate position that women were supposed to occupy in society.[10]

How, then, can we move from an approach centred on famous women to one that seeks to present a wider picture?[11] Even a cursory glance has suggested that the common experience of women is far from impossible to reconstruct. Thus, women have been found to be present in a great range of archival sources in Britain, France, Portugal and Spain alike; in folksong and story; and, finally, and this a fortiori, in large numbers of the memoirs that were published by veterans of the conflict. While the author is the first to admit that there is much more work to be done, it is hoped that that this paper will nevertheless both constitute an appetising 'taster' and suggest that that the female experience of the Peninsular War was anything but the stereotypical picture that is all that has been on offer hitherto.

Before going any further, however, let us first admit that, to a greater or lesser extent, evidence can be found to support most aspects of the heroine/victim syndrome. Beginning first of all with the idea of women as combatants, Agustina Zaragoza is not the only example that we can find of women who took up arms against the French (indeed, she probably is not even the best case to which one can point: there is little firm evidence that she saw much in the way of front-line combat after winning her spurs in July 1808 even in the defence of Zaragoza, the fact being that she appears to have been employed as little more than a kind of a human mascot).[12] At least one British officer speaks of coming across women serving with bands of irregulars as fully fledged combatants. 'One of the Spanish women belonging to Don Julián's corps was very remarkable both for her beauty and her dress, which was a sort of uniform with epaulettes, and a sabre and sash, the latter thrown over one shoulder.'[13] At the same time it is at least possible that, impelled by the murder of her father and brother in the French occupation of Bilbao in August 1808, a young Basque woman named María Martina Ibaibarriaga for a time actually headed a guerrilla band in the Cantabrian mountains and eventually gained a commission in the Spanish army, although it is important to note that she did so disguised as a man, while there are also references to women taking part in skirmishes in the Serranía de Ronda.[14] Finally, here and there are to be found tales of heroines in the style of Agustina de Aragón: in La Palma de Condado (Huelva), for example, according to local tradition, a tavern keeper of the Calle de Escalones named María Marcos (or, to use her nickname, Marímarcos) played a key role in driving out a small force of French troops that was attacked in the town on 9 March 1811.[15] A variant on the theme, here, is the issue of the murder of isolated French soldiers. Travelling to Madrid after the battle of Bailén, for example, the British liaison officer, Samuel Whittingham, was introduced to a peasant woman who was supposed to have killed eight French soldiers by knocking them on the head as they were drinking from her well and then throwing them down its shaft.[16] This case can be dismissed as mere patriotic nonsense, but it is nonetheless interesting that a woman could have persuaded the local community to accept such a claim (and still more interesting that she should have been moved to make it), whilst from time to time rumours also surfaced amongst the French that Spanish women were taking unwary soldiers to their beds so as later to do away with them.[17] If some women fought, meanwhile, others became fierce advocates of the Patriot cause and thereby broke the bounds of the very narrow frame in which the vast majority of Spanish and Portuguese women tended to be constrained. Stationed at Chiclana during the siege of Cádiz, for example, a military pharmacist attached to the corps of Marshal Victor named Antoine Fée who was billeted in the home of a prominent local citizen named Múñoz found himself constantly assailed by one of the household's three daughters, a fiery young woman named María who 'took hatred of the French to a state of exultation'.[18] Meanwhile, still another way for women actively to involve themselves in the patriotic struggle was to become a spy, one such case that has been uncovered being that of María García, a housewife from Ronda who took it upon herself to pass information of all kinds to the local partisans, and two others those of María Isidora de Gastañaga and Manuela Rubín López, both of whom were sentenced to terms of imprisonment for espionage in the Basque provinces.[19] And, finally, there was also always the possibility of engaging in acts of symbolic resistance — the French hussar, Albert de Rocca, saw Andalusian women wearing 'English stuffs on which the pictures of Ferdinand VII and the Spanish generals most distinguished in the war against the French were painted'[20] — or, alternatively, solidarity with the allied cause: when the governor of Seville invited 200 of the leading ladies of the city to a ball celebrating Joseph's saint's day on 19 March 1810, for example, the only ones who turned up were 40 who were 'so dishonest that they were the scandal of the crowd that out of mere curiosity had gathered to inspect the decorations that had been put up to mark the occasion', whilst here one may also cite a number of incidents mentioned in British memoirs in which local girls succoured officers who had been taken prisoner by the French or otherwise fallen upon hard times.[21]

All these examples come from places that were under French occupation, and the fact is that the same can be said of the vast majority of such stories. If this is so, it is no coincidence: to murder French soldiers, turn spy or succour Allied prisoners required a conscious act of courage and, in some cases at least, a willingness to act beyond normal gender expectations, the result being that women who engaged in such actions could not but stand out from the crowd. However, large parts of Spain were never occupied or only saw French occupation for some of the war. If women engaged in activity that was in one way or another supportive of the war effort, in such areas opportunities for positive involvement in the struggle tended to be rather more constricted. Yet here, too, those eager to find proof that women were as much Spanish patriots as men were do not go unrewarded. The participation of women as auxiliaries in the defence of such cities as Zaragoza and Gerona is well known — in the latter instance there even appears to have been a degree of organisation in that 100 or so women were even formed into a unit known as the Companía de Santa Barbara.[22] However, it is not impossible that women also took up arms in the defence of their homes, as witness, for example, the following passage relating to the French sack of Rivadavia in February 1809:

> Under the walls of the town, I saw a horrible tableau that summed up the effects of this odious war. Lying nude and disfigured in the midst of a pile of corpses, I saw the bodies of two women. One of them was middle-aged: beside her lay a musket, whilst she was wearing a cartridge box and a sabre … and had been killed by a bullet in the chest while fighting in the ranks of the Galicians. The other, who was entirely naked and could not have been more than seventeen years old, had evidently joined a group of peasants in trying to pull a mounted officer from his horse: she had been cut down by a blow from a sabre that had split her skull in two.[23]

Service, however, did not need to be nearly so dramatic. A participant in the unsuccessful siege of the castle of Burgos in the autumn of 1812, for example, John Aitchison encountered a pleasing scene when he paid a visit to the town:

> I … was very happy to find a woman at almost every door

busily employed in tearing rags to pieces to make lint for the hospitals. They seem all in great spirits at the prospect of soon being freed from the enemy who ever since the commencement of the siege have kept them in dreadful alarm: the castle completely commands the whole town and looks particularly into the market place.[24]

Involvement in the struggle was naturally accompanied by suffering in the struggle. Examples here are legion, but emblematic enough (and particularly interesting in the manner in which it is recorded) is the description left by Bugeaud of the sack of Lérida in 1810:

The soldiers, greedy for pillage, scatter themselves about among the houses; carnage ceases and gives place to scenes of quite another kind. The conquerors are everywhere to be seen in the arms of the vanquished: Carmelites ... old women, young virgins, all experienced the transports of our grenadiers, and several of them are said to have cried out, 'Oh, if I had known that this would be all, we should not have been so afraid!'[25]

If mass rape was probably not a day-to-day occurrence for the women of Spain, poverty and hardship certainly were. To take just one source of the many that could be cited here, the registry of the petitions handled by the Conde de Montarco during his time as Comisario Regio of Andalucía in the period December 1810–August 1812 contains all too many references such as the following: 'Doña María de los Dolores Rivero, widow of Captain José de Vargas, begs that she might receive assistance on account of her miserable situation ... Doña María Luisa Laglé, widow of Captain José Romero, begs that she be assisted on account of her necessity ... Doña María Teresa Eguía, the wife of Captain Francisco de Paula Serrano, who was taken prisoner in the battle at Durango, acknowledges herself to be indigent and begs for assistance.'[26]

There is, then, no smoke without fire, but the sort of cases we have discussed are but the beginning of the story. As will become clear, this has many other chapters, and to access these it seems sensible first to consider the manner in which women encountered the war in the hope of thereby establishing what may be called a typology of experience. Thus, women became involved in the war by two separate routes: whilst for some women the war was something they travelled to from the outside in their capacity as army wives and, very occasionally, cross-dressers who had succeeded in concealing their sex and enlisting as soldiers, for others the war was something that suddenly arrived on their doorsteps in the form, first, of a distant force that tore away husbands, sons and brothers and brought with it higher prices and food shortages, and, second, the very real presence represented by siege, battle or simply the passage of the rival armies. What we have, then, are two quite different experiences of the Peninsular War in that for the first group the struggle was simply one more episode in a life that was already to some measure set apart from that of the rest of society, a continuation, indeed, of their normality, whereas for the second it came rather as a disruptive force that represented a break in that normality. As time went on, of course, so the two groups to some extent became conflated thanks to the fact that at least some women in the second group responded to the change in their circumstances brought about by the war by leaving their homes and entering the military world as wives or camp followers, but the idea that some women came to the war whilst others found it rather came to them is nevertheless a useful point at which to begin our discussion.

At the heart of the first group, clearly, is in the British army the figure of the army wife and, in the French one, that of the *vivandière* or *cantinière*.[27] Lacking modern logistical services, all armies had since time immemorial depended on women to enable them to take the field, whilst there was, too, at least some rudimentary recognition of the need to look to the morale of the soldiery, and thus it was that they developed a variety of devices to ensure that women could be drawn into the military world. In the

British army the main means of doing this was quite simply to make use of the institution of marriage in that, with the permission of their captains, soldiers were allowed to marry and thereafter to have their wives and children (a useful source of future recruits and camp-followers alike) live with them. However, in the French army and possibly the Spanish and Portuguese ones as well — the Spanish army certainly had *cantineras*, though the story of Agustina Zaragoza suggests that in time of peace soldiers were also allowed to marry in the English style — women were in effect allowed to enlist in their own right by applying for a limited number of posts of sutleresses so that involvement with the army did not come as a result of marrying a soldier but rather as a species of career choice that brought with it the possibility of earning a more-or-less modest living (it should here be noted, however, that the women appointed to these posts were by no means always neophytes in so far as the world of the army was concerned: on the contrary, many of them were probably already soldiers' wives who saw securing one of the new posts as being one of the only ways open to them of avoiding separation from their husbands). Thus, unlike the British-army wife, the *vivandière* or *cantinière* was primarily seen as an economic agent who could supply the troops with food, drink and other services such as washing and repairing clothing and equipment and, unless the authorities were prepared to tolerate a situation that was entirely unregulated — which, of course, they were not — was a necessary invention in a conscript army whose men were likely to spend most of their time of service fighting in imperialistic wars of conquest beyond the frontiers of France.[28] Of course, most such women settled into common-law partnerships or even marriages with soldiers in the regiments to which they had become attached, but, in stark contrast to the situation in the British service, they were licensed business-women first and wives second, whilst their quasi-military status was recognised by the issue of a modified version of the normal regimental uniform.[29]

Armies, then, needed women, and, taking the British army

first of all, for all the evil reputation that pertained to soldiers as a general group, there seems to have been no shortage of young women who were ready to succumb to the charms of the red coat of an infantryman, the green jacket of a rifleman or the blue dolman of a hussar. That young girls should have fantasised about such an ideal is hardly surprising. Dressed in more-or-less splendid uniforms and, at least in the case of the recruiting parties that were the representatives of the armed forces who were most likely to be encountered in, say, the depths of eighteenth-century England, bedecked with plumes, cockades and ribbons, soldiers offered a splash of colour in a world otherwise dominated by drab homespun. At the same time, too, soldiers travelled, saw the world and had adventures, whilst, by virtue of their very profession, the naïve mind might easily invest them one-and-all with notions of honour, courage and vitality, not to mention the hope of social advancement: did not 'Over the hills and far away' — probably the most well-known of all the many ballads that dealt with the military world — speak of the soldiers returning from the wars 'all gentlemen'? In a most literal sense, then, soldiers seemed to offer young girls a way out, and, with soldiers themselves often all too happy to share tales of bravado and in general 'buckle their swash', there must have been many village maidens who thrilled at the arrival of a recruiting party or detachment of troops.[30] Meanwhile, what is quite clear is that, even if the reality of life in the army was one of drudgery and privation — things that were also part and parcel of the daily round in civilian society — there was also a certain freedom from social convention that may have been attracted to young women possessed of an independent disposition. That this was so is suggested from an anecdote recounted by William Graham, an officer of the Forty-Eighth Foot who landed in Portugal in the autumn of 1812 and thereafter made a long journey across the country in search of his regiment. Reaching the town of Lavos, he met an old friend of his named Macleod who was stationed there as a commissary and had taken up with 'a lady named Margaret, a very termagent for temper'. Presumably a soldier's wife who had struck out on her own as a prostitute, this character proved, to put it mildly, a lively acquaintance:

> For some time she behaved well, but broke out one day at dinner, when Macleod happened to say something that displeased her. She then took hold of the table cloth, and madam sent everything on the floor, soup spilt, a smash of dishes, glasses, etc. This, to her, was genteel and in style, and that night she got drunk with brandy, saying [that] it was the finest comfort in nature.[31]

One may assume that on the whole the women of the French army were not creatures of milk and water either — Blayney, indeed, paints a very dark picture: 'In the act of spoliation, the female campaigners are worse than the men, for, being lost to every feminine virtue, they plunder and murder with the greatest coolness and composure'[32] — but there was a crucial difference between them and the British army wife. Whereas the former automatically followed their units to war, for the latter there was no such indulgence. On the contrary, no matter how many soldiers had acquired wives, the latter were only permitted to follow their menfolk to war at a rate of six women to every hundred men. As soon as a regiment was ordered to embark, a ballot was held to choose which women would accompany the troops and which ones would be left behind. This was truly a terrible moment for all concerned: for those who followed the regiment, there was the continued security of the home that it provided and the promise of rations, but for the latter the only assistance was a licence that allowed them to beg their way back to their places of origins. Encumbered with children as they often were, for such women the prospect was a terrible one, and all the more so as they were very often likely to have attracted considerable social opprobrium on account of having taken up with a soldier. A few women doubtless contracted bigamous marriages while others may have contrived to find decent employment, but for many there was no option but to take to the streets as common prostitutes.[33] With such a prospect before them, not to mention the pain of a parting that was almost certain to be forever, the many wives who drew a bad number could not but be thrown into the utmost despair. In a number of folk songs and ballads dating from the era, then, we hear of wives begging their husbands to help them disguise as boys so that they could present themselves as recruits and thereby stay with the regiment, while the memoirs of the period have many affecting descriptions of devoted couples spending their last night together in tears or desperate women going down on their knees and begging sympathetic officers to be allowed to go with the troops.[34]

Given that the straits to which most of the women who were left behind were reduced, the British army wives who accompanied their soldier husbands to the Peninsular War may initially have been relieved. However, whether such feelings of relief were permanent is another matter. Along with the *cantinières* and *vivandières* who were their counterparts on the other side, the women found themselves caught up in a bitter struggle that was nothing like anything that was experienced anywhere else in Napoleonic Europe. One could here advance anecdotes by the dozen to illustrate what they went through, a picture of long marches in extreme heat and icy cold, inadequate rations, disease and starvation, babies born by the wayside and children dying in miserable encampments, extraordinary courage, devotion and resourcefulness, courage under fire, sometimes of prostitution, drunkenness and plunder, and, perhaps least recognised of all, a contribution to the war efforts of all the combatants.[35]

All of this applied to the women of all armies, but, in terms of suffering, it has to be said that the *cantinières* and *vivandières* may have had a particularly grim cross to bear. Thus, while the whole issue of atrocity in the Peninsular War is one that is open to examination, there seems to be no doubt that the women of the French army faced the possibility of dangers that were much less likely to confront their sisters on the other side of the lines. Many

French memoirs have accounts of women suffering appalling deaths at the hands of Spanish guerrillas, while, if some of these stories are a little dubious, there seems no doubt that *cantinières* and *vivandières* who fell into the hands of the enemy could endure periods of captivity of a far darker nature than those that pertained on the other side of the lines (particularly badly off here were the hundreds of women who fell into the hands of the Spaniards following the battle of Bailén: confined in fever-ridden hulks in the harbour of Cádiz for more than a year, they were eventually consigned, along with their menfolk, to the desert island of Cabrera, and with it a régime of neglect and incompetence that led to the death of thousands of the survivors from starvation).[36]

Yet if service with the French army carried with it special dangers, it also offered women opportunities that were quite unique. Thus, if *cantinières* and *vivandières* can on the one hand be seen as forerunners of the uniformed women's auxiliary services of the two World Wars, on the other they were also petty *entrepreneurs* who made their living by providing the troops with goods and services, and this in turn produced the extraordinary spectacle of women emerging as small-scale business tycoons. Let us here trace the story of how this might have worked. In the beginning the *cantinière/vivandière* was just a girl — literally: it should be remembered that many such women were originally *enfants du troupe* — whose stock in trade was limited to what little she could carry, a blanket, a small keg of brandy and a haversack with a little sausage and tobacco and some needles and thread, her own body, and, if she was lucky, quick wits, a pretty face, and a winning smile. Thus equipped, the girl would launch out on a personal odyssey in which success depended above all on establishing a strong rapport with the men of her unit.[37] On the one hand, they were potential clients, of course, but, on the other, they were also vital sources of supply in that, unable to consume or carry with them all the copious plunder they laid their hands upon, they would hand it on to a friendly sutleress in exchange for the promise of, say, a few free drinks; still more so, meanwhile, potentially at least, they were also both protectors and willing hands — men who would come to the rescue in moments of crisis or help put up a tent at the end of a day. When we hear, then, of *cantinières* and *vivandières* dispensing brandy for free on days of battle or taking pity on some hungry conscript by giving him a bit of sausage, we should not think so much of angels of mercy as canny business-women investing in their own futures. And, by the same token, when we hear of girls rushing into the front line to rescue wounded soldiers, encourage the troops or even snatch up a musket, we should think not so much of patriotic viragos, but rather shopkeepers eager to show solidarity with their customers.[38] One can, of course, take all this too far — amongst all the women who served in the French army, there were beyond doubt hundreds of cheerful, generous and even heroic souls who really did conform to the stereotype that has tended to come down to us[39] — but this is neither here nor there. Particularly if she was willing to provide sexual services as well — something that certainly did not always happen — engage in a spot of sharp practice, such as driving up prices when goods were short, or 'fence' articles that had been stolen by the soldiery, it would not be long before the girl would be able to acquire a mule and a tent and thereby start to increase her stock-in-trade and turnover. Next would come, perhaps, another woman — some local girl displaced by the horrors of war, perhaps — and a wagon, and in time one wagon would become two or three or even four. Just to keep such a convoy on the move — a task that obviously required constant negotiation with the military authorities — would have been difficult enough at the best of times, but in Spain and Portugal it was obviously all the harder, even if those countries, by virtue of their very poverty and want of comfort, also offered special advantages to *cantinières* and *vivandières*. The risks were high and the challenges even greater, but with them came the chance of a fame and fortune that was simply inaccessible in any other way of life.[40]

One should not, however, imagine for a moment that the

realities of life for most camp followers were anything other than grim in the extreme. Some soldiers, certainly, treated their wives well enough, but very soon all pretence of romance was lost, for, if their husbands were killed, the women concerned had no option but to take a new husband immediately. The considerable value that attached to their services ensured that there were always many suitors, and in this fashion women might run through half a dozen such partners. Yet few campfollowers were able to escape the trammels of their sex. In the British army, at least, not only were they perpetually condemned to half rations, but they were also absolutely dependent on the protection of an individual soldier, and this last left them vulnerable to a variety of more-or-less degrading treatment. As a German soldier of the King's German Legion named Johan Christian Mämpel remarked, 'I had also the opportunity of witnessing the singular English custom of the sale of wives. A soldier of the Tenth Regiment of infantry sold his wife to a drummer for £2 sterling; he, however, did not keep her long, but parted with her to the armourer of the regiment for 2 Spanish dollars.'[41] As if this was not enough, meanwhile, there was little hope of fair treatment in legal terms in which connection we would do well to cite a grim story from the pen of William Surtees:

> A grenadier of the Eighty-Eighth Regiment (I think it was) had come over from his own division to prevail upon his wife, who had deserted him and taken up with a sergeant of our first battalion, to return with him, she having, as I understand, left him with one or more children, the first of their marriage, which he was anxious she should come and take care of. They had often, I fancy, quarrelled, and he had probably used her ill, but he was now desirous of a reconciliation, and entreated her to return with him to his regiment. He prevailed on her to accompany him to some distance from the bivouac that they might the more freely discuss the subject ... While walking in a field close to the wood in which the bivouac was situated, and, arguing the

point with some heat, and she still persisting in remaining where she was, he became so exasperated at her continued refusal that he, in a rage of jealousy and anger, drew his bayonet and plunged it in her bosom. Her cries soon brought people to the spot, who at once secured him, and he was instantly committed to the provost prison tent, and her body, of course, brought in and buried. Poor creature! She was one of the gayest of the females which graced our rural balls near Ituera only a short while previous and had often danced with old General Vandeleur on those occasions. I believe he was not brought to trial for it, as her ill-conduct probably had been considered as in some measure palliating what he did, and that he might be supposed to have been irritated to a degree of madness when he perpetrated the fatal act.[42]

Thus far we have spoken of women of the lower classes only, but these were not the only females who travelled to the Peninsular War. In both the British and — especially — the French armies, the wives and mistresses of officers and generals appeared in Spain and Portugal in considerable numbers (the appearance of a larger number of French women of this sort can be explained by the fact that the Iberian Peninsula was initially at least seen as an integral part of the French empire and one which would very soon be reduced to order). In general, such women gravitated to the relative safety of garrison cities such as Madrid, Barcelona, Seville and Lisbon. A good example here is the redoubtable Laure Junot, who in 1810 travelled to the Peninsula to join her husband, then a corps commander in the forces of Marshal Masséna, and who, being with child, ended up spending a miserable autumn and winter in the isolated city of Ciudad Rodrigo.[43] Yet even a relatively civilian lifestyle was not without its dangers and privations — Madame Junot was almost captured by guerrillas whilst out riding with the wife of General Thomières near Salamanca, for example, while others found themselves in the direct line of fire when the convoys they were with came under attack or held to ransom by bandits[44] —

while other women habitually travelled with the armies. Thus, amongst the French prisoners at the battle of Bailén were the wives of General Schramm and General Chabert, whilst Marshal Masséna famously invaded Portugal accompanied by a beautiful young woman arrayed in the costume of a hussar.[45] Equally, the young and beautiful wife of Marshal Suchet was often to be observed riding with her husband's headquarters on horseback.[46] In short, for some women of the upper classes, at least, the Peninsular War brought opportunities for travel and excitement that some at least appear to have relished, and with them, if they so chose, the chance to show their mettle on the battlefield: at the battle of Salamanca, for example, the 'delicate and beautiful wife of Colonel Dalbiac ... forgetful of herself, impelled by strong affection for her gallant knight ... rode amidst the enemy's fire, exposing herself to imminent peril'.[47]

For a woman, however, 'imminent peril' was not just a matter of enemy bullets. Less romantically, then, even reasonably genteel camp-followers could easily find themselves at the mercy of both a complete want of privacy and casual sexual harassment: returning to Portugal from leave in England in October 1811, for example, George Bowles found himself sharing a cabin with seven other infantry officers, an officer of the Royal Wagon Train, a commissary, a cavalry veterinary surgeon, an erstwhile officer who had been dismissed from the British service and was travelling out to join the Portuguese army, and, last but not least, the wife and daughter of an officer who was already serving in Portugal. Until the last night of the voyage, the two women endured nothing more but overcrowding and discomfort, but at this point the Wagon Train officer and the man travelling out to join the Portuguese got 'extremely drunk, and, after beating the commissary, offered very improper solicitations to the ladies'.[48]

Having surveyed the varied experiences of the women whom the Peninsular War brought to Spain and Portugal, it is now time to turn to the women to whom the war came.[49] Here, too, we find that the experience of 'the other half' was varied in the extreme. The first and most obvious thing to say is that as the rival armies tramped to and fro across the Iberian Peninsula, they attracted, as they had always done, large numbers of women to their ranks. As early as the autumn of 1808 there were complaints about the crowds of camp followers hanging around the Spanish forces, and it was not long before the French and Anglo-Portuguese forces began to experience the same phenomenon.[50] Some of those who took to following the drum were the wives of men who had enlisted or been conscripted or killed and had no other means of support, while others were mere prostitutes, but still others 'kept the camp fires burning' for reasons that were more complex. First of all, there were women who genuinely fell in love with French or British officers and took to the road with them: the pharmacist, Fée, mentions at least two such cases, while Juana María Dolores de León, a young girl rescued from the sack of Badajoz who married Lieutenant Harry Smith of the Ninety-Fifth Foot, travelled with him for the whole of the rest of the Peninsular War and was eventually, as Lady Smith, commemorated by the town of that name in South Africa.[51] This last case is, perhaps, a very particular one, but that such cases occurred is hardly surprising: in towns across Spain young men of all the different armies were flung into close proximity with the civilian population and, like young men of every age and nation, were all to happy to forge an acquaintance with the proverbial maidens of the parish. Here, for example, is George Bell of the Thirty-Fourth Foot:

> We passed ... the month of September [1812] in the town of Yepes ... There were many pretty girls in the town, all fond of dancing, in which we often indulged of an evening until we became almost of one family; in fact, every young fellow had his sweetheart. The young ladies were charming, barring education: the priest took care to keep them in ignorance and free from the trammels of over-much learning, so that they were generally very idle, but fond of music,

dancing, gossiping and eating grapes and chocolate. However, we thought our fair friends here of a superior race, and
indulged them in every way we could. It was a terrible blank
to those who could not speak their beautiful language.[52]

None of the women encountered by Bell at Yepes made any
attempt to leave their homes when the Anglo-Portuguese army was
forced to evacuate the area in October 1812, but it is quite clear that
the presence of Bell and his fellow officers had nonetheless at
the very least provided them with a break in the monotony of
lives whose dreariness was remarked on by many travellers to the
Peninsula. Here, for example, is Marshal Soult's aide-de-camp,
Alfred de Saint-Chamans, on the women of Andalucía:

> Their spirit is lively, but at the same time marked by little in
> the way of manuals of emulation or lives of the saints; they
> are never trusted with any others except the famous *Don
> Quijote*. The women of Andalucía are idle of all under-
> standing: they are shamefully ignorant and read but little,
> whilst the only books they look at are ordinarily works of
> religion such as the bible, and uncaring: during the heat —
> that is, for seven months of each year — they normally
> spend the mornings and afternoons lounging on their patios
> beside a fountain in a state of undress ... They sing and
> chatter together, but have no interest in anything serious and
> do not even engage in much of the way of needlework.[53]

Rather similar, meanwhile, are the comments of Andrew Blayney,
a British general captured in a bungled disembarkation on the coast
of Andalucía:

> In my intercourse with Spanish families, I could not help
> remarking the listless indolence in which the females doze
> away their lives: never have I seen a book or a needle in
> their hands, and their sole occupation seems to be playing
> with pet animals, particularly cats and dogs. Besides a mon-
> key, several parrots and some pigeons, my landlady [at
> Granada] had four little curs, whose barking and snarling

made them complete nuisances; she had also a large and small cat, for each of which a proportionate sized hole was cut in the bottom of every door, not recollecting, I suppose, that the small cat could pass through the large hole.[54]

Such a life, of course, could not but breed boredom and frustration, and it was, perhaps, a sense that this was so that was the origin of the idea found in many travelogues that Spanish women were avid for sexual adventure. Of this a good example may be found in the writings of Alexandre de Laborde, a French diplomat who travelled extensively in Spain prior to 1808. Thus:

> The females of Spain are naturally beautiful and owe nothing to art ... They are in general well-proportioned, with a slender and delicate shape, small feet, well-shaped legs ... a mouth neither large nor small, but agreeable, red lips, white and well-set teeth ... large and open eyes ... delicate and regular features, a peculiar suppleness, and a charming natural grace in their motions ... Their countenances are open, and full of truth and intelligence; their look is gentle, animated and expressive; their smile agreeable ... They are of a warm disposition; their passions are violent and their imagination ardent, but they are generous, kind and true, and capable of sincere attachment. With them, as with the women of other countries, love is the chief business of life, but with them it is a deep feeling, a passion, and not, as in some other parts, an effect of self-love, of coquetry, or of the rivalries of society. When the Spanish women love, they love deeply and long ... If the Spanish ladies are agreeable, if they are sometimes well-informed, they owe it only to themselves, and in no degree to their education, which is almost totally neglected. If their native qualities were polished and unfolded by a careful instruction, they would become but too seductive.[55]

Even more explicit, meanwhile, was a fellow French diplomat, Louis-François de Bourgoing: 'Depravity knows no bounds. It infects all classes of society and even those whom one would expect at least to have the appearance of shame ... and it is not rare to receive advances from that sex destined by nature not to provoke but to await them.'[56]

Such comments, of course, were based more on cultural prejudice than on reality — indeed, Laborde specifically admits that, whilst Spanish women may have been avid for love inside, on the outside they were careful to abide by the rules of social convention. That said, however, if they were so inclined, then war undoubtedly presented them with many opportunities for dalliance and even adventure, the fact that such a desire for adventure was present being strongly suggested by the following popular song from the region of Salamanca:

Ah, ah, ah, ah, ah, ahhh ...
I ride with a lancer, a-perching on his lance:
Is it that he wants to take me to France?
My lover is a lancer of Don Julián:
If he loves me a lot, I love him more.[57]

In this mixture of fantasy, repression and suppressed desire, there is much to build upon. Indeed, ever eager to present the French army as a liberating force, admirers of Napoleon have always been keen to argue that the coming of French occupation presented those who wished to take advantage of it with a chance of throwing off their chains, while the archives do provide us with instances in which something of the sort appears to have been happening: for example, 'Juan Parra, resident of Rota, petitions in respect of the problems he has been having with his wife, María Aldana, and requests that she be brought to her senses and admonished for her conduct ... Being unwilling voluntarily to re-unite herself with her husband, Miguel Rodríguez, María Manuela Brava ... requests a judicial separation.'[58] Whether large numbers of women really did run off with the invading forces in a bid to start a new life, as such observers have claimed, is unclear, but what is certainly true is that plenty of examples can be found of young women who ended up in the

French camps.[59] On 2 March 1813, for example, we find an officer
of the French Army of the North named Marenghien pleading with
the commander in chief of that force to allow a young Spanish
woman who had been living with him to stay with him rather than
being forcibly returned to her parents, while Louis Fantin des
Odoards describes how in the last days of the campaign in Galicia
he rescued a 19 year-old girl named María from a group of infantry
who had seized her after killing her husband in a skirmish, and
thereafter kept her with him in his billet.[60] Equally, at Andujar
Blayney encountered 'a beautiful Spanish girl of about 18, whose
elegant shape, perfect head and bosom, shaded by ... hair falling in
graceful ringlets over her shoulders, might have entitled her to
sit for the picture of Venus' who had supposedly thrown herself
on the protection of the governor, General Blondeau 'to escape the
brutality of the brigands' and was now acting as his 'housekeeper'.[61]
On top of this, meanwhile, there were the scenes that many British
soldiers witnessed when the Anglo-Portuguese army overran the
French baggage train at Vitoria. To quote George Bell, 'Oceans of
women — wives, actresses and nuns — were captured, but ... all of
them were treated with respect and allowed to follow their husbands
and sweethearts as they found opportunity.'[62]

    Not all women who took up with the invaders necessarily
went to war. On the contrary, many relationships were evidently
rather conducted wholly in the context of garrison life. Of such love
affairs the invaders' memoirs are full. Here, for example, is Charles
Parquin, a veritable *beau sabreur* who by his own account enjoyed
a string of amatory adventures stretching from the frontiers of
Portugal on the one hand to those of Poland on the other:

> At Salamanca my duties as adjutant obtained for me
> excellent quarters in the house of a beautiful Spanish
> noblewoman, Doña Rosa de la N., whose husband, a colonel
> in the Spanish army, had died two years previously. Like
> any widow who still retains a touch of vanity, she had
> instructed her maid to say she was 25 and this was the

answer I received when I sought this detail from the maid. But this little lie, if indeed it was one, was not at all necessary for, whatever my age, Doña Rosa was one of the most enchanting women I have ever seen in her life. She was quite small, but her movements were marked by a supple gracefulness ... She had no children and lived alone with her servants in a house where comfort and even luxury were clearly in evidence. Mine were clearly very good quarters; I could have had none better. Every evening I would spend an hour or two by the fire with my hostess. I had to avoid politics in our conversation as Doña Rosa, who was as proud as any Spaniard could be, would not tolerate contradiction. In the end I persuaded her to banish politics from our conversation. This was a considerable achievement ... Later on, as one can imagine, I did not stop there. I made further requests and, in short, I was happy, very happy indeed.[63]

If French accounts are anything to go by — not to mention events in France herself between 1940 and 1944 — such liaisons were frequent.[64] Fée, for example, remarks that the women 'paid no attention to nationality, but rather let themselves go wherever their sympathy took them', while Heinrich von Brandt, an officer of German extraction serving with the Legion of the Vistula in Aragón, couples this idea with that of both sexual and political liberation. 'Although women, especially the mature ones, bitterly rebuked the French for their lack of religion and for their insatiable appetites, ... on occasion during our wanderings we had the agreeable experience of meeting ardent francophiles, especially young brides with old husbands or ... nuns or novices whose Mother Superiors had set them at liberty on the approach of the French.'[65] If they are not pure invention, however, what did the love affairs written of by the invading forces represent? Genuine affairs of the heart? Encounters with prostitutes or outright rapes sanitised in later life as something less shameful? Attempts by artful local women to secure a protector? We simply do not know, but what is clear is that the frequency of such liaisons cannot in itself be taken as evidence that women were particularly inclined to associate the French with liberation.[66] Indeed, there were those who saw in them nothing more than flightiness and frivolity, though such observations in reality probably reflect simple boredom. To quote George Bowles, 'We arrived at the former of those towns [i.e. Zafra] on the 19th [March 1812] without seeing anything more of the enemy, but in time to postpone a very gay ball which was to have been given that night … in honour of Joseph Bonaparte, and to which I rather believe … a considerable number of the *belles* meant to have gone. As long as women [can] dance, I believe they don't much care with whom.'[67] That the invaders did conquer more Spanish women than did the British, let alone the Portuguese, is probable, but to explain this it is necessary to refer neither to some supposed political dynamic, nor, as at least some British officers did, to superior French cultural adaptability and *savoir faire* (in this last respect, however, it has to be said that figures such as Colonel Browne of the Twenty-Eighth Foot, 'a most wild and eccentric character', did not help: finding himself on the very southern fringes of Spain in a district where the women still swathed their heads in scarves, Moorish fashion, the good colonel amused himself by stopping each woman that he met so dressed and 'made them open the *mantilla* that he might have a fair peep at them').[68] More to the point is surely the fact that the French were in occupation of much of Spain for so much longer than any other force, in Portugal precisely the same advantages which they enjoyed pertaining rather to the British. As Dallas wrote, 'The number of Portuguese women who followed the British army is incredible.'[69] In short, all over the Peninsula women at best traded on their femininity as a means of surviving the conflict and at worst turned more-or-less openly to prostitution, the worse that an area was hit by the ravages of war the more common and, indeed, more general was likely to be this solution to their problems. Writing of one *pueblo* in the hard-hit marches of Spain and Portugal, the

German commissary Augustus von Schaumann wrote, 'As regards morals, I must confess that in all my travels I have never come across such a Sodom and Gomorrah as that place was. The girls and women of the higher as well as of the lower classes were practically all disreputable. Pure virgins were rare.'[70]

As war raged around them, the women of Spain and Portugal became in some instances adventurers, in some instances refugees and in some instances providers (something for which they often faced punishment: following the liberation of Porto in May 1809, for example, one María Margarida Maxima was imprisoned for two months by the town council for the crime of having had French soldiers in her home).[71] Meanwhile, they also found themselves fulfilling other roles. As the French army conquered more and more territory, not the least of these was almost literally to win the hearts of the invaders. Thus, faced by an announcement that Joseph Bonaparte intended to visit their city, the new authorities that had been established in Málaga in the wake of French conquest in 1810 gave orders that the women of the town were to dress in their best, line every balcony along the main street and strew flowers in his path.[72] Meanwhile, just as the young Polish noblewoman, Maria Walewska, had effectively been expected to prostitute herself for her country when Napoleon entered Warsaw in 1806, so something of the sort may explain an incident that is supposed to have taken place at Granada in which 'one of the prettiest women of the town — a member of one of the best families in the province — was so delirious with enthusiasm that she even wrote to [King Joseph] to request the favour of being allowed to visit him in bed.'[73]

On a more humble level, either individually or collectively, female intercession with the authorities was a frequent weapon in the hands of an increasingly desperate populace. For example, we find women petitioning the French authorities to release arrested family members, and travelling to the headquarters of guerrilla bands to secure the release of sequestered sons: as an example of the former, we may cite a petition from one Leonarda de Esparza imploring the French governor of Bilbao, General Thouvenot, to release her husband, Juan María de Iranzu, from imprisonment in Vitoria (according to her, Iranzu had never been a soldier of any kind, but had simply been seized by some French troops without any reason whatsoever near his hometown of Zornoza), while, as one of the latter, we have the mother of the future Spanish statesman, Ramón Santillán, successfully persuading the redoubtable Jerónimo Merino to let him return home after being swept up in a *leva* in his home town of Lerma.[74] Such approaches, moreover, were by no means always personal: in Málaga, for example, the French governor, Jean-Pierre Maransin, was on 15 August 1812 approached by a delegation of 20 women headed by none other than the wife of head of the *josefino* civil administration who had decided to take advantage of the festivities being held to mark Napoleon's saint's day to appeal for clemency for the 44 civilians who had been arrested in the wake of the city's temporary occupation by Spanish regular troops a month earlier.[75] Alternatively, women also had a role in the face of foragers, or at least those of Wellington's army. William Tomkinson, for example, was a cavalry officer who frequently found himself employed in such a role on the frontiers of Portugal in the autumn of 1811:

> The procuring of forage through this winter for the horses was attended with the greatest difficulty … The detachments left their quarters soon after daylight, and were absent from six to eight hours generally, and frequently until dark. The peasants hid their straw with the greatest care, being the only chance of keeping what few oxen remained to them for the purpose of agriculture alive until the spring. They hid their straw behind stores of wood laid by for fuel, which two or three dragoons would remove with several hours' work, and possibly not find above three or four days' supply for three or four horses. The carrying it away was always attended with the complaints and lamentations of the women, who

followed us out of the place saying ... their oxen must now
die.[76]

And, finally, women might also take the lead in efforts to save their
communities from violence. For example, posted with his battalion
of the Twenty-Eighth Foot to assist in the defence of Tarifa, Robert
Blakeney witnessed a scene that was the very antithesis of the heroism of Agustina Zaragoza. Summoned to help defend the walls, the
local town guard had no sooner started to make their way to their
posts than a scene of near bedlam broke loose:

> The streets were instantly crowded with women, one
> seizing a husband, another a son, a third a brother ... all
> endeavouring to snatch them by force from out their war-
> like ranks, loudly and bitterly exclaiming against the British,
> who, they cried or rather screamed, being fond of bloodshed
> themselves, would force others into fighting whether
> willingly or otherwise. At length, urged by some British
> officers and breaking away from their wives, mothers,
> sisters and lovers, in whose hands remained many cloaks,
> coats, hats and even torn locks of hair, the poor nuts arrived
> half-shelled upon the ramparts.[77]

One group of women to whom the war came that is worthy
of special mention consists of Spain's nuns. It would perhaps be
tempting to see the nun as a figure that was especially vulnerable to
the horrors of war, but, to judge from the chronicles which many of
them kept, in fact their experiences varied enormously from one
community to another. Even in parts of Spain that were crossed and
recrossed by the rival armies, good fortune — or, as the nuns
concerned insisted, divine protection — could keep particular
convents free from harm. As an example, one can here cite the
Barefoot Carmelites of Alba de Tormes. Situated right in the main
square, their convent was a prominent landmark in a town that was
repeatedly occupied and fought over by the field armies, and yet
not once did it come to harm, and that despite the fact that both the
other convents in the town were sacked at one time or another.

Following the Spanish defeat at Alba de Tormes in November 1809, French troops poured into the town and slaughtered many Spanish fugitives, but not one enemy soldier even tried to force the doors, whilst their victorious commander even extended the nuns the courtesy of sending them rations of bread and meat the next day. Much the same happened in June 1812 on the night of the battle of Salamanca except this time the French were in retreat, the nuns again being kept from harm by orders that placed the convent under guard until the last troops had left the city. And, finally, in November 1812, the arrival of French forces in the town yet again in the course of their pursuit of Wellington's retreating forces was accompanied by no worse an intrusion than that of two engineer officers who wanted to get a view of the castle (which was being held by a Spanish rearguard) from the convent's roof and could not have been more respectful.[78] Rather similar, meanwhile, was the experience of the Barefoot Carmelites in Seville: not only was the convent left in peace on the arrival of the French forces in January 1810, but friendly French officers even kept the nuns supplied with communion wine (it should be noted here that, whilst in principle the French wished to abolish all religious orders and actually closed down a great many monasteries and friaries, convents were left alone other than a ban being placed on the acceptance of new novices and existing nuns being given permission to apply for secularisation, the hope being that the figure of the nun would ultimately literally die off).[79] However, other communities were not so lucky either in that they encountered much less generosity from the occupying forces — for a good example, one might cite the experiences the convent of Recollective Augustinians in Sala-manca[80] — or in that the war was a time of dispersal, flight and emigration. The Barefoot Carmelites of Burgos decided to abandon their home rather than trust to the tender mercies of Napoleon when he arrived before their city in November 1808 and, sometimes walking all night, travelled on foot through bitter winter weather to sister houses in, first, Lerma, then Segovia, and finally Avila, from whence they dispersed to similar institutions in Palencia and Valladolid.[81] Still more frightening was the experience of the Barefoot Carmelite community at Calatayud: having fled the French troops that had been sent to deal with the uprising in Aragón at the beginning of the war, they took to the road once again in the wake of the Spanish defeat at Tudela. As the community's anonymous chronicler recalled: 'The town emptied anew, and at 11 o'clock in the morning on 27 November 1808 we nuns left our enclosure for the town of Ybides ... in the style of pilgrims, with staves in our hands and bundles on our shoulders ... Though the journey took no more than five hours, it was very difficult.' With the French now in permanent occupation of Calatayud, it was judged too dangerous to return, and eventually the community scattered to the four winds with some of the sisters returning to their old homes and others travelling as far as Valencia and Ibiza.[82] Finally, to add to the greater or lesser travails of becoming a refugee, there was sometimes added the misery of battle: the experiences of the Barefoot Carmelites of the convent of San José in Zaragoza during the sieges of 1808–9 were dramatic in the extreme, while their sufferings were probably increased still further by the fact that, trapped by the demands and expectations of their calling, the nuns concerned could only huddle together in a series of ever more dangerous refuges, of which the last was the great basilica of Nuestra Señora del Pilar:

> In the Pilar basilica ... we felt as helpless as creatures ever could, and could only place our trust in the one God ... All the fire of the enemy was directed at the church ... and we were in the very part of it where most of it seemed to be falling ... As so many bombs were coming down, we crept into a dark little room beneath some stairs ... It was very dirty, and we could not stand upright ... For food we had no more than raw vegetables ... whilst to drink from there was but one jug, and that did not hold enough water for everyone.[83]

Tales of rape and massacre, then, are rare, although there

are certainly a few cases in which dreadful atrocities were certainly perpetrated on convents caught up in the direct wake of storm or battle (by far the worst appear to have taken place at Medina de Río Seco in June 1808 and Badajoz in April 1812, the culprits in the latter instance being British troops who had just come through the horrors of the attack on the walls). Even so few nuns had anything like what could be described as a 'good war' — a further problem worth noting here is the fact that, hit by heavy French demands for money and supplies alike, many communities had to sell off large parts of their patrimony in order to survive[84] — while in those parts of Spain and Portugal traversed by Wellington's army there was the added embarrassment caused by the behaviour of young officers steeped in a Protestant myth that regarded convents with a mixture of fascination and horror and convinced to a man that the 'fair inmates' had been incarcerated in them by cruel brothers or step-fathers. With officers, perhaps, precluded from indulging their sexual needs with the common prostitutes that were the only sources of such solace open to most of them, in every town they came to every convent was soon besieged by scores of subalterns intent on making contact with the nuns or simply indulging their own fantasies. Here, for example, are the recollections on the subject of Jonathan Leach of the Ninety-Fifth Foot:

> Like all towns of any size in Portugal, [Santarem] is full of churches and convents. With the fair inmates of the latter, we had a deal of chit-chat, although the close iron gratings which separated us from our *inamoratas* obscured them in great measure from view. That they were all blessed with sparkling black eyes, I am ready to swear; the rest was left to the imagination. By means of the whirligig concern in which various matters find their way in and out of the convent, these fair ladies presented us with preserved fruits, nosegays and all sorts of fine things, in return for which certain little notes or love letters written in villainously bad Portuguese were transmitted by the same mode of

conveyance to them. They appeared much interested as to the result of the campaign in which we were about to take a part, and two of them, who were heartily tired of their unnatural prison, declared to myself and a brother officer that they were ready and willing to make their escape with our assistance and to share our fortunes in the 'tented field'. When one considers that by so doing they would have brought down on them the vengeance of monks, friars, *padres* and mother abbesses, and that these black-eyed damsels must have calculated on being buried alive or broiled on a grid-iron had they been detected in such an adventure, we must admit that they were heroines of the first class.[85]

Admittedly, matters rarely went so far as they did at Trujillo when the surgeon of the Thirty-Fourth Foot got roaring drunk with a party of other officers and attempted to storm one of the religious houses concerned, only to be repelled by the nun's chaplain, who mounted a staunch one-man defence of the main door that saw him knock down one of the would-be gallants and put the rest to flight but, even so, whatever participants may later have claimed about lonely young nuns returning their affections, the phenomenon was clearly one that was in some ways even more disturbing than the excesses from time to time engaged in by the French.[86]

Yet it would be wrong to think of nuns simply as passive spectators of a struggle that swept over and around them. On the contrary, many communities threw themselves into the war in a spirit of real fervour; indeed, what Leach recalled as flirtation may rather have simply have been attempts to show gratitude towards men who had come to fight for the common cause (it is noticeable, indeed, that Leach specifically notes the nuns' interest in news of the campaign), while at Salamanca Surtees remembered the nuns 'waving white handkerchiefs out of their iron-grated windows' when the Anglo-Portuguese army liberated the city in 1812.[87] Thus, whilst no nun is known to have shouldered a musket, traditional forms of Catholic devotion were often able to give convents a real sense of participating in the war effort, whether it was the Carmelites of Alba de Tormes parading the hand of Saint Teresa through the streets in procession, or their sisters in Seville engaging in a series of spiritual exercises that were ever more punishing in the hope of winning God's favour:

> For a long time the whole community maintained a watch on the Blessed Sacrament in such a fashion that at all times there were two nuns … imploring the Divine Husband to lift the scourge of his justice from we who had so justly merited it. Meanwhile, the processions that were held in the cloister cannot be numbered, and in these each member of the community … practised the most rigorous mortifications, whether it was by carrying a heavy cross on their shoulders or wearing tightly fastened cilices of the most punishing sort, or making use of other devices whose nature would take too long to go into hear; on each occasion, meanwhile, these devotions concluded with a prolonged act of the most strict discipline … Between eleven and twelve each night there was an hour of contemplation for all the community in addition to the two that are already prescribed by our rule for morning and evening, whilst rogations and novenas were going on all the time. On top of all that, who can number the particular and secret exercises with which each one of these chaste Wives of the Lamb attempted to divest the Divine Husband of the righteous anger that sinners had stirred up in him? Bloodthirsty disciplines, cruel cilices, extraordinary fasts … and the denial of all pleasures, even ones that are not only permitted but most innocent, was the daily occupation of all the nuns.[88]

Whether the courage and determination implicit in these words did anything to save Spain and Portugal from their travails is beyond the competence of this author to judge, but what it is clear is that in psychological terms it was vital, binding communities together and giving them the strength to come together once more the French had been ejected from the towns in which they had lived. Often, of course, they returned to buildings that were little more than blackened shells, but very soon even the most battered communities were rebuilding life and cloisters alike. For at least one group of women, war had brought no change whatsoever; the images of convents being put back together stone by stone that close many of their chronicles are a fitting conclusion to this paper.[89]

If that is the case, it is so for two reasons. In the first place, the image is a comforting one, even an encouraging one, in that we see the scars of war being restored and, what is more, restored at the hands of women. However, on another level, the image is a darker one, for, with every brick that they re-laid, the nuns were re-erecting the walls of their prisons, and, or at least so it may be argued, helping to drag their country back into the past. Indeed, for the women of Spain and Portugal as a whole, and, indeed, the vast majority of those who came to it from other countries, the war had in the end meant only suffering and misery. Whilst it had offered a larger or smaller number of unhappy women a chance to escape from their immediate surroundings, the choice that they made was at best a risky one, and one that often involved them in further servitude. Nor in many instances were they even allowed to pursue their new roles for good. Many of the Spanish and Portuguese women who joined the French army as wives or lovers may be assumed to have followed their soldier-partners to France when they retreated across the frontier, but in the British army the situation was very different.[90] Not only were even the miserly pensions allotted to official *vivandières* or *cantinières* noticeable by their absence, but the only women allowed to travel with Wellington's army when it embarked for home in August 1814 were those who could afford to pay for their own passage — essentially officers' wives — and those women who had come out to the Peninsula with British regiments. All the others — and there were almost certainly many thousands[91] — were forcibly cast off and marched back to the Pyrenees in the custody of a column of Portuguese troops. 'The scene which ensued was distressing', writes the Scottish infantryman, Joseph Donaldson, 'the poor creatures running about concealing themselves in the vain hope of being allowed to remain, but it was all to no purpose: although they were willing to have sacrificed country and relations to follow us, the sacrifice could not be accepted.'[92] Following the drum, in short, had not in the end proved much of an option, the most that can be said for it being that it had provided some thousands of women with a means of keeping body and soul together in the midst of a time of near total economic and social collapse. Yet women were not just victims of the conflict. Rather, they had also been participants in it, and in this fashion 'became visible' in a fashion that had never been the case before. As a step on the road to women's liberation it was a small one indeed, but it was nonetheless one that had to be taken.

Were women, however, conscious that they were on such a road? The answer, alas, is almost certainly that this was not the case. In one case only has any evidence been found of women attempting to advance a specifically gender-related agenda. On 22 February 1809 Cádiz was rocked by major riots. These revolved around a number of different issues, but not the least of these was the arrival in the city of a special commissioner named the Marqués de Villel, who had been sent by the Junta Central to galvanise the cause of resistance. Realising that a major priority was control of the streets, Villel imposed a very tough regime on such institutions as taverns, brothels and gaming houses, whilst at the same time putting prostitutes under further pressure by attempting to force women to dress in a modest fashion. Not surprisingly, prostitutes therefore figured prominently among the rioters, one British eyewitness seeing 'a number of women of the lower classes adding all they could by outcries and gestures to the spirit of violence and mischief among the men'.[93] Yet the female voices in the crowd seemingly did not just belong to prostitutes. To quote a letter the British

diplomat, Sir George Jackson, wrote to his mother: 'One peculiarity of the mob … was that very well dressed women, much above
the common class, were observed … actively inciting and encouraging the people in their riotous proceedings.'[94] As to why this was
so, he had no doubts: '[Villel] has been playing the Bishop of
Durham with regard to women's dresses, and has actually sent a
lady to a convent who refused to conform to his orders on that head
and … told him to his face that it was very hot, and that she would
wear no more clothing than she pleased, it being also no object with
her to dress to please him. This has excited all the women against
him.'[95] Evidently, then, there were individual Spanish women who
were resentful of the trammels that society had imposed upon them,
some of whom may even have been radicalised by their experiences
in the Peninsular War, but the fact that so few incidents of gender
conflict of this sort appear to have been recorded suggests that
in 1814 Spanish feminism remained a cause that was waiting to
happen.

References

[1] Such at least is the account of the affair that is currently accepted by leading
Spanish scholars of the Peninsular War; cf. <http://www.1808-1814.org/
persones/agustina.html>, accessed 4 Feb 2009. It will be noted, however, that it
is rather different from the standard version of events. In this, the product, it
appears, of some rather extravagant embroidering of the case by a José Palafox
ever eager to secure good publicity for his defence of the city, Agustina is not
married, but is rather engaged to one of the men serving the battery and, indeed,
snatches up the linstock from his dying hands.

[2] For a convenient means of accessing 'Los desastres de la guerra',
cf. <www.gasl.org/refbib/Goya__Guerra.pdf >, accessed 6 Feb 2010.

[3] The role played by women in the uprising of May 1808 is a subject deserving
of detailed analysis. However, while women were to the fore in many of the
disturbances that took place, this was not a universal reaction: in Cádiz, for
example, facing death at the hands of an angry crowd, the Captain General of
Seville, the Marqués del Socorro, took refuge in the house of a woman of the
propertied classes of his acquaintance; having forced the doors of the building,
the mob burst in, only to find themselves confronted by Socorro's protectoress
brandishing a pistol, the woman eventually being rushed and badly wounded by

a bayonet thrust. Cf. J.B.L. de Crossard *Mémoires militaires et historiques du Baron de Crossard pour servir à l'histoire de la guerre depuis 1792 jusqu'en 1815 inclusivement* (6 vols., Paris, 1829) iii, p. 285.

[4] For some examples of what is available, cf. L.Grant de Pauw *Battle cries and lullabies: women in war from prehistory to present* (Norman, Oklahoma, 1998); *Gender, war and politics: transatlantic perspectives, 1775–1830* ed. K.Hagemann et al. (Houndmills, 2010); A.Venning, *Following the drum: the lives of army wives and daughters* (London, 2005); B.C.Hacker, 'Women and military institutions in early-modern Europe: a reconnaissance' *Signs* 6 (1981) pp. 643–71; J.Lynn *Women, armies and warfare in early-modern Europe* (Cambridge, 2008); F.C.G.Page *Following the drum: women in Wellington's wars* (London, 1986); T. Cardoza *Intrepid women: cantinières and vivandières of the French army* (Bloomington, Indiana, 2010); D.Hopkin, 'The world turned upside-down: female soldiers in the French armies of the Revolutionary and Napoleonic Wars' in *Soldiers, citizens and civilians: experiences and perceptions of the Revolutionary and Napoleonic Wars, 1790–1820* ed. A. Forrest et al. (Houndmills, 2009) pp. 77–95; R. Dekker and L. van de Pol, 'Republican heroines: cross-dressing women in the French-Revolutionary armies', *History of European Ideas* 10 (1989) pp. 353–64.

[5] Cf. E. Fernández García *Mujeres en la Guerra de la Independencia* (Madrid, 2009).

[6] J.M. Calatrava et al., *Contestación por la provincia de Extremadura al aviso publicado por el Coronel Don Rafael Hore en el numero 55 del Redactor General* (Cádiz, 1811) p. 9, Biblióteca Nacional, Colección Gómez Imaz (hereafter BN, CGI). R60036/4.

[7] Cf. Anon. *Representación de las damas españolas a Jorge III, rey de Inglaterra, sobre los vagos rumores de la conducta del gobierno ingles y de sus ejércitos en la Guerra de España* (Cádiz, 1811). Also worth noting here is a decree promulgated by the Junta Suprema Central in condemning the widespread desertion that had taken place among the officer corps and threatening those concerned with dire punishment, amongst the justifications that were given for this being its determination to defend 'the honour of our wives and children, thousands of women have been raped, injured or paraded naked in the streets by the barbarians'. Decree of Junta Suprema Central, 3 Jan 1809, BN, CGI, R6002/2.

[8] *Diario de un patriota complutense en la Guerra de la Independencia* ed. J.Catalina García (Alcalá de Henares, 1894) p. 83.

[9] Cf. *Heroínas y patriotas: mujeres de 1808* ed. I.Castells et al. (Madrid, 2009).

[10] For the story of Manuela Malasaña and its subsequent mythologisation, F.Peyrou, 'Manuela Malasaña: de joven costurera a mito madrileño', in *Heroínas y patriotas*, ed. Castells et al., pp. 155–74.

[11] The work referred to is a study of the French occupation of southern Spain

which is due to be published by Oklahoma University Press.
[12] The service record of Agustina after 2 Jul 1808 is, to say the least, obscure. Whilst she was certainly present in Zaragoza throughout the remainder of its defence, she does not appear to have served with any unit in particular, but rather acted as a species of itinerant cheerleader. Thereafter the story becomes still murkier. Taken prisoner in the wake of the city's fall on 21 Feb 1809, she managed to escape and then travelled to Seville at the invitation of the conspiratorial faction headed by the Palafox family. Hearing that her husband was serving in the garrison of Tortosa, she supposedly travelled there to be with him, only once again to fall into the hands of the French when the city was captured. Escaping for a second time, the story goes that she then served with a guerrilla band in La Mancha, before finally joining the command of General Morillo and fighting with his forces at the battle of Vitoria. Whilst she certainly visited Seville and British troops encountered her in Navarre in the days that followed Vitoria, how much of the rest of this story resembles reality is very hard to say. At least one of the British troops who met her certainly has things to say about her appearance that cannot but call into question the manner in which she was later held up as an icon: 'I saw the heroine of Zaragoza the other day. A heroine of all people ought to be beautiful, and I really should have thought it incumbent upon me to fall in love with her. But nature has bestowed on her a visage so much in opposition to my ideas of beauty that with all my previous determination I could not do it.' Cf. I.Fletcher *For king and country: the letters and diaries of John Mills, Coldstream Guards, 1811–14* (Staplehurst, 1995) p. 62.
[13] G. Bowles to Lord Malmesbury, 3 Mar 1812, in *A series of letters of the first Earl of Malmesbury, his family and friends from 1745 to 1820* ed. J.H.Harris, third Earl of Malmesbury (2 vols., London, 1870) ii, pp. 258–9. It should, perhaps, be pointed out here that there is no certainty that this *guerrillera* actually fought as a man: in the French army, there is at least one case in which a general's mistress habitually affected military-style costume.
[14] References to this case are scanty, but sufficient corroboration exists for it to seem reasonably plausible. For details, <http://www.elcorreo.com/vizcaya/20090306/duranguesado/mujer-armas-tomar-20090306.html>, accessed 9 Feb 2009. For the participation of women in fighting in the Serranía de Ronda, *In the Peninsula with a French hussar* ed. P.Haythornthwaite (London, 1990) pp. 134–5. We should, however, do well to take care in analysing such references. In the summer of 1812, for example, three women were executed in Málaga for the role that they played in serious disorders that broke out in the town after it was temporarily occupied by Spanish troops on 14 July. Were these patriotic heroines who had rallied to the Patriot cause or rather simply looters out to steal the food and money they needed to keep themselves and their families going for a few more days? J.P.Maransin to J.D. Soult, 31 Jul 1812, cited in A.Grasset

Málaga: provincia francesa, 1811–1812 ed. M.C.Toledano (Málaga, 1996) p. 530.

[15] <http://www.scribd.com/doc/27464846/La-Palma-Del-Condado> accessed 10 Feb 2010; whether there is any truth in this story is unknown, but at some point in the nineteenth century the Calle de Escalones was renamed the Calle Marimarcos in honour of the incident.

[16] *A memoir of the services of Samuel Ford Whittingham* ed. F.Whittingham (London, 1868) pp. 39–40.

[17] An interesting variant on this story may be found in the memoirs of a soldier in the Twenty-Second Dragoons named Auguste Thirion. Stationed at Braga after the fall of Oporto, Thirion and three of his friends were enticed out of the convent in which they had been billeted by rumours that there were some particularly pretty whores at an inn in the town. Having found the inn, they settled down to enjoy themselves with the girls, only for Thirion to discover that there were four armed men waiting in hiding in another part of the building. Snatching up the knives from the table that had been set for them, the four men then made a hasty escape and beat a retreat back to their convent. As the author confesses, he and his friends had been very lucky: that same night two other men who had fallen prey to a similar story were murdered. A.Thirion *Souvenirs militaires* (Paris, 1892) pp. 87–91. Highly suggestive, too, is the case of a woman named María Senepe Apri, who was sentenced to a year's imprisonment for complicity when two French soldiers were murdered by insurgents in the house she owned in Alcalá de Gudaira: proclamation of B. de Aranza, 8 May 1810, Archivo Histórico Nacional, Sección de Estado (hereafter AHN, Estado) Legajo 2994.

[18] A.L.A.Fée *Souvenirs de la Guerre d'Espagne, dite de l'Indépendance, 1809– 1813* (Paris, 1856) p. 66.

[19] M.Reder Gadow, 'Espionaje y represión en la Serranía de Ronda: María García, "La Tinajera", un ejemplo de coraje ante los franceses', in *Heroínas y patriotas*, ed. Castells *et al.*, pp. 175–92; *Gazeta de Oficio del Gobierno de Vizcaya*, 27 Apr 1810, p. 3; sentence of the Junta Criminal de Alava, 19 Jun 1812, Instituto de Historia y Cultura Militar (Madrid), Cuartel General del Ejército del Norte (hereafter IHCM, CGEN) 7343.229. In January 1811 two other women, named Ana Gutiérrez and María de la Soledad, were put on trial in Seville with a group of 19 men on charges of espionage and inciting men to enlist in the guerrillas. In the event, neither was found guilty but, with several of the men, they were nevertheless kept in detention pending further investigation, whilst Ana Gutiérrez's husband, an embroiderer named Bernardo Palacio, was sentenced to death. 'Sentencia dada por la comisión militar especial creada en Sevilla en nombre del Emperado y del Rey', 8 Jan 1811, BN, CGI, R60014/79.

[20] *In the Peninsula with a French hussar*, ed. Haythornthwaite, p. 123.

[21] Anon., 'Noticias de Sevilla' (manuscript), n.d., AHN, Estado, Legajo 2994,

No.4. For two cases of feminine generosity towards British officers, G.Bell *Rough notes by an old soldier* (London, 1867) p. 46, and C.Oman , 'A prisoner of Albuera: the journal of Major William Brooke from 16 May to 28 September 1811', in C.Oman *Studies in the Napoleonic Wars* (Oxford, 1929) pp. 185–6. Note, however, that assistance to prisoners of war cannot necessarily be seen as a political act: after the battle of Bailén, for example, women occasionally also came to the help of French captives: J.Roy *Les français en Espagne: souvenirs des guerres de la Péninsule* (Tours, 1856) pp. 149–50, 152–3.

[22] E. Fernández García, 'Las mujeres en los sitios de Gerona', in *Heroínas y patríotas*, ed. Castells *et al.*, pp. 105–28.

[23] J.J. de Naylies, *Mémoires sur la guerre d'Espagne pendant les années 1808, 1809, 1810 et 1811* (Paris, 1817) pp. 63–7.

[24] *An ensign in the Peninsular War: the letters of John Aitchison* ed. W.F.K.Thompson (London, 1981) p. 204. Note, however, the ambiguity of this scene: the women may be glad to be rid of the French, but the suggestion is that this was for negative reasons only, while the sceptical observer cannot but ask whether the women were being paid for their efforts. The image of patriotic heroines doing their duty under fire that the reference conjures up is therefore easily substituted by one of desperate housewives and mothers engaging in menial casual labour to feed their families.

[25] T.Bugeaud to M.A. de la Piconnerie, 4 Jun 1810, in *Memoirs of Colonel Bugeaud from his private correspondence and original documents, 1784–1815* ed. H.D'Ideville (London, 1884) p. 124. It was not just French soldiers who raped Spanish women. Here, for example, is George Bowles on the storm of Badajoz: 'A British officer was shot by one of his own men whom he had endeavoured to prevent ill-using an old woman, [and] nearly a dozen females were actually murdered or died of ill usage.' G.Bowles to Lord Fitzharris, 16 Apr 1812, cited in *Letters of the first Earl of Malmesbury*, ed. Harris, ii, pp. 268–9.

[26] 'Libro donde se sientan los decretos expedidos por el Excmo Sr. Conde de Montarco, Comisario Regio General de las Andalucías por SMC, a las instancias dirigidas a SE colectiva e individualmente como así mismo las ordenes generales e instrucciones dictadas por SE', Archivo Histórico Nacional, Sección de Consejos (hereafter AHN, Consejos), Libro 1741, f. 64. In what is often a rather depressing story, it is pleasing to report that, in response to these appeals, Laglé and Rivero were awarded 200 *reales* and Eguía 300. Conde de Montarco to B. de Aranza, 25 Mar 1811, AHN, Consejos, Libro 1742, f. 51.

[27] Prior to the Revolution, the term in vogue in the French army had been *blanchisseuse*, a washerwoman. *Vivandière* and *cantinière*, meanwhile, appear to have been used indistinguishably from one another.

[28] In the army of the *ancien régime*, by contrast, the British practice seems to have prevailed.

[29] T.Cardoza, '*Vivandières* and *cantinières* in the armies of Napoleon', unpublished conference paper presented at the XXXIII Consortium on Revolutionary Europe, High Point, Feb 2004; and T. Cardoza, 'Habits appropriate to her sex: the female military experience in France during the Age of Revolution', in *Gender, war and politics*, ed. Hagemann *et al.*, pp. 188–205. The governing statute here was a law of 30 Apr 1793. In the eighteenth-century army, the soldiers had taken wives in the English style and the Revolution had greatly augmented the number of such women by removing the need for soldiers who wished to marry to seek the permission of their officers. In the wake of the new law, such women survived, but only at the limited rate of four per company. How far this number was ever enforced is another matter, but as time went on and the French army became dominated by young men raised by conscription, their numbers may be assumed to have fallen sharply.

[30] Of particular interest here is 'A soldier boy for me', an eighteenth-century song in which a young girl reflects on the task of choosing a husband, and specifically rejects a variety of more-or-less respectable alternatives in favour of 'a soldier who marches double quick'. Lyrics accessed at <http://www.mudcat.org/thread.cfm?threadid=53515 >, 7 Feb 2010.

[31] W.Graham *Travels through Portugal and Spain during the Peninsular War* (London, 1820) p. 35.

[32] A.Blayney *Narrative of a forced journey through France and Spain as a prisoner of war in the years 1810 to 1814* (2 vols., London, 1814) i, p. 345.

[33] Such at least is the fate that befalls the heroine of 'Johnny has gone for a soldier', this being perhaps the most famous of all the many eighteenth-century ballads that pick up on the theme of women who are left behind when their men go to war. Lyrics accessed at <http://www.chivalry.com/cantaria/lyrics/shule.html> and <http://www.contemplator.com/america/johnny.html>, 24 Jan 2010.

[34] Page, *Following the drum*, pp. 18–20. For two variants on the theme in song, see the ballads 'The banks of the Nile', lyrics at <http://www.informatik. uni-hamburg.de/~zierke/sandy.denny/songs/banksofthenile.html>, accessed 24 Jan 1810, and 'Susannah Cope', for the text of which, D.Dugaw *Warrior women and popular balladry* (Chicago, 1996) pp. 186–7.

[35] The best documented camp-follower of all is Mary Anton, the devoted wife of a sergeant of the Forty-Second Foot, who accompanied him throughout the campaigns in the Pyrenees and south-west France in the period 1813–14, for whose adventures see J.Anton, *Retrospect of a military life during the most eventful periods of the late war* (Edinburgh, 1841). However, for a rather more larger than life figure, the reader is referred to the redoubtable Mrs Bridget Skiddy in the memoirs of George Bell. Described as 'a squat little Irish woman, as broad as a turtle', she was yet 'a devoted soldier's wife and a right good one, an

excellent forager, and never failed to have something for Dan [her husband] when we were all starving'. Bell, *Rough notes*, pp. 61–134.

[36] Cardoza, '*Vivandières* and *cantinières*'.

[37] Sebastian Blaze provides us with the very epitome of a *cantinière* who had made good in this fashion in the form of a young woman who had marched into Spain with the army in 1808 with nothing more than a cask of brandy on her hip, but made the retreat from Seville in 1812 riding in a fine carriage and dressed in a gown of the finiest black velvet. S.Blaze, *Mémoires d'un apothicaire sur le guerre d'Espagne pendant les années 1808 à 1814* (2 vols., Paris, 1828) ii, p. 251.

[38] The value of cultivating the troops is suggested by a story in the memoirs of Auguste Thirion. He recounts how a young *cantinière*, riding a small mare with a barrel of brandy strapped on either side of her, was swept away when her horse lost its footing crossing the River Esla near Benevente. Fortunately for the girl, the two barrels, which were roped together, came adrift from the horse and, though quickly swept downstream, she was able to cling onto them until such time as a party of dragoons who had galloped along the bank in her wake were able to throw her a rope and pull her ashore (one has to express the hope, however, that what mattered to the men concerned was the girl rather than the brandy!). Thirion, *Souvenirs militaires*, pp. 68–9.

[39] One such who is associated with the Peninsular War may have been Cathérine Baland of the Ninety-Fifth Line who, Lejeune recalls, 'became quite a celebrated character in the army' and was awarded the Legion of Honour in 1813. At the battle of Barrosa, Mar 1811, she is supposed to have gone up and down the ranks of her regiment giving the soldiers brandy and saying, 'Drink, drink ... You can pay me tomorrow.' *Memoirs of Baron Lejeune, aide-de-camp to Marshals Berthier, Davout and Oudinot* ed. A.Bell (2 vols., London, 1897) ii, p. 69.

[40] Again, one should not go too far here. As Cardoza has shown, pension records suggest that most of the women involved in the end gained very little from the war and ended their lives in poverty. At the same time, even during the war the thriving madam was an anomaly. Much more characteristic of the situation of women in the French army is a brief remark that appeared in *The Times* in the context of a report on the siege of Burgos on 27 Oct 1812: 'The besieged are in great want of water. They have got some poor women whom they let down over the wall, giving them 4 *reales* for every bucketful they bring them.' Given the nature of the site, the mission would have been physically very difficult, whilst the women concerned would also have had to run the gauntlet of both musketry and artillery fire, at the same time risking death at the hands of angry residents of the city. I owe my knowledge of this reference to my friend and colleague, Dr Phillip Freeman.

[41] J.C.Mämpel *Adventures of a young rifleman in the French and English armies*

during the war in Spain and Portugal from 1806 to 1816 (London, 1826) p. 324. In this instance we are assured that the woman concerned was well pleased with her various transfers, but, very clearly, this need not always have been the case.
[42] W.Surtees *Twenty-five years in the Rifle Brigade* (London, 1838) pp. 157–8.
[43] For Madame Junot's adventures, L.Junot *Mémoires de Madame la Duchesse d'Abrantes, ou souvenirs historiques sur Napoléon, la Révolution, le Directoire, le Consulat, l'Empire et la Révolution* (4th edition, 7 vols., Brussels 1836–7) iii, pp. 8–104.
[44] Junot, *Mémoires*, iii, pp. 101–2; for an example of such an attack, see the report of Captain Ilarteguí to General Caffarelli, 10 Dec 1812, IHCM, CGEN, 7343.203. In this attack, the wife of a French officer named Journé was captured along with one of her children, but, far from being put to death, they were treated with every courtesy and handed back to the French some days later. P.Thouvenot to J.M.Caffarelli, 21 Dec 1812, IHCM, CGEN, 7343.225. Meanwhile another such convoy story may be found in *Souvenirs militaires du Captaine Jean-Baptiste Lemonnier-Delafosse* ed. C.Bourachot (Paris, n.d.) pp. 85–8; in this instance no women were taken prisoner, but the passage is nonetheless notable for the sense which it conveys of the terror that was inseparable from such experiences. Finally, for an example of bandits holding women to ransom, *Military memoirs of Charles Parquin* ed. B.T.Jones (London, 1987) pp. 114–16.
[45] *Rélations de la campagne d'Andalousie* ed. T.Rouillard (La Vouvre, 1999) p. 121; M. de Marbot, *The memoirs of Baron de Marbot* (London, 1892) pp. 106–7.
[46] S. Larreguy de Civrieux, *Souvenirs d'un cadet, 1812–1823* ed. L. Larreguy de Civrieux (Paris, 1912) pp. 45–6. According to the observer, the sight of Madame Suchet sharing their privations and dangers greatly cheered the troops, while her presence also helped the French commander to forge a variety of social contacts with upper-class women in the province for which he was responsible.
[47] Bell, *Rough notes*, p. 57. The woman described in this anecdote appears to have been made of stern stuff. Named Susannah, she had married her husband in 1804 and thereafter accompanied him constantly, even on campaign. The night before Salamanca, she is supposed to have shared a blanket with him on the ground despite the thunderstorm that drenched the entire army, and narrowly escaped death when a cavalry regiment's horses bolted, while the night that followed saw her combing the battlefield in search of him. *The diary of a cavalry officer in the Peninsular and Waterloo campaigns* ed. J.Tomkinson (London, 1894) p. 188; Page, *Women in Wellington's army*, pp. 56–7.
[48] G.Bowles to Lord Fitzharris, 3 Nov 1811, cited in *Letters of the first Earl of Malmesbury*, ed. Harris, ii, pp. 231–2.
[49] It may here be asked whether the author has not forgotten the issue of cross-dressing (i.e. the well-documented practice of women disguising themselves as

men so as, in some cases at least, to serve in the army). The existence of such women in the Peninsular armies cannot be proved one way or the other, but their numbers were beyond doubt very small. To quote Cardoza, 'Only about five [women serving in disguise] have turned up for Napoleon's reign, suggesting that this practice, if not totally extinct, had become even more rare than before.' Cardoza, 'Habits appropriate to her sex', p. 199.

[50] For a good example of the concerns raised by this subject in the Spanish army, see following order of the day: 'I have regretfully noted the many excesses given rise to amongst the troops on account of their criminal association with the prostitutes who every day flock to the army and, to the general scandal, even accompany it in its marches. These are a serious affront to the holy religion which we profess ... and the fatherland which we hope to liberate, not to mention in every way contrary to discipline. Meanwhile, their consequences have already become all too clear. As well as provoking God's anger in the most extreme fashion, they weaken the soldiers, coarsen their conduct and lessen their readiness to make use of their arms ... whilst at the same time making them imitators of the French. The latter's foul abominations having justly made them hateful not just to God but also the whole world, I therefore command that all women of the sort referred to should be barred from the proximity of the troops and, further, that all those who are currently living with the army should be immediately conducted to the house that used to belong to Don José Romero in the Calle de Sevilla of this city of Utrera so that they may receive due punishment.' Bando of Francisco Javier Castaños, 27 Jun 1808, Archivo de los Condes de Bureta, Papeles de Palafox.

[51] Fée, *Souvenirs*, pp. 68, 104–5. Meanwhile, the history of Juana María de los Dolores de León can best be followed in *The autobiography of Sir Harry Smith, 1787–1819* ed. G.C.Moore-Smith (London, 1910); however, see also J.Kincaid *Random shots from a rifleman* (London, 1835) pp. 292–6.

[52] Bell, *Rough notes*, pp. 59–60.

[53] A. de Saint-Chamans *Mémoires du Général Comte de Saint-Chamans, ancien aide-de-camp du Maréchal Soult, 1802–1832* (Paris, 1896) p. 206.

[54] Blayney, *Narrative*, i, pp. 100–1.

[55] A. de Laborde *A view of Spain* (5 vols., London, 1809) v, pp. 267–70. One feature that may have made the women of Spain particularly exciting in the eyes of foreign observers was that, from an early age, considerable numbers smoked small cigars of ground tobacco, known as *pajitas*, the forerunners of cigarettes. For a detailed discussion of the seductive effect of a habit whose health risks were as yet a very long way from being recognised, Blaze, *Mémoires*, ii, pp. 293–4.

[56] J.F. de Bourgoing *Modern state of Spain exhibiting a complete view of its topography, government, laws, religion, finances, naval and military establish-*

ments, and of society, manners, arts, sciences, agriculture and commerce in that country (4 vols., London, 1808) ii, p. 293.

[57] The sexual tones of this song are impossible to convey in translation: suffice to say that the phrase 'a-perching on his lance' can also mean 'impaled on his lance'. 'Don Julián' was Julián Sánchez, the commander of a force of regular cavalry that harassed the French in the vicinity of Ciudad Rodrigo. For the full lyrics, <http://www.1808-1814.org/poesia/cancion.html>, accessed 11 Feb 2010.

[58] 'Libro donde se sientan los decretos expedidos por el Excmo Sr. Conde de Montarco, Comisario Regio General de las Andalucías por SMC, a las instancias dirigidas a SE coléctiva e individualmente como así mismo las ordenes generales e instrucciones dictadas por SE', AHN, Consejos, Libro 174, ff. 134, 140; for a good example of pro-French apologetics in this respect, J.Elting *Swords around a throne: Napoleon's Grande Armée* (New York, 1988) p. 611.

[59] 'An immense number of the women of Seville', wrote Alexander Dallas, 'became attached to individuals of the French army. The number which left the town during the period of its stay there to accompany their lovers was computed at upwards of 4,000.' A.Dallas *Félix Alvarez or manners in Spain, containing descriptive accounts of some of the prominent events of the late Peninsular War and authentic anecdotes illustrative of the Spanish character* (3 vols., London, 1818) iii, p. 289. Someone else who comments on the immense number of women who took up with the French in Seville and in many cases accompanied them when they evacuated Andalucía in 1812 was the commissary, Sébastian Blaze, for whom the 'army of women' that was so great a feature of the retreat 'just proves that great disorder was occasioned by the war, the fact being that many of these women must have been married'. Blaze, *Mémoires*, ii, p. 254.

[60] Captain Marenghien to J.M.Caffarelli, 2 Mar 1813, IHCM, CGEN, 7343.280; L.F.Fantin des Odoards *Journal du Général Fantin des Odoards: étapes d'un officier de la Grande Armée, 1800–1830* (Paris, 1895) p. 246.

[61] Blayney, *Narrative*, i, p. 157.

[62] Bell, *Rough notes*, p. 94. The presence of so many women at Vitoria was in part explained by the fact that the battle was fought in the context of the wholesale evacuation of France's dominions in central Spain. If most of the women were treated well enough, their experiences were still terrifying: 'Poor Madame Gazan, who had jumped out of her barouche and stuck fast in a field about a hundred yards on one side, had the mortification of seeing the whole of her wardrobe ransacked and dispersed in about 10 minutes.' G.Bowles to Lord Fitzharris, 25 Jun 1813, cited in *Letters of the first Earl of Malmesbury*, ed. Harris, ii, p. 353.

[63] *Napoleon's army: the military memoirs of Charles Parquin* ed. B.T.Jones (London, 1969) pp. 113–14, 121. For a similar story, *Life in Napoleon's army: the*

memoirs of Captain Elzéar Blaze ed.P.Haythornthwaite (London, 1995) pp. 112–14; in this episode, the woman concerned was a bored wife with an aged husband.
[64] That this was so is also suggested by the attempts that one occasionally comes across to demonise any woman who consorted with the French. In 1813, for example, a pamphlet appeared in Córdoba with the catchy title, *El día 8 de enero de 1812 dió muerte esta mujer a sus padres con solimán y veneno, a una hermana suya y una tía que asistía a la cocina por esta resuelta y determinada irse con un oficial de la nación francesa que estaba alojado en su misma casa, y el día 12 de mayo de 1813 fue castigada para ejemplo e escarmiento de otras como vera el curioso lector en este lastimoso romance.* Essentially a penny-dreadful, this told the story of a young girl of 16, who was so denatured by her love for a French soldier who was quartered in her house that she murdered her parents, her aunt and her sister so that she could escape with him. M.C. Simón Palmer, 'De heroínas a traidoras', in *Andalucía en la Guerra de la Independencia* ed. J.M. Cuenca Toribio (Córdoba, 2008) pp. 415–425.

[65] *In the legions of Napoleon: the memoirs of a Polish officer in Spain and Russia, 1808–1813* ed. J.North (London, 1999) p. 87. We shall return to the issue of nuns below. It is worth mentioning here a story that comes from Córdoba. In brief, in September 1810, hearing wild rumours to the effect that a *partida* led by one Francisco Lozano had forced an entire French column to surrender near Lucena, a priest named Francisco de Sales Ramírez made the mistake of remarking to an ex-cloistered nun of his acquaintance that he happened to meet in the street that the guerrillas would be in the city any moment. Unknown to him, however, the nun was relishing her freedom and had therefore become a staunch *afrancesada*. What the priest had done being a breach of the rules laid down in respect of passing on news of the enemy, the woman therefore rushed to report him to the occupying forces, and within 24 hours the unfortunate priest had been arrested and executed. J. Orti Belmonte *Córdoba en la Guerra de la Independencia* (Córdoba, 1930) pp. 148–9.

[66] The same problems present themselves in respect of the response of Spanish women to moments of liberation at the hands of British troops. For example, many British memoirists paint a dramatic picture of the joyful scenes that occurred when Wellington's army entered Madrid on 12 Aug 1812. To quote Charles Cocks, 'I was never kissed by so many pretty girls in a day in all my life.' *Intelligence officer in the Peninsula: letters and diaries of Major the Honourable Charles Somers Cocks, 1786–1812* ed. J.Page (Tunbridge Wells, 1986) p. 191. However, were these women welcoming liberation from the French expressing sexual excitement or simply celebrating the end of many months of misery and famine?

[67] G.Bowles to Lord Fitzharris, 23 Mar 1812, in *Letters of the first Earl of Malmesbury*, ed. Harris, ii, pp. 261–2.

[68] Surtees, *Twenty-five years in the Rifle Brigade*, pp. 110–11; for a good example of a British admission of the superiority of French style and manner, W.Grattan *Adventures of the Connaught Rangers from 1808 to 1814* (2 vols., London, 1847) ii, pp. 95–6.

[69] Dallas, *Felix Alvarez*, iii, p. 294.

[70] *On the road with Wellington: the diary of a war commissary in the Peninsular Campaigns* ed. A.Ludovici (New York, 1925) p. 355.

[71] Order of the town council of Porto, 13 Jul 1809, Biblioteca Municipal do Porto, MS 1773. In Andalucía, meanwhile, the Polish officer, Kajetan Wojciechowski, notes seeing women who had been hanged for the crime of dancing with a Frenchman: K.Wojciechowski *Mis memorias de España* ed. J.S.Ciechanowski *et al.* (Madrid, 2009) p. 106.

[72] J. Mendoza y Rico *Historia de Málaga durante la revolución santa que agita a España desde marzo de 1808* ed. M. Olmedo Checa (Málaga, 2003) p. 132.

[73] A. Bigarré *Mémoires du Général Bigarré, aide-de-camp du Roi Joseph, 1775–1813* (Paris, 1903) pp. 272–3.

[74] Petition of Leonarda Esparza, n.d., IHCM, CGEN, 7343.361; R.Santillán *Memorias de Don Ramón Santillán, 1808–1856* ed. A.Berazaluce (Madrid, 1996) p. 50.

[75] J.P.Maransin to J.D.Soult, 20 Aug 1812, cited in Grasset, *Málaga*, pp. 544–5.

[76] *Diary of a cavalry officer*, ed. Tomkinson, pp. 128–9.

[77] *A boy in the Peninsular War: the services, adventures and experiences of Robert Blakeney, subaltern in the Twenty-Eighth Regiment* ed. J.Sturgis (London, 1899) p. 145.

[78] Francisca Teresa del Espíritu Santo, 'Relación de los prodigios que durante la Guerra de los franceses hizo la intercesión de Nuestra Gloriosa madre, Santa Teresa de Jésus desde el año de 1808 hasta el de 1813 en este convento y villa de Alba de Tormes', cited in *Monjas en guerra, 1808–1814: testimonios de mujeres desde el claustro* ed. J. Sanz Hermida (Madrid, 2010) pp. 11–21.

[79] Elena de Nuestra Señora de la Consolación, 'Relación de lo ocurrido en este convento de Carmelitas Descalzas de Sevilla en la desgraciada época en que los franceses ocuparon nuesrtra España', cited in *Monjas en guerra*, ed. Sanz Hermida, pp. 73–87; for French policy in respect of convents, Blaze, *Mémoires*, ii, pp. 85–6. How many nuns applied for secularisation, it is impossible to say, but some certainly did, a good example being that of Josefa Algaiz, a Concepcionist nun from the convent of San Juan de la Palma in Seville, who requested permission to go and live with a sister who had offered her shelter on the grounds that her community was being reduced to starvation (whether the nun genuinely wanted to be secularised is unclear, but Montarco certainly took it in that sense, and ordered that she be paid the corresponding pension). 'Libro donde se sientan los decretos expedidos por el Excmo Sr. Conde de Montarco, Comisario

Regio General de las Andalucías por SMC, a las instancias dirigidas a SE colectiva e individualmente como así mismo las ordenes generales e instrucciones dictadas por SE', AHN, Consejos, Libro 1741, f. 235. Another case from the same convent was that of María de la Paz Rueda who the same month left the community to return to her family home: Conde de Montarco to acting Bishop of Seville, 29 Jan 1812, AHN, Consejos, Libro 1743, f. 28. In at least one case, they lived to regret their decision. Thus in Nov 1811 the Conde de Montarco received a request from a Dominican nun named Sister María del Rosario Valdivía asking that she be allowed to return to her community in Ronda on account of her fear of the bandits that swarmed on all sides; to this, however, Montarco replied that she should on no account be granted her wish, secularisation clearly being regarded as a one-way street from which there was no return. 'Libro donde se sientan los decretos expedidos por el Excmo Sr. Conde de Montarco, Comisario Regio General de las Andalucías por SMC, a las instancias dirigidas a SE colectiva e individualmente como así mismo las ordenes generales e instrucciones dictadas por SE', AHN, Consejos, Libro 1741, f. 198. Finally, for some of the other women concerned, there was no way back in another sense: on 22 Aug, the acting Bishop of Málaga reported to Montarco that one María de los Dolores Molina, a nun from the convent of San Bernardo, had died in the house of a niece with whom she had taken shelter. Conde de Montarco to Prefect of Málaga, 1 Sep 1810, AHN, Consejos, Libro 1744, f. 48.

[80] María Monica de Jesus, 'Historia de la Comunidad de Madres Agustinas Recoletas de Salamanca durante el periodo de la dominación francesa, años 1808–1814', in *Monjas en guerra*, ed. Sanz Hermida, pp. 123–71. For a particularly grim episode, one might cite the fate of a convent in the *pueblo* of Cienpozuelos whose inhabitants were reportedly gang-raped and then put to the sword by retreating French troops in the summer of 1812, the only survivors being two elderly sisters who managed escape and take refuge in a nearby house. 'The lady abbess, who was 83 years old', writes the author who noted the incident, 'was not safe from their infernal licentiousness, but their conduct saved them the trouble of killing her: she died!' Dallas, *Félix Alvarez*, iii, pp. 154–5, 293.

[81] Anon., 'Salida de la Comunidad de Carmelitas Descalzas de Burgos y trabajos que pasaron en la invasión francesa', cited in *Monjas en guerra*, ed. Sanz Hermida, pp. 23–6. The hussar, Rocca, encountered what was almost certainly a group from this community a few miles outside the city: 'Some of our flank companies met some nuns, who had quitted Burgos during the battle the day before. These poor creatures, some of whom had never been without the precincts of their cloister, had walked in their fright as far as their limbs could bear them without stopping, and had tried to conceal themselves in the groves near the river. On first seeing us at a distance they had dispersed, but on our nearer approach

they gathered together, and remained on their knees, close to each other and with their heads hanging down and enveloped in their hoods. She who had preserved most presence of mind, placed herself upright before her companions. On her face was an air of candour and dignity and that kind of calmness which is given by strong emotions in a moment of despair. The nun who stood up said, as she touched the beads of her rosary ... the only three words she knew of our language: "Bonjour, messieurs François." These poor nuns were left in peace.' *In the Peninsula with a French hussar*, ed. Haythornthwaite, pp. 30–1. For the most part such refugees were given a warm welcome when they arrived in their host convents, but the sudden arrival of large groups of strangers could not but bring with it tensions, and these on occasion became unbearable. For example, 'The Dominican nuns of Santa Catalina de Siena beg to be allowed to return to their old convent on account of the fact that they are completely oppressed in the one in which they are currently living.' 'Libro donde se sientan los decretos expedidos por el Excmo Sr. Conde de Montarco, Comisario Regio General de las Andalucías por SMC, a las instancias dirigidas a SE colectiva e individualmente como así mismo las ordenes generales e instrucciones dictadas por SE', AHN, Consejos, Libro 1741, f. 191.

[82] For all this, Anon., 'Sucesos acaecidos a las Carmelitas Descalzas de Calatayud', in *Monjas en guerra*, ed. Sanz Hermida, pp. 29–36.

[83] Anon., 'Fundación de las monjas carmelitas descalzas de San Jose de Zaragoza: trabajos que padecieron con heroísmo y servicios que hicieron', cited in *Monjas en guerra*, ed. Sanz Hermida, p. 97.

[84] e.g. 'The abbess and nuns of the Convent of La Concepción of the city of Córdoba request permission to sell a number of houses belonging to the convent with a view to meeting their obligation with respect to the contribution ... The prioress and friaresses of the Recollected Carmelite convent of Santa Ana of Seville ask permission to sell a house in the Calle de Laguna with a view to attending to their indigency and paying the contributions which have been required of them', 'Libro donde se sientan los decretos expedidos por el Excmo Sr. Conde de Montarco, Comisario Regio General de las Andalucías por SMC, a las instancias dirigidas a SE colectiva e individualmente como así mismo las ordenes generales e instrucciones dictadas por SE', AHN, Consejos, Libro 1741, ff. 155, 164. Another convent that was badly hit, meanwhile, was that of San Juan de la Palma, the community being reduced to such straits that in February 1812 the abbess was forced to apply to the Conde de Montarco for the money it needed to meet its obligations. Conde de Montarco to abbess of convent of San Juan de la Palma, 4 Mar 1813, AHN, Consejos, Libro 1743, f. 63. For yet another case, we might cite the Madre de Díos convent in San Lucar de Barrameda; in Mar 1813, the prioress wrote to Montarco, outlining the many needs of her community and asserting its complete inability to meet the fresh sum of 24,128 *reales*

that had just been levied on it in respect of the following month's 'contribution',
Montarco responding by writing to the prefect of Jérez, and asking him to do all
that he could to assist the nuns in their tribulations. Conde de Montarco to
J.M.Sotelo, 18 Mar 1812, AHN, Consejos, Libro 1745, f. 119.

[85] J. Leach *Rough services in the life of an old soldier during a service in the East
Indies, at the siege of Copenhagen in 1807, in the Peninsula and the south of
France in the Campaigns from 1808 to 1814 with the Light Division, in the
Netherlands in 1815, including the Battles of Quatre Bras and Waterloo, with
a slight sketch of the three years passed by the army of occupation in France*
(London, 1831) p. 73.

[86] For the affair at Trujillo, Bell, *Rough notes*, p. 41.

[87] Surtees, *Twenty-five years in the Rifle Brigade*, p. 161; *For king and country*,
ed. Fletcher, pp. 160–1. Here, too, is George Bowles on the liberation of Oporto
in May 1809: 'Even the latticed windows of the nunneries were thrown open and
the sacred, though not very fascinating, visages of their antiquated inhabitants
exposed to view for our encouragement.' G.Bowles to Lord Fitharris, 25 May
1809, in *Letters of the first Earl of Malmesbury*, ed. Harris, ii, p. 101. There were,
alas, rather less laudable ways of showing solidarity with the allied war effort: in
at least one convent in Seville, two French nuns who had taken refuge there in the
wake of the French Revolution found themselves not just ostracised by their
fellow sisters, but denied all food. 'Libro donde se sientan los decretos
expedidos por el Excmo Sr. Conde de Montarco, Comisario Regio General de
las Andalucías por SMC, a las instancias dirigidas a SE colectiva e individualmente como así mismo las ordenes generales e instrucciones dictadas por SE',
AHN, Consejos, Libro 1741, f. 180.

[88] 'Relación de lo ocurrido en este convento de Carmelitas Descalzas de Sevilla',
cited in *Monjas en guerra*, ed. Sanz Hermida, p. 74. It is worth pointing out here
that in other senses, nuns remained excluded from the war effort. Thus, the
formation of the provincial juntas in 1808 saw many abbots and priors become
members of these bodies. In no case, however, was the same invitation extended
to their female counterparts.

[89] It is but fair to say that at least some nuns seem to have abandoned their vows
in the cause of the war. Thus, in cities occupied by the French, although convents
were left in peace, it was made clear that nuns were allowed to leave their
cloisters. What happened to the sisters who made this latter choice is unclear. In
principle, they were allotted pensions of varying amounts (the going rate was
anything between 3 and 6 *reales* per day), and this may have allowed a few of
them to survive with the aid of their own resources, though on several occasions
we hear of cases where this was not possible, e.g. those of a Poor Clare named
María de la Merced and of María Felicitas Bevard, an erstwhile nun in the
convent of San Francisco de Paula in Triana — where the money was not paid,

and others where there was clearly financial hardship (in Mar 1812, for example, two secularised nuns from the convent of Santa Isabel de los Angeles in Ronda, named María de Reyes and Josefa Guseme, begged that their pensions be raised from 4 *reales* to 6). 'Libro donde se sientan los decretos expedidos por el Excmo Sr. Conde de Montarco, Comisario Regio General de las Andalucías por SMC, a las instancias dirigidas a SE colectiva e individualmente como así mismo las ordenes generales e instrucciones dictadas por SE', AHN, Consejos, Libro 1741, ff. 136, 151; Conde de Montarco to Joaquín María Sotelo, 6 Nov 1811, AHN, Consejos, Libro 1745, f. 84; Conde de Montarco to sub-prefect of Ronda, 18 Mar 1812, AHN, Consejos, Libro 1745, f. 118. In such instances, it is only too plausible that some of the women concerned became, as Blaze claims, the lovers of French officers: Blaze, *Mémoires*, ii, p. 85.

[90] In the French army, in theory only wives were allowed to travel with the army, but, if accounts of the scenes witnessed after the battle of Vitoria are to be believed, this was at best honoured in the breach, while the naval officer, Jean de Grivel, claims that in his company of Sailors of the Guard several women dressed themselves as soldiers so as to remain with their soldier-lovers and managed to remain undiscovered until after they had returned to France. J.Grivel *Mémoires du Vice-Amiral Baron Grivel* (Paris, 1914) p. 257. The women concerned did not always face a cordial welcome in France: according to the Swiss cadet, Sylvain de Larreguy, his mother refused even to meet the young Extremaduran girl named Josefina Prat y Colomer whom his elder brother, François, a senior official of the customs administration, who attained the post of secretary-general of the military government of Aragón, secretly married while serving in Spain; as for Larreguy and his two other brothers, they cordially hated her, though Larreguy claims that this was less because she was Spanish than because she was possessed of a personality that was as imperious as it was spiteful; Larreguy de Civrieux, *Souvenirs*, pp. 3–4, 56–68.

[91] Mämpel recalls that by the time his battalion left Spain for Sicily in 1813, 'almost all [the] men had either a lawful or a temporary wife'; Mämpel, *Adventures of a young rifleman*, p. 282.

[92] J. Donaldson *Recollections in the eventful life of a soldier* (Edinburgh, 1852) p. 232.

[93] H.Luttrell to E.Vassall, 1 Mar 1809, cited in *The Spanish journal of Elizabeth, Lady Holland* ed. Earl of Ilchester (London, 1910) p. 385.

[94] *The diaries and letters of Sir George Jackson, K.C.H., from the Peace of Amiens to the battle of Talavera* ed. C.C.Jackson (2 vols., London, 1872), ii, p. 386.

[95] *Diaries and letters of Sir George Jackson*, ed. Jackson, ii, p. 386.

CHAPTER 5

The reception of Wellington in Spain, 1808–14
Alicia Laspra Rodríguez

Ever since 1814, the reception of Wellington in Spain has tended to be negative. Even today, criticism and outright hostility to both the Duke and his campaign, fuelled perhaps by historical memories of his men's atrocious conduct in the aftermath of sieges like those of Badajoz or San Sebastian, have led many Spaniards to vent strong feelings of ingratitude when assessing British intervention in the Peninsular campaign. In meetings and conferences held in Spain on the occasion of the bicentennial commerations of the war, question time has often been characterised by members of the audience overtly expressing their hatred of Wellington and the British, as well as undervaluing the role played by the Generalissimo and his countrymen in setting the country free from the imperial yoke.

The damage caused by Wellington's troops to what remained of the china factory in El Retiro (Madrid), in August 1812 appears to many Spaniards to be even more painful than the outrageous plunder of artworks by Joseph Bonaparte and his French agents.[1] Something similar happens with regard to the gratuitous crimes committed by Napoleon's troops wherever they went in Spain, mercilessly killing women, children and the elderly, stealing all they could carry and destroying what they could not, for example, the splendid stained-glass windows of a great many ancient churches.

Those of us who, for the sake of historical accuracy, feel it our duty to confront and challenge such attitudes, often find ourselves in embarrassing situations when lecturing to non-specialist, albeit educated, audiences in forums of the greatest importance for diffusing knowledge and awakening an interest in the troubled history of Spain between 1808 and 1814.

Oddly enough, these attitudes contrast sharply with those of the similarly educated Spaniards of the 1808–14 period. Proof of this is to be found in the numerous occasional Spanish poems and varia written during the war in praise of Wellington, as well as the generous support of Great Britain for a country that had been invaded and which obviously lacked the financial and military resources to stand much chance of success in its fight for survival. This paper reviews a number of these poems and miscellaneous printed writings. They all form part of the Instituto de Historia y Cultura Militar, Archivo General de Madrid, Colección Documental del Fraile (the 'Friar's Collection').[2]

The Colección Documental del Fraile is extensive; it consists of 3,537 documents, most of them written during the Peninsular War: proclamations, pamphlets of many different kinds, poems, sermons, speeches, decrees, daily papers, gazettes, letters, notes, and so on. The collection contains 21 printed items, which include poems (some of them in Latin), plays, essays, etc., written for the most part in praise of Wellington and Great Britain. The documents in prose present a variety of forms: news reports, pamphlets, proclamations; and the poems also offer a great variety, ranging from quite simple bolero-like rhymes to a sonnet, an ode and other more elaborate forms displaying different degrees of learned work. With the exception of a letter written by Wellington to his brother Henry, of which a bilingual version (English and Spanish) was printed, the rest of the documents are all written in Spanish.

While Wellington's 1808 victories in Portugal did not have much impact on the Spanish writers of the time, he merited a mention in Spanish gazettes almost immediately. As early as 20 July 1808, the Gazeta de Oviedo published a piece of news reporting that a 'Sir Astur Bellesley' was on his way to the

Peninsula.[3] However, the Spanish gazettes normally refer to him only in passing. In 1809, and in spite of Talavera, he is not yet the hero later praised by Spanish people, but news about his presence in the Peninsula begins to be widespread. In 1810 and 1811 the only references to him I have been able to find are in newspapers, mainly published in Cádiz. They are not always positive and, on some occasions, Wellington reacts angrily to them, as some of his despatches show.[4]

1812, and more specifically July that year, with the Battle of Salamanca (Los Arapiles), marks the turning point in the Duke's popularity in Spain. Throughout the free areas of the country, he was acknowledged as the glorious hero who had brought hope with him. He became a source of inspiration, and one which was not restricted to academic, learned writings; his popular appeal can be seen in songs which were often sung at banquets and celebrations. In 1813, this continued, and 1814 would also witness manifestations of that positive reception.

The documents discussed below, which constitute the entirety of those referring to the Duke in the Colección del Fraile, are witness to that popularity. This paper is therefore intended as a review of some of the writings inspired by Wellington and published during the Peninsular campaign. Other documents featuring Wellington may be found elsewhere, for example, in the collections of Gómez de Arteche and Gómez Imaz, respectively kept in the Biblioteca del Senado and the Biblioteca Nacional, in Madrid. However, the ones considered here may well illustrate Wellington's popularity.

The 21 documents from the Colección del Fraile have been classified into two groups and organised chronologically. The first group contains seven examples of prose writing, displaying a variety of text forms and layouts. The entries below contain basic information, with the Spanish title and its translation into English, followed by additional information about authorship (where known) and publication details. The second group contains one play and 13 poems. These vary in length and also in literary quality. Some of them are popular songs, others more elaborate poems displaying skillful rhetorical devices; a few are highly learned, in some cases written in Latin and observing rules for metre and rhyme established for the poems of the particular genre. In the following descriptions, all translations are the author's own.

Prose writings

1 *La magnanimidad y generosidad de Jorge III Rey de Inglaterra, de Wellesley y sus generales, la ambición de Bonaparte, y la gratitud de los generosos españoles.* [*The magnanimity and generosity of George III, King of England, of Wellesley and his generals, the ambition of Bonaparte and the gratitude of the generous Spaniards.*] Anonymous, Seville: Imprenta de Hidalgo, 1809. Sketch. 22 pages in quarto. Colección Documental del Fraile, vol. 36/223, ff. 316–27.

The anonymous author of this sketch strongly criticises continental nations, accusing them of acting against Britain from motives of jealousy and rivalry, and explaining that they envy British sea power. The writer begins by reviewing British history from the time of Queen Elizabeth I, whose reign he considers 'brilliant' as a result of sea power and wealth. A temporary decrease in that sea power is associated with revolution and some domestic problems. Admiral Russell's victory over France in 1692 is considered as the turning point for British successful policy. The initial stage of British supremacy at sea is situated at the end of the eighteenth century. A few paragraphs devoted to praising George III open the way to comments on the Peninsular War. The author considers that continental Europe will benefit from British wealth and sea power because the British king, whose generosity is also praised, will help them face the 'monster's abuse'. Mention is made of Sir John Moore and General Beresford before the author starts to praise Wellington.

The introductory section then gives way to the praise of Sir Arthur. Using again a literary device, the author addresses

Wellington directly:

> Illustrious General! The cheers and the happiness you met
> in Lisbon will add to the many tokens of Portuguese
> gratitude: you have raised Portugal from absolute despair
> and from the humiliation of the tyrants; you have softened
> their misfortune and restored their sovereign legitimate
> government. The Portuguese horizon sees itself blurred once
> more and you fly from the banks of River Thames to face
> new dangers on those of the rivers Douro and Tagus in order
> to ensure independence to that grateful country, as well as
> the glory and the wealth that your victories have promised
> them ...

The text goes on to compare Junot's looting in Portugal to
that prompted by Soult in Galicia and establishes a contrast between
the British general, who brings with him all kinds of supplies, and
the French generals who steal everything. After encouraging the
population to oppose the French wherever they are, the author
compares George III's generosity and efforts to restore freedom in
Europe with Napoleon's greed, which has led him to provoke the
ruin of Europe. The terms used to define British positive results
include 'wealth', 'happiness' and 'patriotism'. Those applied to
France include 'ruin', 'misery' and 'slavery'.

The final lines of this text are devoted to criticising
Napoleon's continental system and the text ends up by praising,
once more, British policy and victories. Spanish traitors like
General Morla also merit some lines in this interesting text.

In many respects this text may be assigned a literary nature,
from its lofty tone, careful style and the use of literary images,
mainly personification and metaphor. This is especially brilliant
when the anonymous writer evokes important rivers which act as
mediators of news. The learned character of the author is made
evident on several occasions, as for instance when he alludes to
Icarus' wings melting as an anticipation of Napoleon's fall. The
review of recent events offered by this author shows his concern

for European strategic policy, as well as his insight into Napoleon's contradictions — an offspring of revolution who tries to inflict upon Europe the same things that he had once fought against in Corsica. The author's interpretation of the state of affairs is inspired by powerful insight. He has the ability to identify important differences between the spirit of the French Revolution and that of its most important son, Napoleon, who is considered to betray that spirit. The writer's opinions on the attitude of some European leaders are also discerning.

The sketch is good evidence for the positive feelings generally shared by educated Spanish citizens towards Wellington's character and military skill.

2 *Últimas noticias del Lord Wellington y del estado del exército del rey Pepe, sacadas de* El Redactor de Cádiz. [*The latest reports on Lord Wellington, and on the state of the army of King Pepe, taken from* El Redactor de Cádiz.] *El Redactor de Cádiz*, no. 459, Sevilla: Imprenta Manuel Muñoz Álvarez, 1812. Report. Colección Documental del Fraile, vol. 148/615, ff. 22–3.

This document, from 1812, summarises news reports taken from Spanish papers and gazettes, published in *El Redactor de Cádiz* and extracted for the present pamphlet. Two of those reports refer to Wellington. The first reference, dated Lisbon, 4 September [1812], mentions a letter that Wellington apparently sent from Madrid to Pereira Forjaz in Portugal on 25 August. According to the Spanish version, in his letter Wellington reports the movements of several military commanders and their armies: King Joseph, at La Roda on 19 August, General Maitland, at Monforte on 17 August, General Roche at Alcoy, Suchet at San Felipe and O'Donnell at Yecla, all in the Valencia-Murcia area. Wellington did send a letter on 25 August to Lord Bathurst stating the same facts.[5] An extract, or a duplicate, of that letter may well have been sent to Pereira Forjaz in Lisbon, as the Spanish paper states. A second news report informs us that on 1 September Wellington had marched towards El Escorial where the allied headquarters were to be established.

The interest of this pamphlet lies in the fact that the news about Wellington, though occupying a small proportion of its four pages, is considered significant enough to predominate in the title and thus to be used as a means to attract potential readers. Wellington's popularity was at its highest in Spain at this point. He was to be appointed commander in chief (*generalissimo*) of the Spanish armies by the Cortes very shortly after, on 22 September.

3 *Wellington en España y Ballesteros en Ceuta. Discurso dirigido desde Alicante en 30 de marzo de 1813 a SM Las Cortes Generales y Extraordinarias de España por su electo diputado suplente por la provincia de Aragón.* [*Wellington in Spain and Ballesteros in Ceuta. Speech addressed from Alicante 30 March 1813 to Their Majesties the Cortes Generales y Extraordinarias of Spain by his substitute member elected by the province of Aragón.*] Juan Romero Alpuente, Cádiz: Imprenta Agapito Fernández Figueroa, 1813. Speech. 58 pages. Colección Documental del Fraile, vol. 268/959, f. 187.

The printed version of this lengthy speech, addressed by Juan Romero to the Cortes, is preceded by a quotation from one of the manifestos of the former Junta Central, which reads: 'Winner or looser, a nation that fully entrusts her defence to another nation is the slave either of the enemy that oppresses her or of the friend that defends her.' The inspiration for this speech was the measure adopted by the Spanish government on 2 November 1812, which punished the Spanish General Ballesteros for complaining about Wellington's appointment as *generalissimo* of the allied armies. The 'Aragón Cid', as the author calls General Ballesteros, comparing him to the mythical Spanish warrior, had been relieved of his duties as commander in chief of Andalucía and of the Fourth Army. In addition, he was deported to Ceuta, in North Africa, where he was imprisoned. All this was in effect the Spanish government's reprisal for his opinions against Wellington's appointment. In Romero's words, Ballesteros' complaint had been expressed on the grounds that the Spanish government had taken an important decision without considering, or even requesting, the opinion of either the Spanish generals or the Spanish people. This complaint had been sent to the Spanish Regency and a summary of it had also been published in a gazette.

Romero inserts an extract from another letter sent to the Regency by Ballesteros in which the general complained of the unfair way in which he had been arrested and confined to his house, before being escorted to Ceuta. Romero finds the Regency's measures questionable on the grounds that Ballesteros' main claim had been that the nation should have been consulted before the decision about Wellington had been taken. His plea on behalf of Ballesteros leads him to wonder about the obligation to obey in all cases, quoting the classics to support his doubts.

Romero does not fail to acknowledge Wellington's merit, but he presents serious doubts, both of a legal and a strategic nature, about the appropriateness of appointing a foreigner as commander in chief of the Spanish armies. He goes on to suggest the names of many other Spanish generals who might have been good candidates, equally appropriate, like Enrique or José O'Donnell, Castaños, Del Parque, Montijo, Lacy, Mendizábal, Ballesteros himself, and even some prestigious guerrilla leaders like Longa and Mina. Romero's conclusion is that Wellington has been chosen mainly because Britain's financial support to the Spanish cause has become crucial for an eventual successful outcome to the war. He also rehearses previous attempts to suggest Wellington's appointment, the first made by his brother Richard Wellesley in 1809, and then less straightforwardly by his brother Henry Wellesley later on. In connection with all this, Romero states that Wellington has become more powerful than the Spanish government itself.

Although the British general's qualities and accomplishments are duly acknowledged, there is a point in the speech at which his failures, presented from a Spanish perspective, are the object of

strong criticism, unveiling old and bitter resentment at some of
Wellington's decisions. For instance, he is blamed for his retreat
after the battle of Talavera; and, more controversially, Romero questions whether Wellington and his brother Henry are working for the
benefit of Britain rather than Spain.

As the speech develops, its criticism becomes more and
more resentful, reaching a point at which Britain is no longer
considered an ally, but rather as a harmful friend. Romero accuses
Britain of smuggling along the Spanish coastline, and he lists
the coastal cities controlled by British ships. He questions the
strategies of Moore and Baird, accusing the former of a shameful
retreat, with his soldiers destroying everything in their path. He
criticises Beresford for remaining in Portugal instead of trying to
free Galicia or Castile. He also complains that Wellington did not
pursue Soult into Spain after he had defeated the French marshal.

As for the terms agreed with the Spanish government for
Wellington's command of the Spanish army, Romero goes too far in
his criticism. He is especially critical of the British general's power
to promote and appoint officers. He even dares to predict (wrongly)
that Sir Arthur will appoint British officers to commanding posts in
Spain.

Two interesting points may be derived from this lengthy
text. While Ballesteros' complaint is that his punishment has been
excessive, Romero's text provides good evidence of the extent to
which the decree about the freedom of the press, passed by the
Cortes on 10 November 1810, had been established effectively in
Spain.[6] The second issue is that this is one of the very few documents related to Wellington that offer a negative view of the Duke,
the result of Ballesteros' punishment.

4 *Público desengaño sobre el llamado Convenio del Lord Wellington, o más bien sobre las facultades que se le concedieron quando
se le confirió el mando de los exércitos españoles. [Public
disenchantment about the so-called Agreement of Lord Wellington,*

or rather about the powers granted him when he was entrusted with the command in chief of the Spanish armies.] Co-authored by L.L.L. and the editors ('El Rib°'), Madrid: Fuentenebro, 1813. Pamphlet, 12 pp. Colección Documental del Fraile, vol. 342/1139, ff. 139–44.

This pamphlet was written in response to an article published in a well-established Cádiz newspaper, *El Diario Mercantil*, on 21 November 1813. The author is a Spaniard who identifies himself only as 'Juan'. He makes a strong attack on the Spanish government for having entrusted Wellington with the command of the Spanish armies on the basis of what he considers an unacceptable agreement.

The pamphlet was published separately on 20 December 1813: its text had already appeared in the Cádiz newspaper *El Conciso*. This was one of the many papers established in Cádiz in 1810 and it was characterised by its conspicuous presentation of news items. This, together with its low cost, made it extremely popular at the time.[7] The author of the pamphlet, identified as L.L.L., is very angry with Juan's article and has decided to reprint his response with a view to making sure that, by printing it once more, it will counterbalance the negative effects of Juan's text.

The author of the pamphlet reviews Juan's opinions and refutes them one by one. This is a good example of the common practice of handling public controversy so characteristic of the time. The main reason why the author reprints his text is an important issue currently under discussion in Cádiz: whether Wellington's request to quit his appointment to command the Spanish armies should be accepted or not. Naturally, L.L.L. is in favour of Wellington remaining at the head of all the allied armies. For that purpose, he reviews four articles included in the initial agreement signed by Wellington and the Spanish government; and he justifies the terms that both parties had come to. Wellington's qualities as a leader and as a soldier are also praised.

The final part of this pamphlet is a note of clarification by the editors. It is devoted to reporting part of a meeting of the Cortes on the night of 28 November, which lasted until 2 a.m. During that session, the deputies considered the points requested by Wellington as a prerequisite to him continuing at the head of the Spanish armies. The lengthy discussion concluded that the terms of the initial agreement could not be more reasonable for a general in charge of freeing Spain from her enemies. Three proposals for an answer were the subject of controversy, as the positions of the deputies show. The first proposal was to ask the government (the Regency) to request the Duke to remain in his post at least until his request could be fully studied. The second proposal was to request the Duke to continue on the same grounds as before. The third proposal was to add to the latter the following words: 'in order to provide the nation with more glorious days'. The first proposal was supported by all the deputies but two: Antillón (a deputy from Aragón) and Canga Argüelles (a deputy from Asturias). The third proposal was unanimously accepted. The second proposal was supported by 59 deputies and rejected by the remaining 54. Two lists are then given, naming the deputies voting for and against the proposal.

The final, impassioned paragraph is intended to warn readers, and the Spanish people in general, against the dangers of paying attention to those so-called patriots, the pro-French enemies of the country, who only want to abuse innocent Spaniards in order to lead the nation towards slavery.

The main points of interest in this document lie again in the controversy related to Wellington's appointment as *generalissimo*, mainly rejected by the most radical, pro-liberal deputies, whose names are given to the readers. The small margin in favour of the second proposal also illustrates the way in which the Cortes, and indeed Spain, were divided into two groups, with opposing ideologies, symbolising a traditional division that remains to the present day.

5 *Proclama que hizo el gran Lord Wellington a los exércitos* *aliados a la entrada de Francia, y recuerdo que hace la España a sus guerreros y fieles hijos.* [*Proclamation addressed by the great Lord Wellington to the allied armies on entering France, and recollections addressed by Spain to her warriors and faithful sons*]. Seville: Imprenta Padrino, 1813. Address. (The text of the proclamation is divided into two parts, with a long poem inserted in between). Colección Documental del Fraile, vol. 256/900, ff. 75–7.

This proclamation is very likely apocryphal. Neither its tone nor its contents fit Wellington's style or feelings. It is initially presented as an address, of a highly literary nature, delivered by Wellington to the allied armies under his command on their arrival in France after a victorious campaign. He congratulates all of them for their recent victories in Salamanca and Vitoria. The compliments he apparently pays to his addressees include flattering references to Cuesta and Ballesteros, probably the Spanish generals he disliked most.

Wellington explains the importance of treating properly the French inhabitants whose cities the army will occupy as it marches into the enemy's territory. There comes a point in the address at which the Duke starts to utter a sentence intended to direct measures against those who might misbehave and fail to show good will towards the defeated enemies. But he suddenly interrupts himself and the sentence remains unfinished. An external narrator then continues the address indicating that at that point Wellington has sat down and is listening to 'Spain' addressing her children.

A poem is then inserted which recounts the main events in the history of the war.[8] At its conclusion, the narrator takes the floor again to pass it to Wellington, who then continues his address and gives orders to ensure a dignified attitude on the part of the soldiers who are about to invade France, threatening anybody who might dare disobey his orders. He also promises rewards to all those who may deserve them. Then the narrator reappears and reports the excitement and happiness of the armies as well as their agreement to obey Wellington's orders.

This document is especially interesting as it focuses on Wellington's concern at the possibility of a vengeful attitude on the part of the successful allied armies, ironically one of the reasons why he eventually left behind most Spanish soldiers before entering France.

6 *Carta del excelentísimo señor duque de ciudad Rodrigo al señor embajador de S.M.B. cerca del Gobierno español relativa a las causas que dieron margen a que se destinasen tropas inglesas a las plazas de Cádiz y Cartagena; y orden para su relevo.* [*Letter from His Excellency the Duke of Ciudad Rodrigo to His Britannic Majesty's Ambassador in Spain, relative to the reasons for having posted English* [sic] *troops at Cádiz and Cartagena; and orders for their withdrawal.*] ed. D.R.Howe, Cádiz: Imprenta Patriótica, 1813. Despatch. Bilingual version, English and Spanish, of Wellington's letter to Sir Henry Wellesley, dated St Jean de Luz, 7 December, 1813, 8 pp. Colección Documental del Fraile, vol. 504/1620, ff. 32–5.

The English text of this document is in fact the printed version of a letter written by Wellington to his brother Henry Wellesley, which was later published in Gurwood's edition of Wellington's papers.[9] The letter was written to rebut widespread suspicion in Spain at the presence of British garrisons in Cádiz and Cartagena. Wellington was indeed very annoyed at that suspicious attitude of his Spanish allies. The final paragraph includes his suggestion that this letter be published, as it contains a full account of all the transactions that took place between the commander in chief of the allied armies and the Spanish government. Following this suggestion, D.R.Howe was in charge of having this bilingual version published in Cádiz, with the texts side by side. The translation is of excellent quality. Unexpectedly, two clarifying notes, which are not included in Gurwood's edition, were added to both versions. The first of these was added to Wellington's words stating that, when he decided to send a detachment of British troops to co-operate in the defence of Cádiz, at the 'pressing' request of the Spanish Regency, he had transmitted a statement of the conditions on which he had agreed to send the troops. One of those conditions was that they should be fed from Spanish stores. The note reads as follows: 'It must be observed that although the Spanish government consented to this condition, yet that at the end of the first month the authorities of Cádiz having declared that they were unable to furnish any longer for the subsistence of the British troops, they were from that time fed at the expense of the British government.' The second note relates to the troops sent to Cartagena. It refers to a paragraph in which Wellington states that his brother Henry is in possession of some documents on this subject which show that there 'could be no sinister view in sending British troops to that station'. The note reads as follows: 'Although Lord Wellington was apprized that the Spanish government was desirous that the British troops should be sent to Carthagena, yet he positively refused to send them, unless they were applied for officially.'[10] The author of these notes, especially the second one, was probably the editor of the letters. The intention, most likely, was to make sure that Wellington's explanations were fully supported by additional evidence and also fully understood.

The interest of the document lies in the fact that it was Wellington himself who wanted the information made public, and it is the only record in the collection of which a bilingual version was printed and distributed. Wellington's interest in both the British and Spanish populations in the Peninsula being fully informed of the process by which the ports were garrisoned with British troops is quite remarkable, especially if we take into account that this letter was written at a point when he was already in France and the war was practically won.

7 *Brindis en el gran convite que el prefecto de Tolosa, Mr Des Thoutes, dio en [24] de abril al Lord Wellington. [Toasts given at the great banquet offered by the Prefect of Toulouse, Mr Des Thoutes* *on 24 April to Lord Wellington.*] Anonymous, Madrid. Seville (reprinted): [   ], 1814. News report. Colección Documental del Fraile vol. 306/1056, ff. 144–51.

This is a report on the celebrations marking the convention signed in Toulouse by France, Britain and Spain, bringing hostilities to an end. It mentions some of the toasts given at the main banquet offered by the French prefect of the city, and it includes sarcastic references to the reaction of the guests at the toasts given by Marshals Soult and Suchet. As the text records, the agreement was signed by Major General Sir George Murray, Field Marshal Ludwig Wimpffen and Colonel Richard of the staff of Marshal Suchet.[11] The document records the erection of an obelisk-shaped arch ('un arco en forma de obelisco'), on which two inscriptions included references to Wellington. The toasts, naturally with Bordeaux wine, were addressed to the Pope, the Prince Regent, the Church, France, Freedom, the British, Louis XVIII, the glory of Spain, etc. Soult's toast, 'To general peace', was met with little enthusiasm and some laughter, while Suchet's toast, 'To the union of the French and the Spaniards' was followed by total silence.

Drama and poetry

The next group of material consists of 14 items or a literary nature. Most of them are poems, some are lyrics, written to be sung, and there is a one act verse play which is completed with two song lyrics and which, in fact, contains three items. The literary quality of this set is uneven. Some songs, rhymes and lyrics are of a popular nature, while some poems, like sonnets, epigrams (in Latin) and other pieces are the work of learned writers and composers. In some cases, the sheet music has also been found.

8 *Canción Patriótica en loor del héroe de Europa, el Excmo. Sr. Duque de Ciudad Rodrigo.* [*Patriotic song in praise of the hero of Europe, His Excellency the Duque of Ciudad Rodrigo.*] Anonymous, Cádiz: Imprenta Viuda de Comes, 1812. Song with chorus, 4 pp. Colección Documental del Fraile, vol. 256/899, ff. 73–4.

The title of this document speaks for itself: it is a popular, patriotic song in praise of the hero of Europe. Wellington was mainly referred to as the Duque of Ciudad Rodrigo in Spain, the title awarded to him in January 1812. The song has 14 stanzas of four lines, each line having 8 syllables, using the rhyme scheme identified with the Spanish 'copla' metre. The rhythm is very apposite for a song in Spanish.[12] The song begins with a chorus wishing Wellington long life and then the different verses recount his victories from 1810 onwards: Torres Vedras, Albuera, Almeida, Ciudad Rodrigo, Badajoz, Salamanca and Tormes. His main opponents, Masséna, Soult, Phillipon and Marmont, are duly ridiculed.

> *Viva, viva Wellington*
> *Del galo domador,*
> *El consuelo de España,*
> *Nuestro libertador*
>
> En las líneas del Tajo
> Humillaste a Masséna,
> Haciendo sus ardides
> Juguete de tu ciencia.
>
> *Viva, viva Wellington,* etc.[13]

9 *A la Inglaterra* [*To England.*] Anonymous, Cádiz: Imprenta Viuda de Comes, 1812. A Spanish 'silva'. Colección Documental del Fraile, vol. 503/899, f. 75.

This poem follows the metre and pattern for the Spanish poetic form known as a 'silva'. The use of the article 'la' ('the') in the Spanish title adds to the solemn, archaic flavour to the piece. The length of a silva may vary according to the author's choice. This poem is rather short (only 9 lines), but it is quite elaborate.[14]

A La Inglaterra
Feliz mil veces, patria venturosa
De un héroe militar, cuyas hazañas
Resonando el clarín en las campañas,
Su fama el eco extenderá gloriosa:
Feliz, vuelvo a decir, patria dichosa,
Pues que puedes gloriarte
Serlo de un nuevo Marte,
Que descubrió el secreto
De poner á los galos en respeto.[15]

10 *Estrofas en honor del duque de Ciudad Rodrigo para cantarse en la función que dan en su obsequio los Grandes de España en la noche del día 4 de enero de 1813. Se acomoda especialmente a la música de la marcha nacional: Españoles, la Patria Oprimida.* [*Stanzas in praise of the Duke of Ciudad Rodrigo to be sung at the performance held in his honour by the Spanish Grandees on the night of 4 January 1813. It may be performed to the tune of the Spanish march: 'Spaniards, our homeland oppressed'.*] J.B.A., no publisher, no place of publication, 1813. Song with chorus. Colección Documental del Fraile, vol. 805/3013, f. 56.

This patriotic poem was written in honour of Wellington to be sung at a performance organised to praise the Duke. The author is Juan Bautista Arriaza, a well-known poet of the time, associated both with neo-classicism and romanticism, and a firm supporter of Ferdinand VII's absolutism. In an introductory note, the poet specifies that the lyrics may be performed to the melody of another patriotic song, also written by him, 'Españoles, la patria oprimida', intended to encourage the Spaniards to join in the fight. Arriaza's patriotic songs were transmitted orally and were commonly sung by the Spanish resistance movement. The original song is still well-known in present day military circles, probably thanks to its inspired, march-like melody. This version devoted to Wellington consists of three stanzas of two quatrains each, and a chorus of four lines. The text is lyrical and learned, with references to the classics, and to mythological characters and deities. The tone is quite solemn. Of the poetry written in Spain during the Peninsular War, this is no doubt one of the poems which most sincerely show gratitude to Wellington.

¡O quán dulce es a un Héroe glorioso,
Que triunfó con justicia y valor,
Presentarle el tributo amoroso
De ternura, de aprecio y de honor!

1   Ved qual llega a gozarse en el seno
De la Ibera leal gratitud
El que oímos de lejos qual trueno
Dar a Gades victoria y salud.
       Hoy se muestra apacible y triunfante
Y ayer bravo; y con fiero tesón
Los tiranos lanzaba adelante
Qual las nubes el duro Aquilón.
Chorus

2   Acojamos al Héroe bizarro
En los muros que él mismo libró;
Y descienda del bélico carro
A gozar de la paz que nos dio.
       No la oliva a su frente neguemos,
Ni la rosa de alfombra a sus pies:
Que él sabrá quantas flores le demos
En laureles volverlas después.
Chorus

3   Él unió con el nuestro su brazo
Para hazañas de precio inmortal:
Mire pues en tan ínclito lazo
El injusto opresor su dogal.

Y en el templo de eterna memoria
Y en los fastos de la última edad
Se unirá de Wellington la GLORIA
Con la hispana feliz LIBERTAD.
Chorus[16]

11 *La Batalla de Los Arapiles o Derrota de Marmont* [*The battle of the Arapiles or Marmont's defeat.*] Francisco Garnier-González, Madrid: Imprenta Álvarez, 1813. A one act verse drama, concluding with two songs (12 and 13 below), 56 pp. Colección Documental del Fraile, vol. 905/3309, ff. 24–50.[17]

The title of this literary piece anticipates much of its contents. The front page of the printed version also provides information about the date of its first performance in Madrid, 23 July 1813, as well as the fact that it was the first play to be published in the Spanish capital to honour the 'celebrated Field Marshal Wellington' ('en loor del célebre field Mariscal Wellington'). The printing details are given at the foot of this same page.

The text is preceded by an introductory address to Wellington, written by the author, whose decision to print his name in full makes plain the initials given on the title page: Don Francisco Garnier-González. The play was first performed in Teatro del Principe in Madrid. In the introduction, Garnier expresses his gratitude to the British hero, who has freed Spain and all Europe, and he also shows his admiration for the Duke. The main characters naturally include generals Marmont, Bonet, Vouvant and Lilli, along with Wellington and his favourite guerrilla leader, Julián Sánchez, 'el Charro' who, incidentally, was from Ciudad Rodrigo. There are also other minor characters. It is a lengthy piece, containing 11 scenes and running to 55 pages.

The first two scenes present Marmont and his generals speaking about what they consider as the opportunity to take revenge on the man who overwhelmed Masséna in Portugal. The only character bold enough to offer a pessimistic view — in contrast to the over-optimistic expectations of Marmont — is General Bonet. At the end of Scene 2, Julián Sánchez's visit is announced. Scene 3 begins with the guerrilla leader's attempt to dissuade Marmont from battle. The French marshal rejects that proposal and confirms that he will give battle the next day. Scene 4 begins with the French General Lilli trying to persuade Sánchez to defect to Napoleon's lines but, when El Charro reproves him and asks him to be honourable, Lilli praises his interlocutor's patriotism and laments ever having joined Napoleon, as he feels deceived by him. The scene ends with Lilli himself defecting to Sanchez's forces. Scene 5 presents Marmont haranguing his army before his generals. In Scene 6, Marmont offers a reward of 100,000 pesetas for Wellington's head and 50,000 pesetas for those of General España and General Sánchez. Scenes 7 to 8 show troops in movement, off-stage voices and the sounds of trumpets and the firing of artillery. A defeated, bleeding Marmont comes on stage with his broken sword, feeling dishonoured and blaming Napoleon for his excessive ambition. Off-stage voices shout: 'Long live Wellington.' Scene 9 is mainly given over to British soldiers, carrying the corpses of French officers. Scene 10 is devoted to Wellington, who appears on horseback while military music is played. The Duke is at the centre of the last scene, giving a triumphal speech. The passage concludes with a grenadier requesting a reward. While Sánchez says that glory should be its own reward, Wellington agrees that the soldier deserves it and appoints him colonel. Some women then sing two songs (12 and 13 below).

12 *Al héroe cantemos*. [*Let's sing to our hero.*] Francisco Garnier-González, Madrid: Imprenta Álvarez, 1813. Song ('Letrilla'). Colección Documental del Fraile, vol. 905/3309, ff. 51–3.

This popular song and poem is identified by the author as a 'letrilla'.[18] It is a satirical and burlesque poetic work, characterised by a humorous tone. It was written to be sung immediately after a play (11) by six village girls. A chorus, normally intended to repeat one idea or feeling, follows every stanza. The chorus here is devoted to Wellington:

> Let's sing to our hero
> Who in battle won
> The fierce giants
> Of the Seine and the Rhine

Despite the popular tone of the poem, the rhythm is solemn. The first two stanzas are pastoral and patriotic, describing the surroundings of the river Tormes (in Salamanca) . The third stanza, however, is special. It mentions Wellington, England, George III and the 'horrible Corsican'. Apart from being mainly devoted to praise of the British, it is given more prominence than the rest of the song because it is to be sung solo, as a sign of gratitude and respect:

> Honor a Wellington,
> Honor a Inglaterra,
> De la triste España
> Protectora tierna,
> Y a Jorge tercero
> Cuya real firmeza
> Juró al corso horrible
> El odio y la guerra.[19]

13 *Coplas de la Batalla de Los Arapiles.* [*Stanzas about the battle of the Arapiles.*] Francisco Garnier-González, Madrid: Imprenta Álvarez, 1813. Song ('Letrilla'). Colección Documental del Fraile, vol. 905/3309, ff. 54–6.

As the author states in the printed version of this new popular rhyme-song, inserted immediately after 12 as one more element of the volume, it was written to be sung on the days following the opening night of the play (11). It is probably the most popular war song of the time. The several differing versions of the lyrics which were also printed at the time are the result of that widespread popularity. From a formal point of view, it follows the standard pattern of the Spanish 'octavilla quebrada'.[20] It is funny and sarcastic. This version here includes nine stanzas, most of them containing at least one line devoted to Wellington. Two of the most popular stanzas read as follows:

Belintón en Arapiles
A Marmont y sus iguales
Para almorzar les dispuso
Un gran pisto de tomates;
Y tanto les dio
    Que les fastidió
    Y a contarlo fueron
    A Napoleón
    Viva Belintón!

Cuando a Marmont vio su esposa
Que iba herido de un balazo
Le preguntó compungida
'Te falta algo más que el brazo?'
    Y el la respondió
    No querida, no,
    Y esto se lo debo
    Al Lord Belintón.
    Viva el español![21]

The chorus consists of one line, which is repeated several times with a rising tune. It has the peculiarity that it does not always include the same lyrics. The variations are: 'Viva la nación', 'Viva Belintón' and 'Viva el español' ('Long live our nation', 'Long live Wellington' and 'Long live the Spaniard'). The popularity of this very amusing piece has helped preserve its musical score, which was recovered for the bicentennial celebrations. There are now recordings of brilliant choir and orchestral arrangements.

14 *Sevilla o Romulea al Excmo. Sr. Duque de Ciudad Rodrigo, Grande de España de Primera clase, Gran Collar del Toisón de*

*Oro, Gran Cruz de la Orden de San Fernando, Generalísimo de los
Exércitos de la Liga, el Lord Wellington. Poema cogratulatorio con
ocasión de su retorno a aquella capital para unirse a los exércitos.*
[*Seville or Romulea to His Excellency the Duque of Ciudad
Rodrigo, Grandee of the First Class of Spain, Grand Collar of the
Golden Toisón, Grand Cross of the Order of San Fernando,
generalissimo of the allied armies, the Lord Wellington. A
congratulatory poem on the occasion of his return to that capital to
join the armies.*] José Gabriel de Lozada, Sevilla: Imprenta Agustín
Muñoz, 1813. Heroic ode. Colección Documental del Fraile,
vol. 256/898, ff. 67–72.

This is allegedly a learned, literary poem, written by José
Gabriel de Lozada, who claims to be a poet and lawyer in Seville.
It is, in fact, a pompous, heroic ode where the classics are quoted in
some places. The poem is preceded by a Latin quotation from
Virgil's *Aeneid*, which does not make much sense with reference to
Wellington: 'Heu, miserande puer, si quafata aspera rumpas, tu
Marcellus eris.'[22] Five clarifying footnotes provide information, in
some cases about matters connected with Roman culture, that are
superfluous for an educated reader. The ode was written in praise of
Wellington and Britain. The sixth stanza mentions several relevant
Peninsular rivers (Tormes, Tagus, Betis, Douro and Ebro) which,
in a process of personification, adore Lord Wellington and kiss his
feet. The seventh stanza predicts glory for Wellington and his
family when he returns to Britain. The ninth stanza makes explicit
reference to those who envy and do not trust Wellington and also to
those who accuse him of trying to deprive Spain of her liberty. The
author then requests jealousy to cease. The value of this poem lies
in the huge effort made by its rather naïve author, with the aim of
contributing, in an 'elevated' way, to praise Lord Wellington for his
victories. The last stanza is a direct address to Britain:

> Feliz tú Gran Bretaña,
> Que hoy proteges a España
> De un cruel enemigo, fascinado

En llenar mil proyectos ambiciosos,
Rompiendo la balanza
Que limita el poder desordenado!
Si España sucumbiera! ¿Qué espantosos
Resultados daría tal mudanza?
Temblaras, Albión, por tu existencia,
Rindiendo el cuello altivo a su influencia,
Y acaso, acaso, la potente Rusia
Cayera cual cayó la triste Prusia ...
Tú, reyna de los mares, por tu amiga
Mira, entre penas y congojas pobre,
que época llegará en que la sobre
Con qué premiar quien su dolor mitiga.[23]

15 *Wellington Caudillo de Tres Naciones sobre la Antigua Mantua Carpetana.* [*Wellington, leader of three nations, upon the Mantua Carpetana of old* [Madrid]] Eliso Barcíneo, Oviedo: Cándido Pérez Prieto, 1813. One canto poem. Colección Documental del Fraile, vol. 256/901, ff. 78–88.

This poem is a long, single canto of 15 regular sections, preceded by a shorter one. The type of stanza corresponds to what is called in Spanish 'octava real' or 'octava rima'.[24] The author, who calls himself by the pseudonym Eliso Barcíeno, was in fact the Asturian lawyer and archaeologist Pedro Canel Acevedo. He was a humanist who wrote in Latin as well, and who always used a pseudonym for his writings. His canto único is just a single canto. The poem is preceded by a Latin quotation from Virgil's Aeneid which, in contrast to Lozada's, is appropriate: 'Nec pietate fuit, nec bello maior et armis.'[25] There then follows an introductory address to potential readers. Canel justifies writing the poem on the grounds that he was full of gratitude and interest after having witnessed Wellington's achievement at Ciudad Rodrigo. His gallantry, as well as the discipline, brotherhood and bravery of the Spanish and Anglo-Portuguese soldiers in Salamanca added afterwards to the poet's motivation. The highly literary nature of this poem is self-evident. There are examples of almost all literary figures, from metaphor, personification, oxymoron, simile, parallelism, metonymy, to direct appeal. It is also full of references to classical and mythological characters.

The poem begins by referring to the damage caused by the French in Spain and to their cruelty. These things moved Wellington to take revenge by raising a three-headed army, formed by British, Portuguese and Spanish soldiers. At one point the author mentions Marmont by the rivers Adaja and Douro, now red with blood. When Wellington is chasing the fugitive enemies, a goddess turns up and advises him to give up the pursuit. She then presents him with a vision of Mantua (Salamanca), encouraging him to free it. The poet mentions Generals Carlos de España and Julián Sánchez. After continuous fighting, both sides showing fierceness and determination, the allies manage to get into the city, but the fight continues until the French give in and beg for their lives. The rivers Manzanares and Tagus hold a conversation about the possibility of carrying French corpses out to the sea to obviate their damaging effects. Meanwhile, some Tritons and Nereids reach Britain with the news. London's Thames then passes the news to the Seine of Paris. Napoleon and 'Josefa' wake up and, hearing of that news, they realise their throne and lives are in danger.

The following extract, from section 8, stanzas 1 and 2, illustrates the 'modern' — as opposed to the classical — features of the poem.

> Llegan presto al Retiro, y la batalla
> Empiezan vengadores animosos;
> Más del broce al abrigo y de muralla
> Opónense los galos jactanciosos
> A su extremo valor, y de metralla
> Y balas lluvia arrojan sanguinosos,
> Fulminando sus ojos de tal suerte,
> Que infernales despiden ira y muerte.

Sus tiros despreciando los aliados
Al pie del alto muro se aproximan.
La vida prometiendo a los malvados
De la plaza entrega les intiman
Pero a muerte o vencer determinados
De Wellington la oferta desestiman
Y añaden del cañón recio al fuego
Del mortero y el obús el pronto fuego.[26]

16 *Colecioncita de seguidillas boleras, unas en reconocimiento y gratitud a la nación británica, y al Excmo. Sr. Duque de Ciudad Rodrigo. Y otras joco-serias al errante rey Pepe y a sus satélites.* [*A small collection of 'seguidillas boleras', some intended to acknowledge and express gratitude to the British nation and to His Excellency the Duque of Ciudad Rodrigo. Others, half in jest, half serious, to the wandering King Pepe and his satellites.*] P.D.M.M.R., Málaga: Imprenta Calle del Marqués, no date. Song. Colección Documental del Fraile, vol. 905/3310, ff. 83–9.

This piece contains a combination of 'seguidillas' and 'boleras', commonly sung and danced, typically in Castile and Andalucía.[27] The songs begin by making reference to Wellington's worldwide fame, Britain's generosity and Spain's gratitude. The typical, sarcastic tone begins when Marmont is first mentioned. His defeated soldiers are depicted crying and in flight. The author wishes death to Joseph and Napoleon, and a long life to George III. There follow praise and expressions of gratitude to Wellington and also encouragement to chase the French into France.

El clarin de la fama
Desde el oriente,
Publique de Wellington
Hasta occidente
Que en todo el orbe
No halla quien le resista,
Ni quien le estorve.

La Albión generosa
Con sabia mano,
Te ha preparado triumfos
Contra el tirona.
La eleccion viva,
Y tu memoria en mármol
La España escriba.[28]

17 *Ad Wellingtonem, victo Napoleone, epigramma.* [*Epigram for Wellington, on the defeat of Napoleon.*] N.M. de S., no place of publication, no publisher given, [1814]. Epigram. Latin. Colección Documental del Fraile, vol. 503/1606, f. 142.

This item, like 18, is a Latin epigram.[29] 17 and 18 were probably written by different authors. We do not know who wrote 17; the publisher, who as is explained below is likely to be the author of the second epigram, adds to this one a Spanish translation. The original Latin version is given here.

Napoleo ex orco, superas dimissus ad auras,
In coelum, et terram bella cruenta movet.
Hic dux tartareus, se jactans omnipotentem,
Credidt e coelo pellere posse Deum.
Sed, duce Wellington, summo dejectus Olimpo,
Extemplo rabido dente momordit humum.
Hinc populis est parta quies, pax reddita mundo,
Ex Wellingtoni gloria summa duci.[30]

18 *In laudem Wellingtonis.* [*In praise of Wellington.*] Agustín Muñoz Álvarez,[31] Seville, no publisher given, [1814]. Epigram. Latin. Colección Documental del Fraile, vol. 503/1607, f. 144.

The name of the author of the second epigram, Agustinus Munnozius, corresponds to the Latinised version of the name of a Seville printer, Agustín Muñoz who has been mentioned above as the printer of Gabriel Lozada's pretentious poem. Here Muñoz, apart from translating his name into Latin, provides additional information about himself. It is from this that we know he was a priest who, apart from being the author of the epigram — he declares he has sung it, 'canebat' — claims to be a teacher of the Spanish, Greek and Latin languages. Wellington's name only appears explicitly in the title of the poem, but there is another reference to him in the epigram as 'invicti'.

Monstrum horrendum, orbis timor, atque infia gentis
Corsorum, invicti victus ab ense, cadit.
Plaudite, mortales; Jani jam claudite portas.
Ille jacet; terris, credite, parta quies.[32]

19 *Soneto* [*a Wellington*]. [*Sonnet* [*to Wellington*]]. Anonymous, no publisher or place of publication. Colección Documental del Fraile, vol. 503/1605, f. 141.

A further literary work in this second group is an interesting sonnet: it is not only skilfully written from the point of view of form, as it follows the canonical pattern, but also, and most especially, because of the way in which the contents are gradually presented. Using a solemn tone, the anonymous author leads the reader from top to bottom until the poem reaches its climax in the very final lines, where Wellington is mentioned for the first and last time. The impact of Wellington's voice, when he orders Napoleon to disappear, is so decisive that Bonaparte becomes invisible as the poem ends. The sonnet's 14 lines contain a masterly summary of the Peninsular War, the Corsican origins of Napoleon and his imperialist policy, the initial, universal response, followed in most cases by his violence and deceit. As the poem unfolds, British power arises to help the only daring nation that faces the invader. Napoleon's cruel offensive operations prove fruitless and he incredulously tries to find out who his enemy is. Wellington only needs to express an order for Napoleon to face complete defeat. The writer's modesty has unfortunately deprived us of his identity.

Irguió el Corso feroz su altiva frente,
Y á su opresión y servidumbre dura

El orbe todo reducir procura,
Y el orbe á su ambición no es suficiente.
Violencia, ardides de otra gente
Vuelan, y ya triunfante se figura:
A los unos la alianza no asegura,
A los otros domó guerra inclemente.
Albión resiste, ya a la fiel España,
Que al opresor se opone, auxilio ofrece:
El tirano en horror todo lo envuelve;
Y dice al ver lo inútil de su saña
¿Quién contra mí? WELLINGTON: desparece
A esta voz; en vapores se resuelve.[33]

20 *Sueño que asegura la felicidad de España y ruina de Francia con una silva en honor y obsequio de Lord Wellington, Generalísimo de las tropas Anglo-Hispano-Lusitanas, Duque de Ciudád-Rodrígo, etc.* [*A dream ensuring the happiness of Spain and the ruin of France, with a poem in honour of and as a gift to Lord Wellington, Generalissimo of the English, Spanish and Portuguese troops, etc.*] Juan Maria Morcillo Quevedo, Zaragoza: Imprenta Andrés Sebastián, 1813. (Silva.) Colección Documental del Fraile, vol. 462/1500, ff. 109–10.

This poem is another example of the 'silva' stanza form. Curiously enough, it is inserted in a much longer poem written in praise of Samuel Whittingham, a British officer who commanded a Spanish division during most of the Peninsular War. This 'silva' consists of an unusually large number of lines, though it follows the pattern that characterises that poetic form. This is an inspired and learned piece, full of mythological references, mainly deities, and also references to the classics, as well as employing many literary devices. It is a complex text to read, even for Spanish speakers; its language is sophisticated and hard to express in translation. Even with such refinement, it does not compare to the freshness and simplicity of the popular songs noted above.

The poem reviews the history of the occupation of the Peninsula, paying attention to the looting, crimes and plunder carried out by the invaders. The author acknowledges the thirst for revenge, but he finally reminds his readers that the war is against Napoleon and not against the population of France. The seventeenth-century Spanish poet, Francisco de Quevedo, is mentioned with nostalgia in the poem, suggesting that had he been alive, he would have joined the poets of the time in celebrating Wellington's genius. Incidentally, Quevedo was a keen exponent of the 'silva', the form chosen by this anonymous poet.

O Welington! A el que gloriosa fama,
A el que Lides Marciales le tributan
El premio, el honor, y la grandeza
Que es propia de virtud a la belleza:
Lord Welington, cuyos magnos timbres,
De Quevedo a la pluma, a la rudeza
No es dado describir, ni permitido,
Por temple, por razón, por la fiereza
Del tiempo proceloso, en quien la Patria
Avasallada gime, horrenda pena!
O Deydad sempiterna!
Del Parnaso que habitas las florestas,
Entre amorosos sauces y violetas,
Allá en qualquiera siglo haced que sea,
Ansiosa alma lo desea,
De la Fama en el Templo resonante
Un General triunfante,
Tháctico Campeón, que, en nuestra España,
Destruyendo la raza mas estraña,
Pomposos triunfos, placeres, alborozo,
Conducirá a la Iberia entero gozo.[34]

21 *Recuerdo*. [*Recollection*.] Poem inserted in the middle of an address (5, above), apparently given by Wellington to the allied armies. Copla. Colección Documental del Fraile, vol. 256/900, ff. 76–7.

This poem was inserted in the middle of an address, which is presented as if it were given by Wellington to the allied troops when they were on the point of entering France, in 1813 — but it is very unlikely to have been written by the Duke. The poem is introduced by a narrator who states that it is addressed by the Spanish nation to her children. This digression had been anticipated in the second part of the title of the complete document. Adopting the form of a 'copla', and a solemn tone, the poet summarises the most important events in the Peninsula since the first moments of the French invasion. The main protagonists and some of their most important actions there are duly mentioned. Murat and the events of 2 and 3 May 1808 open the way to Dupont's looting in Andalucía and La Mancha. Then follow Moncey's plunder of Valencia and the occupation of Castile by Bessières. Slightly out of place, Junot's crimes are then mentioned, with some reference as well to his 'thieves'. Finally, Duhesme's killings in Cataluña, followed by Napoleon's slaughter, are explained by association with the devil. A summary of their atrocities and cruelty closes what may be considered the first part of this statement. The second part begins with Wellington's defeat of Marmont and putting the French to flight. The British general, referred to as 'The one never defeated', is mentioned several more times. Tribute is also paid to Spanish generals, including Castaños, Murillo, O'Donnell, Girón, Mendizábal and Mina. The final part of the poem begins by acknowledging the need for revenge and the *lex talionis* is even mentioned. At this point, a negative parallel between the main characters is established by associating a series of opposites. Thief and Napoleon are set against the generous, human and kind Wellington; bloodthirsty Suchet against a compassionate Girón; an unbeaten Mina against a defeated Soult. Although the poet goes on to remind the soldiers that they should bear in mind that the war is against Napoleon, and not against the French population, the imbalance between the many lines devoted to revenge and those few intended to ask the Spaniards to be generous gives the poem an ironical tone which the poet does not try to hide. The explanation for this may have a basis in Wellington's reluctance to allow Spanish troops into France at that moment, a decision which did not please his allies at all.

* * *

The documents discussed in this chapter reflect Wellington's popularity in Spain: though at first modest, it reached its height with the battle of Salamanca (Los Arapiles). Most of the popular songs written in his honour include references to the Arapiles. The Duke's popularity reached all social levels and cultural layers, involving learned and illiterate people alike. Other voices were raised against the *generalissimo*, but they were mostly restricted to some army officers and their supporters, that is, the groups that opposed Wellington did not have such a broad base, socially, as those who were in his favour. The events that inspired the writers of these texts, as well as their tone, show a widespread feeling of sincere gratitude, both to Britain and the Duke. In the last two centuries, paradoxically that feeling has shifted into an attitude towards Wellington that is predominantly suspicious, at least in the popular mind. Most present-day Spanish academics, however, do fully acknowledge his efforts and merits.

References

[1] Although some authors assign the destruction of the factory to Napoleon's troops, it was actually the result of action by Wellington's soldiers. Murat had done nothing but turn the factory into a military target by fortifying it with three defensive lines. The attack of the British in the Battle of El Retiro (13 August 1812) was so violent that bullets and uniform fragments can still be found. The French Colonel Lefond surrendered 2,500 soldiers, 289 pieces of ordnance, 2,000 rifles and important amounts of ammunition and supplies. The remains of the factory were destroyed on Hill's orders as part of the evacuation programme (31 October), including the blowing up of the building and its magazines; the

Spanish authorities ignored the measure without trying to prevent it. See further Alicia Laspra, 'Del mito a la Historia. Las perfidias de Albión en la Península (1808–1814)', *Desperta Ferro* (September 2012) pp. 3–6.This paper is related to the Spanish I+D+i National Research Project MCI FFI2011–23532.

[2] For a catalogue of the collection, see A.M.Freire *Índice bibliográfico de la Colección del Fraile* (Madrid, 1983).

[3] Alicia Laspra *La Gazeta de Oviedo. Primera época* (Oviedo, 2009) p. 155.

[4] See, for instance, AW to Sir Henry Wellesley, Pero Negro, 11 Nov 1810, *WD*, vi, pp. 610–13. In this particular case, he reacted against strong criticism directed towards the Spanish general, the Marquis of La Romana, who stayed in Portugal supporting Wellington from Oct 1810 until La Romana's death in Jan 1811.

[5] *WD*, ix, pp. 379–81.

[6] For a sound analysis of the issue, Emilio Laparra *La libertad de prensa en las Cortes de Cádiz* (Valencia, 1984), also available on-line at Biblioteca Virtual Miguel de Cervantes http://13.0.4.19/servlet/SirveObras/hist/56818403212381663654679/p0000001.htm

[7] Beatriz Sánchez de Hita, 'La imprenta en Cádiz durante la Guerra de la Independencia y su relación con la prensa periódica' in *La guerra de pluma. Estudios sobre la prensa de Cádiz en el tiempo de las Cortes (1810–1814)* ed. Mariet Cantos-Casenave et al. (Cádiz: Universidad de Cádiz, 2009) i, p. 50.

[8] See document 21.

[9] *WD*, xi, pp. 351–3.

[10] Pages 4–5 and 6, respectively, of the bilingual version revised.

[11] The event was recorded in the *Gentleman's Magazine*, supplement to vol. 84, p. 763, which in turn had taken it from the *London Gazette*, extraordinary issue dated 27 Apr 1814, p. 1.

[12] The 'copla' is a very popular poem type in Spain. It is normally written to be sung and it consists of a varying number of 4 line stanzas. The rhyme pattern is [4- 4a 4- 4a]. Lower-case letters indicate that the poem corresponds to the so called 'arte menor' verse type, where each line contains 8 or fewer syllables; upper-case letters reflect a poem of the 'arte maior' verse type, where lines contain more than 8 syllables. Contrary to what happens in English, which is stress-timed language in terms of rhythm, Spanish is a syllable-timed language. In the case of the copla, all the verse lines contain 8 syllables. The rhyme is of the so-called 'asonante' type, which means that it only affects the final vowel sounds of the corresponding lines.

[13] 'Hail, Hail, Wellington / Tamer of the French, / Spain's comfort, / Our liberator. / On the banks of the Tagus / Masséna you humbled, / Turning his tricks / Into your realm's toy. / Hail, Hail, Wellington, etc.'

[14] A 'silva' is a poetic form consisting of several 7 and 11 syllable lines with a free rhyme scheme for all lines, as long as it corresponds to the so-called 'consonant'

rhyming type, affecting both final vowel and consonant sounds of every line. The rhyme scheme here is [11A 11B 11B 11A 11A 7C 7C 7D 11D].

[15] To England: 'A thousand times happy, venturous nation / Of a military hero, whose deeds, /The bugle resounding in the campaigns, / His fame the echo will gloriously spread: / Happy, joyful land, I say again, / As you can feel glorified / By being that of a new Mars, / Who the secret uncovered / Of how to force the French to obey.'

[16] The rhyme scheme is [10A 9B 10A 9B 10C 9D 10C 9D] for the stanzas, and [10A 9B 10A 9B] for the chorus. Formally, this poem does not correspond to a particular type. As the author himself states, it is a series of different stanzas. [Chorus] 'Oh, how sweet it is to present a glorious Hero / Who triumphed with justice and valour / with the loving tribute / Of tenderness, esteem and honour! [Stanza 1:] Behold how comes to rejoice in the bosom / Of Iberia's loyal gratitude / He whom we heard from the distance like thunder /Give Gades victory and health. / Today calm and triumphant he appears / Yesterday courageous, and with fierce effort / Charging against the tyrants / As tough Aquilon does with clouds. / [Stanza 2:] Let us receive the gallant hero / Within the very walls he himself freed / And let him get off the war chariot / To enjoy the peace he gave us. / Let's not deny his forehead the olive / nor his feet the roses carpet / Since he will know well all flowers we give him/in laurels to turn later on. / [Stanza 3:] He joined to ours his arm / For immortal prize deeds / See then in such illustrious bond / The unfair oppressor his noose. / And in the eternal memory temple / and in the celebrations of posterity / Wellington's glory will join / fortunate Spanish Liberty.'

[17] The battle of the Arapiles is the name given in Spain to what is known in Britain as the battle of Salamanca. The Arapiles are two hills where the main fighting took place.

[18] 'Letrilla' is the popular name given to most poem types written to be sung. This one corresponds formally to the so-called 'octavilla' type because each stanza contains eight lines. The 'octavilla' has connections with the copla poem type in terms of rhyme scheme [6- 7a 6- 7a 6- 7a 6-a]. All the stanzas present 'asonante' rhyme type, thus affecting final vowel sounds only. The lines vary in number of syllables. In this case, six and seven syllable lines alternate.

[19] 'Honour Wellington, / Honour England, / Of sad Spain / A tender protector, / And George III, / Whose royal firmness / To the horrible Corsican / Hatred and war swore.'

[20] An 'octavilla quebrada' is an 'arte minor' poem, often written to be sung, characterised by a varying number of eight line stanzas. The first four lines contain eight syllables each, and the remaining four lines usually contain six syllables each. The author is free to establish the rhyme scheme of his own choice as long as it is regularly repeated all through the poem. In this case, Garnier

applied the [8- 8a 8- 8a 6b 6b 6-6-] rhyme scheme.

[21] 'Wellington in Arapiles / For Marmont and his equals / To have breakfast prepared / Great amounts of tomato sauce; / And he gave them so much / That they were very annoyed / And then they went to tell / Napoleon / Long live Wellington! / When Marmont's wife saw him / He had been shot in the arm / Very worried she asked him / 'Have you lost anything else?' / And he answered her / No, darling, no, / And this I owe / To Lord Wellinton. / Long live the Spaniard!'. Published recording: *Concierto 'Bicentenario de la Guerra de la Independencia'*, Auditorio Nacional de Madrid, 13 Feb 2008. San Agustín Choir and Municipal Choir of Pinto. Music Unit of the Infantry Regiment 'Inmemorial del Rey' No. 1, CGE. Conductor: Lt. Col. D. Enrique Blasco.

[22] 'Alas, unfortunate child! If thou evade thy evil star, Marcellus thou shall be', *Aenied*, Book IV, Chapter 32. This ode consists of 10 irregular stanzas containing a variety of verse lines in each case. The shortest stanza is No. 3 (10 lines) and the longest is No. 6 (33 lines). The author's rhyming technique is rather pedestrian, making use of striking liberties, misspelling some words for the sake of easy rhyme, as when the writer employs 'respetoso' for 'respetuoso'.

[23]'Happy are you, Great Britain / Spain you protect today / From a cruel enemy, fascinated / To fulfil a thousand ambitious plans / Tipping the scale in his favour / That restricts unbalanced power! / Should Spain yield! What horrendous / Results would such alteration bring? / You could tremble, Albion, for your existence, / Yielding your pride to his influence, / And perhaps, perhaps powerful Russia / Could fall as also once fell sad Prussia ... / You, queen of the seas, of your friend / Take care, among sorrows and grief wretched, / For a time will come when she'll have plenty / To reward those who her pain relieve.'

[24] Section one contains three stanzas. Sections 2 to 16 contain four. In all cases the stanzas are formed by means of eight 11-syllable lines, the rhyming scheme being [11A 11B 11A 11B 11A 11B 11C 11C]. This was the most frequently used type of stanza in the Renaissance period. It was created by Boccaccio in Italy and then introduced in Spain by Garcilaso and Boscán.

[25] 'Neither more merciful nor mightier in war and combat.' The quotation is an extract of Virgil's description of the qualities of his hero, Aeneas, to whom nobody can compare. *Aeneid*, Book I, Chapter 31.

[26] 'Soon they reach El Retiro, and the battle / They start by revenge encouraged; / But by weapon and wall protected / The boastful French oppose / Their extreme gallantry, and of grapeshot / And bullets rainfall they send brutal, / In such a way their eyes withering, / That like hell they spread anger and death. / Their shots ignoring the allies / The foot of the high wall approach. / Promising life to the wicked, / The town they request them to give in / But, determined to die or win / Wellington's offer they reject / And to the cannon strong fire they add / Of mortar and hotwizer fire fast.'

[27] The 'seguidilla' is a very popular four verse stanza where verses 1 and 3 have seven syllables and verses 2 and 4 have five syllables. The rhyme scheme may vary, which involves a sub-classification into finer categories. The one used here, [7- 5a 7- 5a], is called a 'seguidilla arromanzada' (romance-like seguidilla). Additionally a seguidilla which, like this one, contains three more lines, of which lines 1 and 3 have five syllables and line 2 has seven syllables, is known as a 'seguidilla compuesta' (compound seguidilla). The rhyme scheme is [5a 7b 5a].

[28] 'The bugle of fame / From the East / Divulge of Wellington / To the West: / That in the whole world / Is found no one to resist him / Nor one to molest him. / Generous Albion / With her wise hand, / Has prepared your triumphs / Over the tyrant. / To the choice long life / And on marble your memory / Spain write.'

[29] A canonical epigram is a brief, witty or satirical poem which conveys a single thought, usually a memorable statement.

[30] 'Napoleon, sent from Hell to the World, / Declares bloody war on Heaven and Earth, / This infernal leader, boasting of omnipotence, / Thought he might expel God from Heavens; / But knocked down by General Wellington from high Olympus / He soon bites the dust with furious teeth. / From that the nations have recovered rest, obtained peace for the world, / And General Wellington immense glory.'

[31] A priest from Seville, a teacher of Latin in St Isidore's School.

[32] 'A horrendous monster, fear of the world and disgrace / of the Corsicans, defeated by the sword of the invincible, has fallen. / Mortals, celebrate: Close now Janus' doors. / He is already dead. Believe me, there is peace on Earth.'

[33] The poem is difficult to render into English: 'Raised the fierce Corsican his proud forehead, / And under his hard bondage and oppression / The whole world he tries to subdue, / And the world is not enough for his ambition. / Violence, tricks fly from one nation to another, / And triumphant he imagines himself: / To some the alliance he does not ensure, / The others merciless war has tamed. / Albion resists, and to faithful Spain, / Who the oppressor confronts, she offers help: / The tyrant wraps all in horror; / And when he sees the uselessness of his fury: / Who against me? WELLINGTON: disappear / At this voice, in vapours he melts.'

[34] 'Oh Wellington! who glorious fame, / Who martial fights profess / The reward, the honour, and the greatness / That suits virtue and beauty: / Lord Wellington, whose great deeds / Quevedo's pen is not able / To describe, nor roughness allowed / For courage, for reason, and for the ferocity / Of wild times, when the subdued homeland / moans, horrendous grief! / Oh, everlasting deity! / That in Parnasus' forests dwells / Among loving willows and violets / Far away, any century make it be, / An anxious soul longs for it, / Of Fame in the resounding Temple / A triumphant General / Of tactics Champion who, in our Spain, / Destroying the weirdest race, / Magnificent victories, pleasure, mirth, / Will lead to Iberia full happiness.'

CHAPTER 6

The depiction of the Duke of Wellington in the broadside ballad
Karen Robson

The broadside ballad, the *Waterloo soldier defeated*, opens with the line 'My name is Arthur, I'm known quite well.' This was probably something of an understatement as the so-called 'saviour of Europe' was, from the time of the Peninsular War period onwards, a widely recognised public figure. Indeed Wellington was perhaps 'the most portrayed Briton in his own lifetime',[1] the subject of some 300 paintings and 180 published engravings. As the subject of caricatures, he far outstripped his contemporaries: Richard Gaunt has calculated that he appeared in 5%, or over 800, of the 17,500 satires in the British Museum's collection for this period.[2] He was similarly popular as the subject of song. A comparison of the Bodleian Library's collection of broadside ballads identifies Wellington directly as the subject of twice as many ballads as that other great soldier hero, the Duke of Marlborough, and a third more than Napoleon. While he was in turn outflanked by Lord Nelson, a figure to whom Wellington was sometimes compared, if ballads relating to battles are taken into account, in which Wellington appears as a 'supporting player', then the number of appearances in song considerably outweigh all those of others.

A focus on similar subject matter was just one of the areas of cross-fertilisation and overlap between the graphic art of the caricatures and the written format of the broadside ballads. As the two formats were essentially aimed at very different sections of society, for reasons we shall come to shortly, it could be argued that the broadside ballads helped to permeate the imagery taken from caricature into the wider national consciousness. The impact of both depended on the recognition of a particular reference or personality. Their conspiracy of understanding was facilitated by the use of various symbols and stereotypes which had been inherited from a European polemical tradition and into which new emblems, such as Britannia or symbols of other European countries, were assimilated to compose elaborate allegorical tableaux.[3] The language in the broadsides played directly off the graphic imagery and repertory of forms used within caricatures, whilst the imagery of the caricatures sometimes played on descriptions or phrases used within the ballads. The consistent use of imagery of symbols and stereotypes both in visual and verbal form reinforced their meaning, creating a useful shorthand for the producers and consumers of the products.

The broadside ballads were part of what has been termed 'street literature'. They were cheap, somewhat crudely produced, with rough language and woodcuts, often sensational in subject matter, and were a strange mix of truth, untruth and sheer banality. The broadsides developed as a genre from the topical ballads of the sixteenth and seventeenth centuries, were hastily issued for commercial purposes and took the place now filled by the tabloid press.[4] They shared with the modern tabloid press a love of the sensational: never was there an execution of a celebrated highwayman or a catastrophe without it becoming the subject of a broadside.[5] Broadside ballads were essentially popular songs, usually printed on one single side of paper, that were designed to be read, unfolded and posted in public places. Whilst there was commonality across the broadsides produced in the United Kingdom, regional differences remained. In Wales *baled* was a term which could also mean poems, including songs woven into dramatic productions known as *anterliwtiau* or 'interludes',[6] but it increasingly was used to encompass a wide range of orally transmitted songs, broadsides included. In Wales, the broadsides were differentiated by language:

there were Welsh broadsides, and progressively more English or bi-lingual versions as the nineteenth century progressed. Nor did broadsides from Wales necessarily follow the prescribed format of a single sheet of paper, instead retaining the multiple sheet format of chapbooks. The ballad produced by John Evans of Corwen in 1813 relating to Wellington is one example of this four page pamphlet format.[7]

The broadsides produced across the United Kingdom in the eighteenth and nineteenth centuries existed alongside a burgeoning newspaper industry; they developed into commentaries on topical events or on personalities, rather than presenting new information, or 'news', as they had in earlier centuries. While they changed subtly in focus over time, until the 1850s the broadsides and chapbooks, as well as other forms of 'street literature', met the need of the mass of the population for information that was not supplanted until the introduction of an affordable popular press.[8] Broadside ballads had begun to be circulated at all levels of society from the eighteenth century and there was a cross-fertilisation of popular and sophisticated literature.[9] Sir Walter Scott developed a genuine love of balladry and chapbook histories and Wordsworth was familiar with genre.[10] Yet ballads were always associated with a low standard of life and were considered culturally unspeakable.[11] While the growing division between the socially and politically privileged and wider society was not altogether impassable for isolated individuals, for most it was a chasm.[12] The market for broadside ballads developed a focus on the common people, the lower classes and the expanding literate or semi-literate urban population.[13] Unlike the popular ballads, which had been mainly rural entertainments, the broadsides were more the preserve of the urban population.[14]

The influence of broadsides went beyond the burgeoning literate population. Broadsides might connect with the illiterate: their contents was performed by street sellers, the items were often illustrated and used easily recognisably symbols, and they were produced as souvenirs of events rather than as solely literary items, sought after, for example, as wall decorations.[15] Indeed, contrary to the belief that the development of the printed form marked the death of the oral tradition which had existed in the pre-literate population, there is evidence that publishers of broadsides, such as James Catnach, sought out performers and writers of old broadsides and are said to have paid men to collect ballads.[16] Catnach in effect used technological developments and the increasing size and literacy of the urban population to preserve rather than destroy the oral tradition of the countryside by introducing this new industrial society to the songs of previous generations.[17]

The broadsides, which cost either a ½*d*. or 1*d*. apiece, were the main printed works within the means of the working class or even lower middle classes. The hand-coloured intaglio prints used for caricatures, for instance, at more than 2*s*. each, could never be a 'mass' medium.[18] Despite printing and technological developments in the early part of the nineteenth century, which led to cheaper newspapers, the tax on newspapers was not reduced until 1836 and not finally abolished until 1855, making their cost prohibitive for many. Moreover, newspaper distribution was poor: copies might not be found closer than the nearest market town, which meant rural workers had difficulty securing a regular supply.[19]

In format, the broadsides were pages of text with either forceful headlines or illustrations. In general these illustrations were made with crude woodcuts. The style and the range of images would necessarily have been limited given the cheapness of the printing process and these stock images did not change over a considerable period. Images were repeated constantly or copied from elsewhere — such as the use of Hunt's cartoon *The man wot drove the sovereign* with the broadside ballad *My homeland*[20] — and did not necessarily correlate with the text. The size and sophistication of images developed with time and certainly some of the broadsides produced at the time of Wellington's death used detailed images that had been designed specifically for them.[21] Nevertheless, whatever the quality of their design, it is worth noting that the broadside ballads exercised a considerable influence on printing. Modern, cheap newspapers derived their format of alternating text and illustrations and using forceful headlines from the nineteenth-century broadsides.[22]

While they might have some merit in terms of their visual style, the broadsides had few distinctive verbal qualities. Indeed, at times they seemed to have no style at all: they were realistic rather than romantic, contemporary rather than timeless, moralistic and subjective rather than detached, clichés were used to fill out stanzas rather than advance the story, they were often too detailed, and the language could be flat and non-poetic.[23] Yet in skilful hands they could be riveting. It was certainly true that ballads had always had more influence than polite literature; they were quick, uncomplicated and capable of instant application.[24] They catered to a widespread interest in the newsworthy and sensational, and told their story in a straightforward manner that everyone could understand.[25]

Broadsides were works of commerce and depended on enterprising publishers or printers to produce them. Printers tended to be specialists who diversified into other street literature, such as tracts and chapbooks. The production of this literature was focused on urban centres, which increasingly reflected the development of new industrial conurbations and the largely urban consumer market. In Scotland, Glasgow exerted a considerable influence on the publication and distribution of street literature. Meanwhile in Wales, although publishers remained scattered across the country, the rapid industralisation and massive expansion of the population in the valleys of south-east Wales led to an explosion in the market and in ballad printing.[26] London, as the capital city, housed the largest number of printers of this literature, including Birt, Catnach and other firms based in Seven Dials and Brick Lane. There also were printers who specialised in this literature in regional urban centres, some of them newly industrialised: they could be found, for example, in Newcastle, Belfast, Manchester, Banbury, Durham, Bath and Preston.

The authorship of broadsides and chapbooks was largely anonymous, but many were versifiers who earned an uncertain living carrying out commissions for printers.[27] Yet these anonymous authors had to reflect popular interests and attitudes if they were to sell their wares.[28] For this reason there was a remarkable consistency in this type of ballads above all others. Although all had cultural hallmarks, broadside ballads in Welsh, English, French, Breton and German, for instance, shared a similarity of style and subject matter.[29] The ballads fed on a mix of fact and fiction and their authors could be said to both provide the knowledge that informed the worldview of their public as well as reflecting a form of public opinion.

Some of the printers distributed their own wares, but most depended on pedlars, hawkers and street criers, who would buy their goods from the printers and then sing or shout about them on streets or carry them to markets and fairs. In his *London labour and the London poor* (1861–2) Henry Mayhew gave a wonderfully detailed picture of how these broadsides were sold:[30]

> All these men state that the greater the noise they make, the better is the chance of sale, and better still when the noise is on each side of a street, for it appears as if the vendors were proclaiming such interesting or important intelligence that they were vie-ing with one another who should supply the demand with must ensue. It is not possible to ascertain with any certitude what the patterers are so anxious to sell, for only a few leading words are audible. One of the cleverest of running patterers repeated to me, in a subdued tone, his announcements of murders. The words 'Murder', 'Horrible', 'Barbarous', 'Love', 'Mysterious', 'Former crimes', and the like, could only be caught by the near, but there was no announcement of anything like 'particulars'... The

running patterers describe, or profess to describe, the contents of their papers as they go rapidly along, and they seldom stand still ...

Certain sellers became well-known figures, such as Dougal Graham and William Cameron – known as 'Hawkie' – in Glasgow,[31] and the affectionately remembered eccentric 'Zozimus', who was the pre-eminent minstrel of Dublin city's streets in the early nineteenth century.[32] Charles Dickens, who was praised for recording London 'life as it is', introduces us in *Our Mutual Friend* to Silas Wegg, a one-legged man selling ballads on street corners. William Tinsley, the publisher of *Tinsley's magazine*, in his memoirs recalled ballad sellers selling murder broadsides visiting his Hertfordshire village regularly, as it was near to London.[33] It was often a meagre living, and there is evidence that it was seen as a form of begging and classed as vagrancy.[34] Officials in Birmingham were fairly typical in their attitude when they gave public notice that 'they are come to a determined resolution to apprehend all strolling beggars, ballad singers, and other vagrants within this parish.'[35] Some ballads were specifically printed with a message describing the seller as an ex-soldier deserving charity, so as to circumvent the charge of begging.

Broadside ballads depicting Wellington fall into two main groups: military and political. The way that the Duke was portrayed in the ballads varied considerably, depending on whether they focused on his military triumphs or on his politics, but there were recurrent images or themes. These had resonance with imagery used in the art of caricatures, as well as feeding into the street language and literature to which the broadsides belonged. In the military ballads, for instance, the imagery included Britannia, bulldogs or lions, which became synonymous with, and shorthand for, an emerging sense of British national identity. The bulldog transposed into the representative of the British nation, John Bull. The lion, which lay at the feet of Britannia, became the servant of the monarch and the nation. In these celebratory and commemorative broadsides Wellington was presented as the personification of a British hero and of the positive values of a great British nation. For the political ballads the tone tended to be less deferential, paralleling closely the satirical wit of many of the political cartoons. A recurrent image was that of 'Lord Nosey', a satire of Wellington instantly recognisable from the visual media. Yet if the broadsides featuring the Duke as a soldier were more celebratory and deferential than those of a political nature, like the political ones the military broadsides were composed as a response to events and based on popular opinion. As many of the military broadsides dated from the period Wellington's death, the opinion they reflected was of the world coloured by developments of the mid-nineteenth century rather than those of the Peninsular War, with a mid-century, rose-tinted view of what constituted a British national hero.

The military broadsides tended to have a number of different strands interwoven within the same ballad. Central to many was the depiction of Wellington as the representative of the idealised, heroic, British soldier. The soldier hero has been one of the most durable and powerful forms of idealised masculinity in western tradition since antiquity.[36] Wellington, in becoming the most successful British general of his generation, defeating the Colossus that was Napoleon, fitted neatly into this role. That many of the broadsides casting him in this idealised role were written at the time of his death, when sentiment overwhelmed criticism, added considerably to this process. Lord Nelson was similarly the subject of many ballads praising him and his achievements because he died victorious in battle in the service of his country.[37] This reverential treatment of Wellington and Nelson linked with ideas that dated from antiquity about the creation of heroes, and concepts of death and honour and the commemoration of personal sacrifice.

The representation of Wellington as an idealised national hero also fitted with a trend in caricatures, which developed in the wake of the French Revolution, when a kind of mythology was created centred on personalities. Napoleon and Wellington were both subjects of this process and English caricature built up the myth of the little Corsican even as it derided it.[38] While he was treated with derision in caricatures such as *The Corsican spider in his web*, by Woodward, published by Thomas Tegg in 1808, *Modern Prometheus, or the downfall of tyranny*,[39] or songs such as *The devil and Buonaparte*,[40] the act of cutting Napoleon down to size was taken to extremes in the 1830s by a flea circus exhibited by Signor L.Bertolotto at the Cosmorama Rooms at Regent Street, London. For the grand finale of the circus, three minute figures in full uniform appeared representing Napoleon, his aide de camp and Mameluke Roustan, all mounted on fleas.[41] By creating such comparisons between two great military leaders and the two nations, the caricatures and ballads touched upon a second major theme: that of nationhood. It has been claimed that war was the midwife of national unity, that the hundred years of warfare which ended with Waterloo also witnessed the creation of the modern nation and that 'Great Britain' was an invention forged above all by war.[42] As heroic masculinity became fused in an especially potent configuration with representations of British imperial identity,[43] heroic military figures such as Wellington, and Nelson before him, were represented as personifications of the great British nation.

One way these themes manifested themselves in the broadsides was through the use of symbols and emblems, developed as part of visual art and recognisable from caricatures and illustrations. Britannia made her appearance in a number of ballads. Those dating from the time of Wellington's death represented her as a figure, seemingly modelled upon Queen Victoria, mourning the double loss of a great British hero and her country's protector. *Wellington at Waterloo* contains the lines:

> Britannia justly mourns! All Europe weeps!..
> He who is Britain's boast
> Is now to Britain lost ...[44]

In further ballads, Wellington 'was the glory and pride of Britannia',[45] and the defender of the nation.[46] Representations of

Wellington and Victoria illustrated concepts of national identity, the British empire and the role of the army and the monarchy within them. The depiction of Wellington as the martial hero and as the protector of his Queen associated imperial patriotism with the virtues of manhood and war. This placed the Duke squarely in the context of the reign of Queen Victoria, the country and empire of the 1850s, when the ballads were written, rather than in the era of Waterloo. Britain by the 1850s had become a nation waging aggressive warfare to maintain an empire.[47] The military were seen as a symbol of the power and prestige of the monarchy. Queen Victoria took a keen interest in military matters, even appearing in military-style costume at army reviews.[48] The representation of the weak feminine Britannia and her defending hero also fitted the concept of masculinity created within British national identity: martial masculinity complemented domestic femininity which needed protection.[49]

Other symbols that had a resonance with British nationalism and pride, likewise employed in the visual art of caricatures, were British lions and British bulldogs. A ballad commemorating the battle of the Pyrenees, for instance, contained the line 'the lions of Britain, their duty have done'.[50] Wellington was elsewhere described as the 'lion hearted hero'.[51] In a ballad marking the action at Bayonne, the bulldog and the lion both appeared: the British bull-dogs' 'teeth look quite venomous like lions they roar'.[52] A version printed by J. and W.H.Sweet of the well-known ballad *The soldier's tear*, which depicted the departure of the brave soldier off to do his duty in defence of his country taking leave of his sweetheart, was illustrated by a lion.[53] Through symbols synonymous with Britishness and the British nation, found in other patriotic ballads of the period, Wellington was claimed for the nation and presented as an idealised and potent symbol of the glory of that nation. It was a British nation, it should be noted, that was very much English in its construction. Indeed, in contrast to the political broadside ballads, Wellington's Irish ancestry was, with very few exceptions, never mentioned in the military ones. This was because the depictions of the Irish, or Welsh or Scottish come to that, were usually negatively stereotypical and used to emphasise the greatness of English qualities. Thus Wellington became English by default to personify the glorious characteristics of the British hero and nation. And in casting him in the role of the protector of Britannia/Queen Victoria in the ballads, he became the hero of an empire, not merely of a nation.

The creation of a mythology around an idealised figure of Wellington was achieved by a number of means. There was the use of particular language and of comparisons with other heroic figures, as well as links made with antiquity and the adaptation of more ancient oral traditions of which the ballads were an inheritor. The depiction of Wellington the lionheart in the broadsides, which had placed him squarely in a heroic British warrior tradition, was one means used to create this mythology. Certainly he was praised as a great hero:

> He who was the joy and the pride of the earth
> The chief and the hero of the wonders.[54]

Equally, he was acclaimed a great soldier, 'the warrior chief, the nobly brave',[55] and 'Guardian invincible of freedom!'[56] Comparisons with other great military heroes, such as Marlborough, Nelson and Wolfe, as well as Sir Francis Drake,[57] who had occupied the symbolic centre of English national identity,[58] added to the lustre of Wellington's reputation. Further comparisons with Caesar[59] showed the importance of antiquity to concepts of honour and nobility and to a construction of heroism which should not be underestimated.[60] The depiction of Wellington as a hero from antiquity extended into a range of artistic formats, such as sculpture.[61] Within the ballads he was 'the warrior of old Britain' and the 'immortal Wellington',[62] who sent out thunderbolts to vanquish the French.[63] Another ballad bore the line: 'His shot and his bombs they rattled in the air like thunder.'[64] The language of heroic narratives seen here, containing resonances of Homeric descriptions of gods and mortals in battle, appeared again in a description of Wellington at the battle of Waterloo, where he was presented as an invincible hero warrior:

> Before that valiant proud Napoleon
> He stood that day at Waterloo
> What man on earth could e'er be bolder
> To fight the French in armour bright
> While men and generals all around him
> The great Napoleon he put to flight.[65]

Such overblown language with idealised descriptions of glory and honour in war was echoed in other military broadsides of the period, including those featuring great British military leaders, such as Marlborough, and a rehabilitated Napoleon. A typical example is *With a helmet on his brow*, in which the soldier was described as mounting on his gallant steed

> To conquer or to die
> His plume like the pendant stream
> In the wanton winters wind
> In the path of glory still
> A bright plume shall he find
> Bright as his own good sword.[66]

Lord Marlborough contains the lines 'I must go face my foe with glittering sword and shield' and 'Tthe sun was down, the earth did shake, we'll gain the field or die.'[67] While Napoleon was seen not only as soldier who was 'valiant' and noble of heart,[68] but as 'bolder than Mars'.[69]

In using language of the heroic narratives of martial exploits that had developed over many centuries, the broadside ballads fused together ancient and contemporary depictions of heroes. They built on ideas of heroism which dated back to antiquity. They linked to sculpture and ideas of commemorative art which developed in the nineteenth century and with contemporary trends of caricatures and the cult or mythology of personalities. And the broadside ballads built on their own origins as an oral and storytelling tradition. Oral tradition contained many examples of tales of heroic deeds and warrior heroes vanquishing evil. Heroic narratives celebrating the deeds of military heroes had invested their heroes with the new significance of serving their country and glorifying its name. The stories became myths of nationhood itself.[70] The representation of Wellington fitted neatly into this pattern, mythologised as a figure who transcended time and place, a link in a chain of national heroes and the personification of the greatness the nation.

The comparison between Wellington and Napoleon, and by extension Britain and France, was part of the process of reinforcing a sense of national identity and of Britain's place in the world. Within the broadsides, the comparisons were universally positive towards Wellington, who was after all the potent representative of all that was glorious about the British nation, and designed to elevate both Wellington and Britain. Where Napoleon was celebrated in broadsides, such as the *Hero of war* —'no force could withstand him' and 'a terror to all Europe'[71] — or in the *Ashes of Napoleon*,[72] these were used to emphasise Wellington's achievements in defeating his rival. The 'gallant'[73] Wellington became a symbol of British justice against foreign tyranny: 'thou was the sword which justice draws'.[74] He was:

The glory and pride of Britannia
He made tyrants to quake[75]

whilst Napoleon was derided as the 'greatest scourge', 'the tyrant' and 'the Gallic chief unmindful of the wretched men he'd onward to destruction led'.[76] In creating these clear comparisons between the two men, and hence the two nations which personified, the ballads underscored the development of a constructed national identity that evolved during the nineteenth century. In this process, English/British identity created another identity that represented the anti-type of the Englishman,[77] thereby emphasising the superior qualities of the English and their nation.

The idea of the superiority of one nation, by making another its anti-type, was used further in the depictions of Britain and France in battle. Just as Wellington became the symbol of justice against tyranny and rebellion, so the British army were cast in the same role: the British lions deflected the French forces — 'Hark! Hark! How the lion is roaring'[78] — and the British bulldogs made 'French rebellious dogs to fly'.[79] The superiority of the British soldiery over the French, casting derision on French bravery, was the theme of a number of broadsides. The French were depicted as a lightweight force, prone to crumble in the face of the stout British resistance: 'The Frenchmen's ranks like chaff they break'[80] or were made 'to dance'.[81] Another broadside, entitled *Boney's total defeat and Wellington triumphant*, spoke of how the brave British troops, 'our brave lads of old England', defeated the French who 'prick'd by the bayonet they stagger'd and reel'd'.[82] And in a broadside about Pamplona, the French were derided for hiding 'like foxes in their holes'[83] until that great British hunter, Wellington, forced them out to engage the British forces. By the use of stereotypes, by making the French a crude negation of what are seen as positive British/English characteristics, by picking symbols and emblems that would be familiar to the audience, the broadsides sought to glorify the achievements and the sense of superiority of their own nation.

In the political broadside ballads, the tone and representation of Wellington was considerably different. This was partly due to the fact that the aims of the two categories were very different. The military broadsides were celebratory or commemorative. They did not merely celebrate the victory of the British army in battle, but marked the burgeoning sense of British national identity and the mythology that was created around the soldier hero and British superiority. Although they focused on Wellington and his military exploits, his depiction in them was more in the abstract, as a symbol of Britishness and of the British nation. The military broadsides ranged widely in date, they were not necessarily written contemporaneously with events they depicted: indeed a con-siderable body of work was produced at the time of Wellington's death. The political broadsides, in contrast, were an immediate reaction to events that they represented. They were satirical in tone, much more direct, unflattering and personal in their depiction of Wellington. They shared a point of view, imagery and nuance of political caricatures of the period. Politics was a cruel arena and within this sphere Wellington was shown as mortal rather than god-like, a Colossus with feet of clay. They subverted qualities which were seen as positives and celebrated within the military broadsides. Hunting, for instance, a noble skill in a military hero, since it was one of the elements of militaristic manhood, became a means of oppression in the political broadside ballads. This was a manifestation of an image that arose of Wellington as a military dictator, riding roughshod over his opponents.

Cross-fertilisation between the political broadside ballads and caricatures was evident in the commonality of representations of Wellington, as well as in the way that imagery seeped from one medium to the other. It has been argued that reform excitement meant that politics permeated social satire as never before.[84] Certainly reform produced a concentration of broadsides which paralleled the caricatures on the subject, but it was also true that imagery transferred from graphic registers to verbal ones, and vice versa, over a range of topics. For instance, the broadside *The man of the tight little island*,[85] which was produced in 1828–9, talked of Wellington as blind to poverty. This was followed in 1830 by William Heath's cartoon, *Blind man's buff*, which is subtitled 'There is none so blind as him who will not see.'[86] Wellington and Robert Peel, left without employment in the wake of the Whigs taking office in 1830, were the subject of a number of caricatures as well as the subject of song.[87] Robert Peel the Ratcatcher (or parliamentary whip) who appeared in broadsides[88] was based on an image used in William Heath's *The man wot's appointed rat-catcher to the king*.[89] A broadside marking the repeal of the corn laws, in which Wellington was described as the boasting cock of Waterloo,[90] used the image of Canning as a game cock from a caricature produced in 1827 on the formation of Canning's government.[91]

Wellington was endowed with a Roman nose, a distinguishing physical feature that was a blessing to the caricaturist and very rapidly adopted widely. Accepting that Wellington could indeed be recognised by his nose, the broadside ballads also concentrated on this distinguishing physical feature.[92] 'Nosey' was quickly adopted as verbal shorthand for the Duke in broadsides. A broadside that appeared attacking Robert Peel and Wellington in the aftermath of the passing of the reform act was entitled *Bob and Nosey's lament on the passing of the English reform act*.[93] Other examples include *Repeal and Erin go Bragh*, which referred to Orange Peel and Nosey with all the Tory crew;[94] *The British servants*, which contains the line 'Nosey the King of Waterloo and his row dow dow iddy iddy pipe clay nose';[95] and *John Bull and his rhubarb* and the comment 'Poor old King Nosey is getting old'.[96] *The man of the tight little island*, produced during Wellington's premiership, in 1828–9, described him thus:[97]

He is betray'd by his long nose
Which might do well to frighten the crows
Derry-down Nosey

This repetition of the imagery was a sign not of poverty but of invention, of political shorthand. Just as the repetition of imagery worked in cartoons to satirise and comment upon the behaviour of the political establishment, so it worked in the context of broadsides as street literature, presenting a popular 'tabloid', non-establishment point of view. This was the art of the excluded, of politics seen from below, which expressed an insolent contempt for the mighty rather than a sense of powerlessness.[98]

Repeated references to Wellington as king in the broadside ballads, as in *John Bull and his rhubarb* or *The British servants*, played on widely held views of him as an over-mighty subject and of his relationship with the Crown. This imagery was found in caricatures produced during Wellington's premiership, where it was commonplace to imply that he was a military dictator in the vein of

Napoleon or Cromwell.[99] 'Old Nosey will govern old Billy again' is a line in the ballad *Resignation of His Majesty's ministers*, produced in 1832;[100] while *The Waterloo soldier in power again* by its very name conveyed the idea of a military dictator.[101] *The Waterloo solider in power again* was one of a number of ballads that also focused on Wellington's relationship with the Crown. *Billy Barlow's breeches,* for instance, worked with the idea of the hen-pecked King William cast aside whilst Wellington and Queen Adelaide 'will again rule the land'.[102] Queen Adelaide was cast in *Billy Barlow's breeches* both as a German broom and in the role of Mrs Barlow, playing on the idea of her sweeping out the Whigs from power and commenting on her perceived close relation with Wellington. The image of a broom was used as satirical shorthand for Queen Adelaide in a number of other ballads.[103]

The representation of Wellington in these political broad-sides was a subversion of the image of the British national hero presented in the military broadside ballads. This subversion was carried further by the use of the images of John Bull and of Billy Barlow. One of the symbols of Britishness from the military broad-sides was that of the British bulldog. The character of John Bull could be seen as an extension of this bulldog figure, becoming the representation of the ordinary British public. In setting Wellington against John Bull — as in *The Waterloo soldier in power again* — the political broadsides underscored the notion that he had become an over-powerful subject, no longer a bulldog alongside his fellow soldiers. This idea was taken further with the use of the character of Billy Barlow. Billy Barlow was a comic figure, a ne'er do well, a droll who appeared in street theatre and who fancied himself as some great personage.[104] The character was recognisable to the public as a figure of ridicule and of overweening pride; the satirists and broadside writers were making very clear points by connecting him with Wellington. Billy Barlow also appeared in song as a soldier, indeed in later broadsides he was described as 'a bully old soldier'.[105] In associating Wellington with him in this military context, the ballads were able to build further on the image of Wellington as a military dictator.

Wellington's military career, his martial qualities and associations with the army were used in the political broadsides to represent a hated political figure, a military dictator, an over-mighty subject and a bluff soldier unsubtle in his dealing with politics. This was the shorthand of political comment, used in the same way that the image of a jackboot in cartoons became adopted as a symbol of a hated ministry.[106] Indeed, Wellington's military uniform and the Wellington boot became the easily recognisable replacement for the jackboot in the oppression of the masses. In *Parliament's closed and you can't come in and it's no use knocking at the door*, the Waterloo Duke does not stand on ceremony but 'kicked at the door with a Wellington boot'.[107] In *John Bull and his party*, which concerned Great Britain and Ireland, Old Nosey is in his cocked hat and feather, 'his cannons rattled as it 'twas in battle'.[108] The repeated refrain of Wellington as the victor of Waterloo chimed with the image of him as a military dictator, while also exposing the disparity between Wellington's less adept endeavours in the political arena and those on the battlefield.

Despite the fact that the British army made a significant contribution to the development of the British nation and empire, and Wellington was extravagantly praised in the military broadsides for his contribution, soldiers were not universally popular. Wellington's military associations were the subject of censure in the political broadsides. The derision with which he was described as someone who would 'lay with a knapsack and musket'[109] fed into the caricatures of him in military uniform and the associations with jackboots and oppression. This developed further into caricatures of Wellington as a lobster, a popular form of derision for soldiers.[110] But, in the French context, the lobster also referred to revolutionary propensities; and the idea circulated in 1830 that Wellington supported Polignac's unpopular regime in France.[111] While ironic in one sense, since Wellington feared revolution and disorder, this a belief arose from his wish to maintain a status quo. He was described in this way by Shelley in his sonnet *England in 1819* as one of the:

> Rulers who neither see, nor feel, nor know,
> But leech-like to their fainting country cling ...[112]

Wellington's actions in the face of the possibility of unrest and revolution coloured the image of him as an oppressor or military dictator, no more so than in the wake of Peterloo in 1819. Named ironically after the great military victory at Waterloo, the incident occurred when the crowd attending a meeting held at St Peter's Church, Manchester, on 9 August 1819 to discuss reform, at which the radical reformer Henry Hunt was speaker, was charged by the yeomanry cavalry. Eleven people were killed and hundreds injured. In the aftermath, Wellington worked to save the country from further agitation, regardless of how reactionary and oppressive his measures might appear. It was feared by the Whigs that the supply of additional military forces indicated that the army was being primed to act independently of the old constitutional authorities in preparation for a role supporting 'a government disposed to despotism'.[113] But Wellington felt that firm action needed to be taken. He wrote to Mrs Arbuthnot that 'it is clear to me that they [the agitators] won't be quiet till a large number of them "bite the dust" as the French say, or till some of their leaders are hanged, which would be the most fortunate result.'[114] In a letter to Major General Sir John Byng, who was in charge of the Northern Command, he made suggestions for the best disposition of forces in the north of England should there be an uprising inspired by the radicals.[115] He was also one of 13 ministers who supported a letter of thanks to the magistrates after Peterloo, because he did not think that magistrates would act again in similar circumstances if not supported. According to Lady Shelley he approved of their conduct, with the exception of the reading of the Riot Act.[116] Later, as Commander in Chief of the army, Wellington was cast in the role as the main source of oppressive force.

Depictions of Peterloo in ballads and caricatures resonated with the image of hunting, but subverted this from the positive connotations found in the military context. In the political arena, the bold hunter of French soldiers became either the self-serving and cruel politician using force to oppress any opposition or hunting for his own gain. As the military were responsible for imposing order at Peterloo, Wellington as a leading soldier was seen as ultimately responsible for the actions of the force. The song *With Henry Hunt we'll go*, set to the tune of the *Battle of Waterloo* (the opening line of which is 'With Wellington we'll go') was much sung around Manchester in the aftermath of the affair.[117] S.W.Fores' caricature of the event showed aggressive cavalry soldiers trampling innocents under hoof and attacking others with sabres.[118] The cavalry charge and hunting motif is taken up in *Charlie Grey's come again* to reiterate the image of Wellington as someone who would trample on the necks of those who opposed him.[119] And the description of Wellington, alongside Peel, as an unfeeling politician who would 'feed us all on paving stones',[120] had the resonance of the trampling of the oppressed into the ground. It was not a great leap of imagination from here to the image of Wellington as the bogey man in a child's ballad. In this the naughty child was told to behave or he would be beaten and then eaten by the Duke:

> Baby, baby if he hears you
> As he gallops by the house
> Limb from limb at once he'll tear you
> Just as pussy tears a mouse
> And he'll beat you beat you beat
> And he'll beat you all to pap
> And he'll eat you, eat you, eat you
> Gobble you, gobble you, snap, snap, snap.[121]

This particular manuscript could be a play on invasion threat ballads, but also clearly based its imagery on that of Wellington as a bully and oppressor found in broadsides and cartoons in the post-Peterloo era. It also fitted with William Hone's *The political house that Jack built* (London, 1819), which was set in the style of a nursery rhyme and featured a violent Wellington, who would resort to arms and force to achieve his aim:

> [Reform] This word is the watchword —
> The talisman word
> *That the WATERLOO-MAN's to crush*
> With his sword.

The other hunting theme that emerged from the broadsides was that of the self-serving politician who was a hunter of honours and who had betrayed the brotherhood of soldiery. It was a sentiment that found expression in other print forms. Byron's *Don Juan*, Canto Nine,[122] for instance, contains the lines 'And I shall be delighted to learn who, save you and yours, have gained by Waterloo?' *The political 'A, apple pie;' or the extraordinary red book* (London, 1820) noted:

> Great Wellington certainly had much to do
> In beating Napoleon at fam'd Waterloo;
> And so well has his country rewarded his skill
> Should he eat all we've given him, I'm certain it will,
> If not burst him outright, make him terribly ill.[123]

There was a similar expression of disquiet in the broadside ballads at the perceived excess of honours granted to Wellington. In the *Political fishing net* Wellington was described as:

> Duke Conkey is a shark
> That has followed many a bait[124]

Another broadside contained the comment that 'Folks talk of his services done for the state, but then they forget a' his riches an' plate!'[125] The analogy in the *Political fishing net* is that of sea creatures, yet describing Wellington as a shark is a clever play on two different images. A shark is a sea creature, a voracious carnivore and predator, a creature that could be equated with the image of Wellington as an oppressor and voracious collector of honours. A shark is also an unscrupulous person who swindles others; here Wellington might be seen as the betrayer of his fellow soldiers, as depicted in further broadside ballads.

The lack of affinity Wellington as politician showed to his fellow soldiers in the post-Waterloo period was conceived as a particularly bitter betrayal. Despite sometimes being treated with derision, the soldier was a potent symbol of idealised masculinity and closely associated with national identity and might. The idea that the patriots, who did their duty and served their country, would not be rewarded for their sacrifice was a heavy blow. The fact that Wellington gained honours whilst his former comrades in arms suffered privations and loss of income added to this sense of betrayal. In the ballad, *Sportsmen*, Wellington's own situation was contrasted with those of his fellow soldiers:

> And Wellington to Waterloo he had the best of luck
> He hunted from a lieutenant till he became a duke
> Men that did fight well for him and did him honours again
> He tried all that he could do to have their pensions ta'en.[126]

The theme of Wellington as a betrayer, or 'traitor' as he is described here, is found in the broadside *The triumph of reform*:

> Let Wellington think on the days of Spain and Waterloo
> When the Shamrock, Rose and Thistle join'd
> Great Bonny to subdue
> Although we never ran from him
> From our cause he ran away,
> And like a traitor wanted to
> Pull down the soldiers' pay.[127]

Sandy the Waterloo man contained the lines 'Sleep on ye brave dead, whilst your country so grateful will cherish your widows and fatherless babes', which enshrined the commonly held idea that the state should support those or the families of those who had served their country.[128] It was no coincidence that a scathing ballad commenting on Wellington's political career, *The last look, or Nosey's tear*,[129] was a play on the well-known ballad *The soldier's tear*,[130] which told of the brave soldier going to war. The satirical nature of the former was a pertinent reminder of how the sweet, sentimental ideas of the military and warfare engendered in patriotic songs had soured in the realities of the post-Waterloo peacetime. This shift paralleled that of the image of Wellington from idealised British national hero to derided politician. Depicting him at odds with his fellow soldiers starkly illuminated this change.

Given the paucity of other sources available for the lower classes for a long period of time, and effectively until the mid-nineteenth century, the broadside ballads have real value as a reflection of popular politics. They provide a tangible sense of what going on and public opinion: they did not necessarily provoke public action, as in earlier centuries, but were a protest literature of their time; and they created a climate of opinion and sentiment.[131] While the extent to which broadside ballads reflected or expanded politicisation depended to a considerable degree on the growth of literacy in this period, the impact of this extended far beyond the minority who could read and write, reaching through them to many who listened to texts read aloud.[132] Always more popular than serious literature and with a much wider reach, the broadsides were not only a link between earlier cultural forms and the later popular cheap newspapers, but were to have a lasting influence on typography and format of the newspapers that succeeded them. The broadsides did not exist nor function in isolation. They were also to have an influence on other, contemporary, media formats; there was cross-fertilisation of images and themes between the street literature of the broadside ballads with caricatures and cartoons as well as with the classical forms of art, such as sculpture. Depictions of Wellington in the broadsides were very much a mirror of public opinion, reflected in the style and form of this type of street literature. They were, in effect, the tabloid press of the time. The different Wellingtons that emerged from the spheres of the military and political broadsides were not only contemporary satirical responses to events, but represented emerging ideas of national identity and nationhood that coloured the military broadsides. Both Wellington the national military hero or crudely drawn political villain were reflections of contemporary public opinion; they were products of two very different aims and purposes. The one was framed by sentiment and rose-coloured contemporary images of nation, the other by satirical political opinions of contemporary events.

References

[1] P.Jupp 'Pictorial images of the first Duke of Wellington' in *Avenues to the past. Essays presented to Sir Charles Brett on his 75th year* ed. T.Reeves-Smyth and R.Oman (Belfast, 2003) p. 110.

[2] R.Gaunt, 'Wellington in petticoats: the Duke as caricature', in *Wellington Studies IV* ed. C.M.Woolgar (Southampton, 2008) p. 140.

[3] D.Donald *The age of caricature: satirical prints in the reign of George III* (New Haven, 1996) p. 47.

[4] A.Bold *The ballad* (London, 1979) p. 66.

[5] R.D.Altick *The English common reader: a social history of the mass reading public 1800–1900* (Chicago, 1967) p. 28.

[6] *Ballads in Wales (Baledi yng Nghymru)* ed. M.A.Constantine (London, 1999) p. 2.

[7] National Library of Wales, Cerddi Bangor 9(16), *Can o ddiolchgarwch; Dduw am bluddugoliaethau a ennillwyd ar fyddinoedd Ffraingc yn Russia a Hispaen gan Arglwydd Wellington ac amryw rai eraill ynghyd ac ychydig o hanes y frwydr* (Corwen, [1813]).

[8] R.Collison *The story of street literature: forerunner of the popular press* (London, 1973) p. 10.

[9] L.Shepard *The history of street literature* (London, 1973) p. 114.

[10] Shepard, *History of street literature*, p. 114.

[11] Bold, *Ballad*, p. 73.

[12] Shepard, *History of street literature*, pp. 113-14.

[13] See D.Dugaw *Warrior women and popular balladry 1650–1850* (Cambridge, 1989) p. 20.

[14] Bold, *Ballad*, p. 66.

[15] G.Crabbe *The parish register*: Crabbe commenting on one of the less salubrious dwellings notes that 'Here are no books, but ballads on the wall ...': *The poetical works of the Rev George Crabbe, with letters and journals of his life, by his son* ed. G.Crabbe (8 vols., London, 1834) ii, p. 151.

[16] C.Hindley *The life and times of James Catnach, ballad monger* (London, 1878) p. 383.

[17] D.Vincent, 'The decline of the oral tradition in popular culture' in *Popular*

culture and custom in nineteenth-century England ed. R.D.Storch (London, 1983) p. 29.

[18] Donald, *Age of caricature*, p. 21.

[19] Collison, *Story of street literature*, p. 9.

[20] Edinburgh UL, Collection 47, Broadsides, *My fatherland*.

[21] Examples include: Bodl., Broadside Ballads, Hardy B 13(262), *An elegy on the death of His Grace the Duke of Wellington*; Firth c.14(376), *General Wellington*.

[22] Shepard, *History of street literature*, p. 115.

[23] G.M.Laws Jr *The British literary ballad* (Carbondale, 1972) p. 13.

[24] Shepard, *History of street literature*, p. 35.

[25] Laws, *British literary ballad*, p. 13.

[26] See E.Wyn James, 'Watching the white wheat and that hole below the nose: the English ballads of the late-nineteenth century Welsh jobbing-printer' at http://www.cardiff.ac.uk/insrv/libraries/scolar/digital/welshballads/whitewheat.html; originally published in *Bridging the cultural divide: our common ballad heritage* ed. S.Riewerts and H.Stein (Hildersheim, 2000) pp. 178–94.

[27] Collison, *Story of street literature*, p. 3.

[28] T.Downe 'Popular ballads: revolutionary rhetoric and politicisation' in *Ireland and the French revolution* ed. H.Gough and D.Dickson (Dublin, 1990) p. 139.

[29] *Ballads in Wales*, ed. Constantine, p. 2.

[30] From H.Mayhew *London labour and the London poor* (4 vols., London, 1861–2), quoted in Shepard, *History of street literature*, p. 72.

[31] NLS, *The Word on the Street*: http://www.nls.uk/broadsides

[32] Shepard, *History of street literature*, p. 98.

[33] W.Tinsley *Random recollections of an old publisher* (2 vols., London, 1905), quoted in Shepard, *History of street literature*, p. 99.

[34] Bold, *Ballad*, p. 74

[35] *A touch on the times: songs of social change, 1770-1914* ed. R.Palmer (London, 1974) p. 13.

[36] G.Dawson *Soldier heroes: British adventure, empire and the imagining of masculinities* (London, 1994) p. 1.

[37] Examples include: Bodl., Broadside Ballads, Firth c.12(43) *Death of Nelson*; Harding B 11(1532), *The hero of Trafalgar or the death of Nelson*; Curzon b.24(79), *A new song on the grand funeral procession of the late gallant Lord Nelson*.

[38] E.L.Smith *The art of caricature* (London, 1981) p. 68.

[39] *Modern Prometheus or the downfall of tyranny*, produced by Cruikshank (London, [July 1814?]).

[40] *The devil and Bonaparte: or the emperor's last tumble, as sung by Mr*

C.Taylor, written by T.Evans (London, [1813]).

[41] L.Bertolotto *The history of the flea: with notes and observations* (2nd edition, London, 1835), quoted in *Boney: Napoleon through English eyes*, catalogue of the exhibition prepared by the Devon Library Services, 1985 at http://www.devon.gov.uk/localstudies/100304/1.html

[42] M.Paris *Warrior nation: images of war in British popular culture 1850–2000* (London, 2000) p. 14.

[43] Dawson, *Soldier heroes*, p. 1.

[44] Bodl., Broadside Ballads, Firth c.14(36), *Wellington at Waterloo*.

[45] Bodl., Broadside Ballads, Johnson Ballad 492, *Death of the Duke of Wellington*.

[46] Bodl., Broadside Ballads, Firth c.16(423), *The death of the Duke of Wellington*; Firth c.14(36), *Wellington at Waterloo*; and Firth c.16(422), *The death of His Grace the Duke of Wellington* which contained the lines: 'Midst the wreck of the world, old England can boast / That she basked in the blaze of the sun, / For her chief was a wall of defence round the coast — / His name made the universe run.'

[47] Paris, *Warrior nation*, p. 13.

[48] Quoted in Paris, *Warrior nation*, p. 17.

[49] Dawson, *Soldier heroes*, pp. 1–2.

[50] Bodl., Broadside Ballads, Harding B 25(143), *Battle of the Pyrenees, gained by Field Marshal Wellington*.

[51] Bodl., Broadside Ballads, Firth c.14(34), *Lines in memory of the Duke of Wellington the hero of an hundred fights*.

[52] Bodl., Broadside Ballads, Harding B 25(1145), *Lord Wellington's success near Bayonne. A new song*.

[53] Edinburgh UL, Broadsides Collection, 47.

[54] Bodl., Broadside Ballads, Firth c.16(422), *The death of His Grace the Duke of Wellington*.

[55] Bodl., Broadside Ballads, Firth c.14(36), *Wellington at Waterloo*.

[56] Bodl., Broadside Ballads, Johnson Ballads 1235, *To His Grace the Duke of Wellington*.

[57] Bodl., Broadside Ballads, Harding B 17(331a), *We shall never see his like again*, contains comparisons with Marlborough, Nelson and Wolfe; Johnson Ballad 1384A, *Wellington's victory: a new song*, mentions Wolfe and Caesar; Harding B 30(15), *Wellington and Blucher*, and Firth c.16(422), *The death of His Grace the Duke of Wellington*, mention Nelson; Firth c.14(307), *Darby Kelly*, contains mention of Marlborough and Wolfe; and NLS, LC1270(016), *The ashes of Napoleon*, refers to Marlborough, Nelson, Jarvis, Howe, Blake, Wolfe and Abercrombie.

[58] Dawson, *Soldier heroes*, p. 1.

[59] Bodl., Broadside Ballads, Johnson Ballad 1235, *To His Grace the Duke of Wellington, KG*, and Johnson Ballad 1384A, mentioned in n. 57.

[60] Bold, *Ballad*, p. 7

[61] See D.Arnold *The Duke of Wellington and London: the Thirteenth Wellington Lecture* (Southampton, 2001).

[62] Bodl., Broadside Ballads, Firth c.14(34), *Lines in memory of the Duke of Wellington, the hero of an hundred fights.*

[63] Bodl., Broadside Ballads, Harding B 25(143), *Battle of the Pyrenees gained by Field Marshal Wellington.*

[64] Bodl., Broadside Ballads, Harding B 25(908), *The invasion of France by Lord Wellington.*

[65] Bodl., Broadside Ballads, Firth c.14(34), *Lines in memory of the Duke of Wellington, the hero of an hundred fights.*

[66] Bodl., Broadside Ballads, Harding B 16(311b), *With a helmet on his brow.*

[67] Bodleian Library Broadside Ballads: Firth c.14(8) *Lord Marlborough*

[68] NLS, LC1270(016), *The ashes of Napoleon.*

[69] Edinburgh UL, Broadsides Collection 47, *Hero of war.*

[70] Dawson, *Soldier heroes*, p. 1.

[71] Edinburgh UL, Broadsides Collection 47, *Hero of war.*

[72] NLS, LC1270(016), *The ashes of Napoleon.*

[73] Bodl., Broadside Ballads, Harding B 3(86), *Bonaparte's disasters in Russia: a new song*, and Johnson Ballads, 1384AA, *Wellington's victory: a new song.*

[74] Bodl., Broadside Ballads, Johnson Ballads 1293, *Ode to be sung at the dinner given by the gentlemen from India to Field Marshall the Duke of Wellington, KG, Monday July 11 1814.*

[75] Bodl., Broadside Ballads, Firth c.16(424), *The death of the Duke of Wellington.*

[76] Bodl., Broadside Ballads, Harding B 3(86), *Bonaparte's disasters in Russia: a new song*, and Firth c.14(376), *General Wellington.*

[77] G.Porter, '"Who talks of my nation?": the role of Wales, Scotland and Ireland in constructing "Englishmen"' in *Imagined states: nationalism, utopia and longing in oral cultures* ed. L.Del Giudice and G.Porter (Logan, 2001) p. 103.

[78] Bodl., Broadside Ballads, Firth b.26(211), *The standard of England and the banner of France.*

[79] Bodl., Broadside Ballads, Harding B 25(1145), *Lord Wellington's success near Bayonne. A new song.*

[80] Bodl., Broadside Ballads, Harding B 13(188), *England and Napoleon.*

[81] Bodl., Broadside Ballads, Harding B 25(908), *The invasion of France by Lord Wellington.*

[82] Bodl., Broadside Ballads, Harding B 12(6), *Boney's total defeat and Wellington triumphant.*

[83] Bodl., Broadside Ballads, Harding B 25(908), *The invasion of France by Lord

Wellington.

[84] *From Hogarth to Cruikshank: social and political caricature — the catalogue: an exhibition of original prints at Canterbury College of Art and Camden Arts Centre* (London, 1985) p. 1.

[85] Bodl., Broadside Ballads, Johnson Ballads 34, *The man of the tight little island.*

[86] See E.Du Cann *The Duke of Wellington and his political career after Waterloo — the caricaturists' view* (Woodbridge, 2000) p. 65.

[87] Sharpshooter [?J.Phillips] *Partial distress or the old cabinet maker and his man Bob out of employment*: see Du Cann, *Duke of Wellington*, p. 64; Bodl., Broadside Ballads, Johnson Ballads 40, *The odds and ends of the year 1830.*

[88] Bodl., Broadside Ballads, Harding B 11(469), *The British servants.*

[89] Du Cann, *Duke of Wellington*, pp. 80–1.

[90] Bodl., Broadside Ballads, Harding B 14(315), *A new song on the repeal of the corn laws.*

[91] H.H[eath] *The game cock and the dunghills*, reproduced in Du Cann, *Duke of Wellington*, p. 40.

[92] Bodl., Broadside Ballads, Harding B 11(1739), Images, 'Great as Roman was he ... Everybody know'd him well by de nose!'; Harding B 11(2788), *Old England for ever! And do it no more*, 'He will be known by his nose.'

[93] Bodl., Broadside Ballads, Harding B 27(48), *Bob and Nosey's lament on the passing of the English reform act.*

[94] Bodl., Broadside Ballads, Harding B 12(243), *Repeal and Erin go bragh.*

[95] Bodl., Broadside Ballads, Harding B 11(469), *The British servants.*

[96] Bodl., Broadside Ballads, Johnson Ballads 98, *John Bull and his rhubarb.*

[97] Bodl., Broadside Ballads, Johnson Ballads 34, *The man of the tight little island.*

[98] Donald, *Age of caricature*, p. 51.

[99] Gaunt, p. 156

[100] Bodl., Broadside Ballads, Harding B 14(323) *Resignation of His Majesty's ministers*

[101] Bodl., Broadside Ballads, Johnson Ballads 2047 *The Waterloo soldier again in power* contains the lines: Wellington "will make John Bull like the devil rue as I did poor Boney at Waterloo"

[102] Bodl., Broadside Ballads, Harding B 14(85) *Billy Barlow's breeches*

[103] For example Bodleian Library Broadside Ballads: Harding B 27(48) *Bob and Nosey's lament on the passing of the English reform bill*

[104] *Brewer's Dictionary of Phrase and Fable* ed. I.H.Evans fourteenth edition (London, 1992)

[105] For US civil war version of a ballad *Billy Barlow* by E.Clifford (1863), see Library of Congress Rare Book and Special Collections American Song Sheets

Series 1, vol. 1: digital version at http://barlowgenealogy.com/Arts/
BillyBarlow.html
Examples of British songs relating to him include *Billy Barlow: the favourite
comic song* arranged by G.L.Saunders (Edinburgh, [c.1835]) and *Billy Barlow:
the wounded Hussar* (Songs) (London, 1840)

[106] The jackboot became the symbol for Lord John Butea and its use turned it into
a symbol of a hated ministry: Donald, *Age of caricature*, pp. 50-1.

[107] Bodl., Broadside Ballads, Harding B 11(2939) *Parliament's closed and you
can't come in and it's no use knocking at the door*

[108] Bodl., Broadside Ballads, Harding B 14(290) *John Bull and his party or, Do
it again*

[109] Bodl., Broadside Ballads, Firth c.16(44) *Old Nosey is going to get married.*

[110] Gaunt, 'Wellington in petticoats', p. 156.

[111] Gaunt, 'Wellington in petticoats', p. 156.

[112] P.B.Shelley *Sonnet: England in 1819*, in *The complete works of Percy Bysshe
Shelley* ed. R.Ingpen and W.E.Peck (10 vols., London, 1965) iii, p. 293.

[113] Graham to Lambton, 23 Oct 1819, quoted in A.Aspinall *Lord Brougham and
the Whig party* (Manchester, 1939) pp. 278–9; and D.Read *Peterloo: the
'massacre' and its background* (Manchester, 1973) p. 194.

[114] AW to Mrs Arbuthnot, 27 Aug 1819, quoted in E.Longford *Wellington: pillar
of state* (London, 1972) p. 62.

[115] AW to Major General Sir John Byng, 21 Oct 1819, WP1/629/20.

[116] *The diary of Frances Lady Shelley* ed. R.Edgecumbe (2 vols., London,
1912–13) ii, p. 68.

[117] K.Kitson *Traditional tunes* (Oxford, 1891) p. 161.

[118] See R.Palmer *A ballad history of England from 1588 to the present day*
(London, 1979) p. 96.

[119] Bodl., Broadside Ballads, Harding B 27(23), *Charlie Grey's come again.*

[120] Bodl., Broadside Ballads, Firth c.22(64), *Hard times and no beer.*

[121] West Sussex Record Office, Add. MS 22249.

[122] Lord Byron *Don Juan*, canto 9: see *Lord Byron: the complete poetical works*
ed. J.J.McGann (7 vols., Oxford, 1980–93) v, p. 410.

[123] See *Radical squibs and loyal ripostes* ed. E.Rickword (London, 1971)
pp. 135–66.

[124] Bodl., Broadside Ballads, Harding B 14(358), *Political fishing net.*

[125] Bodl., Broadside Ballads, Harding B 11(3682), *Subterranean oratory, or a
lyrical dozen for the hero of Waterloo.*

[126] Bodl., Broadside Ballads, 2806 b.11(283), *Sportsmen.*

[127] NLS, APS 4.87.11, *The triumph of reform.*

[128] Edinburgh UL, Broadsides Collection 47.

[129] Bodl., Broadside Ballads, Johnson Ballads 1073, *The last look, or Nosey's*

tear. A parody on the Soldier's tear.
[130] Edinburgh UL, Broadsides Collection 47; see also British Library, Music Collections H1601.n.(18), *The soldier's tear* (sung in the new interlude *Sold for a song) The poetry by Thomas Haynes Bayly* (3rd edition, London, *c.*1830).
[131] Shepard, *History of street literature*, p. 125.
[132] Downe, 'Popular ballads', p. 142.

CHAPTER 7

A hero's welcome: attitudes to Wellington and the army, 1814–23
Rory Muir

When Wellington returned to England in June 1814, after five years in which he had led his army from the ramparts of Lisbon across Spain and the Pyrenees and deep into the heart of southern France, he received a rapturous welcome. Cheering seamen manned the yards of all the ships in the harbour at Dover; coastal batteries and warships alike fired a ceremonial salute; and a large crowd carried the hero of the hour to the inn where he breakfasted. Similar scenes greeted his arrival in London while he was virtually mobbed when he went on to Portsmouth to attend the Prince Regent. The long war against France was finally over and in the summer of 1814 the public was in the mood to celebrate a victory which had seemed little more than a forlorn hope only two years before. The allied sovereigns, generals and ministers who visited Britain at the time were fêted and acclaimed by good humoured crowds, but after weeks of applauding foreigners, there was a special relish in singing the praises of Britain's own triumphant general.

The following month was filled with grand state occasions and fashionable balls and revels in which the grateful nation gave thanks to the Almighty, to Wellington, and to the army, for its success. When the government proposed a grant of £300,000 to Wellington to support his ducal dignity, the Opposition, led by the radical Samuel Whitbread, increased the figure to £400,000. The Common Council of the City of London, which only a few years before had been a venomous critic of Wellington, accusing him of fighting unnecessary battles for base motives, now gave a splendid dinner in his honour, with speeches eulogising his achievements. Large crowds turned out to meet the new duke wherever he went, in London or the country, and far from disdaining them he cheerfully shook hands with everyone he could reach and listened to their compliments with great good humour.

It was not only Wellington who was greeted with such delight: soldiers of all ranks were welcomed home with great gusto. When Rowland Hill returned to Shrewsbury the streets were filled with thousands of cheering onlookers; 1,300 children of charity and Sunday schools were arrayed to welcome him; the local yeomanry formed his escort; and a splendid formal dinner at the Guildhall was followed by a fête in a beautiful garden in the town in which the mild-mannered general was almost crushed by the multitude.[1] At the other end of the military hierarchy a drummer in the Royal Welch Fusiliers recalled that he and his comrades were

> cheered, fed and regaled as though each man ... were some illustrious hero; until it seemed like dreamland to the poor fellows after having had years of fighting and starving and marching in inhospitable climes ...
>
> In almost every town they passed through they were treated to as much meat and drink as they could use by their fellow countrymen, who were not only joyful at peace, but delighted to have amongst them the gallant soldiers who had won it for them ...[2]

The euphoria did not last, and by the following spring London was gripped by protests against the Corn Laws. Napoleon's return from Elba provoked other disagreements, and Whitbread launched an extraordinary personal attack on Wellington over the declaration of the allies in Vienna that Napoleon was an outlaw. The Opposition was divided in its response to the crisis with many of the most active and radical members affecting to regard it as a matter purely of internal French politics in which other countries had no right to interfere; while the less articulate bulk of the party agreed

with the government that Napoleon had breached his treaty obligations by leaving Elba and that his return to power inevitably meant
war.

News of Waterloo and the collapse of Napoleon's new
regime confounded the dire predictions commonly made by the
Whigs of a prolonged and bitter conflict; and the country, while
mourning the long list of casualties, breathed a sigh of relief. Only
five days after the battle ministers moved thanks to Wellington and
the army in Parliament. Lord Lansdowne, a prominent Whig peer,
supported the motion, describing the victory as 'one of those events
which formed the most valuable part of the national property and
history', while in the Commons the vote was passed unanimously
and with 'loud and long cheering'.[3] Specific motions thanking the
officers, non-commissioned officers and private soldiers of the army
and Britain's allies were also passed, with leading radicals such as
Sir Francis Burdett and Whitbread speaking in their favour: the
latter now going out of his way to heap praise on Wellington's
courage and skill. The non-conformist MP for Norwich, William
Smith, not only supported the grant of an additional £200,000 for
Wellington, but said that he would support an even larger grant
to ensure that a palace equal to Blenheim in magnificence was
constructed, rather than see the money used to purchase an existing
house, and this was supported by William Wilberforce.[4]

There was more interest in 1815 than previously in the
contribution of junior officers and ordinary soldiers to the victory.
When Castlereagh proposed a national monument to those who
had been killed or mortally wounded in the battle Charles Wynn
expressed a wish that 'the name of every man who fell in the battle
should be commemorated'.[5] A fund to make grants to the wounded
and the families of the fallen raised almost £500,000 by public
subscription in a few months: a huge sum by the standards of the
day.[6] And for the first time a commemorative medal was issued, not
just to senior officers, but to all British soldiers who had taken part
in the battle. No British victory, not Trafalgar nor Blenheim, had

ever been celebrated so lavishly or would gain such renown.

Nonetheless critical voices did not stay silent for long, and before some of the soldiers wounded at Waterloo had returned to the ranks the memory of their triumph was overlaid by a tide of hostility and abuse directed at Wellington and the army. This reaction came largely from the government's political opponents, ranging from extreme proletarian radicals, through journalists and artists like Cobbett and the Cruikshanks, to radicals and Whigs in Parliament, and extending even to include groups such as the fundamentally conservative Grenvilles and independents like Wilberforce. It was fuelled by a widespread genuine popular feeling of disillusionment that peace had resulted not in prosperity but economic hardship and dislocation, and by a rebellion against the government's attempt to keep in place the property tax.

Napoleon's defeat had been followed by the second restoration of Louis XVIII, a result which, while certainly not unpopular with the bulk of the British people, was viewed with dismay by many radicals. George Cruikshank expressed their view with satirical brilliance not far short of Gillray at his best. As early as November 1815 he produced a print significantly titled 'The Afterpiece to the Tragedy of Waterloo' in which Wellington and other allied leaders tied a feminine embodiment of France to the ground in order to torture and rape her, while literally forcing the Bourbons down her throat.[7] And the following August Cruikshank produced 'The Royal Shambles or the Progress of Legitimacy & Re-establishment of Religion & Social Order – !!! – !!! – !!!', the largest and most complicated caricature of his career. While directed primarily against the Bourbon restoration, which is depicted as a triumph of religious bigotry and political oppression, Wellington is also a target as the ally of the ultra conservatives in France, and the instrument, with his army, of despotism.[8]

Remarkably Cruikshank's work was scarcely more violent or extreme than the line pursued by the Opposition in Parliament. Lord Grenville of all people opposed the presence of British troops in the Army of Occupation of France on the curious grounds that it would expose them to 'debauchery & vice', and that, because the expense was met by France, it undermined Parliament's constitutional control over the army.[9] The young Lord John Russell went further, arguing in Parliament in February 1816 that,

> It might happen that evil counsellors should persuade a King of France to trample on his subjects, and British soldiers might be engaged as the instruments of detested tyranny. Already in Spain the prediction had been nearly verified. Sir William Blackstone had held, that the army existed for the protection of the people; and after having been employed successfully in France in quelling the rising energies of a great people, our soldiers on their return would be well qualified to act the same disgusting scenes in England.[10]

The idea that the British army posed a danger to the constitution and traditional freedoms was taken up by many speakers in Parliament in 1816. Lord Lansdowne called for an enquiry into the size of the army, arguing that statesmen of all parties in the previous century had agreed that a large standing army was a threat to civil liberties.[11] Lord Milton complained of the use of troops to police the streets on court days, protesting that this was a new and alarming innovation and that a trooper in the Horse Guards had, that very morning, behaved in an insolent manner to him. This trivial incident was used as the peg for a lengthy debate with George Tierney accusing the ministers of attempting to accustom the populace to the sight of the soldiery being used on ordinary occasions. It was then raised in the Lords with Grenville, Grey and Holland — the most senior members of the Opposition — all treating it as a matter of great significance. Lord Holland declared that 'it was of the last importance that the people of the metropolis should not be familiarised to the sight of troops acting on such occasions without the control of the civil power, lest they should begin to look upon the military, not as their servants, which they really were, but as their masters.'[12] In another debate the radical Lord Folkestone went even further, stating his apprehension that 'a military government was growing up in this country, and that there existed in certain quarters a wish and design to substitute a military despotism for the free constitution of this country.'[13]

In such a climate it is hardly surprising that the proposal to establish a London club for officers of the army and navy was viewed with grave suspicion, even though its chief proponent was Sir Thomas Graham, who was not only one of Wellington's most distinguished subordinates, but a lifelong Whig. Graham put forward the idea in May 1815 and received support from the Dukes of York and Wellington, as well as a considerable number of senior officers. But even in November 1815, before the Opposition had begun their attacks on the army in Parliament, the Prime Minister was sensitive to the way such a club might be portrayed, and refused to lease it Crown Land, describing it as 'a most ill-advised measure, and so far from its being serviceable to the army, it will inevitably create a prejudice against that branch of our military establishment, and we shall feel the effects of it even in Parliament.'[14] He was right. On 4 March 1816 Thomas Foley, a Whig MP and a colonel in the militia, presented a petition from the inhabitants of Leominster in Herefordshire expressing their alarm at the news of the formation of the club and humbly hoping that the House of Commons 'will watch over, with a true constitutional jealousy, the proceedings of such a formidable military body, which appear to the petitioners to be too well calculated to render the military power of the country a body too distinct from the people, and consequently with the principles of a free government.'[15] Opposition speakers supporting the petition dominated the lengthy debate which followed and hammered away at the same theme: that the army as the instrument of the ministers and the Crown threatened to undermine the free constitution of the country and replace it with a military despotism.[16]

Some of these fears may have been no more than rhetoric designed to gain party political advantage in Parliament, but it is clear that even in private the Whig leaders felt great suspicion, dislike and distrust of Wellington and the army. Lord Holland accused Wellington of arranging the judicial murder of Marshal Ney from jealousy as he had never been able to defeat him in battle, thus showing surprising ignorance of Busaco, Quatre Bras and Waterloo as well as of Wellington's character.[17] And Lord Grey wrote in a private letter in the autumn of 1816 that,

> Everything seems to me to be tending, and is pushed by Burdett and his adherents, to a contest between the crown and the mob; in which those who ought to be the leaders of the people, and would be so if they could, will be drawn from a sense of their own security to the support of the Crown; the success of which, with the assistance of the Duke of Wellington, and the worst army in spirit and principle that I believe ever existed in the world, will be probably the utter extinction of all liberty.[18]

It is hard to know what effect these attacks had on the general public. On the one hand we are told that when Wellington visited England in 1816 he was 'follow'd and Huzza'd' as much as he had been in 1814;[19] but on the other, the petitions which flooded into Parliament denouncing the property tax also frequently condemned the retention of a large standing army as, to quote one example, 'hostile to the spirit of the *British* Constitution, and highly injurious to the best interests of society.'[20] What is striking is the weakness of the government's defence against these charges: none of the ministers rose to the occasion and rejected the allegations with scorn or indignation. They did little to defend the honour and reputation of the army, or even make the obvious point that many of those who claimed to fear the establishment of a military despotism in Britain were open admirers of Napoleon, the very model of a military despot. Faced with incessant calls to slash spending on the army there was little effort to beat the patriotic drum and remind the House that the regiments which would be reduced, and the soldiers who would be discharged, were the very same who had triumphed at Waterloo less than a year before. The British army had never been as good as it was in 1813–15; substantial reductions were undoubtedly necessary to place it on a peace establishment and the government's finances in order, but Palmerston, the responsible minister, did nothing to make MPs and the country feel that these reductions were a painful necessity and not something intrinsically desirable. Whether from weakness or cool judgement that the spirit of the times was running too strongly in the other direction, the ministers abandoned their best ground without a fight and left the initiative almost entirely to their ideological opponents.

Throughout the post-war years the radical press disparaged Wellington and derided his achievements. For example, on the second anniversary of Waterloo, 18 June 1817, when most of London was pre-occupied with the festivities associated with the opening of the new, 'Waterloo', bridge over the Thames, Wooler's *Black Dwarf* published a poem 'The Waterloo Man' denouncing the miseries of war and suggesting that the battle was a victory, not for freedom and justice, but for oppression.[21] When reports began to circulate in late 1818 that Wellington was to join the Cabinet, the *Examiner* declared that 'The Duke of Wellington is a mere soldier, who manages things well enough when they are in a barrack-state, but no further.'[22] The *Black Dwarf* went further:

> This Duke is a very fortunate fellow! The King of France has rewarded his services to that country by a blue cord, and a diamond worth *twenty thousand pounds sterling!* To be sure His Grace has helped a little in the glorious endeavour to thin France of its population as much as possible; and it is but fair that he should have his share of the spoil produced by the friendly executions of Ney, Labedoyère, etc; but one could hardly think it would have amounted to Twenty Thousand Pounds! Besides a rope![23]

The following year saw the publication of the first cantos of Byron's *Don Juan* which opened with a sly dig at Wellington:

I want a hero: an uncommon want,
    When every year and month sends forth a new one,
Till, after cloying the gazettes with cant,
    The age discovers that he is not the true one.

The poet's sharpest barbs, however, were to appear a few years later in Canto IX.[24]

1819 was, of course, the year of 'Peterloo': the 'massacre' in which 11 unarmed, peaceful demonstrators were savagely cut down and killed while hundreds more were knocked to the ground and trampled by brutal soldiery. At least that is the radical account of events which was repeated by a liberal press and given visual form in Cruikshank's famous print, the 'Massacre at St Peter's or Britons strike home',[25] which has all too often been reproduced as an accurate illustration, rather than as a crudely partisan piece of political propaganda. The very name 'Peterloo' with its implicit equivalence between the 11 civilian deaths in Manchester and the battle four years before in which more than 11,000 men were killed and over 50,000 wounded, was coined by a journalist within days of the event, and reflects both the over-blown rhetoric of the moment and the radical desire to discredit the achievements of Wellington and the army.

In the heightened atmosphere which followed, the government felt obliged to support the magistrates and the forces of authority throughout the country, while the radicals and radical whigs intensified their ideological assault. The army and Wellington were again prominent targets, along with the government, the church, magistrates in general and those of Manchester in particular, taxation and, above all, the Prince Regent. George Cruikshank depicted John Bull as a bull, shackled to the ground and laden with a huge pyramid of placemen, office holders and soldiers, with corpulent bishops at the top supporting an enormous heavy crown. Wellington, wearing a butcher's apron over his uniform, holds an axe erect ready to slaughter the bull if it attempts to free itself of its burden.[26] A few weeks later another print accuses Wellington, or 'Waterloo Man' of corruption, support for the Spanish Inquisition and — best of all — of not having been at Waterloo because he lingered in Brussels.[27] Wellington also appears on the title page of the hugely successful tract *The political house that Jack built*, where he is shown throwing his sword into the scales on the side of repression; and in its sequel, *The man in the moon*, there is an illustration of soldiers thrusting their bayonets into the open mouths of protestors under the clever caption 'steel lozenges' — an allusion to a patent medicine popular at the time.[28]

The extravagance of these claims and the fear of revolution following Peterloo produced a long overdue conservative response to the tide of radical polemic. In one such work, *The real or constitutional house that Jack built*, Wellington is the most prominent of a group of patriots 'the heroes of Britain — the gems of her crown'. Yet even here, he is the only soldier: Nelson and Duncan represent the navy, while Burke, Castlereagh and Canning the conservative side of politics, Pitt having already been given a more prominent place.[29] Attempts to establish a conservative newspaper had little success until December 1820 when *John Bull* was founded and quickly made a name for itself by attacking the leaders of Whig society with the same scurrility and venom which radical writers and cartoonists had employed for years against their opponents. This was in the wake of the Queen Caroline affair in which passions aroused by the reaction to Peterloo had been whipped into a new fury and then burnt themselves out. At the height of the Queen's trial, Wellington was repeatedly hissed and booed by the crowds filling the streets leading to Parliament; one day an attempt was made to pull him from his horse, while on another occasion the windows of his carriage were broken. Dispassionate observers were shocked by news of such scenes with Sara Hutchinson, Wordsworth's sister-in-law, writing 'Only think of the D. of W. being *insulted* so late their idol — but it is ever so and why wonder? Alas how soon are benefits forgot!'[30]

It is likely that feelings such as these played a part in the reaction which followed the Queen's affair, but broader influences were also at work, mostly notably an improving economy which reduced discontent and disturbances in the industrial parts of the country. Radicalism had also lost much of its charm and novelty: the most extreme radicals had been discredited by the Cato Street conspiracy, while the moderates were damaged by the failure of the defence of the Queen to result in any tangible benefit for their supporters. And there were other, less explicitly political shifts in taste and opinion at work. Between 1815 and 1821 military memoirs had generally been dismissed as boring and worthless by reviewers, although one work of real merit, the anonymous *Journal of a soldier of the Seventy-First*, had sold well. But the publication of Moyle Sherer's *Recollections of the Peninsula* in 1823 and G. R. Gleig's *The subaltern* in 1825 were marked by enthusiastic reviews and inaugurated a vogue for military literature, both memoirs and fiction, which lasted for more than a decade. Both works were unusually well written and vividly described the life and experiences of junior regimental officers on campaign, blending elements of picaresque, adventure and travel writing into a whole that owed more than a little to the style and tone of Scott's immensely popular Waverley novels.[31] At the same time, in 1822, David Wilkie's painting 'The Chelsea Pensioners' was exhibited at the Royal Academy and drew large crowds and much praise. Wellington had commissioned the work four years previously, but it was Wilkie who added the rather too appropriate device of showing the assembled veterans of Britain's earlier wars reacting to the news of Waterloo. Traditional military art had fallen from favour in Britain over the preceding generation, but Wilkie's fresh approach revealed a more democratic, and more sentimental, way of viewing military triumphs; and although it attracted a good deal of political criticism from radicals, the work was immensely popular with a wide public.[32] This was also the year in which a large statue of Achilles was erected in Hyde Park to commemorate Wellington's victories. Paid for by a subscription from 'the ladies of

England', its fine physique and nudity (a fig leaf was added after some discussion) aroused much ribald comment, which probably had the effect of deflecting political criticism of its central purpose.[33] Taken together these examples point to a clear shift in the mood of the times: the anti-militarism of the post-war years had run its course and 'respectable' opinion was again happy to view Wellington and the army as a bulwark of the state and not a threat to the constitution.

The Opposition to the government had faced a problem in 1814–15. It had always been half-hearted and defeatist in its attitude to the war, while many on the radical fringe were open in their sympathy for Napoleon. This put it at odds with the great bulk of the public who were delighted with the victory and predisposed to give the credit for it to the ministers who had kept their nerve through so many difficulties. One way in which the Opposition could regain political momentum was to recast the debate and depict the army and Wellington not as military heroes who had triumphed over the country's enemies, but as a financial burden on the struggling taxpayer, and as a threat to civil liberties and an instrument of oppression and despotism. This line of attack proved extra-ordinarily effective, partly because it tapped into a long-standing British tradition of anti-militarism which dated back to the seven-teenth century. The financial position of the country was genuinely difficult, and the government accepted the need for large spending cuts which inhibited ministers from taking a more assertive line in defence of the army. And the press, caricaturists and at least a slice of the public were strongly inclined to favour liberal and even radical views. There is no reason to believe that the Opposition took this line cynically – on the contrary, the private correspondence of senior Whigs suggests that they really believed that the Regent, his ministers, Wellington and the army were a danger to the consti-tution, just as, a few years earlier, they had really believed that Napoleon was a man of peace and liberal views whose outlook on the world reflected the values of the Glorious Revolution of 1688.

Finally two points may be noted explicitly: Wellington was the subject of intense political controversy long before he returned from the Continent and joined the Cabinet at the end of 1818; and second, he reacted to these attacks with some hurt and disdain, but without bitterness, and subsequently established good personal relations with some of those who had made the most exaggerated and hostile attacks upon him in these years. He was not a man to bear grudges any more than he was to overthrow the constitution and proclaim himself emperor.

References

[1] E.Sidney *The life of Lord Hill, G.C.B., late Commander of the Forces* (London, 1845) pp. 291–4.

[2] Drummer Bentinck, quoted in Donald E. Graves *Dragon rampant. The Royal Welch Fusiliers at war, 1793–1815* (London, 2010) pp. 225–6.

[3] *Parliamentary Debates*, xxxi, cols. 976–7, 986.

[4] *Parliamentary Debates*, xxxi, cols. 987–8 (Burdett), 991 (Whitbread), 992 (W. Smith) and 1054 (Wilberforce).

[5] *Parliamentary Debates*, xxxi, col. 1052.

[6] Thomas Rowcroft to Wellington, 17 Nov 1815, *SD*, xi, pp. 238–9.

[7] M.D.George *Catalogue of political and personal satires preserved in the Department of Prints and Drawings in the British Museum.* Vol. 9: *1811-1819* (London, 1949) pp. 592–3, no. 12,620.

[8] George, *Catalogue of political and personal satires.* Vol. 9: *1811-1819*, pp. 692–4, no. 12,797; M.D.George *English political caricature. A study of opinion and propaganda* (2 vols., Oxford, 1959) ii, pp. 173–4; John Wardroper *The caricatures of George Cruikshank* (London, 1977) p. 61.

[9] James J. Sack *The Grenvillites 1801–1829. Party politics and factionalism in the age of Pitt and Liverpool* (Urbana, IL, 1979) p. 162.

[10] *Parliamentary Debates*, xxxii, col. 845.

[11] *Parliamentary Debates*, xxxiii, col. 319 (15 Mar 1816).

[12] *Parliamentary Debates*, xxxiii, col. 956 (5 Apr 1816).

[13] *Parliamentary Debates*, xxxiii, col. 243 (13 Mar 1816).

[14] Liverpool to Huskisson, 25 Nov 1815, in Alex M.Delavoye *Life of Thomas Graham Lord Lynedoch* (London, 1880) pp. 750–1; see also Major General Sir Louis Jackson *History of the United Service Club* (London, 1937) pp. 1–6.

[15] *Parliamentary Debates*, xxxii, cols. 1068–9.

[16] *Parliamentary Debates*, xxxii, cols. 1069–78.

[17] Henry Richard Vassal, third Baron Holland *Further memoirs of the Whig party 1807–1821* (London, 1905) p. 226; AW to E.Cooke, Paris, 17 Dec 1815, *WD*, viii, pp. 319–20.

[18] Grey to Holland, 6 Oct 1816, quoted in E.A.Smith *Lord Grey 1764–1845* (Stroud, 1996) p. 209.

[19] William Wellesley-Pole to Charles Bagot, 5 Jul 1816: Joceline Bagot *George Canning and his friends* (2 vols., London, 1909) ii, pp. 29–31.

[20] Quoted in J.E.Cookson *Lord Liverpool's administration. The crucial years 1815–1822* (Edinburgh, 1975) pp. 47–8.

[21] *Black Dwarf*, 18 Jun 1817.

[22] *Examiner*, 13 Dec 1818.

[23] *Black Dwarf*, 9 Dec 1818, p. 701.

[24] George Gordon Byron, Baron Byron *The complete poetical works* ed. J.J. McGann and B. Weller (7 vols., Oxford, 1980–93) v, pp. 9, 409–35.

[25] George, *Catalogue of political and personal satires*. Vol. 9: *1811–1819*, p. 918, no. 13,258; George, *English political caricature*, ii, p. 181, attributes it to Robert rather than George Cruikshank; cf. Wardroper, *George Cruikshank*, p. 79.

[26] George, *Catalogue of political and personal satires*. Vol. 9: *1811–1819*, pp. 942–3, no. 13,288.

[27] George *Catalogue of political and personal satires*. Vol. 9: *1811–1819*, p. 957, no 13,346.

[28] *Radical squibs & loyal ripostes. Satirical pamphlets of the Regency period, 1819–1821* ed. Edgell Rickword (Bath, 1971) pp. 35, 94.

[29] *Radical squibs & loyal ripostes*, ed. Rickword, p. 66.

[30] Sara Hutchinson to Mrs Swaine and Mrs Wordsworth, 19 Sep [1820]: *The letters of Sara Hutchinson* ed. Kathleen Coburn (London, 1954) p. 208.

[31] Neil Ramsey 'The military author and romantic war: British military memoirs and the emergence of the soldier hero, 1809–1835' (Australian National University, Ph.D. thesis, 2008) chapters one and two.

[32] Allan Cunningham *The life of Sir David Wilkie* (3 vols., London, 1843) ii, pp. 68–78; H.Miles, 'Sir David Wilkie' *ODNB*, lviii, pp. 965–70 ; David H. Solkin *Painting out of the ordinary. Modernity and the art of everyday life in early nineteenth century Britain* (New Haven, 2008) pp. 198–204; Brian Winkenweder, 'The newspaper as nationalist icon, or how to paint "imagined communities"' *Limina* 14 (2008) pp. 85–96, and Linda Colley *Britons: Forging the Nation, 1707–1837* (New Haven, 1992) pp. 364–7, all give interesting discussions of the patriotic themes inherent in the composition.

[33] George, *Catalogue of political and personal satires*. Vol. 10: *1820-1827* (London, 1952) p. 297; Alison Yarrington *His Achilles heel? Wellington and public art* (Southampton, Tenth Wellington Lecture, 1998) pp. 12–13.

CHAPTER 8

Fearing 'the bold unflinching McBeath': Ultra Tory concerns about the Duke of Wellington and his administration in the aftermath of Catholic relief
Douglas Simes

I

While the golden glow of mid-Victorian adulation, the Winterhalter-Tennyson effect, may have faded a little, the Duke of Wellington remains a national icon, to whom few would deny the label of 'a great man'. Judging by the biographies of the last half century there is also little variation of opinion as to the constituent elements of his greatness. That he was a famous military leader and war hero is generally a given. His political career is less widely acclaimed, since 'his political views were widely regarded as anachronistic, or just plain wrong'.[1] Still it was redeemed by an 'act of great political courage', Roman Catholic relief,[2] or by 'the sincerity of his intentions as he applied himself to his duty as he saw it'.[3]

It was not his achievements alone though that enabled him to stand 'like a colossus' over early nineteenth-century Britain.[4] His character and style were integral to his reputation and stature. His imperturbability, courage, honesty, modesty and stern sense of duty were, and are, generally lauded. The Countess of Longford provides a veritable checklist of his admirable qualities:

> The Great Duke's chief virtues are not in dispute: the truth-
> fulness, courage, honesty, fairness and simplicity; the

directness, straightforwardness, decision and realism that made him so extraordinarily sensible; the repeated proofs that personal ambition … had no power to move him and that all he responded to was service, duty and patriotism, on whose tide he was carried forward.[5]

It is a glowing testimonial, and contested by most subsequent biographers only in detail.

In the face of such consensual admiration, in many respects well founded, it seems almost churlish to draw attention to the carping of early nineteenth-century critics, usually lesser men, and especially to the Ultra Tories, whose own reputation, if improving slightly, remains less than stellar. The persistent negativism of their comments, especially as the Duke's erstwhile friends, remains for some a mystery and for others a proof of Ultra inadequacies. Nevertheless the Ultra critique needs fuller consideration than it has received, not because it was right or just, but because it was persuasive and had a significant influence on events.

The 'heightened rhetoric' of the Ultras,[6] which led them to couch their criticisms in intensely emotive language, has long been, and remains, a barrier to full understanding of their viewpoint. Still the epithets they chose to fling, even if overwrought and not altogether apt, do provide clear indicators as to the sources of their unease about the Duke. Stanley Faber, a well-regarded and highly literate, if opinionated, Anglican controversialist, searching for an image to express his irritation and concern found it in Shakespeare. The Duke reminded him of 'the bold, unflinching McBeath [*sic*]'.[7] Others compared him to Cromwell, Warwick the Kingmaker, or even the King of Dahomey; or resorted to generalised allusions to despotism, tyranny, or military rule.[8]

The common thread linking the epithets and allusions, the Duke's commanding personality and abilities being readily conceded, was alarm at his military values and support networks, his ruthless methods, and his overweening ambition. In the eyes of many Ultras, from the King downwards, he was an over-mighty subject pursuing his own agendas. As a widely quoted versifier put it:

>   In England rules King Arthur,
>   In Ireland rules King Dan,
>   King George of Windsor Castle,
>   Dethrone them if you can.[9]

As the rift deepened, and hostility intensified, they came to see him not just as a threat to the constitution in Church and State, but as a continental-style authoritarian with scant respect for English liberties, whose economic and social policies threatened the general welfare, and even the nation's political stability.

The obvious excesses of this political rhetoric have tended to distract the attention of historians from both its essential sincerity and its appeal to contemporaries. Intellectually coherent and stylistically presented, it became a commonplace of some of the leading newspapers and periodicals of the day. However outré it may now appear, it resonated with their readers. As a consequence it had a significant impact on politics at a crucial and climacteric period.

Historians have, by and large, paid scant attention to the Ultra case against the Duke and his administration, and have usually addressed it only briefly and indirectly. In some well-researched and influential monographs, indeed, the Ultras virtually disappear between 1829 and 1830 or become camouflaged as 'country gentlemen'.[10]

A generation ago, leaders in the field of early nineteenth-century political history confidently provided their readers with a narrative in which Ultra Tory separatism was essentially an aberration, shallow in its motivation, and predestined to end, as in fact it did end, in reunion with the vastly wiser Wellington-Peel Tories, under a new and 'decontaminated' brand name. The Ultras were foredoomed by their backward-looking inadequacies and intellectual aridity. Thus Norman Gash asserted that they had 'no policies commensurate with the real problems of the time'.[11] Robert

Blake was of the opinion that all they had to offer was the inflexible adherence to shibboleths such as Protectionism, Protestantism and No-Popery.[12]

Despite recent advances in research, strong elements of this viewpoint persist, even, and somewhat surprisingly, in the work of those who have enhanced our knowledge of Ultra organisation and the Ultra press. James Sack, for example, contends that 'an overwhelming hatred of Catholicism' was what drove an [unspecified] section of Ultras into progressive principles, 'at a general variance with the normal image ... of a Tory world view'.[13] Frank O'Gorman, by contrast, and even more briskly, dismisses them as 'reactionary'.[14]

A constant theme throughout has been, and remains, an emphasis on shallow emotionalism. Ultra opposition to the Duke is variously characterised as resentful, angry, vindictive, spiteful, snobbish and actuated by a spirit of revenge and grievance.[15] While there can be no denying that emotional negativism did play a role in Ultra discourse and behaviour, it needs to be kept in perspective, as it usually is in discussions of the nature of Whig, Huskissonian or Radical oppositionism. It was only one element in a complex melange of Ultra Tory ideas and responses.

A better-balanced view of the Ultra Tories and their opposition to the Duke in 1829–30 requires less stress on emotion and more on principled dissent. Some steps have certainly been taken in this direction, especially in relationship to particular issues such as the currency and distress.[16] More remains to be said about the cohesiveness and relevance of Ultra ideas, about their dissemination and popularity, and about the crucial role they played in unseating the Duke.

II

The reasons that the Ultra Tories are often imperfectly understood and, as a corollary, partially misrepresented, are complex. Certainly the values they espoused, and the language in which they couched them, are important factors. It has been a long time since pietism, agrarianism, protectionism and paternalism of the privileged have had much of a following in academia.

More importantly, perhaps, there are significant befogging problems of definition and conceptualisation. This is true even if the focus is, as is usual, only the parliamentary party. Few Ultras identified themselves as such and contemporary lists rarely tally exactly. Division lists can be especially difficult to interpret, as the various estimates of Ultra votes on the crucial Civil List division attest.[17] This leads on to reliance on the speeches, letters, and diaries of 'safe' sources. Thus an over-confident letter of Sir Richard Vyvyan, or an emotional outburst by the Duke of Newcastle in a diary never intended for publication, can be assumed to be authoritative or characteristic.

The difficulties are compounded in any discussion of Ultra Toryism beyond Westminster. That there were Ultra Tory writers, organisers, readers and voters is beyond question. That they were better organised than their competitors is at least arguable. The 'party', or proto-party, was, however, decentralised, disparate and loosely linked together, both in Parliament and beyond. Mapping the underlying networks of family, personal and group relationships is a major exercise in the collection and analysis of scattered minutiae.

Nevertheless it is quite clear, and it was obvious to contemporaries, that there was in the late 1820s and early 1830s a political entity, certainly closer to a party than to an aristocratic connection or faction, which was widely and popularly dubbed 'Ultra Tory'. At its heart lay a self-consciously separate, if indifferently organised, parliamentary party, whose membership and wider appeal fluctuated in the very fluid politics of 1829–30 and beyond. Behind the party at Westminster, and closely associated to it, were a significant press and periodical interest spanning the whole country, and a noteworthy collection of clerical and literary intellectuals, with their own networks. Beyond this again there were corporations, electoral clubs, such as many of the Pitt and True Blue Clubs, and popular organisations dominated by Ultra leaders, which included the Orange Institution, the Brunswick Clubs and in later years many Conservative Associations. Support was probably also forthcoming as a result of 'entryism' in an array of pressure groups: agrarian, humanitarian, protectionist, and religious. Examples would include the Reformation Society, the Protestant Colonisation Society, the Labourers' Friends Society, the Ten Hour Movement and even (at least initially) the Birmingham Political Union.[18]

This Serbonian bog of complexities is difficult to chart or navigate, but it cannot be ignored with impunity. When ascertaining Ultra attitudes to the Duke, or tracking their anti-governmental activities, it is necessary to look beyond the parliamentary 'big beasts'. What Michael Sadler said to the shipbuilders at Whitby, or Charles Boyton to the newly re-organised Conservatives of Dublin, can be as relevant as what Knatchbull wrote to Vyvyan. So too can a reflective article by David Robinson in *Blackwood's Magazine,* or an Alexander editorial in the *Morning Journal.*

If a wide range of extra-parliamentary sources, which are very varied and numerous, is brought into play alongside the contributions of the leadership, a stronger and clearer light is shed on the nature and depth of Ultra antagonism to the Duke and his administration. It becomes apparent that a great deal more was involved than mere factiousness and vindictiveness, and that rapprochement, before the shared trauma of the Whig measure of parliamentary reform and the ensuing 'great smash', was improbable on any terms the Duke was likely to offer. The prospects, moreover, were steadily receding throughout 1829 and 1830.

III

While antagonism to the Duke did not develop in its full intensity overnight, there can be no doubt that the concession of Catholic relief was a pivotal moment. The grounds on which Ultras opposed the measure were varied, though an Anglican confessionalism that feared for the safety of the Established Church was fairly general. Almost as widespread, among both seceders and waverers, was a concern about the methods by which the measure was carried. The secrecy of its gestation, the speed of its introduction, the high-handed approach to the Crown and public opinion, the pressure tactics in Parliament and especially in the Lords, all seemed suggestive of a military strategic approach to problem solving ill-suited to a constitutional state.[19] While a few had been uneasy about the Hero of Waterloo as early as 1827–8, their lone voices now became part of a swelling chorus.

Disillusionment with the Duke, although especially intense, needs to be seen as part of a wider phenomenon. The reiterated refrain of the Ultras, easier to understand now perhaps than a generation ago, was 'the collapse of confidence in all public men'.[20]

'All faith in public men is gone', asserted William Maginn, and 'trickery, fraud and dishonesty are revealed as the prerequisites for holding political office.'[21] Although the whole *classe politique* was suspect, the apostate ministers were especially singled out. David Robinson in *Blackwood's Magazine* spoke for many:

> Ministers gained office by deluding the country with the conviction that they would defend particular laws and institutions of the very highest importance: almost immediately on gaining office, they audaciously cast from them their faith, and altered those very laws and institutions.[22]

This broad-brush alienation from the *classe politique*, and office-holders in particular, was to persist. As the months passed, however, increasing stress was placed upon the Duke, the greatest of public men, as uniquely dangerous.

Robert Peel was certainly reviled by many Ultras as equally responsible for the emancipation measure. However, it was possible to dismiss him as just another politician, 'a smartly-dressed, sneering, middle aged man, who has little more between him and family than £150,000 of public money'.[23] It was believed his career was effectively over and that he was no future threat. He was assailed primarily as a symbol of systemic failure, apostasy, nepotism and 'old corruption'.[24]

The Duke, 'the bold unflinching McBeath', was quite another matter. Certainly there were those who asserted that his 'Irish family never heard of 30 years ago' had done very well out of public office.[25] However, this had to be offset against the unquestionable worth of his military services to the nation. He was, after all, one of the greatest military commanders of the age, 'the Hero of Waterloo'. While few Ultras ever spoke ill of the Duke's military career, they were unquestionably troubled by his subsequent role as a soldier in politics. In their eyes Catholic emancipation had revealed in him the will, focus, strategic planning, driving ambition and ruthlessness of a great commander. The characteristics that had made him formidable on the battlefield were latently menacing in constitutional politics. As Thomas Powell commented in *Fraser's Magazine*:

> A soldier like the Duke of Wellington is little qualified for the civil government of a nation. He has no condescension, no conciliation. Every measure of his administration is according to those values which are dearest to the heart of a great military commander. Nothing is done to bind people to him by love of his person ... His way is to force the inclinations of men; to make them bend to his wishes; either to urge them by the appliance, as it were, of brute force, to become the servants of the government, or to buy them heart and soul, by the golden dispersion of ministerial patronage.[26]

Military allusions and analogies became a standard part of Ultra critiques of the Duke. They were often linked to unflattering estimations of his character. He was, wrote Robert Alexander in words that helped wreck his newspaper, the *Morning Journal*, proud, overbearing, grasping, unprincipled and dishonest.[27] *The Standard* found him 'an imperious and engrossing spirit, who aimed to be not only prime minister, but sole minister'.[28]

The Cabinet, which should have been a check on his power, was perceived as merely 'a cabinet of cyphers' who 'were no more than aides-de-camp or orderlies to be dismissed at the slightest resistance ... to orders.'[29] The Duke had military protégés 'placed in clusters around his own person'.[30] The civilian ministers, with the partial exception of the discredited Peel, were placemen and clerks, 'political *condottieri*', 'underlings under the management of an autocratic minister'.[31]

Similarly the Duke controlled Parliament through 'the corrupt and servile majorities'[32] in both Houses of Parliament. Catholic emancipation had shown that the parliamentarians ignored public opinion and represented the nation neither actually nor virtually. 'As for those', wrote Stanley Faber, 'who before voted ... or expressed themselves against that measure [Roman Catholic relief], when I hear it alleged against *them*, that without a single reason being given for their change, they wheeled about at the mere word of command of our military premier, I confess myself puzzled to excuse them.'[33]

Others were less circumspect. 'An ignoble assembly ... mean, servile, pedling [*sic*], corrupt and cowardly', sneered one *Fraser's* essayist.[34] 'A horse-racing, club-house haunting, opera-loving assemblage of joint stock traders and stock-exchange graduates', complained another writer.[35] 'If', acidly observed S.L.Giffard in the *Standard*, 'there was less stock-jobbing, less dandyism, and a smaller number of hungry adventurers in Parliament, the affairs of the nation would surely go on none the worse.'[36]

The autocratic and ruthless minister, dominating a cabinet of non-entities and a corrupted Parliament of 'fribbles', military protégés and self-aggrandising 'mere money men', was integral to Ultra thinking. Even among those who participated at Westminster there was a growing willingness to assert that the Duke and his administration were the by-products of a flawed system.

In an attempt to make sense of what was occurring, especially as new issues arose in the wake of emancipation and the government proved unamenable to reasoned complaint from erstwhile supporters, a number of Ultra commentators sought a wider framework of explanation.

Some surmised that the government had abandoned its traditional Tory support base, 'the working clergy, the sturdy yeomanry, the inferior gentry, the independent inhabitants in the towns'.[37] Instead of the traditional middling orders, they had embraced a restructured *classe politique*, composed of the beneficiaries of recent trade and monetary policies — the great office-holding families with their dependent pensioners and annuitants, international traders, export-oriented manufacturers, stockbrokers, speculators, contractors, and fund holders.[38]

Others, such as Sir Richard Vyvyan, sought an explanation in international politics.[39] There was a strong vein of British exceptionalism and John Bullishness in the Ultras, who suspected the internationalist proclivities of the inner circles in London. It was feared that they were all too ready to abandon British interests, whether Protestantism, strategically vital industries, or traditional liberties, to please their continental allies, friends and customers.[40] Comparing the Duke to Polignac, and welcoming the revolution of 1830, may not have been entirely characteristic, but neither was it an isolated aberration. Those who eulogised the constitution of 1688 often thought Protestantism and liberty were inseparable, and that Roman Catholicism and autocracy were also a matched pair.

While Ultras may have differed as to the exact details of the challenge they faced, they were generally all of a mind that it transcended 'politics as usual' and that merely cosmetic changes to the existing ministry would not suffice as a remedy for the deep-seated ills. From the outset, and increasingly as time passed, they sought to articulate, awaken and organise public opinion to ensure

not only a change of men but also a wide-ranging change of measures. In this they were far from the timid aristocratic clique of the
stereotype. Indeed a case could be made out that they were most
zealous parliamentary advocates of the constitutional expression of
popular opinion throughout most of the Wellington administration's
tenure of office.

IV

To understand fully Ultra expectations of the role that the constitutional expression of public opinion might play as a check on
arbitrary and high-handed government, and as a catalyst for
change, it is necessary to look back to the struggle over Catholic
emancipation.

Any hopes they had harboured of the government voluntarily yielding ground to the expression of electoral opinion on the
issue were dashed by the Oxford by-election in which Sir Robert
Peel was defeated by the Ultra, Sir Robert Inglis. The opinion of
one of Britain's most extensive and best-educated electorates was
then ignored. Peel simply moved to the rotten borough of Westbury
and the government proceeded as before. While Oxford was never
forgotten, the Ultras found themselves obliged to abandon any
prospect of an electoral strategy.

They had recourse to other forms of constitutional protest
and pressure. There was, as General Gascoyne asserted, 'a voice as
powerful as the Cabinet ... the voice of the people'.[41] The Ultras
put a great deal of effort into stimulating and channelling that voice.
The Orange Lodges and Brunswick Clubs, among other Ultra-
dominated groups, encouraged a wave of meetings and petitions.
These might constitute a kind of informal referendum of public
opinion, which could prove as worthwhile as an election.[42]

Appeals for extra-parliamentary support were launched in
the press by public letters from the party magnates. That of the Earl
of Winchilsea was characteristic:

Let the voice of Protestantism be heard from one end of the country to the other, let it be heard from hill to hill and vale to vale. Let the tables of Parliament groan under the weight of your petitions, and let your prayers reach the foot of the throne.[43]

The response was gratifying in all three kingdoms. Widespread meetings were held, producing a flood of petitions, numerously signed by a wide cross-section of society.

The contempt for these petitions, common to both the government and High Whiggery, elicited an Ultra response which shows the degree to which they were supportive of the constitutionally appropriate expression of popular opinion. 'The poorest man', argued Sir Thomas Gooch, 'had as good a right to express his opinion upon this question as his betters.'[44] 'From the substantial farmer to the lowest labourer', their sentiments should be heard in Parliament, agreed Colonel Sibthorp.[45] 'He trusted', said George Moore, MP for Dublin City, 'that he should never live to see the day when public opinion, generally, calmly, but fearlessly expressed, would cease to have its due weight with that House.'[46] 'The humblest individuals ...', he reminded the Commons, 'had feelings, wishes, rights and privileges, to be consulted, which were as dear to them as the feelings, wishes, rights and privileges of the highest classes of society.'[47]

What was true for unenfranchised men was also true of women. 'Both men and women', asserted Colonel Sibthorp, 'were bound to come forward on a subject so deeply interesting to the welfare of the community.'[48] General Gascoyne agreed. He 'saw no objection to the signatures of females to such petitions; for they were as much interested in this important subject as the other sex'.[49]

As long as public opinion, including unenfranchised opinion, was couched in traditional forms and not associated with disorder, the Ultras positively endorsed it and utilised it. It did not, perhaps because of timing, suffice to block or even to modify the government's relief measure. It did, however, render the Ultra minority in Parliament more formidable than they would otherwise have been. The lesson was not lost on them when they decided to persist as a separate party. Unlike the 'red-tape' Tories who followed Wellington and Peel, the Ultras always had, and retained, a populist tinge. There is nothing whatever to suggest they were more snobbish or cliquish than other parliamentary groupings; indeed, the evidence rather suggests the opposite, especially when they are compared with the Wellington-Peel Tories.

V

It appears to have been the Duke's hope and intention that the passage of Catholic relief should be followed by a reconciliation of Tory factions. That this did not occur certainly owed something to spitefulness and revanchism in Ultra ranks, as well as among the Ministerialists. However the differences between the two increasingly distinct parties were not superficial and were not confined to Catholic emancipation alone. The emergence of the Ultras as an Opposition party, utilising the methods of mobilising public opinion learnt during the emancipation controversy, was a natural, if not an inevitable, development. Their distrust of the Duke, his government and his system was intense, and showed little sign of abating.

The passage of Catholic emancipation deprived the Ultras of their most salient and emotive issue. Their response was to counsel obedience to the new law and to keep a watching brief on the impact (and anticipated failure) of 'the healing measure'.[50] Until that should become readily apparent they re-oriented their efforts, focusing on social and economic issues, and the ineptitude and selfishness of the Wellington government in handling them. The prevailing distress, especially among the labouring poor, provided a good deal of grist to the Ultra mill. The Ultra press thundered anathemas, their intellectuals debated causes and consequences, and the parliamentarians attended meetings, encouraged petitions, moved motions of inquiry and crusaded in support of favoured remedies. Much of the time they were the most vocal and effective Opposition group.

It is easy to dismiss their endeavours, as has frequently been done, as faction or posturing. Predictably there were elements of that. However, key individuals, such as Sadler, Southey, and Robinson, had long track records as social paternalists, as did leading journalists such as Giffard, Alexander and Maginn. The same was true of a good many MPs and peers. Even the great magnates of the party (Richmond, Newcastle, Mansfield, Cumberland and Eldon, for example) had a sense of social and/or religious obligation.[51] Certainly the Ultras wished to harass and embarrass an administration they disliked. That, however, did not preclude a sincere concern for those they perceived as victims of a corrupted and uncaring government, which they viewed as effectively representative only of the *classe politique* and committed to the economic liberalism it favoured, regardless of the consequences for others.

The government admitted in 1829–30 that there was distress, but insisted that it was partial and temporary. The Ultras responded that it was general, structurally embedded and unsusceptible to early or easy remedy. They were especially concerned about the plight of the labouring poor, such as silk workers and farmhands.[52] The refusal of the government even to concede an inquiry was met with genuine indignation.

> … this distress — this poverty — this insolvency is the work of the King's Servants. To them alone we owe this pitiable state of things. They have plunged us into our difficulties by these insensate policies and they must relieve us by changing their measures.[53]

Callous indifference was what was to be expected of an administration insensitive to British interests and characterised by a dogmatic adherence to the tenets of economic liberalism. In particular Ultras pointed to the destructive and socially damaging consequences of the government's free trade and monetary policies.

The Ultras were, with few exceptions, committed and consistent protectionists, who thought that Britain ought to maintain self-sufficiency, for strategic reasons (grain, shipbuilding) or social cohesion (e.g. silk weaving). They viewed free trade as an ideological speculation, unsuited to the real world of competing nations. While a few powerful interests might benefit, at least in the short term, it was likely to harm many others. Huge quantities of capital would be lost, and large numbers of working people lose their jobs.[54] The plight of the silk weavers of Coventry and Spital-fields, on the verge of starvation as a consequence of French imports, proved an especially emotive issue,[55] given the widespread Francophobia prevailing outside elite circles in London.

Opposition to the government's monetary policies was almost as widespread as opposition to free trade. The return to the gold standard, closely associated with Robert Peel, was seen as benefiting primarily the *classe politique*.[56] It had 'given a monopoly to the hoarders of stock and ready money; doubling the value of their money, doubling the value of all fixed salaries, annuities and pensions'.[57] Loans and salaries contracted in war paper currency were now to be (re)paid in gold. The losers from this policy, it was argued, included all those who borrowed to improve or expand, or to tide over periods of recession, and all those who were dependent on them.[58] Difficulties were compounded, especially for small manufacturers, artisans and shopkeepers, by the Act suppressing small banknotes, which constricted credit and impeded small transactions.[59] Collectively those adversely affected were a major source of employment. Their difficulties translated into mass unemployment and growing social tensions.

While free trade and monetary policies, and their deleterious social consequences, headed the litany of Ultra complaints against the government, they were not their only criticisms. Irresponsible government expenditure and high, poorly conceived and inequitably distributed taxation were also assailed.[60]

Although the Ultras certainly placed stress on the reversal of recent trade and monetary policies, retrenchment and restructured taxation as practical solutions to distress, it is important to note that, initially at least, they were far from inflexible. They began by asking for an acceptance of the fact of a crisis and an inquiry into its causes.[61] The refusal of the government to concede that much gave the initiative to hardliners and enthusiasts. At the same time the sheer rigidity of the government on such issues, probably attributable to Robert Peel, but easily blamed on the autocratic Duke and his system, hardened Ultra antagonism, especially outside Westminster, to a regime that appeared unsusceptible to public opinion, however constitutionally expressed. Suspicion grew, and was increasingly voiced, that this was a government that did not listen and would prefer coercion to compromise.

VI

In the latter part of 1829, and throughout 1830, the Ultras convinced themselves, and others, that the government was indifferent to British liberties and interests, and that it was drifting towards continental modes of control and repression. The crusade against Peel's police force, orchestrated by the *Standard*, was motivated by the fear that it was a gendarmerie, set up as 'a body of spies', and potentially dangerous.[62] As early as April 1828 the *Standard* published a letter from 'Macasius' that asserted in part:

> It is possible that the new police regulations may be destined to forward the view which HIS IMPERIAL HIGHNESS, THE GRAND DUKE ARTHUR may have towards the attainment of a power that has only once in the annals of this country been held by a subject.[63]

In October of the same year, S.L.Giffard, the most powerful and influential of Ultra newspapermen, editorialised that the police were 'an army not kept by any authority of Parliament and not in any way controlled by those who pay for it'.[64] By December the

Standard was highlighting a *Foreign Review* article which asserted that 'It is obvious with 20,000 such satellites that a minister, skilful, bold and enterprising, choosing well his time, might make a daring attempt against the subjects.'[65]

The *Standard* was certainly influential in Ultra circles and its concerns were picked up and reinforced by other newspapers of the same persuasion. Misgivings were also expressed in Parliament. Sir Richard Vyvyan, who admitted the new police had advantages, nonetheless complained that 'it was a large force, which might be increased to a great extent — the funds for which were not under the control of Parliament.'[66] He did not like it because it was under the control of a government which appeared 'intent on superseding the ancient institutions of the country'.[67]

While the crusade against the police may have gained less traction than Giffard probably hoped, it was not therefore unimportant. It contributed effectively to the general unease about the leadership and direction of a government which could be presented as not quite British in its aspirations and practices.

VII

Concerns about a potentially sinister new police force meshed very nicely with another, and more effective, Ultra crusade: in defence of their own press interest and freedom of the press more generally. The government attack on the *Morning Journal* antagonised and re-energised even some of the most malleable and passive Ultras (for example, the Lowther connection).[68] It also aroused public interest and sympathy well beyond their normal support base.

The Ultra Tory press was an essential weapon in the party's armoury. It was a crucial element in their organisation as well. Leading journalists had close working relationships with MPs and peers. S.L.Giffard, for example, dined with the Duke of Newcastle and had privileged access to the Duke of Cumberland. The Sheehans, of the *Dublin Evening Mail* and the *Star of Brunswick*, stayed at Lord

Farnham's home, and had his support in their social aspirations.[69]

The newspapermen tended to be more militant and trenchant than the politicians, who were [usually] restrained by parliamentary conventions and the prevailing social concepts of good taste. Especially uninhibited in his slashing attacks on 'apostates' was Robert Alexander, editor of the daily *Morning Journal*. Alexander, of Scots Covenanting descent, was a fierce Protestant and a vehement social paternalist. Despite some almost Cobbettite outbursts, he was also a lifelong and consistent Ultra Tory. He was no respecter of persons, he was extremely blunt and he was disconcertingly honest in expressing his opinions.

An erstwhile admirer of the Duke, he had come to the conclusion that 'there never was a more ambitious or dangerous minister in England than the Duke of Wellington.'[70] Exposing the Duke as a potential dictator governing through military methods, bullying the King, and undermining the constitution and British liberty, became a constant refrain of the *Morning Journal*. Alexander, characteristically, ventured into even more dangerous territory. He alluded to the Duke's morals and slighted the Duke's military career.[71] On 18 June 1829, referring to Waterloo, he informed the Duke:

Better you had fallen on that day
And lain where many thousands lay.[72]

A little later he wrote in his editorial that 'Waterloo has not conferred upon England the price of its blood.'[73] Not surprisingly Ultras such as Eldon and Mansfield drew back from such journalistic excesses.[74]

The Duke, angry with some cause, was anxious to make an example of an offending Ultra print. His preference would have been to move against the *Standard*. It, however, had secure finances, and an editor with a DCL, who was prepared to accept full responsibility for whatever was published, thus protecting the proprietors.

Unlike Giffard at the *Standard*, Robert Alexander was an

editor/proprietor, which helped ensure that a successful action would damage further the paper's operations, financial base and viability. Having determined to act, the government struck hard at its chosen target. A private prosecution by Lord Lyndhurst for criminal libel elicited Alexander's defence. Lyndhurst's action was then discontinued, and followed by three *ex officio* actions on behalf of the government, and two personal actions by the Duke.

Alexander was placed in a very difficult situation. Facing, initially, a legal team of six, including the Attorney General, the Solicitor General and Henry Brougham, he had to pay the costs of his defence, meet bail, and respond to an immediate demand for payment of Stamp Tax of £800. Forced by financial exigencies to conduct his own defence, he had simultaneously to function as editor. Pressures continued to mount as assets were seized, including the printer's press. There were even claims of harassment by the new police.[75] After a long drawn-out and complex set of proceedings Alexander was found guilty on several counts and imprisoned. His newspaper was placed under the administration of a hostile journalist[76] and was eventually, despite assistance from leading Ultras,[77] forced to close. Various aspects of these proceedings, including the role of the Attorney General, the cumulative nature of the actions, the element of double jeopardy, and the vagueness and inclusiveness of some of the grounds of action aroused concern at Westminster Hall and in the *Law Journal* and elsewhere.[78]

The remainder of the Ultra press, closely and strenuously supported by the parliamentary Ultras, inveighed fiercely against the threat to press freedom. The *Standard* 'doubted very much whether any newspaper was ever issued from the press, which with well-directed affidavits might not be made the subject of criminal [action] by an imaginative and vindictive projector'.[79] The *Age* observed that 'without strictures on the attributes of ministers and measures of the government, the public press would be of no benefit to society, nor would there be any restraint on bad men, or the execution of bad measures.'[80]

On this occasion sympathy for the Ultra viewpoint was widespread. Henry Brougham, despite his role in the proceedings, expressed concern at the outcome, and joined Richard Vyvyan in warning of the dangers of an English Polignac.[81] The editor of the *Elgin Courier*, who disliked both Alexander and his cause, noted that he was 'literally a martyr'.[82] The great metropolitan dailies, the *Herald, Globe* and *Morning Chronicle*, all sounded the alarm. Eventually even *The Times*, usually seen as the government's favoured journal, added its voice. The periodicals were of the same mind.[83]

This was a significant, if unintentional, publicity coup for the Ultras in their campaign against the military and autocratic minister, his 'un-British' attitudes and continental aspirations. There was widespread agreement that little respect had been shown for one of the most basic of British freedoms and one of the most vital to the effective functioning of a constitutional state.

While the government succeeded in crushing the *Morning Journal,* it was a pyrrhic victory. It did not put an end to intemperate attacks on the Duke and his ministers. It revivified the antagonism of the Ultras, including some who had lapsed into inactivity. It helped facilitate co-operation among the various opposition groups. Above all, it further strengthened the Ultras in their conviction that there was nothing to be hoped for from a Prime Minister who appeared to be fulfilling their gloomiest prophecies.

VIII

Initially a number of Ultras, like some of the Ministerialists and almost all of the band of waverers who floated between the two, had hoped for a Tory reunion, based upon a ministerial reconstruction and an adjustment of measures. Even before the death of George IV, however, this had become unlikely. The Duke would not take in any group *as a group*, he would not abandon Peel, and Peel would not yield an inch on such issues as distress and the currency.

The Ultras for their part were entrenching and deepening their opposition. Although the parliamentarians were moving more slowly than the intellectuals and the provincials, even at Westminster there was a drift towards favouring a complete change in government and, beyond that, towards a moderate reform of the system that had sustained it.

Ultra rhetoric against a government which slighted constitutional expression of public opinion, assailed the freedom of the press, threatened traditional liberties and pursued anti-national social and economic policies, became ever more emotive. The government was 'a club of borough-mongers and parasitical clerks',[84] who had 'placed the resources of the country entirely under the control of those who had the least interest in it: loan-brokers, contractors, all the lenders of money; all the unprincipled jobbers of the stock exchange'.[85] The parliament was dominated by MPs 'as ignorant as they are unprincipled', 'as venal as they are reckless'.[86] It was 'totally incapacitated from protecting our rights and our achievements'.[87]

To effect the change they increasingly believed to be an urgent necessity, the Ultras strengthened their contact with both Whigs and Huskissonites. This was not an altogether palatable option for many, but since George IV had failed to effect change from above and the election of 1830 had shown the limited electoral impact of public opinion under the existing system, a joint effort to bring down the Duke was the most plausible strategy remaining.

The problem with an opposition coalition was finding common ground that did not entail abandoning core interests and values. A general dissatisfaction with the government would not in itself suffice. This gave salience to two issues where united effort might be practicable: retrenchment and parliamentary reform. From the Ultra viewpoint, the first was an easy option; the second was more problematical. On neither issue has the Ultra standpoint always been well understood.

IX

At one point the Ultras designated themselves the 'Country Party', although the label never stuck.[88] This is perhaps a pity, since 'Ultra Tory' is in some respects misleading and has proved a considerable distraction to subsequent generations of historians. The Ultras were natural enemies of metropolitan influence, big government and its patronage chains, and systemic corruption. Retrenchment was, for them, largely uncontroversial. As the *Standard* remarked, support for it 'was almost self-ensured when applied to the [Ultra] party, the ground of whose dissent and the bond of whose union is a preference of principle to place'.[89] The few likely to be adversely affected, such as Lord Kenyon, remained silent.

The government on the other hand, was easily assailable on issues of 'old corruption'. Peel was already under attack for his role in 'the Swan River job', and the patronage grabbing of both Peels and Wellesleys was easily highlighted (and overstated).[90] A 'sea of corruption', it was argued, kept afloat the Wellington administration.[91] 'In the executive government, and its pensioners and dependents ... there is nothing but venality and corruption, treachery being deemed the mark of talent, and dishonesty and subserviency the avenues to power.'[92]

Although as usual, press and provincial Ultras were more strident in tone than the parliamentarians, there was little substantive difference of opinion. Some of the most assiduous and determined opponents of 'old corruption' were Ultra MPs such as T.B.Fyler and Colonel Sibthorpe. On key issues such as the treasurership of the navy, the paymastership of marines, the Bathurst and Dundas pensions and the emoluments of Privy Councillors, the party could, and did, muster in numbers.

An element of vindictive personal politics in the Ultra

espousal of retrenchment can be assumed, but it was not the only motivation. The Ultras believed in small and 'clean' government. They felt the corrupt use of patronage was helping to underpin in office a government that they had come to despise.[93] Their vote on the Civil List was a logical corollary. It may very well be, since the issue was not obviously one of confidence, that they did not expect the government to resign. A few might, as Ellenborough believed, have had regrets.[94] It is unlikely that this was very general, since the Ultras had a healthy contempt for 'expediency' where matters of principle were at stake, and for the Ultras this was as matter of principle. It was later suggested by some that it was the wrong issue on which to vote down the government, but that was with the benefit of hindsight. At the time an anti-corruption issue fitted seamlessly into the Ultra campaign against the Duke and his system. It was not internally disruptive and above all it was successful. The rule of McBeath was brought to an end on an issue that appeared optimal from their viewpoint.

X

At the meeting at which the Ultra MPs decided to vote against the Civil List, they also discussed an alternative or supplementary proposal to endorse some measure of parliamentary reform. They adjourned, intending to resume the discussion later. That may well have been a fatal mistake, but it was not obviously such at the time. Because, subsequently, the majority of Ultras opposed the Whig bill and were almost destroyed by reform hysteria, it has sometimes been assumed that they were opposed to all parliamentary reform as a matter of principle. That is a fundamental misunderstanding. For the Ultras, Westbury, the pocket borough where Peel took refuge after his defeat at Oxford, was more symbolic than Old Sarum. It seemed to highlight the way in which the abuses of the old system thwarted public opinion and even the expert opinion of the educated.

The Ultra press, both reflecting and shaping extra-parliamentary opinion, moved steadily and progressively towards support of some measure of parliamentary reform. As early as April 1829 the *Belfast Newsletter* claimed, somewhat prematurely, that Catholic Emancipation 'had convinced the leaders of the Protestant interest of the necessity of modified parliamentary reform, and of abolishing what Cobbett had long denounced as "the beastly boroughmongering system"'.[95] By 3 June the *Standard*'s editorial commented:

> So very little sympathy has been manifested between the House of Commons and the people, so very little vision, not to speak of other qualities, has been evinced by the conduct of that House … that the knot can never be severed without a generous reform of the manners and principles or in the constitution of that body.[96]

The following day the *Edinburgh Examiner* asked the rhetorical question, 'What was to prevent a High Tory from desiring to see that close and rotten boroughs be got rid of?'[97] In the weeks and months that followed, the *Morning Journal*, the *Age*, *Fraser's Magazine* and the leading political essayist, David Robinson of *Blackwood's magazine*, as well as many provincial prints, repeated the refrain.[98]

The parliamentarians were more hesitant. They after all were participants in the existing system, and some, such as the Duke of Newcastle and the Earl of Falmouth, had a significant amount of money invested in it. There were also Ultra MPs, often enough intellectuals, such as Inglis and Sadler, who gloried in the complexity, diversity and equipoise of the old system. For the parliamentary party more generally there was always the need to balance press and provincial demand for parliamentary reform with the need to avoid secessions on the issue.

The early endeavours of the Marquis of Blandford, which did much to keep the issue on the political agenda in 1829, elicited little direct support in Parliament. Similarly Ultra involvement with the foundation of groups such as the Birmingham Political Union went beyond what most would have favoured. Later, though, as Ultra antagonism hardened towards the Duke, his government, and the system that kept them in office, the lineaments of an Ultra reform position began to emerge. It was to be rational and not revolutionary, 'a safe and prudent reform', which respected existing rights.[99] Their objection was not to parliamentary reform as such, but to the kind of sweeping radicalism which for many (although not all) was to be epitomised by the eventual Whig bill.[100]

While many Ultras were supportive of disfranchising insignificant boroughs and corrupt voters, they wanted to keep this to a minimum. The Earl of Walsingham was 'opposed to every kind and species of disfranchisement'.[101] Sir Charles Wetherell thought it 'a monstrous principle'.[102] Colonel Sibthorpe, a doughty defender of ancient right voters, objected to 'annihilating hosts who have done no harm, committed no fault'.[103] John Fane thought taking away their votes would reduce the labouring classes to 'mere hewers of wood and drawers of water'.[104] The Duke of Richmond and William Duncombe, among others, defended even the rights of Irish 40*s*. freeholders.[105]

The Ultras were also, in general, cautiously supportive of some enfranchisement measures. General Gascoyne represented petitioners who 'did not oppose the transfer of the elective franchise from insignificant places to large and populous towns and cities'.[106] Richard Vyvyan was of the same mind,[107] while S.L.Giffard, opposing the disfranchisement of East Retford, wrote in his editorial:

> Manchester is unrepresented — Leeds is unrepresented — Birmingham is unrepresented. In the name of common sense what has this to do with the rights of East Retford? If the great towns want representation, as we believe they do, let them be represented.[108]

Given that Ultras sat for urban centres with large populations or extensive electorates, such as Liverpool, Exeter, Bristol, Coventry,

York and Dublin, it was not obvious in 1829–30 that they need fear a moderate degree of enfranchisement. Popular Protestantism and social paternalism could potentially have translated into votes and seats.

It was entirely possible that at the meeting of 14 November, or some subsequent one, the Ultras might have evolved a distinctively Ultra reform proposal, or negotiated adjustments to the one proposed by Henry Brougham. What is certainly true is that, as a group, they were most unlikely to have been propitiated by a dogmatic pronouncement against all parliamentary reform. With a few exceptions they no longer believed in the perfection of the existing system. Had the government not chosen, somewhat unpredictably, to go out on the Civil List question, it seems likely that it would have been defeated on a moderate reform proposal, backed by many of the Ultras, shortly thereafter.

The Ultras were by no means blindly antagonistic to parliamentary reform, which many of them believed was necessary to unseat an authoritarian and dysfunctional administration, impervious to public opinion, and to preclude the recurrence of such a government. That approach entailed adjustment to the electoral system which had helped to sustain the Duke and which might do so again in the future. Earl Grey recognised that the Ultras were not diehard anti-reformers. He noted, with some irritation, that their opposition to reform 'concedes the principle, … admits the necessity, and having given this advantage to the advocates of reform, disappoints all their expectations'.[109] Though this showed more insight into the Ultra stance than the Duke of Wellington ever managed to muster, it was, nonetheless, still skewed and severe. The Ultras were advocates of moderate reform in a context where moderation was at a discount. The fatal flaw of the Ultras was not a diehard determination to resist all change, but rather an inflexible and principled moderation, combined with a poor sense of timing.

XI

While it has long been realised that the secession of the Ultras, and their persistence in opposition, were pivotal to the fall of the Wellington administration and the advent of 'the Age of Reform', the nature of the split in Tory ranks has been dealt with rather cursorily. It has often been assumed that the rift was essentially over Catholic emancipation and that otherwise the differences were superficial. The Ultras, in this view, were factious, spiteful, and revenge seeking, and, in the end, self-immolating. 'Had Zimri peace who slew his master?' inquired Michael Brock, parsonically and rhetorically.[110]

Yet virtually all the extensive corpus of Ultra speeches and writings suggests that their differences with the Ministerialists were more extensive and deeper than is frequently asserted. That they were prepared to vote down the Duke of Wellington and his government, not on a religious issue but on one of retrenchment and potentially on one of parliamentary reform, is surely indicative of a chasm within Toryism that was close to unbridgeable by 1830. It would take a transformation of the political landscape, of landslide dimensions, to close the gap.

The Ultras' passionate denunciation of the Duke was more than personal malice. He was given due deference as a great military commander and a national hero. Rather they saw that military greatness did not necessarily translate into sound political leadership. Their criticism over Roman Catholic emancipation was not just about apostasy, but about political methods. The Duke's strategic planning, use of secrecy and surprise, ruthless tactics and expectation of soldierly obedience by fellow Tories, all suggested to them a military intelligence largely honed on conflict outside Britain.

The Ultras were also concerned about the short shrift the Duke gave to the Church, the universities, the Crown and constitutionally-expressed public opinion, where they conflicted with his agenda. His lack of respect for constitutional niceties and impedimenta suggested to them a would-be dictator, a potential Cromwell. This was excessive and overwrought, and subsequent generations have rightly given it little credence; but it was not altogether groundless and, since it was sincerely believed and widely disseminated, it was more than just spiteful triviality. It had a significant impact on erstwhile supporters of the Duke and, as a consequence, helped destabilise his government.

While Catholic emancipation was obviously a pivotal issue in prompting Ultra secession and in defining attitudes to the Duke and his supporters, it was never the only issue. There was always a strong vein of agrarianism and protectionism among the Ultras, which ramified into hostility to the government's trade and taxation and monetary policies. The onset of acute distress, especially among the labouring poor in 1829–30, consolidated criticism of economic policies and management, and also brought to the surface a current of social paternalism. Increasingly the Ultras provided an alternative Toryism to that of the government. Sometimes referred to as 'Old Toryism', it certainly rejected most of what David Robinson called 'the new liberal system'.[111] It was, nevertheless, evolving quite rapidly itself, and the gap with the Ministerialists was widening on both sides.

The unwillingness of the Ministerialists to make concessions to electoral or constitutionally-expressed popular opinion, not just on Catholic emancipation and religious or constitutional issues, but across the whole range of Ultra concerns, intensified anti-government rhetoric. The new police and the perceived threat to freedom of the press indicated to the Ultras a drift towards continental-style autocratic practices and a contempt for British liberties. The refusal of Parliament to hearken to public concerns over social distress, or even to inquire into its causes, seemed indicative of a callous mixture of authoritarian politics and economic liberalism, which deferred to the wishes of a *classe politique* revamped and reinforced by the beneficiaries of recent trade and monetary policies.

There was an increasing conviction, especially among Ultra intellectuals, that the Duke and his allies represented a stain on the fundamental constitutional fabric. There followed a willingness to assail the patronage that enabled the Duke to hold on to power, and the 'borough-mongering' which had disturbed the electoral process and, as a corollary, produced a servile and ineffectual House of Commons. By November 1830 the Ultra parliamentarians had more or less reached the same conclusion and were ready to act upon it.

The Ultras voted against the Civil List; they would probably have supported a modest measure of parliamentary reform. By late 1830 they had rejected the Ministerial leadership, scathingly criticised its parliamentary supporters, expressed dissent on a wide range of issues of importance and begun to attack the political system they believed sustained the current inept and dysfunctional administration. They had articulated a different and alternative brand of Toryism, and they were utilising a wider and more 'populist' range of political methods to spread it. They had, in short, diverged so far from the Ministerialists that, despite would-be conciliators on both sides, rapprochement no longer seemed feasible. Nor was it much sought after. To many Ultras, even Whiggery had come to seem preferable.[112] This was an illusion, no doubt, but one that took some time to dispel.

XII

While Ultra criticism of the Duke, as a political leader, was not entirely without foundation and should not be utterly dismissed, it was certainly too wide-ranging and couched in overly emotive language. The Duke was a military man, and was shaped by the values of his profession and his experiences as a soldier. He was inclined to be authoritative, impatient of dissent and constitutional obstruction, and contemptuous about the press and inconvenient manifestations of popular opinion (however traditional and legal).

That did not, though, make him a would-be dictator. His rather high-handed treatment of George IV and the occasional nasty remark about the royal family did not make him an incipient Cromwell or an alternative King Arthur either. Bold and unflinching he may have been, but he was no Macbeth. Such claims, widespread enough in the febrile politics of 1829–30, soon became an embarrassment, inconsistent with a new need for reconciliation, and were generally and quickly abandoned.

Nevertheless the scathing Ultra critique of the Duke and his administration was of considerable significance, both in its immediate impact, and as a harbinger of things to come. The Ultras showed considerable skill in articulating and disseminating their view, and it was plausible enough to undermine the government's credibility and its support base amongst erstwhile adherents. It was also destructive of the internal cohesion and morale of the administration. It played a key part in the successful Ultra strategy to bring down the Duke.

The Ultras had, of course, envisaged as an alternative an Ultra-led government or a coalition with an influential Ultra component. Had this eventuated they would have pursued their own reform agenda, which would not have been without its merits, especially in terms of social cohesion. If they had gone down this path not travelled, it was unlikely it would have led them back to reconciliation with the ministerial Tories in a re-branded Conservative Party. Outmanoeuvred by the more politically adroit Whigs and almost destroyed by a wrong-footed response to parliamentary reform, that became their best option by default. It was not, however, an altogether satisfactory outcome. The differences of principle, which had initially provoked their rift with the Wellington-Peel Tories and their attack on the Duke, persisted and some of the resentments festered on. After little more than a decade of recurring friction, such discordant views would help to wreck the Conservative Party in a welter of recriminations reminiscent of 1829–30. In the long struggle for the heart and soul of the Tory/Conservative party, the Ultra attacks on the Duke, even if overstated and in part misdirected, were neither aberrant and anomalous, nor merely superficial and malicious. Rather they made manifest virulent incompatibilities which were to be troublesome for years to come. In subsequent affrays the Duke, who was gradually slipping into the linked roles of elder statesman and national icon, was almost never the primary target of verbal assault by the Ultras and their successors.

They largely transferred their attention to his successor as party leader, that 'man of respectable talents, moderate acquirements, unquestionable propriety, undeniable self-complacency and brilliant and boundless wealth',[113] Sir Robert Peel. The fall of Peel was to be, in many ways, a repeat performance. He, however, was no 'colossus' or war hero, and so his critics, while vehement enough, rarely resorted to the colourful hyperbole of the attacks on the Duke. Not even the most fervent Protectionist saw Peel as the King of Dahomey, or the 'bold, unflinching McBeath'. Even in defeat, and in the rhetoric of his enemies, the Duke attracted, and warranted, imaginative superlatives.

References

[i] Dick Leonard *Nineteenth century premiers. Pitt to Roseberry* (Basingstoke and New York, 2008) p. 148; Neville Thompson *Wellington after Waterloo* (London, 1986) p. 1.

[2] John Severn *Architects of empire. The Duke of Wellington and his brothers* (Norman, 2007) p. 538.

[3] Thompson, *Wellington after Waterloo*, pp. 1–2.

[4] Thompson, *Wellington after Waterloo*, pp. 1–2.

[5] Elizabeth Longford *Wellington: pillar of state* (London, 1972) p. 405. For a briefer but congruent list, Richard Holmes *Wellington: the Iron Duke* (London, 2002) p. 301. For contrast, see [George Croly?], 'The Duke of Wellington and domestic politics', *Monthly Magazine* 7 (Sep 1829) pp. 241–50, and [William Maginn?] 'The downfall of the Wellington administration', *Fraser's Magazine* 2 (Dec 1830) pp. 592–603.

[6] J.C.D.Clark *English Society 1660–1832* (Cambridge, 2000) pp. 548–9.

[7] Revd G.S.Faber to Thomas Burgess, Bishop of Salisbury, 23 Jun 1829, Bodleian Library, Oxford, Burgess MSS, C135, ff. 28–9A.

[8] [David Robinson], 'The breaking in upon the constitution of 1688', *Blackwood's Edinburgh Magazine* 25 (Apr 1829) pp. 503–24, at p. 505; 'Notes of the month on affairs in general', *Monthly Magazine*, new series, 8 (Aug 1829) pp. 195–208, at p. 201; 'Notes of the month', *Monthly Magazine*, new series, 8 (Sep 1829) pp. 316–28, at pp. 320–1, 323; *Standard,* 25 Apr 1829; *Morning Journal*, 15 Jun 1829, 16 Jun 1829, 18 Jul 1829, 24 Jul 1829, 31 Jul 1829, 25 Aug 1829, 15 Sep 1829.

[9] *Star of Brunswick*, 6 Jul 1829. The original source is [J.G.Lockhart and William Maginn], 'Noctes Ambrosianae, No. XLIV', *Blackwood's Magazine* 153 (Jun 1829) pp. 769–803, at p. 803.

[10] e.g. Phillip Harling *The waning of Old Corruption: the politics of economical reform in Britain, 1729–1846* (Oxford, 1996).

[11] Norman Gash, 'From the origins to Sir Robert Peel', in *The Conservatives: a history from their origins to 1965* ed. N.Gash (London, 1977) pp. 59–60.

[12] Robert Blake *The Conservative Party from Peel to Churchill* (London, 1970) pp. 19–21.

[13] James Sack *From Jacobite to Conservative. Reaction and orthodoxy in Britain* (Cambridge, 1993) p. 248.

[14] F.O'Gorman *The long eighteenth century: British political and social history 1688–1832* (London, 1997) pp. 359–60. For a similar view, Peter Jupp *British politics on the eve of reform. The Duke of Wellington's administration 1828–30* (Basingstoke, 1998) p. 3.

[15] Robert Stewart *The foundation of the Conservative Party 1830–1867* (London, 1978) pp. 44, 50–1. M.Brock *The great Reform Act* (London, 1973) p. 63; J.Cannon, *Parliamentary reform, 1640–1832* (Cambridge, 1973) p. 191; Jupp, *British politics*, p. 87.

[16] For example, Boyd Hilton *A mad, bad and dangerous people. England 1783–1846* (Oxford, 2006) pp. 406–7; Jupp, *British politics*, pp. 274–90. Jupp places undue emphasis on Jewish relief, an issue on which Ultras disagreed significantly.

[17] Stewart, *Foundation of the Conservative Party*, p. 57 (29); Jupp, *British politics*, p. 290 (32); O'Gorman, *Long eighteenth century*, p. 360 (33); B.T.Bradfield, 'Sir Richard Vyvyan and the country gentlemen, 1830–1834' *English Historical Review* 83 (1968) pp. 729–43, at p. 729 (34); Hilton, *A mad, bad and dangerous people*, p. 419 (40+); D.G.S.Simes, 'The Ultra Tories in British politics, 1824–1834' (unpublished University of Oxford DPhil thesis, 1974) p. 474 (50).

[18] There is no entirely satisfactory discussion of Ultra Tory organisation, either parliamentary or extra-parliamentary. Jupp, *British politics*, pp. 274–90, provides the best account of the party at Westminster. Sack, *Jacobite to Conservative*, pp. 107–11, discusses 'right wing organisations'. The Ultra press is addressed by the same author in 'Wellington and the Tory Press, 1828–1832' in *Wellington: studies in the military and political career of the first Duke of Wellington* ed.

N.Gash (Manchester, 1990) pp. 159–69. Douglas Simes, '"The champions of the Protestant cause will not lightly abandon it": the Ultra Tory press and the Wellington administration', in *Wellington Studies IV* ed. C.M.Woolgar (Southampton, 2008) pp. 299–312, also discusses the press. For an extended but dated overview, see Simes, 'Ultra Tories in British politics', pp. 152–235.

[19] *Morning Journal*, 12 Feb 1829, 17 Feb 1829, 4 May 1829; [Samuel O'Sullivan], 'Colloquies in Ireland regarding recent measures' *Blackwood's Magazine* 25 (Jun 1829) pp. 752–70, at p. 756; [David Robinson], 'An opposition' *Blackwood's Magazine* 25 (Jun 1829) pp. 782–6, at p. 782; 'The coronation oath and the Cabinet' *Monthly Magazine*, new series, 7 (Apr 1829) pp. 337–44, at pp. 341–4; *Morning Journal*, 2 Jan 1829, 1 Jan 1830.

[20] [William Maginn], 'The Dead Parliament', *Fraser's Magazine* 2 (Aug 1830) pp. 111–18, at p. 117; 'The conversazione' *Monthly Magazine*, new series, 2 (Jun 1829) pp. 596–602, at p. 598.

[21] [Maginn], 'Dead Parliament', p. 117.

[22] [David Robinson], 'The assembling of Parliament' *Blackwood's Magazine* 25 (Mar 1829) pp. 271–87, at p. 282.

[23] *Standard*, 23 Jul 1829.

[24] *Morning Journal*, 10 Feb 1829, 12 May 1829, 8 Jun 1829; *Standard*, 23 Apr 1829, 6 Jun 1829; 'The coronation oath and the Cabinet', p. 341; [Lockhart and Maginn], 'Noctes Ambrosianae XLV' *Blackwood's Magazine* 26 (Jul 1829) pp. 120–42, at p. 126.

[25] *Standard*, 10 Jun 1830, 30 Sep 1830. There was an article in the *Monthly Magazine* about the same time, which is frequently referred to, but which I have not been able to see.

[26] [Thomas Powell], 'Thoughts on the Wellington administration' *Fraser's Magazine* 1 (Jul 1830) pp. 729–37, at p. 729.

[27] *Standard*, 11 Sep 1829. More generally, *Morning Journal*, 24 Jul 1829, 31 Jul 1829, 25 Aug 1829.

[28] *Standard*, 20 Jul 1829; *Morning Journal,* 11 Sep 1829.

[29] [Maginn?], 'Downfall of the Wellington administration', p. 594.

[30] [Powell], 'Thoughts on the Wellington administration', pp. 730–1.

[31] [Powell], 'Thoughts on the Wellington administration', p. 729.

[32] [W.Maginn], 'Placemen, Parliament-men, penny-a-liners and parliamentary reporters' *Fraser's Magazine* 2 (Oct 1830) pp. 282–94, at p. 282; [ex-MP], 'The prospects of the ministry' *Fraser's Magazine* 1 (Sep 1830) pp. 190–9, at p. 195; [Robinson], 'An opposition', p. 782; 'Notes on the month in general' *Monthly Magazine*, new series, 6 (Apr 1829) pp. 401–16, at p. 402.

[33] Revd G.S.Faber to the Bishop of Salisbury, 23 Jun 1829, Bodleian Library, Burgess Papers, C 135, ff. 28–9A.

[34] [Maginn], 'Placemen, Parliament-men', p. 282.

[35] *Standard*, 24 Jun 1829.

[36] *Standard*, 5 Sep 1829.

[37] [Maginn], 'Dead Parliament' *Fraser's Magazine* 2 (Aug 1830) pp. 111–18, at p. 117; *Age*, 9 Aug 1829.

[38] [Ex-MP], 'Prospects of the ministry', p. 195; [W.Maginn?], 'Machinery and the manufacturing system' *Fraser's Magazine* 2 (Nov 1830) pp. 419–30, at p. 425; [W.Maginn?], 'The burnings in Kent and the state of the labouring classes' *Fraser's Magazine* 2 (Dec 1830) pp. 572–81, at pp. 575–76.

[39] Sack, *Jacobite to Conservative*, pp. 247–8; *Parliamentary Debates*, new series, xx, cols. 522–3; *Morning Journal*, 9 Sep 1829.

[40] [Maginn], 'Machinery and the manufacturing system', pp. 419, 421, 424; [Powell], 'Thoughts on the Wellington administration', pp. 733–4; *Standard*, 21 Oct 1829, 9 Feb 1830, 28 Oct 1830.

[41] *Parliamentary Debates*, new series, xx, col. 96.

[42] *Parliamentary Debates*, new series, xx, cols. 146, 149–50, 589; W.A.Hay, *The Whig revival 1808–1830* (Basingstoke, 2005) p. 169.

[43] *Morning Journal*, 10 Feb 1829; *Enniskillen Chronicle*, 19 Feb 1829.

[44] *Parliamentary Debates*, new series, xx, col. 981.

[45] *Parliamentary Debates*, new series, xx, col. 860.

[46] *Parliamentary Debates*, new series, xx, col. 71.

[47] *Parliamentary Debates*, new series, xx, col. 1054.

[48] *Parliamentary Debates*, new series, xx, col. 1085.

[49] *Parliamentary Debates*, new series, xx, col. 653.

[50] *Manchester Courier, Sheffield Mercury, Dublin Evening Pacquet, Belfast Newsletter*, quoted in the *Standard*, 20 Apr 1829; *Felix Farley's Bristol Journal, Birmingham Journal*, quoted in the *Standard*, 21 Apr 1829; Marquis of Chandos at Aylesbury public dinner, quoted in the *Standard*, 20 Jun 1829; Hugh Dick at the Maldon True Blue Club dinner, *Standard*, 4 Feb 1829; Earls of Eldon and Harewood at the Pitt Club dinner, *Standard*, 29 May 1829; Marquis of Chandos at Aylesbury public dinner, *Standard*, 20 Jun 1829. The *Standard* and the *Morning Journal* reported negative news from Ireland on an almost daily basis, often drawing on the reports of Irish Ultra newspapers such as the *Dublin Evening Mail* and the *Warder*. The *Standard* also collected references from Catholic newspapers (16 Jun 1829). The *Age* set the results of Catholic emancipation alongside quotations from politicians about 'the healing measure': *Standard*, 14 Sep 1829.

[51] *Parliamentary Debates*, new series, xxiii, cols. 475–85, 490–6, 496–501, 534–5; H.Twiss *Life of Lord Chancellor Eldon* (3 vols., London, 1844) iii, p. 122; diary of the fourth Duke of Newcastle, 13 Feb 1830, Nottingham University Library. For philanthropy in practice, see *Morning Journal*, 1 Jan 1830, for a partial list of Newcastle's Christmas benefactions to the poor.

[52] For example, *Standard*, 6 May 1829, 2 Jun 1829, 3 Jun 1829, 9 Jan 1830,

11 Jan 1830, 13 Mar 1830 (Winchilsea and Stanhope at Kent county meeting), 15 Apr 1830; *Parliamentary Debates,* new series, xxiii, cols.116, 231, 385, 806–7, 1268; [Maginn], 'The burnings in Kent'.

[53] *Morning Journal*, 25 May 1829.

[54] *Parliamentary Debates*, new series, xxi, cols. 744–6, 751, 962–82; [David Robinson], 'Debates in Parliament on the silk trade' *Blackwood's Magazine* 25 (Jun 1829) pp. 685–700, especially pp. 685, 699; *Standard*, 2 May 1829, 27 Jun 1829 (quoting *Glasgow Courier*), 26 Aug 1829, 29 Aug 1829, 14 Sep 1829, 15 Sep 1829.

[55] *Morning Journal*, 23 Jan 1829, 30 Jan 1829, 3 Feb 1829, 4 Feb 1829, 8 May 1829, 3 Jun 1829, 16 Jun 1829; *Standard*, 7 May 1829, 17 Jun 1829, 19 Sep 1829; *Parliamentary Debates,* new series, xxi, cols. 596, 744–60, 866, 903, 914–19, 962–82; [Robinson], 'Silk trade', pp. 685–700.

[56] [David Robinson], 'The working of the currency' *Blackwood's Magazine* 25 (Feb 1829) pp. 135–52. Mathias Attwood put the Ultra case, *Parliamentary Debates*, new series, xxv, cols. 166–7. This was endorsed by Knatchbull and Vyvyan, *Parliamentary Debates*, new series, xxv, cols. 170–1.

[57] [Maginn], 'The burnings in Kent', pp. 574–5.

[58] [Maginn], 'The burnings in Kent'.

[59] *Parliamentary Debates*, new series, xxv, cols. 101–41, 170–1; [Robinson], 'Working of the currency', especially p. 151; *Standard*, 9 Jun 1829, quoting *Felix Farley's Bristol Journal.*

[60] [Robinson], 'Machinery and the manufacturing system', pp. 419–30; [Maginn], 'The burnings in Kent', p. 580; *Parliamentary Debates*, new series, xxii, col. 1317; xxiii, cols. 483–5, 494–5, 903, 952–3; Colonel Sibthorpe at Lincolnshire county meeting, *Standard*, 9 Jan 1830.

[61] *Parliamentary Debates*, new series, xxii, cols. 13, 940–3, 969–70; xxiii, col. 476.

[62] *Standard*, 29 Sep 1829.

[63] *Standard*, 25 Apr 1829.

[64] *Standard*, 17 Oct 1829.

[65] *Standard*, 3 Dec 1829.

[66] *Parliamentary Debates*, new series, xxv, cols. 359–60.

[67] *Parliamentary Debates*, new series, xxv, cols. 359–60.

[68] Lonsdale to Lowther, 8 Oct 1829, 17 Jan 1830, 21 Feb 1830, Cumbria Record Office, Lonsdale Papers.

[69] Captain Cottingham to Lord Farnham, 18 Jul 1831, National Library of Ireland, Farnham Papers 18610(4)

[70] *Morning Journal*, 14 May 1829.

[71] For example, *Morning Journal*, 29 Jun 1829, 24 Jul 1829, 31 Jul 1829, 11 Sep 1829, 15 Sep 1829; Newcastle diary, 1 Sep 1829, Nottingham University Library.

[72] *Morning Journal*, 18 Jun 1829, 10 Jul 1829.

[73] *Morning Journal*, 29 Jun 1829.

[74] Twiss, *Eldon*, iii, p. 70; Mansfield to Newcastle, 5 Dec 1829, Nottingham University Library, Newcastle MSS 5147.

[75] D.G.S.Simes, "'The champions of the Protestant cause will not lightly abandon it": the Ultra Tory press and the Wellington administration', in *Wellington Studies IV* ed. C.M.Woolgar (Southampton, 2008) pp. 311–12.

[76] S.C.Hall *Restrospect of a long life* (2 vols., London, 1883) i, p. 131.

[77] General J.Litton Crosbie to Lord Salisbury, 6 Aug 1829, Hatfield House, Salisbury MSS 2M, quoted in Jupp, *British politics*, p. 351; *Morning Journal*, 14 Jan 1830; Newcastle diary, 9 Jul 1829, 12–18 Oct 1829, Nottingham University Library.

[78] *Annual register or view of the history, politics and literature of the year 1830* (London, 1831) p. 119.

[79] *Standard*, 30 Jun 1829.

[80] The *Age*, as quoted in *Morning Journal*, 1 Jul 1829.

[81] *Cobbett's register*, quoted in *Morning Journal*, 1 Jan 1830; *Parliamentary Debates*, new series, xxii, cols. 1228–30, 1233 (Althorp, O'Connell, Hume).

[82] *Morning Journal*, 7 Jun 1830. The *Morning Journal* reproduced supportive editorials, beginning 1 Jul 1829 with the *Carlisle Patriot, Berkshire Chronicle* and the *Age*. As further examples, on 5 Jan 1830 it quoted the *Manchester Courier, Durham Advertiser, Dublin Evening Mail, Dublin Warder, Leeds Patriot*, and the *Cork Constitution*. On 6 Jan 1830 it added the *Edinburgh Evening Post, Paisley Advertiser* and the *Dublin Evening Paquet*.

[83] *Standard*, 14 Sep 1829 (*Globe*), 4 Oct 1829 (*Spectator*), 10 Dec 1829 (*Herald*), 10 Feb 1830 (*Morning Chronicle*). [Unidentified], 'The late prosecutions of the press' *Monthly Magazine*, new series, 7 (Aug 1829) pp. 137–44; ['M'], 'Star Chamber and the liberty of the press' *Monthly Magazine*, new series, 8 (Oct 1829) pp. 396–409; John Wilson, 'Noctes Ambrosianae XLVII' *Blackwood's Magazine* 26 (Dec 1829) pp. 845–78, at pp. 855–6.

[84] [Maginn?], 'Downfall of the Wellington administration', p. 603.

[85] [Maginn], 'The burnings in Kent', p. 575.

[86] *Morning Journal*, 5 Jun 1829.

[87] *Morning Journal*, 5 Jun 1829.

[88] Diary of the fourth Duke of Newcastle, 12–15 Feb 1830, Nottingham University Library, Newcastle MSS; *Parliamentary Debates*, new series, xxii, col. 466.

[89] *Standard*, 23 Sep 1829, 29 Jan 1830, 24 Mar 1830, 17 Jul 1830.

[90] For example, 'Affairs in general' *Monthly Magazine*, new series, 6 (Jun 1829) pp. 635–52, at pp. 637–9; 'Notes of the month on affairs in general' *Monthly Magazine*, new series, 7 (Jul 1829) pp. 317–28, at p 323; *Standard*, 23 Apr 1829, 4 May 1829, 8 May 1829, 12 May 1829, 8 Jun 1829, 16 Jun 1829, 10 Jun 1830,

30 Sep 1830.

[91] [Ex-MP], 'Prospects of the ministry', p. 190.

[92] [Maginn], 'The burnings in Kent', p. 576.

[93] Powell, 'Wellington administration', pp. 729–30; 'The state of the empire. Police, press, popery and foreign relations' *Monthly Magazine*, new series, 8 (Oct 1829) pp. 361–9, at p. 367; *Standard*, 23 Apr 1829, 22 Jan 1830, 20 Mar 1830, 26 May 1830; [ex-MP], 'Prospects of the ministry', pp. 194–5.

[94] Political journal of Lord Ellenborough, 16 Nov 1830, cited in B.T.Bradfield, 'Sir Richard Vyvyan and the country gentlemen' *English Historical Review* 83 (1968) pp. 729–43, at p. 731, from MS copy at TNA.

[95] Quoted in the *Standard*, 20 Apr 1829.

[96] *Standard*, 3 Jun 1829.

[97] Quoted in the *Standard*, 16 Jun 1829.

[98] [David Robinson], 'The reform of the House of Commons' *Blackwood's Magazine* 27 (Apr 1830) pp. 640–58; *Morning Journal*, 16 Jun 1829; [anon.], 'Parliamentary reform proceedings before the Committee of Privileges, and in the case of the Cinque Ports' *Fraser's Magazine* 2 (Dec 1830) pp. 612–37; *Age*, quoted in the *Standard*, 8 Jun 1829; *Morning Journal*, 27 Jul 1829.

[99] *Parliamentary Debates*, 3rd series, iii, cols. 31–3.

[100] *Parliamentary Debates*, 3rd series, iii, cols. 122, 633, 733, 745.

[101] *Parliamentary Debates*, 3rd series, iii, col. 1471.

[102] *Parliamentary Debates*, 3rd series, iii, col. 884.

[103] *Parliamentary Debates*, 3rd series, iii, col. 1203.

[104] *Parliamentary Debates*, 3rd series, iii, cols. 1090–1.

[105] *Parliamentary Debates*, 3rd series, iii, cols. 31–3.

[106] *Parliamentary Debates*, 3rd series, iii, col. 1236.

[107] *Parliamentary Debates*, 3rd series, iii, col. 1764. See also *Parliamentary Debates*, 3rd series, iii, col. 644: 'I never was of opinion that such large towns should be without representatives; but in advocating their interests I wish not to destroy those of others.'

[108] *Standard*, 6 May 1829.

[109] Earl Grey to King William III, 22 Mar 1831: *The Reform Act of 1832. The correspondence of the late Earl Grey with His Majesty King William IV and with Sir Herbert Taylor*, ed. Henry Grey, Earl Grey (2 vols, London, 1867) i, p. 185.

[110] Brock, *Great Reform Act*, p. 129.

[111] [David Robinson], 'The condition of the empire' *Blackwood's Magazine* 26 (Jul 1829) pp. 97–119, at p. 97. Robinson's indictment of the new system was expounded consistently and at some length. See also, for example, 'The taxes' *Blackwood's Magazine* 27 (Mar 1830) pp. 487–500.

[112] This would include the 10 pro-Reform Act MPs identified by Stewart, *Foundation of the Conservative Party*, p. 57, plus others returned on an Ultra platform

in 1830 (Bayntun, Schonswar), and, of course, peers such as Richmond and Manvers. Others initially leaning to the Whigs included Newcastle (Newcastle diary, 1 Dec 1830), and Winchilsea. See Brock, *Great Reform Act*, p. 104 for Vyvyan; G.M.Willis *Ernest Augustus, Duke of Cumberland and King of Hanover* (London, 1954) pp. 208–9, for Cumberland; 'A general feeling of satisfaction', *Carlisle Patriot*, quoted in *Standard*, 22 Nov 1830.

[113] [Anon.], 'The decline of Mr Huskisson and the approaching Parliament' *Fraser's Magazine* 2 (Oct 1830) pp. 251–63, at p. 262. For a similar judgement, see note 23.

CHAPTER 9

Wellington, Peel and the Conservative Party
Richard A. Gaunt

The first Duke of Wellington and Sir Robert Peel occupy a unique
position in early nineteenth-century British history, as the dominant
Conservative political figures of their age. Given the extraordinary
(and atypical) status of both men, this might be said to be an
incongruous, if not altogether contradictory, outcome. Wellington
was a soldier-politician, whose natural métier was the battlefield and the Horse Guards, and whose accommodation to the
compromises entailed in political life was never complete. Peel, by
contrast, came to be associated with precisely those accommoda-
tions of principle which contemporaries believed corrupted the
political virtue of succeeding generations. This charge, based largely
on Peel's role in returning Britain to the gold standard (through
'Peel's Act' of 1819), passing Catholic emancipation in 1829 and
overseeing the repeal of the Corn Laws in 1846, was levelled with
the greatest force and severity by Lord George Bentinck and
Benjamin Disraeli, chief amongst Peel's Conservative political
critics in the spring of 1846.[1] However, it found its echo in the work
of novelists such as Anthony Trollope. In *The Three Clerks,*
Trollope delivered a damning verdict upon what he perceived to be
the consequences of Peel's political immorality:

> Who has given so great a blow to political honesty, has done
> so much to banish from men's minds the idea of a life-
> ruling principle, as Sir Robert Peel? ... He has taught us as
> a great lesson that a man who has before him a mighty
> object may dispense with those old-fashioned rules of truth

to his neighbours and honesty to his own principles, which should guide us in ordinary life.Thrice in his political life did Sir Robert Peel change his political creed, and carry, or assist to carry, with more or less of self-gratulation, the measures of his adversaries. Thrice by doing so he kept to himself that political power which he had fairly forfeited by previous opposition to the requirements of his country ... posterity will point at him as a politician without a policy, as a statesman without a principle, as a worshipper at the altar of expediency, to whom neither vows sworn to friends, nor declarations made to his country, were in any way binding.[2] To their contemporary admirers, however, Wellington and Peel represented, 'with little stretch of fancy ... the two great spirits of the age'. Wellington, the exemplar of 'brave, undaunted, and courageous patriotism', seemed to find his perfect foil in Peel, the 'representative of enlightened political and social progress'. Wellington, through his incomparable military exploits, 'gained peace for England', whilst Peel, 'by his liberal policy [showed] the way in which England could best derive the most advantage from that peace'.[3]

It followed from these two, contrasting, interpretations of their conduct that issues of reputation, honour and consistency were crucial in the self-presentation of Wellington and Peel. This was undoubtedly so during their lifetime and has lately become a keynote in historical considerations of their lives and political conduct. Both men carefully prepared the groundwork for future historians by instituting editions of their correspondence, despatches and memoirs.[4] Wellington's well-known habit of speaking of himself as if in the third person — for after all 'he was the Duke of Wellington' — was more than an affectation born of his increasingly heroic reputation; rather it was a carefully constructed political strategy to reinforce the essential rectitude and integrity of the positions he adopted in civilian political life. Wellington's habitual self-defence, for whatever political compromises he made during the period 1818–46, was summed up in the memorable political aphorism 'How is the Queen's government to be carried on?' — a sense that the stability of government itself demanded almost any compromise, consistent with the security of the state. Peel's self-defences (for multiple 'infringements' of principle required multiple defences) were more complex and more tortuous and continue to be the subject of fierce historical debate. These too were given a particular edge, especially in the years after 1846, when Peel's extra-parliamentary reputation rose, amongst some sectors of the population, because of his role in achieving Corn Law repeal. Almost any public pronouncement made by Peel, during these years, was seized upon with alacrity for indications of his future political conduct. This situation continued until Peel's tragic death in the summer of 1850, the circumstances of which served somewhat to increase the romantic aura surrounding the departed statesman. The great 'what if?' of history — Peel's possible, future conversions — thus remained unanswered, although Trollope, for one, had few doubts as to Peel's likely course of action:

> Had Sir Robert Peel lived, and did the people now resolutely desire that the Church of England should be abandoned, that Lords and Commons should bow the neck, that the Crown should fall, who can believe that Sir Robert Peel would not be ready to carry out their views?[5]

Perhaps unsurprisingly, the Conservative Party has never been entirely sure what place to assign Wellington and Peel in the pantheon of its political heroes. Whilst Wellington left no sustained political legacy, in a party political sense, Peel's legacy has been at turns appropriated, aggregated and abrogated in equal measure. The navel-gazing exercise undertaken by political commentators, historians and biographers as to whether Peel or Disraeli was the true 'founder of modern Conservatism' has served to deflect scholars somewhat, forcing them away from considering more interesting tensions within nineteenth-century Conservatism.[6] Of these tensions, one of the more under-emphasised is the strained political relationship between Wellington and Peel themselves. Though this has often been acknowledged by historians and biographers of the two men, it has been insufficiently appreciated by those who have examined the subject in any depth. Norman Gash, who as the biographer of both men was uniquely placed to understand the relationship, acknowledged the occasional squalls between them but, perhaps understandably, absolved Peel of much responsibility for them.[7] Conversely, Frederick Mather was concerned with elevating Wellington's status in the couple's partnership after 1832; stressing the lack of personal chemistry between the two men would have been, in this respect, counter-productive.[8] More recently, Douglas Hurd has followed a distinguished line of academic historians of the Conservative Party (notably Robert Blake and his former doctoral student, Robert Stewart), in regarding Wellington principally as the 'last Tory' Prime Minister, whose removal from office in November 1830 coincided with the emergence of the new nomenclature of 'Conservative' (in an article in the *Quarterly Review* in January 1830) and the subsequent political ascent of Robert Peel. Wellington is thus associated with a particular type of Toryism (sometimes equated with Ultra-Toryism) as a road-block on the way to reform.[9]

However, one of the more interesting aspects to emerge from recent historical work on the Duke of Wellington's political career is the extent to which Wellington and Peel were necessary but uncomfortable partners in a joint Conservative political enterprise. In life, Wellington and Peel co-operated and competed with each other for the leadership of their followers and the gratitude of the nation. For most of the period between 1827 and 1846, necessity made them indispensable to one another. However, by the end of their lives, their unique respective positions in standing above the normal rules of political engagement had driven the relationship to breaking point and changed its focus away from present political exigencies to securing their future good standing with posterity. Though they were perfect allies as the predominant civilian and military figures of the age, the evolving reputations of Wellington and Peel meant that, increasingly, they were competitors in the battle for the hearts and minds of the mid-Victorian mourning public: the constituency which, in the decade after their deaths, subscribed to the statues, public amenities, medals and libraries of working men's books with which they were commemorated.[10]

* * *

On 30 June 1851, almost a year to the day since Peel's death and a little over 15 months before Wellington's demise, the Lord Chamberlain purchased, on Queen Victoria's behalf, a dual portrait of Wellington and Peel by the artist Franz Xavier Winterhalter (front cover image). The picture had been painted 'at the command of Her Majesty, from life, in 1844', and was exhibited at the premises of Messrs Paul and Dominic Colnaghi and Co., 13 and 14 Pall Mall East, only a few months before. The image was popularised for wider consumption through a mezzotint engraving by James Faed, issued by Messrs Colnaghi during the same period. Contemporaries expressed ecstasies of delight over the portrait. A number of press commentators remarked that Wellington and Peel had been captured (in the words of the *Globe*) 'in attitudes beautifully characteristic' of their habits in life. Others noted 'the firm hold of the ground which the Duke takes with both legs' and his 'hair of venerable white', which contrasted pleasingly with Peel's positioning 'with one leg forward and his hands resting in each other before him'. According to the commentators, these poses would 'strike as familiar those who have had opportunities of noticing the peculiarities of each [man]'. 'No picture ever before', the *Daily News* enthused, 'gave so completely the character of both, with the additional interest accruing from the proximity of two men so long connected in life, and now brought together on the same canvas.' This fact was the more telling because, aside from Sir Thomas Lawrence's famous portrait of Peel of 1825, it was the only major portrait for which Peel sat.[11]

The appearance of Winterhalter's portrait was accompanied by a prospectus for Faed's engraving, issued by Colnaghi and Co., which offered readers what the *Examiner* called 'a sketch of the political and personal intimacy of the Duke and Sir Robert'. 'In a few pages devoted to remarks illustrative or explanatory of the origin of the painting in question', the *Morning Advertiser* noted, 'some extremely interesting and curious observations are made respecting the political intimacy existing to the last between the Duke of Wellington and the late Sir Robert Peel.'[12]

In fact, the prospectus offered a paean of praise to the perceived intimacy and unity of interest it believed to have subsisted between the two men and observed that Winterhalter's portrait had paid testament to a friendship which it would 'appropriately record'. According to the prospectus, respect for Wellington was 'a religion' with Peel 'that pervaded his whole being … and was cherished by him until the last moment of life':

> The importance of this connection is visible in all the great measures which have occupied the attention of the present generation, whilst to the influence of their friendship may be traced the identity of purpose characteristic of all the public acts of these statesmen … From the hour in which [they] were first associated in the administration of public affairs, the mind of either would appear to have adopted that of the other as his guide, and moral appeal.[13]

* * *

In spite of the self-promotional 'puffing' of Messrs Colnaghi and Co., it is hard to avoid the impression that, unconsciously or not, Winterhalter's portrait had in fact captured something of the underlying tension which marked relations between Wellington and Peel. The image undoubtedly has all the warmth and affection of Winterhalter's other compositions, and plays up the physical stature of the two men. Yet for all the physical equality and proximity between them, there appears to be a detachment and distance which is reinforced by the fact that each man's gaze is crossing, rather than meeting, that of the other. Undoubtedly, some of the formality and fixity of position adopted by the subjects is reflective of the fact that the portrait was copied from a much larger canvas commissioned to commemorate the reception of Louis-Philippe, King of the French, at Windsor Castle (8 October 1844), in which the two men were stood with their gaze drawn to the King and his entourage.[14]

At the time the original portrait was commissioned, in 1844, Wellington and Peel had been political comrades-in-arms for nearly 20 years. Peel, then at the height of his powers as Prime Minister, was approaching 60, whilst Wellington, happily restored to his position as commander-in-chief of the army since 1842, had just turned 75. Though the two men had been cabinet colleagues under Lord Liverpool during the 1820s, it was the formation of George Canning's administration, in 1827, which forced them together, creating a political partnership which neither man found it possible to dispense with thereafter. According to Colnaghi's prospectus, from this period could be traced 'the development of those mutual sympathies destined by Providence to influence the government of the world'.[15]

However, as one of the leading 'Liberal Tories' of the period, Peel was in many respects closer to George Canning's political views at this time and, during the opening months of Wellington's ministry in 1828, was on better terms with the Canningite ministers Huskisson, Grant, Palmerston and Dudley, than almost anyone else in the Cabinet.[16] It was shared hostility to Catholic emancipation which bound Wellington and Peel together in opposition to Canning's ministry and which continued to be the hallmark of the Duke's administration, until the spring of 1829. Peel's sacrifice in staying in office to lead the Catholic Relief Bill through the House of Commons, after 20 years of hostility to such a measure, created a debt of honour which Wellington later repaid by standing alongside Peel during the repeal of the Corn Laws in 1846.

That Peel remained in office after Emancipation had passed and did not retire to the backbenches to rebuild relations with his erstwhile followers was entirely characteristic of his executive view of government and a tacit recognition of his indispensability to the government's management of the House of Commons. That is why Wellington flirted with resigning the premiership to Peel in the summer of 1830. Denis Le Marchant made a pointed reference to the joint nature of the ministry's leadership, as well as the strained relations between the two men at this time, when he observed that neither Peel nor the Duke had 'social habits. Indeed they even associate very little with each other, and keeping themselves also aloof from the subordinate members of *their* government, they [know] very little of what [is] going on.' Palmerston had made much the same observation two years before.[17]

By this point, each man had become *primus inter pares* in their own chamber and this made them the inevitable part of any Conservative government which either afterwards attempted to form. As Wellington commented, with evident exasperation, at the end of December 1830, 'What is the use of talking of *my* making bargains or arrangements? Can *I* execute them? Will Peel consent to anything? Can *I* do anything without Peel [?]' Lady Salisbury put the matter more crisply, three years later: 'It is evident the Duke feels he cannot do without [Peel], though he never can entirely depend upon him.'[18]

Rather than being a source of strength, the two men's individual dominance in their respective chambers created tensions which were reinforced by a sense of constitutional etiquette. As Wellington explained to Charles Arbuthnot in November 1840:

> The truth is that he in the House of Commons and I in the House of Lords cannot originate a communication, either with the other, upon the particular business of the House, in

which each takes a part; and there can be no natural communication till the business of the two requires communication or is likely to clash ... All this naturally separates me from Sir Robert and his councils, and I don't meet him excepting by accident or when the cause of the public renders our communication necessary.[19]

For his part, Peel frequently cited the different strategies required to lead the Commons, as compared with the Lords, during the Conservative Party's years in opposition from 1835 to 1841, as a reason for his many tactical disagreements with the Duke.[20] In this respect, it is perhaps telling that Sir James Graham, who had seceded from the Whig government in 1834 along with Lord Stanley and other members of the 'Derby Dilly', and who afterwards refused to join Peel's 'Hundred Days' ministry precisely because of Wellington's prominent role within it, had by 1840 come to hold so high an opinion of Wellington's indispensability to the Conservative Party that he was at pains to negotiate, through Arbuthnot, some form of rapprochement between the Duke and Peel.[21]

Viewing Wellington and Peel as indispensable counterweights to one another's governments helps to explain three things about their relationship after 1827: first, the tremendous degree of influence exercised by Peel during Wellington's government of 1828–30 over an increasingly wide range of domestic issues; second, Peel's ability to frustrate Wellington's attempt to form a government in the final stages of the Reform Bill during the 'Days of May' in 1832; and third, the essential role played by Wellington in the autumn of 1834, when he effectively installed Peel as leader of the Conservative Party by accepting the premiership from William IV on an interim basis. It also explains why an increasingly deaf Wellington remained in Peel's second ministry, without official portfolio, during the period 1841–6, lending the weight and authority of his name and presence to the government.[22] To adapt a famous observation of Margaret Thatcher, Peel found that 'every

Prime Minister needs a Welly' — a dependable, loyal and trust-worthy buffer between the vast mass of Conservative backbenchers and a detached, authoritarian leader. According to John Campbell,

> [Thatcher] meant two rather different things … First, every Prime Minister needs an authoritative deputy to chair committees, resolve disputes and ward off trouble. But she also meant that a Prime Minister needs one senior colleague with no ambition of his own to guard his (or her) back against the plots of jealous rivals.

The same might be said (with some reservations) about Wellington and Peel.[23]

The essential function which Wellington played, in this respect, is well illustrated in a letter from the fourth Duke of Newcastle to his daughter Lady Charlotte Pelham-Clinton, immediately after Peel's resignation as Prime Minister in April 1835:

> It is all over, Sir R. Peel has resigned! What on earth could have induced him to adopt such a course — it will be productive of certain ruin & destruction to the country. I most deeply lament the event — and I cannot in language express how intensely I deplore it — The Revolution will now go grand train under every possible disadvantage to ourselves — God preserve us, his good providence can alone do it — and will eventually do so, if we deserve it. After leaving my lawyers I walked with [your brothers] William and Robert to the Duke of Wellington's, hoping to see him and to enlist him on my side, or at all events to know what he desired on which I should have shaped my course and either have persevered or despaired.[24]

Given the querulous political relationship which Wellington and Newcastle enjoyed, it is a remarkable testament of the Duke's abilities to make Peel's leadership palatable to even the most unrepentant of Ultra-Tories to find him acting the part of diplomatist and peacemaker. It was a role which Wellington quietly

but resolutely undertook, with all shades of opinion within the
Conservative Party, time and again, in succeeding years.[25]

* * *

Wellington's ability to empathise with others' misgivings about Peel
may have been heightened by an awareness of his own brittle and
occasionally fractious relationship with him. As the Duke observed,
somewhat pointedly, in February 1833:

> it is possible for two men to serve the public ... but there
> must exist candour, truth and fairness in the views of both;
> and the line of proceeding of each should be taken without
> the desire of contradicting and opposing himself to the
> views of the other.[26]

Wellington and Peel's relationship was always marked with a sense
of respect, mixed with the sort of detachment which Winterhalter
captured in his portrait of the two men. Peel's periodic, public
declarations of praise for Wellington, at major set-piece orations
such as the Mansion House dinners of 1835 and 1849, were
regarded, by more than one contemporary, as garnered for effect.
In the first, Peel somewhat exaggeratedly observed that he and
Wellington had 'never been [for] one moment estranged by any
difference on political subjects', nor their relationship 'embittered
by the slightest effusion of petty jealousy'.[27] In fact, there were
extended periods of acrimony, recrimination and misunderstanding
between them. That much of this is recorded from Wellington's
perspective tells us something about his own sensitivities, where
Peel was concerned, as well as the tremendous (almost crippling)
degree of self-discipline which Peel seems to have exercised over
his own emotions and his restraint in recording them.

Much of this ill-feeling was the consequence of Wellington's resignation as Prime Minister in November 1830. In one
of several, heated epistles to Mrs Arbuthnot, after the event,
Wellington fumed:

You may be very right respecting the principle of any government to be formed under our auspices in the future. But I come back to the old story. What will Peel say or do? Recollect that I was always ready to go on. I did not break up the government. To use a vulgar expression, I did not dirty my own nest by way of excuse for quitting it. Before we talk of any system for the future, we must see how the gentleman is disposed to act who did these things, and who must have it in his power to choose whether he will do them again.[28]

At the heart of the dispute was a disagreement as to the correct manner and timing of the government's resignation. The same issue re-surfaced at the end of Peel's 'Hundred Days' ministry in April 1835, and again in June 1846. On each occasion, Wellington's argument was essentially the same: a perception of being placed in a danger 'which for our own characters and the safety of the country we must remain as long as we could'. On each occasion, Peel ignored his advice not to resign.[29]

Peel's unwillingness to launch a frontal assault on the Whig ministry, during the 1830s, was also castigated by Wellington as a weak policy. In October 1833, he told Lady Salisbury that Peel was 'afraid — afraid of everything' — a comment which echoes his later commentary on the Repeal of the Corn Laws: 'rotten potatoes have done it all, they have put Peel in a damned fright.'[30]

Both men accused one another of lacking moral courage in their political conduct. Peel is reported to have said that 'the last man who has [Wellington's] ear, always has him', whilst Wellington told Lady Salisbury that 'if [Peel] will not come forward and sacrifice himself for the public good, we must make it without him.' This was empty rhetoric, in the circumstances, as the failure of Wellington's abortive 'May Days' government of 1832 and his own actions at the end of November 1834 had proved, and was in any case rather hard on Peel, who had sacrificed a good deal of his reputation for consistency in helping to achieve Catholic emancipation in 1829.[31] Nevertheless, whilst Wellington told Lord Camden, at the end of December 1832, that he and Peel 'were upon the best terms as we have always been', only two months later he concluded that they 'would never again serve the public in the same council'; a perception which Peel appears to have shared. Charles Greville thought it was all part of an ill-concealed conceit: 'Peel and the Duke are ostensibly great friends, and the ridiculous farce is still kept up of each admiring what he would not do himself, but what the other did.'[32]

What Greville called the 'ill blood' between the two men was also kept up by Wellington's closest confidants, headed by Charles and Harriet Arbuthnot. Lady Salisbury thought that the couple made 'the worst of all Peel does in the eyes of the Duke' in order 'to persuade him that he intends to slight or neglect him in trifles where I am sure no such intention exists'. In an effort to bring the two men together, she was asked to mediate between them. The difficulty, as she observed, was that neither was known for their sociability with others, let alone with each other. Wellington, she observed pointedly, 'is so accustomed to be courted, and [Peel] has so much sensitiveness and plebeian pride that they are easily led to take mutual offence'.[33]

The low-point in relations was reached in late 1833 and early 1834. Wellington confessed to Charles Arbuthnot that he had not had any communication with Peel 'for some time upon any subjects, excepting the mere forms of society'. Their estrangement was solidified by Wellington's acceptance of the Chancellorship of Oxford University — a position which Peel might have considered himself eligible for, considering his own academic and political connections with the University, had the dons not turned against him for his part in helping Wellington achieve Catholic emancipation. Peel subsequently left for his Italian holiday, in the autumn of 1834, having had little formal communication with the Duke for months.[34] When he returned, as a result of Wellington's recommendation to King William IV, he found himself thrust in to the leadership of the

Conservative Party, the premiership and a general election which his own instincts opposed but which he was forced to accept. Little wonder that so many correspondents pressed Peel with flattering appraisals of Wellington's handling of affairs in the intervening period, for they had helped to achieve what no-one else, least of all Peel himself, had contemplated: Peel's own explicit assumption of leadership over the Conservative Party.[35]

* * *

Though the *froideur* between the two men was an evident cause of dissatisfaction for their friends and followers, it might reasonably be asked how far the lack of communication between Wellington and Peel affected the Conservative recovery of the 1830s, or the subsequent ministry of 1841–6, given that, as Wellington himself admitted (on more than one occasion), 'I generally, indeed always, find that without any previous communication he and I are found upon the same ground' on most important measures.[36] The largest area of disagreement between them, perhaps unsurprisingly, arose in matters of foreign and defence policy; Portugal in 1833, Canada in 1840, and the state of the coastal defences at the end of 1845. On the subject of the currency, where Peel's views in favour of the gold standard were fixed, as Boyd Hilton has argued, to the point of doctrinal rigidity, Wellington knew better than to intercede — however much he was urged to do so.[37]

Whilst Wellington dutifully marched his troops into line behind Peel for the final great battle of repeal, at the start of 1846, this was from the traditional vantage point of supporting the Queen's government, in the absence of all reasonable alternatives, rather than from extolling the virtues of the measure itself.[38] In stark contrast with the position in the House of Commons, Wellington fulfilled his duty to Queen Victoria as well as to Peel by ensuring the legislation passed safely through the House of Lords, whilst bequeathing to Lord Stanley, his successor as leader of the

Conservative peers, a party much better oriented towards affecting a re-union with its Peelite minority and creating a meaningful opposition to the incoming Whig administration of Lord John Russell. Wellington's retirement from the leadership of the party in the Lords, after 18 years, was thus adroit and diplomatic. He had won over Stanley (who had voluntarily gone to the Lords, effectively as Wellington's deputy, in 1844, as much out of frustration at his own relationship with Peel as from a sense of frustrated ambition) as he had earlier won over Graham, helping to thwart a potentially cataclysmic Protectionist revolt under his leadership. Perhaps because Wellington saw the issue of repeal less dogmatically than Peel and was less personally associated with the defence of the Corn Laws up to that point, the Duke was able to ensure stability for the legislation, the Lords and the party; under the circumstances, this was quite an achievement.[39]

By contrast, the scale of Conservative hostility to Peel in the House of Commons, the personal abuse which he suffered on the occasion and his very individual identification with the repeal measure, divided MPs much more severely. Peel relied on the votes of the opposition to secure the bill's passage and, in the course of the next four years, proceeded to occupy an almost unprecedented position in British political life. The Peelites returned about 90 MPs in the 1847 general election and held the balance of power, allowing the government to remain in office where the combined Conservative MPs could have defeated them. It was an anomalous and uncomfortable position for many of the Peelites and some of them, notably Gladstone, were not shy of recording the fact.[40] Nor was this outcome inevitable. Wellington had unsuccessfully tried to prevent Peel's resignation at the end of June 1846, advising him to divide his opponents — who were then mustering in readiness to defeat the government's Irish Coercion Bill — with a vote on the sugar duties. Peel ignored the advice and went down to defeat at the hands of what Wellington famously described as a 'blackguard combination' of disgruntled Protectionist, Irish, Radical and

Whig-Liberal MPs.[41]

A month later, the breach between the two men was brought home visibly by an episode which Lord Ellenborough relayed to Lord Clare:

> The other day the Duke [of Wellington] riding down to the Horse Guards saw Peel riding towards him and clearly intending to pass him with a 'How d'ya do, Duke?'. This the Duke determined should not be the case, so he stopped him, and asked him to ride back with him which Peel did. The Duke then gave him his full confidence — spoke of the position of the government — of his own, of Peel's, and of the course to be pursued. To all this Peel replied not one word and, at the Horse Guards, turned round saying, 'Goodbye, I am glad to see you so well.'

The impact of this incident upon Wellington was signified by the fact that, in addition to Ellenborough, the Duke subsequently relayed the story to his son and heir, Lord Douro, his confidante, Lady Westmorland, and his Boswell, Lord Mahon, each of whom recorded it in separate accounts. The meeting was the only one between the two men for some time after repeal and the memory of it lingered. That it penetrated the Iron Duke's usual defences is signified by a telling outburst to Ellenborough: 'This is the man, for whom I have been sacrificing myself during the last six months!'[42]

It was precisely this feeling of resentment, on Wellington's part, and incomprehension, on Peel's, which drove the two men apart during the final years of their lives. Peel's unexpected death, as the result of a riding accident, on 2 July 1850, set this aside — as most tragic and unexpected political deaths invariably do — giving rise to a moving tribute from Wellington in the House of Lords in which he stated that he had 'never ceased to enjoy [Peel's] friendship'. However, as Greville rather tartly observed:

> Notwithstanding the friendly and eulogistic terms in which he spoke of Sir Robert Peel … it is very certain that the

Duke disliked him and had a bad opinion of him [and] in his heart bitterly lamented and disapproved of his case about repeal of the Corn Laws ... because it produced a fresh and final break-up of the Conservative Party which he considered the greatest evil that could befall the country.[43]

It was exactly this last point which has been most under-appreciated by historians of the Conservative Party. Given that Wellington had been describing his colleagues (in opposition to Canning) as a *parti conservateur* in 1827, was still ostensibly the party's leader when the *Quarterly Review* used the term 'Conservative' on the first major occasion in 1830 and was the preferred choice for Prime Minister of both William IV in 1834 ('Hundred Days') and Queen Victoria in 1839 ('Bedchamber Crisis'), there is good reason for suggesting that, rather than the 'last Tory' Prime Minister of Britain, Wellington might truly be regarded as the first leader of the Conservative Party and thus its first Prime Minister.[44] Wellington enjoyed better relations with the Crown and the House of Lords, over a longer period, than Peel ever achieved, and had a fuller sense, insofar as the Conservative Party was concerned, of the need to meet the contingencies of the present whilst planning for the future. This was evident both in Wellington's dexterous handling of the Conservative peers in the House of Lords between 1832 and 1841, when the inbuilt Conservative majority threatened to ride roughshod over its more liberal counterparts in the House of Commons, as well as in the Duke's handling of the Corn Law crisis. Though Wellington may not have shared Disraeli's prescription for privileging the claims of party above all else, his fears for a political future which lacked its stability were apparent throughout his management of the Conservative peers in 1846. Wellington exhibited none of what might be called Peel's 'scorched earth' policy towards his followers in the House of Commons. Far from being, as Norman Gash argued, the 'least political' of party leaders, Wellington was, in fact, one of the most political, exhibiting a political mindset which remained undiminished in subsequent years.[45]

Wellington was particularly critical of Peel's attempt to shore up Russell's Whig government after 1846, rather than face the prospect of a Protectionist government under Stanley and Bentinck. In this, he shared something in common with Peel's leading Peelite supporters, not least Gladstone himself.[46] Moreover, Wellington lived to see a minority Conservative government installed under Stanley's leadership (as fourteenth Earl of Derby) in 1852. Indeed, he unwittingly sent it down to posterity as the 'Who? Who?' ministry as, increasingly deaf, he strained to hear the names of the somewhat unfamiliar individuals who comprised its leading officers. This was an outcome which unsettled Wellington less than it would have done Peel. In 1849, Wellington is reported to have:

> abused Peel, on whom he lavished all sorts of execration. He said that free trade had ruined the country: that he had supported all their measures against his will in order to keep out Cobden and Company — and that he feared change now for the same reason.[47]

* * *

By contrast, Peel's role in the repeal of the Corn Laws transformed him, in some quarters, from a mere politician in to a personality who stood above the normal rules of political engagement. This process was consciously encouraged by Peel, both through his over-generous praise of Richard Cobden, the leader of the Anti-Corn Law League, in his resignation speech, and in the anomalous position he occupied in British politics in the period 1846–50. Peel's death reinforced this process with a rash of populist commemorations, ranging from penny subscriptions for a working man's library to commemorative pottery, public parks, towers and statues.[48] This popular apotheosis was something which Wellington lived long enough to see. An edition of Peel's speeches was rushed out in 1853, whilst Peel's literary executors, Philip Mahon and Edward

Cardwell, advanced plans for the publication of Peel's *Memoirs*, a posthumous defence of his role in Catholic emancipation and Corn Law repeal.[49] Whilst there were political objections to the immediate publication of the volume dealing with the Corn Laws, considering the possibility of a revived political battle over the issue, there were none in respect of the volume concerning emancipation. This could be published immediately, subject to the approval of those, like Wellington, whose correspondence formed an integral part of it. Otherwise, as Mahon observed, it would have to 'await the period which in the course of nature cannot I fear be very many years delayed, of the termination of [Wellington's] glorious career'.[50]

Meanwhile, Wellington's reputation, commemorated in his latter days in a diverse number of ways, including the controversial Wellington Monument, was secured almost wholly in connection with his military career, with only a grudging nod to his political role after 1818. The lack of an edition of his papers for the post-1832 period reinforced this sense of neglect; regrettably so, given that, as Disraeli commented, Wellington's *Dispatches* for the period 1819–32 were the 'best reading he had ever had'. The keynote for interpretations of the Duke's political career was struck, early on, by *The Times,* whose famous obituary article on the Duke praised him with faint damns, observing that, in politics, he 'had to deal with events over which no individual mind can exercise a commanding influence'. Equally, an otherwise admiring essayist, Sir William Fraser, was moved to observe:

> That [Wellington] did his best no one can doubt: that his best was a failure few will hesitate to say ... The Duke ultimately surrendered his position in relation to any measure, however much he disapproved.[51]

Interpretations of Wellington and Peel have moved on somewhat from Fraser's day, influenced largely by the deposit of the two men's personal papers in the British Museum (afterwards British Library) in the 1920s, in the case of Peel, and the University of

Southampton in the 1980s, in that of Wellington. It is only comparatively recently that the full import of Wellington's political role, after 1819, has come to register within the historiography of nineteenth-century British politics.[52] That both men were titanic figures — dominant, egotistical, self-assured, aware of their place in history and destiny — may not be doubted, but historians have a greater understanding of the crucial difference in temperament which influenced their calculations and affected their strategies as politicians. As Richard Davis has perceptively observed, Wellington 'put a comparatively low value on his own opinions and consistency — in marked contrast to Peel. That is because he put the highest value on what he called necessity, which can roughly be translated as the national good.'[53] For all the rigidity implied by the ferrous qualities of the epithet 'Iron Duke', Wellington was actually more willing to concede (in a political sense) than many contemporaries (other than Ultra-Tories of the Newcastle variety) appreciated, whilst Peel, as recent scholarship has suggested, was more dogmatic than the castigations of Disraeli and Trollope might suggest. This meant that, for different reasons, both Wellington and Peel became increasingly pre-occupied with how future ages would regard their honour and reputation. If Peel's credentials as a man of heroic political vision are no longer unassailable, the transformation in Wellington's historical fortunes, insofar as his political conduct after 1818 is concerned, is attributable to the opening up of the Wellington Papers and the meticulous scholarship to which this has given rise, over the past three decades.[54] The Conservative Party may yet find cause to commemorate Wellington's long-term contribution to the strength and stability of the party. That this has not, hitherto, been the case is a salutary reminder that posterity takes the long view.

References

[1] R.A.Gaunt, 'Disraeli, Peel and the Corn Laws. The making of a Conservative reputation' *The Historian* 97 (2008) pp. 30-3. Also see Lord Lexden, 'Peel and

Disraeli' at <http://www.alistairlexden.org.uk/news/peel-and-disraeli> (accessed 14 September 2011).

[2] A.Trollope *The three clerks* (London, 1858) chapter 29.

[3] *Criticisms on the engraving by Samuel Cousins, ARA of the late Right Honourable Sir Robert Peel, Bart, MP Painted by Sir Thomas Lawrence, PRA and of the engraving by James Faed of Field Marshal the Duke of Wellington, KG and the late Right Honourable Sir Robert Peel, Bart, MP painted by Winterhalter* (London, n.d., but clearly late 1850), p. 12.

[4] R.A.Gaunt *Sir Robert Peel. The life and legacy* (London, 2010); C.M.Woolgar, 'Wellington's *Dispatches* and their editor, Colonel Gurwood' in *Wellington Studies I* ed. C.M.Woolgar (Southampton, 1996) pp. 189–210.

[5] Trollope, *Three clerks*.

[6] Gaunt, *Peel*, chapter 5.

[7] N.Gash *Sir Robert Peel: the life of Sir Robert Peel after 1830* (London, 1986) pp. 33–5, 52–3, 61–4, 71–4, 140–1, 177–8, 244–8. It is worth recording here that Gash (who died on the 240th anniversary of Wellington's birth, 1 May 2009) became increasingly interested in and to an extent sympathetic towards Wellington. This process culminated in Gash's entry on the Duke in the *ODNB*, lviii, pp. 1–29.

[8] F.C.Mather, '"Nestor or Achilles?" The Duke of Wellington in British politics, 1832–1846' in *Wellington: studies in the military and political career of the first Duke of Wellington* ed. N.Gash (Manchester, 1990) pp. 170–95, and 'Wellington and Peel: conservative statesmen of the 1830s' *Transactions of the Peel Society* 5–6 (1985–6) pp. 7–23.

[9] D.Hurd *Wellington and Peel: from Tory to Conservative* (Southampton, 2006); R.Blake *The Conservative Party from Peel to Major* (London, 1997) pp. 30–1; R.Stewart *The foundation of the Conservative Party* (London, 1978) pp. 49–58.

[10] D.Read *Peel and the Victorians* (Oxford, 1987); P.W.Sinnema *The wake of Wellington. Englishness in 1852* (Ohio, 2006).

[11] *Criticisms on the engraving by Samuel Cousins*, p. 11; O.Millar *The Victorian pictures in the collection of Her Majesty the Queen: text* (Cambridge, 1992) pp. 288–90, 320–1. The larger canvas from which the dual portrait is derived is at Windsor Castle, the separate portrait of Wellington and Peel is at Buckingham Palace. A portrait of Peel's head, copied from the dual portrait, was presented (at the command of Queen Victoria) to Julia, Lady Peel, in 1851, as a mark of respect and affection for the departed statesman. The portrait is still held by Peel's descendants.

[12] *Criticisms on the engraving by Samuel Cousins*, pp. 10, 12.

[13] *Field Marshal the Duke of Wellington, KG and the Right Hon Sir Robert Peel, Bart MP* (London, 1850), frontispiece, pp. 1–2.

[14] Millar, *Victorian pictures in the collection of Her Majesty the Queen,*

pp. 288–90, 320–21.

[15] Hurd, *Wellington and Peel*, p. 3.

[16] Gaunt, *Peel*, pp. 74–80.

[17] E.A.Smith *Reform or revolution? A diary of Reform in England, 1830–32* (Stroud 1992) p. 32 (italics added); Palmerston to Laurence Sulivan, 20 Sep 1828, in *The letters of the third Viscount Palmerston to Laurence and Elizabeth Sulivan, 1804–1863* ed. K.Bourne (Royal Historical Society, Camden, 4th Series, 23; London, 1979) p. 215.

[18] AW to Harriet Arbuthnot, 26 Dec 1830, in *Wellington and his friends* ed. Gerald Wellesley, seventh Duke of Wellington (London, 1965) p. 92; Lady Salisbury's diary, 22 Dec 1833, in *Prime Ministers' papers: Wellington, Political Correspondence, Volume I: 1833–1834* ed. John Brooke and Julia Gandy (London, 1975), [hereafter, *PMP*], p. 397.

[19] AW to Charles Arbuthnot, 16 Nov 1840, in *The correspondence of Charles Arbuthnot* ed. A.Aspinall (Royal Historical Society, Camden 3rd Series, 65; London, 1941) pp. 223–4. For an earlier example of the same issue, AW to Arbuthnot, 23 May 1834, *PMP*, p. 541.

[20] C.S.Parker *Sir Robert Peel from his private papers* (2nd edition, 3 vols., London, 1899) iii, pp. 366–7.

[21] *Correspondence of Charles Arbuthnot*, pp. 217–20; I am indebted for this point to B.P.Arnold, "'A Whig and something more": Sir James Graham, party and politics, *c*.1810–1846' (unpublished DPhil thesis, University of Oxford, 2011).

[22] P.Jupp *British politics on the eve of Reform: the Duke of Wellington's administration, 1828–30* (Basingstoke, 1998) and R.W.Davis *Wellington, Peel and the politics of the 1830s and 1840s* (Southampton, 2002).

[23] <http://www.independent.co.uk/arts-entertainment/books/reviews/splendid-splendid-the-authorised-biography-of-willie-whitelaw-by-mark-garnett-and-ian-aitken-604683.html> (accessed 14 September 2011).

[24] Newcastle to Charlotte Pelham-Clinton, 8 Apr 1835, University of Nottingham, Manuscripts and Special Collections, NPC 2/17/1.

[25] *Unrepentant Tory. Political selections from the diaries of the fourth Duke of Newcastle-under-Lyne, 1827–1838* ed. R.A.Gaunt (Woodbridge, 2006).

[26] AW to Charles Arbuthnot, 12 Feb 1833, *PMP*, p. 74.

[27] E.Ashley *The life of Henry John Temple, Viscount Palmerston, 1846–1865, with selections from his speeches and correspondence* (2 vols., London, 1876) ii, pp. 119–20; Hurd, *Wellington and Peel,* pp. 5–6.

[28] AW to Harriet Arbuthnot, 28 Dec 1830, *Wellington and his friends*, pp. 92–3.

[29] Ellenborough diary, 26 Mar 1835, TNA, PRO 30/12/28/5, pp. 230–9. Elsewhere, Ellenborough noted that Wellington was 'annoyed at Peel's mode of dealing with his recommendations' for patronage (14 Dec 1834, p. 71).

[30] Lady Salisbury's diary, 25 Oct 1833, *PMP* pp. 345–6; *The diaries of Charles*

Greville ed. E.Pearce with D.Pearce (London, 2005) p. 241.

[31] *Disraeli's reminiscences* ed. H.M.Swartz and M.Swartz (London, 1975) p. 121; also see *The journal of Mrs Arbuthnot, 1820–1832* ed. F.Bamford and G.Wellesley, seventh Duke of Wellington (2 vols., London, 1950) ii, p. 230 (5 Jan 1829).

[32] AW to Camden, 8 Dec 1832, Centre for Kentish Studies, Maidstone, Camden Papers U840/C266/17; AW to Charles Arbuthnot, 12 Feb 1833, *PMP*, p. 74; Greville's diary, 31 May 1832, in Smith, *Diary of Reform*, p. 133; Greville's diary, 26 Oct 1832, in C.Hibbert, *Greville's England. Selections from the diaries of Charles Greville, 1818–1860* (London, 1981) p. 105.

[33] Lady Salisbury's diary, 11 May 1834, *PMP*, p. 529; Ellenborough's diary, 19 Feb 1835, TNA, PRO 30/12/28/5, notes Peel would not dine with Wellington at the Salisburys: 'This, I think, looks ill.'

[34] AW to Charles Arbuthnot, 23 May 1834, 23 Aug 1834, in *PMP*, pp. 541, 641.

[35] Gaunt, *Peel*, pp. 87–99.

[36] AW to Charles Arbuthnot, 16 Nov 1840, *Correspondence of Charles Arbuthnot*, pp. 223–4; AW to Camden, 8 Dec 1832, Centre for Kentish Studies, Camden Papers U840/C266/17,

[37] Mahon to AW and reply, 15–16 Mar 1833, *PMP*, pp. 124–6; Gaunt, *Peel*, chapter 3.

[38] For one interpretation of these events, see I.McLean, 'Wellington and the Corn Laws 1845–6: a study in heresthetic', in *Wellington Studies III* ed. C.M.Woolgar (Southampton 1999) pp. 227–56. Also see Robert Morton's chapter, below, pp. 286–98.

[39] On Wellington and Stanley, see R.W.Davis *A political history of the House of Lords, 1811–1846* (Stanford, 2008) chapter 23, and A.Hawkins *The forgotten prime minister. The 14th Earl of Derby* (2 vols., Oxford 2007) i, chapters 5–6.

[40] Gaunt, *Peel*, chapter 7; also see R.A.Gaunt, 'Gladstone and Peel's mantle', in *William Gladstone: new studies and perspectives* ed. R.Swift, R.Quinault and R.Clayton Windscheffel (Farnham, 2012) pp. 31–50.

[41] AW to Peel, 21 Jun 1846, Parker, *Sir Robert Peel*, iii, pp. 365–6. Richard Cobden also advised the dissolution of Parliament, though for different reasons: Gaunt, *Peel*, p. 130.

[42] Ellenborough to Clare, 9 Aug 1846, TNA, Ellenborough Papers, PRO 30/12/21/1–2, ff. 356–8; Lady Westmorland to Lord Westmorland, 23 Jul 1846, in *Correspondence of Lady Burghersh with the Duke of Wellington* ed. Lady Rose Weigall (London, 1903) p. 177; P.H.Stanhope, fifth Earl Stanhope *Notes of conversations with the Duke of Wellington 1831–1851* ed. E.Longford (London, 1998) p. 247; Broughton diary, 14 Apr 1848, in *Recollections of a long life by Lord Broughton (John Cam Hobhouse). With additional extracts from his private diaries* ed. Charlotte Carleton, Lady Dorchester (6 vols., London, 1909–11), vi, pp. 217–18.

[43] Hurd, *Wellington and Peel,* p. 8; Greville diary, 18 Sep 1852, in *Diaries of Charles Greville,* ed. Pearce, p. 290.

[44] A point first made by N.Gash, 'Wellington and Peel' in *The Conservative leadership, 1832–1932* ed. D.Southgate (London, 1974) p. 35.

[45] Gash 'Wellington and Peel', p. 36.

[46] Gaunt, 'Gladstone and Peel's mantle'.

[47] Disraeli to Lady Londonderry, 30 Apr 1849, in *Benjamin Disraeli: letters* ed. J.A.W.Gunn *et al.* (8 vols, Toronto, 1982–2009), v, p. 175.

[48] Gaunt, *Peel,* chapter 8.

[49] *Speeches delivered in the House of Commons by the late Rt Hon Sir Robert Peel* (4 vols., London, 1853); *Memoirs of Sir Robert Peel* ed. P.H.Stanhope, fifth Earl Stanhope (Lord Mahon) and Edward Cardwell (2 vols., London, 1856–7).

[50] Mahon to Cardwell, 11 Oct 1851, TNA, Cardwell Papers, PRO 30/48/53, ff. 64–6. Wellington commended Peel's choice of literary executors, remarking to Mahon that 'he knew that you would make no improper use of [his papers] — that you would use them only for the use of history': Stanhope, *Notes of conversations with ... Wellington,* p. 247.

[51] *The Times,* 18 Nov 1852; Sir William Fraser *Words on Wellington* (London, 1889) pp. 86, 110, 142.

[52] This is not to under-emphasise the importance of E.Longford *Wellington. Pillar of State* (London, 1972), the first full-scale biography to be based upon the (then privately held) correspondence, which gave due weight to Wellington's role in civilian life after 1815. Like R.Blake's *Disraeli* (London, 1966), it combined solid and original research with a highly readable style. As a Pakenham (by marriage), Lady Longford could claim to be part of a tradition of family hagiography towards Wellington, epitomised in the successive works of the seventh Duke of Wellington as historian and editor (for example, nn.18, 31 above). This tradition has lately been revived in J.Wellesley *Wellington. A journey through my family* (London, 2008). For an alternative reading of Wellington's post-1815 career, see N.Thompson *Wellington after Waterloo* (London, 1986).

[53] Davis, *Lords of parliament,* p. 258.

[54] In addition to those published works already cited, key developments to emerge from this process include the annual Wellington lecture (since 1989) and *Wellington Studies* (5 volumes since 1996), as well as the database of the first Duke's papers, at <http://www.southampton.ac.uk/archives/catalogue-databases/wellintro.html> (accessed 14 September 2011).

CHAPTER 10

A melancholy sight: Wellington and the Protectionists
Robert Morton

The Protectionists presented the Duke of Wellington with a series of painful dilemmas at the end of his life. While he largely agreed with their political outlook, he hated them for splitting the Conservative Party and for destabilising the political scene. Many statesmen as distressed as Wellington was by the fracturing of the Tory party in 1846 would have stepped back from the fray. He was in his late seventies, still Commander-in-Chief of the army, and had nothing to prove. But Wellington was prevented from retiring from public life by a powerful sense of duty, coupled perhaps (as Disraeli alleged) with a need to be in the thick of the action.[1] So Wellington soldiered on miserably, sometimes supporting the Protectionists, at other times opposing them and, from time to time, intentionally or not, undermining them. This paper charts the ambivalent relationship Wellington had with the Protectionist party and its two main leaders, Lord Stanley (from 1851 the fourteenth Earl of Derby) and Disraeli.

In common with many of his contemporaries, Wellington had very different views of Stanley and Disraeli. Wellington rated Stanley's talents highly, and saw in him the man who would take over the leadership in the Lords, and probably the party. Disraeli was ignored by the Duke; they had just three exchanges of correspondence — long before Disraeli achieved anything in the political sphere — and a search failed to find a single reference to Disraeli in any of Wellington's papers or speeches from 1840 to

1852.

Disraeli was respectful to Wellington in his few direct dealings with him in the 1830s. He claimed — not very convincingly — in 1835 that he was only fighting for the seat of High Wycombe for a third time 'unwillingly', because he felt it 'a point of duty to yield to the solicitations of that great man, who has delivered Europe and saved England'.[2] After he lost, Disraeli told the Duke: 'if the devotion of my energies to your cause, IN or OUT, can ever avail you, Your Grace may count upon one, who seeks not greater satisfaction than that of serving a really great man.'[3]

Disraeli had strange ideas of what service to a great man involved. In the Commons from 1837, he shared the general Tory annoyance at Wellington's often supportive approach to the fading Whig government of Lord Melbourne. For example, on 20 January 1838, he wrote of how 'Our peers mustered thick ... but the Duke of Wellington rose and spoilt all with his generosity and all that. Great disgust in Tory ranks, even among the highest.'[4] Disraeli published a blunt letter addressed to Wellington, signed 'Atticus', in *The Times* on 11 March 1841, in which he challenged the Duke over this support for Melbourne. He told Wellington that he had 'performed a greater number of great exploits than any living man', but he had 'never achieved a deed more remarkable or more difficult than keeping the Whigs in office'.[5] This letter contains the usual knockabout of political discourse (albeit expressed with some literary style), but nonetheless is striking for its mixture of mockery and faint praise for the man who was the greatest hero of his day from a young Tory who aspired to hold high office.

While Disraeli was hiding behind a pseudonym in the letter to *The Times*, there was no mystery as to the authorship of the novels *Coningsby* and *Sybil*, published in 1844 and 1845 respectively. Yet in these books, Disraeli is even more disparaging about Wellington. The Duke is portrayed as being tactically incompetent, ignorant of the nation and spineless in the defence of its institutions. Disraeli's most sustained passage about Wellington appears in

Sybil. Writing of the situation in 1830, Disraeli asks:

> How comes it, then, that so great a man, in so great a position, should have so signally failed? Should have broken up his government, wrecked his party, and so completely annihilated his political position, that, even with his historical reputation to sustain him, he can since only re-appear in the councils of his sovereign in a subordinate, not to say equivocal, character?

Disraeli's answer is that Wellington did not know England, adding, 'His Grace precipitated a revolution which might have been delayed for half a century, and need never have occurred in so aggravated a form.'[6] According to Disraeli, this revolution — the passing of the first Reform Bill — overthrew the aristocracy, but did not emancipate either the Crown or the people. Disraeli was, of course, ignoring the fact that Melbourne's Whig governments were every bit as aristocratic as their predecessors and that the landed interest continued to dominate in the Commons, even if people at the time thought this must no longer be the case.[7] He was also ignoring the fact that his own election to the Commons added one more middle class member.

Disraeli claims in *Coningsby* that the future historian would be 'perplexed to ascertain what was the distinct object which the Duke of Wellington proposed to himself in the political manoeuvres of May 1832', and asserts that it was the blunders of the Duke that allowed power to fall into the hands of the Whigs.[8] In fact, as he was writing, Disraeli was in the process of helping the same thing to happen again. Soon after *Coningsby* and *Sybil* were published, the debates over the Corn Laws started, which were to rip apart the Conservative party once more.

Unlike Disraeli, Wellington's one overriding object during the crisis over Corn Law repeal was to keep the party together. He told Aberdeen on 23 December 1845, when Peel's administration was about to be re-formed, that he had been 'making every effort in my power to keep the government together for the Queen during the last two months'.[9] To the Duke, the words 'for the Queen' are key. The diplomat Henry Pierrepoint reported that Wellington saw himself as 'one of the rank and file, ordered to *fall in*, and he set about doing his duty, and preparing for battle', having been, along with his colleagues, as he saw it, ordered to resume office by the Queen's command.[10] On Wellington's death, Greville was not far wrong when he wrote that there was 'no duty, however humble, he would not have been ready to undertake at the bidding of his lawful superiors'.[11] At the same time, Wellington was angry and resentful and complained vociferously to anybody who would listen. For example, to Lord Beaumont, he said 'it is a damned mess, but I must look to the peace of the country and the Queen.'[12]

At the beginning of 1846, Wellington set out his view of the political situation to Lord Ellenborough. He started with his familiar refrain that it was better to have the government 'in the hands of gentlemen instead of in the hands of such men as Cobden'. He went on: 'It is but too true that those who will upon this occasion discontinue their support of the government will in acting over again the scene of 1830 ... expose themselves and the country to the same dangers once again ... I confess that reflection on this state of things annoys me beyond measure.'[13] His overwhelming desire was for a strong Conservative party, which he believed was the best means of ensuring the wellbeing of the Queen, the Church and the other institutions of the country, and the happiness and security of the people. Should the Tories fail, a stable Whig government was acceptable if it prevented instability and the creation of an opportunity for radicals to take power.

Consequently, he was constantly urging people to look at the bigger picture. As he told Croker, 'the existing Corn Law is not the only interest of this great nation'.[14] To Stanley, he pointed out that posterity would make a favourable judgment on the achievements of Peel's government: 'resolution of the finance of the country; the settlement of the banking system; the revival of commerce; the settlement of the Corn Law question, the success in

Ireland ... the universal tranquility prevailing throughout Great Britain'.[15] This last point was the crucial one — Wellington was obsessed with the security of the realm, and tended to see dangers lurking around every corner both from within and from overseas. Arbuthnot said that worries about the defence of the country 'haunted the Duke and deprived him of rest'.[16] For Wellington, the repeal of the Corn Laws was a small price to pay for a calm nation.

Peel also believed that the safety of the nation was at stake over Corn Law repeal. He scared Prince Albert with the thought that 'Lord Stanley, with the aristocracy as his base, would bring about an insurrection ... and the ground on which one would have to fight would be this: to want to force the mass of the people, amidst their great poverty, to pay for their bread a high price, in favour of the landlords.'[17] In the minds of Peel and Wellington, the stakes could not have been higher.

So Wellington asked that if Stanley had to oppose the repeal of the Corn Laws, he would do so with moderation and restraint. It looked like Wellington's wish would be granted; when Stanley had moved to the Lords in 1844, *Fraser's Magazine* pointed out that it was impossible to 'recognise in the quiet, unobtrusive minister who now sits under the wing of the Duke of Wellington ... the fierce, fiery leader who was named the Hotspur of the Conservative forces'.[18] But even the Duke could not stop Stanley breaking away from the party over the repeal of the Corn Laws. In February 1846, he offered Stanley the leadership in the Lords, with the lament that Peel had broken up a noble party, and that it was for Stanley to 'rally it again'.[19] But Stanley had to tell him that it could 'only be ... rallied in opposition to the measures of your own government'.[20] Nevertheless, when Stanley did assume the leadership of the Protectionists, Wellington gave him unwavering support, in spite of disagreements. Wellington's loyalty bolstered Stanley's position, but also made it more difficult for Stanley to oppose him.

A sign of how this would limit Stanley can be seen when he told Lord Montrose that for the second reading of the bill for the repeal of the Corn Laws, 'from deference to the Duke', he would 'abstain from taking any active step, or seeking to influence the decisions of other peers'.[21] However, he came under intense pressure from Protectionist peers to oppose the bill more actively and in the event, spoke on the measure for three hours, with a mixture of reasoned argument, forensic dissection and impassioned plea. However, unlike Disraeli, Stanley did at least largely avoid personal attacks — he went out of his way to express his high regard for the Duke ('however deeply I may deplore the course he has pursued') and said that he did not doubt the sincerity of Peel's conviction that this measure was called for by 'a great exigency' (the famine in Ireland).[22] It is conceivable that if Wellington had had a similar influence over Disraeli, and could have persuaded him to refrain from making personal attacks on Peel, the party may not have broken up — or that it at least could have been re-formed after the Protectionists had dropped Protection. Certainly Stanley avoided leaving the trail of bitterness that Disraeli (and Bentinck) did. This bad feeling greatly limited Stanley's options when trying to form governments, Peelites being reluctant to forgive the way their leader had been treated and join his Cabinet.[23]

The repeal of the Corn Laws was not the only matter over which the Protectionists found themselves on the other side of the argument from Wellington. A great surprise to them was Wellington's support for the Russell government's Time of Service in the Army Act (known as the Enlistment Bill) in 1847, which they were opposed to. Army enlistment was for 21 years, giving it the character of a long prison sentence, which, it was thought, was putting off potentially good recruits. This bill would reduce the period to 10 years. The measure looked as if it would be anathema to Wellington, and Greville tells us that the bill's opponents were sure that the Duke was with them. When Stanley was told that Wellington was not, he said 'he must be very much changed since I talked to him about it', the Duke having told Stanley: 'they have got a damned good army, and they want to make it a damned bad one.'[24] However, in return for his change of heart, Wellington had gained a major concession from Russell and Grey (Secretary of State for War and the Colonies), which was that men would be able to re-enlist after 10 years. The Duke believed that soldiers would indeed re-enlist when their 10 years was up (he was right: more than half did), so, having satisfied himself that the bill would make no real difference, he spoke for it. His support was, however, very half-hearted. With respect to Grey's central contention that superior men would enlist in the army as a result of it, the Duke told the Lords, 'I sincerely hope that such a result will follow from the adoption of the measure; but I confess I very much doubt it.'[25]

Stanley, determined to oppose the bill, had the problem of having to manoeuvre around the Duke's support for it, it being very difficult for him to oppose Wellington on a matter connected with the army. The best that Stanley could do was to tell the Lords that Wellington had decided not to oppose the bill 'in his public character', although 'the noble Duke's private opinion was, that the measure was one of doubtful utility, and of no inconsiderable hazard'.[26]

A much greater divide between Wellington and Stanley opened up over the Duke's support for the repeal of the Navigation Acts in 1849, another attempt to repeal protectionist legislation and therefore an assault on the core tenet of Stanley's party. In the case of the repeal of the Corn Laws, Wellington had been supporting his party leader; in the case of the Enlistment Bill, he had gained con-cessions in exchange for his support. Neither of these pertained over the repeal of the Navigation Acts and, probably as a consequence, a new element of bitterness crept in. As with the Enlistment Bill, Greville tells us beforehand that Wellington was going to vote against it.[27] However, Wellington had concerns about how the Queen's government would be carried on if the bill was defeated, Russell having said that his government would resign if it lost the vote on this measure. Stanley's declaration that he would fight the bill to the utmost 'regardless of consequences' was taken as a sign that he wanted to bring down Russell's government, although, as became evident in 1851, the Protectionists' severe lack of potential ministerial talent in the Commons meant that they were scarcely in a position to form a credible government.[28] The issue became whether it was right for Stanley and Disraeli seriously to attempt to defeat Russell's government, without having a reasonable alternative to put in its place. Stanley, knowing how the Duke felt, would later assure him: 'I am sure we have only the same objects at heart, the interests of the country, irrespective of party, and the stability of the institutions.'[29] Sometimes, Wellington must have felt, his actions told a different story.

Wellington seems to have been even more ambivalent over the repeal of the Navigation Acts than he had over the Enlistment Bill. He said that he would help the government pass the bill, but in the event, he failed to speak in the debate and did not try to talk any peers around. He did, however, vote for it, helping it to scrape through its second reading in the Lords with a majority of 10. In spite of the Duke's passivity, during the debate, Stanley, addressing a crowded House of Lords, confronted Wellington over his support for this measure far more aggressively than he had ever done before. He expressed his

> deep regret, that adherents as attached, troops as staunch, and hearts as devoted as ever bled under his command, and died on the field of battle to raise him to the highest pinnacle of glory, should now, while struggling in another field for the maintenance, not only of the honour and glory, but the existence of this country — now, while fighting for principles which I will not but believe that the noble Duke in his own heart approves, be chilled and saddened by finding him ... standing coldly aloof from their exertions, or even casting the weight of his mighty name and influence into the ranks of their opponents.[30]

It reads insultingly, with its implication that troops died for the purpose of glorifying the Duke, and Greville considered it 'unjustifiable and in bad taste'.[31] It appears to have hit home, however; the old man, according to Stanley's son, 'appeared moved, turned restlessly in his seat, and covered his face with his hands'.[32] Indeed, Wellington was reported to have pronounced the speech 'not only the finest which he had ever made, but the finest ever delivered in Parliament'.[33] Very likely he did not hear it properly, but he took Stanley's point. It was the moment at which his 'peculiar position in the House of Lords', as he put it, was tested to destruction.[34]

One of the difficulties in working with the Duke was that he was not terribly concerned about consistency with respect to men, measures and party, unlike Stanley and indeed almost any conventional politician. Another was that deafness and old age were taking their toll. Greville comments that, at the end of his life, 'his prejudices had become so much stronger and more unassailable, that he gave great annoyance and a good deal of difficulty to the ministers who had to transact business with him'.[35] As ever, his duty to the nation and Crown — as he saw it — were what mattered. This made him support, and enabled him to persuade others to support, policies he was known to disagree with and many of his friends found deeply objectionable. It also made him unpredictable — while his backing could make or break a bill in the Lords, particularly on any matter related to the army, it was difficult to know which way he would go as he would send out different messages to different people. For example, in February 1851, to Prince Albert, he expressed his dread of a Protectionist government with a dissolution, believing it might lead to civil commotion.[36] Wellington told the Prince that he could not forgive the Protectionists for their role in bringing down Russell's government, adding, as the Prince recorded it, 'he had no feeling for Lord John Russell's Cabinet, measures, or principles, but he felt that the Crown and the country were only safe in these days by having the Liberals in office, else they would be driven to join the Radical agitation against the institutions of the country.'[37] Yet in a conversation with Stanley a month later, he was deploring the recent advances of Liberalism.[38] Perhaps both Albert and Stanley had some difficulty communicating with him, and therefore tended to think that he agreed with them.

Wellington certainly agreed with both Stanley and Prince Albert about the fact that the Protectionists were not capable of forming a government in 1851, but he put a positive gloss on it, saying that it was good that they had failed, in that the Whigs had had the burden of office thrown back at them — the Whigs 'are in the mud, and now you can look around you'. Disraeli, never having held office, did not agree, commenting: 'The Whigs might be in the mud, but it was clear to me, that another party was not in a more clean predicament.'[39]

Relationships are said to founder when the two sides want different things. Disraeli and Stanley wanted to form a Protectionist government and were prepared to risk political instability in order to achieve that. The Duke's priority was a secure, stable kingdom and power kept out of the hands of Radicals, meaning that a strong government composed of 'gentlemen' was more important than any other consideration. Consequently, their views of the break up of the Conservative party and how the Russell government was to be opposed were very different. Disraeli had been content to see his party divide and greatly benefited from it, being catapulted from the backbenches, after Bentinck's death in 1848, to the position of effective leader of his party in the Commons. To Stanley the split in the Tory party was a sad necessity. To both of them the goal was to prolong the steadily weakening Russell administration just long enough for the Protectionists to work themselves into a position to form a government. However, to the Duke, a weak government at a time of revolutions on the Continent, Chartist demonstrations in Britain, famine in Ireland and the risk of an invasion from France, was a source of the deepest concern, perhaps second only to the break up of the Conservative Party in the anxiety it caused him. That had

been the greatest calamity that could have befallen the country —
and a 'melancholy' sight 'to one who has served the country for 50
years, who has seen the approach of this danger and has made every
effort in his power, and every sacrifice to avoid it'.[40]

References

[1] Addressing the Duke in a letter to *The Times*, 11 Mar 1841, Disraeli told him,
'The sublime vanity of a mind like yours will not suffer that any great transactions shall be conducted in your lifetime without your special interference.'

[2] Benjamin Disraeli to John Matthie, 1 Jan 1835, *Benjamin Disraeli: letters* ed.
J.A.W.Gunn *et al.* (8 vols, Toronto, 1982–97), ii, p. 362.

[3] Benjamin Disraeli to AW, 7 Jan 1835, *Benjamin Disraeli: letters*, ed. Gunn *et
al.*, ii, p. 363. Three days later, Disraeli received this curt reply: 'The Duke of
Wellington presents his compliments to Mr Disraeli, and has received his letter
of Wednesday night, for which he is much obliged. He very much regrets the
result of the election at Wycombe.' (W.F.Monypenny and G.E.Buckle *The life of
Benjamin Disraeli, Earl of Beaconsfield* (2 vols, revised edition, New York, 1929)
ii, p. 279.

[4] Benjamin Disraeli to Sarah Disraeli, 20 Jan 1838, *Benjamin Disraeli: letters*, ed.
Gunn *et al.*, iii, p. 8.

[5] *The Times*, 11 Mar 1841.

[6] B.Disraeli *Sybil: or, the two nations* (London, 1845), Book 1, Chapter 3.

[7] As Joseph Meisel states, 'Historians have conclusively refuted the nineteenth-
century belief that the social composition of the Commons changed dramatically
after 1832': J.Meisel *Public speech and the culture of public life in the age of
Gladstone* (New York, 2001) p. 62.

[8] B.Disraeli *Coningsby; or, the new generation*, (London, 1844), Book 1,
Chapter 7.

[9] AW to Aberdeen, 23 Dec 1845, WP2/135/25.

[10] C.C.F.Greville *Greville memoirs (second part): a journal of the reign of Queen
Victoria from 1837 to 1852* (3 vols, London, 1885) ii, p. 351, 13 Jan 1846.

[11] *Greville memoirs (second part)*, iii, p. 475, 18 Sep 1852.

[12] J.H.Harris, Earl of Malmesbury *Memoirs of an ex-minister: an autobiography*
(London, 1885) p. 123, 19 Feb 1846.

[13] AW to Ellenborough, 2 Jan 1846, WP2/135/88.

[14] AW to John Wilson Croker, 6 Jan 1846, WP2/135/88.

[15] AW to Stanley, 19 Feb 1846, WP2/138/39–44.

[16] *Greville memoirs (second part)*, iii, pp. 75–6, 10 Apr 1847.

[17] Memorandum by Prince Albert, 7 Dec 1845, *The letters of Queen Victoria 1837–1861* ed. A.C.Benson and Viscount Esher (3 vols, London, 1911) ii, p. 50.

[18] *Fraser's Magazine*, Nov 1845.

[19] Malmesbury, *Memoirs of an ex-minister*, pp. 122–3, 19 Feb 1846.

[20] Stanley to AW, 18 Feb 1846, WP2/138/15–16.

[21] Stanley to Montrose, 2 Mar 1846: A.Hawkins *The forgotten Prime Minister: the 14th Earl of Derby* (2 vols, Oxford, 2007–8) i, p. 307.

[22] *Parliamentary Debates*, 3rd series, lxxxvi, cols. 1130–1.

[23] For example, Lord Aberdeen refused Stanley's offer to join a Protectionist Cabinet in 1851, not over free trade (he confessed to Prince Albert that he did not pretend to understand the question), but because he felt it his duty to stand by Peel, who had died the previous year: memorandum by Prince Albert, 22 Feb 1851, *Letters of Queen Victoria 1837–1861*, ed. Benson and Esher, ii, p. 291.

[24] *Greville's memoirs (second part)*, iii, p. 78, 30 Apr 1847.

[25] *Parliamentary Debates*, 3rd series, xci, col. 1339.

[26] *Parliamentary Debates*, 3rd series, xci, col. 1346.

[27] *Greville's memoirs (second part)*, iii, p. 283, 1 Apr 1849.

[28] *Derby, Disraeli and the Conservative Party: journals and memoirs of Edward Henry, Lord Stanley, 1849–69* ed. John Vincent (Hassocks, 1978) p. 5, 30 Apr 1849.

[29] Stanley to AW, 15 Mar 1851, WP2/168/68.

[30] *Parliamentary Debates*, 3rd series, cv, cols. 109–10.

[31] *Greville's memoirs (second part)*, iii, pp. 287–8, 11 May 1849.

[32] *Derby, Disraeli and the Conservative Party*, ed. Vincent, p. 7, 6 May 1849: this date is incorrect — Edward Stanley is referring to the Navigation Bill debate, in which his father spoke on 8 May (cf. *Parliamentary Debates*, 3rd series, cv, cols. 83–111). There were no sittings in the House of Lords on 5 or 6 May.

[33] *Derby, Disraeli and the Conservative Party*, ed. Vincent, p. 7, 7 May 1849. As with the previous reference above, this date is incorrect. The comment was made to Lord Wilton, who passed it on to the younger Stanley.

[34] AW to Aberdeen, 23 Dec 1845, WP2/135/25.

[35] *Greville's memoirs (second part)*, iii, pp. 474–9, 18 Sep 1852.

[36] He was not the only person who held this view. Sir James Graham had told the Queen that if Stanley formed a Protectionist government, there would be a struggle between the aristocracy and the democracy of the country, 'very perilous to the former'. She told him she entirely agreed with the opinion: *Greville's memoirs (second part)*, iii, pp. 283–5, 1 Apr 1849.

[37] Memorandum by Prince Albert, 23 Feb 1851, *Letters of Queen Victoria 1837–1861*, ed. Benson and Esher, ii, pp. 295–6.

[38] *Disraeli, Derby and the Conservative Party*, ed. Vincent, p. 56, 16 Mar 1851.

[39] Disraeli's Memoirs, *Benjamin Disraeli: letters*, ed. Gunn *et al.*, v, p. 537.

[40] AW to Ellenborough, 2 Jan 1846, WP2/135/88.

CHAPTER 11

'Bury the Great Duke': thoughts on Wellington's passing
R. E. Foster

In December 1852 Charles Dickens was asked for his opinion on a collection of 12 sonnets that had just been submitted to Messrs Macmillans. Their subject was the recently-deceased Iron Duke. Dickens' assessment was mixed. Intrinsically, he considered the sonnets not without merit. The content matter, however, he deemed regrettable for 'it strikes me that no topic ever considered since the earth was without form and void, has been so exhausted as the Death of the Duke of Wellington.'[1] Anybody who trawls the print media for the last quarter of 1852 will readily understand his caveat. Charles Greville, who can usually be relied upon to write voluminously about anything, confessed in his journal on 18 September that the coverage had been 'so able and so elaborate in all the newspapers, that they leave little or nothing to be said'. Two days later, he did at least manage to venture the observation that 'The sensation and regret have been unparalleled, and even the French press has been more just and moderate than could have been expected.'[2] Anything that might have been left unsaid might reasonably be presumed to have been included in the *Annual Register* which, in addition to its detailed chronicle of preparations for the funeral, appended an even longer supplement on the funeral procession and service itself.[3]

Perhaps partly for this reason, early histories and biographies of the Duke tended to say little about his passing. Thus Justin McCarthy's *A history of our own times,* though acknowledging that Wellington's death had 'created a profound public emotion', said nothing about the funeral. Gleig's biography, already in its third edition in 1864, devoted just over three of its 438 pages to Wellington's final illness and funeral combined, consistent with its author's intention of drawing 'a veil over all that followed' his death.[4] Modern writers, by contrast, would seem to have ripped that veil asunder. Elizabeth Longford, Neville Thompson, Christopher Hibbert and Richard Holmes all treat his passing as both a literal and metaphorical final chapter. The events of the funeral, in particular, have also attracted interest in their own right. The seventh Duke, for example, making use of hitherto unused family correspondence, produced a piece on its centenary.[5] More recently, Thompson returned to the subject in his review of the literary outpourings prompted by Wellington's passing, most of them, it must be said, fairly awful. Of far superior quality is John Wolffe's chapter in his overview, *Great deaths*, whilst Peter Sinemma's *The wake of Wellington* also has much to say.[6]

Is there then anything more to add? In arguing for the affirmative, the present essay attempts to do three things: firstly, to identify what it was that contemporaries found so striking at the time of Wellington's passing; secondly, as contemporaries could not, to put Wellington's obsequies in the context of other state funerals; and thirdly, to suggest the combination of circumstances which made Wellington's funeral unique in modern British history.

I

Although Wellington was 83 and had to some extent withdrawn from public affairs, he was still very much in harness when he died. As lord lieutenant of Hampshire, for example, he had left his usual summer residence of Walmer Castle for a brief period in mid-August 1852 to assist his deputies in Winchester as they set about raising the militia in the face of uncertain events in France. He had also agreed to meet Lieutenant Colonel Peter Hawker, of the

North Hampshire regiment, to listen to the latter's suggestions for technical improvements to firearms. Notwithstanding increasing deafness and the fact that he had suffered a series of strokes from 1839, he was reported to be in good health.[7] Back at Walmer, however, in the early morning of Tuesday 14 September, he experienced a series of epileptic attacks from about 6 a.m. In the presence of his second son, Lord Charles Wellesley, and his wife, Lady Sophia, servants and doctors, he died at around 3.20 p.m. that afternoon.[8]

Some contemporaries sentimentalised the news of Wellington's passing. Thus the stylised sketch of the Duke's last moments which appeared in the *Illustrated London News* or Greville's reflection that 'Nothing, but so easy and unlingering a death, was wanting to complete the felicity of such a glorious life.'[9] For many more, however, notwithstanding his advanced years and indifferent health, the event came as a shock. Hawker, the more so since he had only recently met with the Duke, confessed that, 'The event quite cut me up'; whilst Dickens, who was actually walking in Walmer even as events unfolded, 'little thought that the great old man was dying or dead'. Gladstone, at home in Hawarden in North Wales, only heard the news on Thursday 16 September, confiding to his diary that 'We were astounded in the morning with the news of *the Duke's* death.' Queen Victoria, holidaying at Balmoral, initially refused to believe the telegrams, until they were confirmed by her house guest and prime minister, Lord Derby.[10]

The Queen and prime minister, together with Prince Albert, very quickly agreed as to how to dispose of some of Wellington's many offices and titles: Lord Hardinge became Commander-in-Chief, whilst Lord Dalhousie succeeded as Lord Warden of the Cinque Ports and Lord Londonderry took the vacant Garter.[11] They were less definite about the detailed arrangements for the Duke's funeral. In general terms, the question had been considered at cabinet level since at least 1839, shortly after Wellington's first serious stroke; but no firm course of action had ever been agreed.

There was also media speculation about where Wellington would be buried. The *Hampshire Chronicle,* for example, reported that 'it is said always to have been the wishes of His Grace that he should be interred privately at Stathfieldsaye', in order to lie alongside the Duchess. Gleig, however, claimed that Wellington had expressed the wish to be buried where he died ('Where the tree falls, there let it lie'), which presumably would have meant Walmer. In all probability, Wellington was never greatly vexed by such questions, and there may well be something in the idea that he kept his silence on the matter in the knowledge that his passing might be made use of: a final act of state by the selfless pillar of state.[12]

In the end it was Derby who insisted upon St Paul's Cathedral as being the most appropriate final resting place for the Duke. Derby it was, too, who made the suggestion of a state funeral to the Queen. She readily agreed. On her instruction, the prime minister wrote to the Wellesley family on 17 September conveying his sovereign's wishes. The Wellesley family, headed by Lord Charles Wellesley in the new Duke's absence abroad, probably inclined to a relatively quiet private family affair, but replied by expressing themselves ready to defer to Queen and country. As the new Duke subsequently put it, 'If the country has desired that which in real good taste is not reverential, at least it has an opportunity of displaying unexampled respect, and attachment while it perhaps violates our feelings.' Public anxiety and speculation on the matter was finally laid to rest when Derby's letter of 20 September to the home secretary, Spencer Walpole, was made public. 'The great space which the name of the Duke of Wellington has filled in the history of the last 50 years', Derby wrote, 'his brilliant achievements in the field — his high mental qualities — his long and faithful services to the Crown — his untiring devotion to the interests of his country — constitutes claim upon the gratitude of a nation which a public funeral, though it cannot satisfy, at least may serve to recognise.'[13]

The national gratitude, however, had to wait two months

before being given expression. The delay is usually said to be the consequence of the fact that Parliament, whose sanction was required for a public funeral, was not sitting. This may well be true, but Derby showed no desire to have Parliament briefly re-summoned for the purpose, whilst he was perfectly happy for sums to be spent on the funeral preparations in advance of parliamentary approval. This at least hints at an element of political calculation on his part. His administration, formed the previous February, enjoyed only a minority status in the Commons: one can hardly blame him for wanting to prolong the truce of parties that was likely to prevail pending Wellington's burial. But perhaps this is too cynical. The grand affair which the Queen wanted was bound to take time and at least one official complained privately of 'the miserably small period allowed by the Privy Council at Windsor'. As it was, castings for the funeral carriage had to be farmed out to a number of firms to get the work completed on time, with 50 female students from the School of Art completing embroidery work only early on the funeral day itself.[14]

Derby, it should also be remembered, had questions of greater moment to occupy him: specifically the diplomatic tensions created by possible French designs against Belgium, and the fact that on 4 November the French Senate announced that a plebiscite would be held on the question of whether or not Louis Napoleon should be elevated to imperial status. The unburied Duke would have thoroughly approved of the Admiralty estimates being increased by £800,000. Thus, although Derby presided at the cabinet meeting of 16 October which fixed the funeral for 18 November, and whilst his papers contain correspondence with the Earl Marshal and a draft of the ceremonial, the detailed planning for Wellington's funeral passed to others.[15] They were principally Prince Albert, the Duke of Norfolk as Earl Marshal and head of the College of Arms, the Marquis of Exeter as Lord Chamberlain, and the Dean of St Paul's, Henry Hart Milman.

II

For ordinary mortals, meanwhile, the main topic of debate in the days after Wellington's death was what it was that his passing represented. Most obviously, there was a sense of his greatness. William Spicer described the Duke's passing as 'the sudden demise of the greatest man in the universe'. Few others went quite that far, but Charles Greville's more considered assessment of Wellington as 'in spite of some foibles and faults ... beyond all doubt, a very great man — the only great man of the present time — and comparable, in point of greatness, to the most eminent of those who have lived before him', came close. In similar vein, Hamlet's lament for his father, 'Take him for all and all, we never shall look upon his like again', was much quoted in the press.[16]

Justin McCarthy, whilst not disputing the Duke's claims to greatness, later wrote that Wellington had outlived his era, that 'he belonged so much to the past at the time of his death ...' That was not how contemporaries saw it. Rather, Wellington was seen to embody the age, having outlived his earlier unpopularity, the nadir of which had been reached in the early 1830s, to become the living legend that nearly all now wanted to laud. This was apparent even before he died. The Chartist, Thomas Cooper, admitted to detouring from his home some mornings in the hope of catching sight of Wellington as he left Apsley House: 'What a fascination, what an irresistible attraction there was about that grand old man! How all the memorable doings of our century seemed to gather around him, as you looked at his rigid, stern figure!' Cooper ranked only the Queen above him, a judgement in which he found an unlikely ally in Greville, who wrote that Wellington's 'position was eminently singular and exceptional, something between the royal family and other subjects'.[17] It followed, therefore, that Wellington's passing represented the closing of an age. 'He was', wrote Cooper, 'an institution in himself. We all felt as if we lived, now he was dead, in a different England.' Wellington's longevity, after all, meant that nobody less than 50 would have grown up without the Duke being part of their national consciousness. 'I seemed to myself', concluded Cooper, 'to belong now to another generation of men; for my very childhood was passed amid the noise of Wellington's battles, and his name and existence seemed stamped on every year of our time.'[18]

There was also widespread agreement that Wellington's life had spanned a remarkable period in the nation's history, or as Disraeli put it, that Wellington was 'not only a great man, but the greatest man of a great age'. That age was now felt to be passing. The *Daily News* reported that 'The knell that tolls for this great man's death tolls also the death of a remarkable period of history.' For most, that future promised optimism, but not for all. How would the nation cope without Wellington in face of a new Napoleon? And was Chartism really dead? None put it better than Wellington himself when he told Croker shortly before he died that 'it is some consolation to us who are so near the end of our career that we shall be spared seeing the ruin that is gathering about us.'[19]

Most thoughts in 1852, however, dwelt more on past glories than future anxieties, and inevitably focused on the Duke's and the nation's exertions against Revolutionary and Napoleonic France. Much, too, was made of his long years of service to the state. 'The Nestor of the state has bowed his venerable head in death', was how the *Salisbury and Winchester Journal* began its tribute. However, given Wellington's political stances, notably over reform, the obituaries were less than hagiographical in their assessment. 'He leaves to us the working out of principles which he once vainly sought to oppose, but which he had the wisdom afterwards to recognise', was how the *Daily News* chose to put it. Less charitably, the *Morning Chronicle* judged that he could be prejudiced and obstinate, the *New York Courier* that 'there was no liberality in his notions and maxims of civil policy. He had no great faith in the progress of humanity, no lively feeling in the strength and majesty of moral powers.'[20] Overwhelmingly, however, writers identified countervailing qualities which aggregated to make Wellington a unique human being. In a speech to the East Cumberland Agricultural Association in Carlisle on 18 September, Sir James Graham opined that 'devotion to his country, his never-ceasing patriotism, his self-denial, and his love of duty ... were the qualities which made the Duke of Wellington what he was.' Former political opponents followed suit. Lord John Russell, on receiving the freedom of Stirling, acknowledged Wellington's incomparable achievements and exhorted his listeners to aspire to imitating his personal qualities, 'that sincere and unceasing devotion to his country — that honest and proud determination to act for his country on all occasions ... that vigilance in the constant performance of his duty ... that unostentatious piety by which he was distinguished at all times in his life.' This was surely more than a long-rehearsed formula for public consumption, as Palmerston's private remark to his brother amply testifies: 'our great Duke', he wrote, 'is a great loss to the country. His name was a tower of strength abroad, and his opinions and counsel were invaluable at home. No man ever lived or died in the possession of more unanimous love, respect and esteem from his countrymen.'[21]

Wellington, in short, was held to personify the virtues of Englishness. These were identified by the *Daily News* as being chiefly simplicity (epitomised by his lifelong preference for his army camp bed), honesty, truth, probity and patience. Above all else, Wellington's life was seen to be characterised by a devotion to duty. The *Morning Chronicle* wrote of his 'unwavering recognition of duty'; the *Examiner* that 'The idea of the Duke of Wellington's life was duty'; the *Salisbury and Winchester Journal*, less pithily, that the Duke was 'unstained by the imputation of a corrupt or unselfish motive, and in every circumstance, and at all conjectures, steadfast and unwavering in his allegiance to DUTY'. Tennyson's famous *Ode on the death of the Duke of Wellington* mentioned duty no fewer than five times.[22] Small wonder that Disraeli, pondering what to say in leading Parliament's tribute on 15 November, confessed to his wife that he was 'a little disturbed by the Duke of Wellington, all the world expecting a great speech from me. And I at least resolved that I will make one without the word "duty" appearing.' Perhaps the resulting anxiety contributed to his celebrated *faux pas* in which he used words very similar to those which had been uttered by Thiers in his tribute to Marshal St Cyr in 1829. It was an error for which he was much pilloried. Moreover, in subsequently declaring that 'I will not say of England that he has revived here the sense of duty — that, I trust, was never lost', he was not altogether successful.[23]

III

Some, such as Sir Charles James Napier's daughter, Elizabeth, would have liked to have seen Wellington's supposed virtues inform the planning for his funeral. This was never probable. The funeral inevitably focused on the Duke's military achievements, though much of the detail was dictated by precedent as determined by the Earl Marshal and the College of Arms. This coincided with the Queen's hope that it might serve a diplomatic purpose too, by reviving memories of the grand coalitions against France, and through them deter any renewed dreams of French imperialism.[24] As it turned out, the Austrians were to boycott the proceedings in protest at General Haynau's treatment in London in September 1850, a reminder instead therefore of how fragile the coalitions had been. The Queen was, understandably, not amused. A related but hitherto overlooked point, was that in staging the funeral 'as a continuity with the glories of the national past', it might stir men to volunteer for the militia, the act for reviving which had only been passed in June 1852, and the implementation of which Wellington had been so keen to effect. As one MP who opposed the proposal for a state funeral put it, it might 'stimulate the military spirit of the people, and make militiamen come forward'.[25]

Queen Victoria's main aspirations for Wellington's funeral,

however, were early conveyed to Derby when she wrote that she was 'anxious that the greatest possible number of her subjects should have an opportunity of joining in it', and that the proceedings 'should be deprived of nothing which could invest it with a thoroughly national character'.[26] These public proceedings at last got under way in the second week of November. First, Wellington's embalmed body inside its three coffins of lead, oak and mahogany, lay in state at Walmer Castle. An estimated 9,000 people queued to file past it there on 9–10 November.[27] From Walmer, it was taken by train to London and placed in the hall of the Royal Military Hospital at Chelsea during the early hours of 11 November. Here it lay in state for a week. The black-draped hall was lit by over 50 large candles in 7-foot holders which surrounded the Duke's coffin, covered in red velvet. His military decorations were placed on a table at its foot. A few found this display distasteful. Samuel Carter, MP for Tavistock and a former Chartist, declared that 'the feeling in his mind was only one of deep disgust, to see the clay of a departed man hung round with all the emblems of heraldry.'[28] Most, however, were duly impressed. Admission on the first two days, 11 and 12 November, was by ticket only. The Queen herself headed the visiting dignitaries on the first day and was so overwhelmed that she stayed only briefly. Hawker, who had come up from Hampshire on 10 November to queue for a ticket from the Lord Chamberlain's office, was amongst those who attended early on the second day. Perversely, the dreadful weather of those days added to the occasion for him. 'I had', he wrote, 'the closest possible stare at the cortège. An incessant pour of rain all day; but it was fun to see the silk-stocking flunkeys (for whom nothing is good enough) obliged to trample through the mud like a brood of young ducks.' When he finally got to see the lying in state, however, it 'was the most magnificent spectacle I ever saw'.[29] The four days of viewing for the general public, 13–17 November, were less memorable for the spectacle than the unexpectedly large scale of the public response. Some 260,854 people were to pass through the hall in total, with two women, Sarah Bean and Charlotte Cooke, crushed to death on the first day. According to the *Annual Register*, some five people perished in all. The new Duke was so disgusted by such an 'exhibition devoid of taste and feeling' that he privately rued the family's decision to agree to a public funeral in the first place.[30]

Concerns over public safety played a part in Greville's decision to follow up his visit to the lying in state on 16 November ('fine and well done, but too gaudy and theatrical'), with a visit to St Paul's Cathedral, where round-the-clock preparations were nearing completion for the Duke's funeral. Messrs Cubitt & Co. had been instructed by the First Commissioner of Woods and Works to set up seats for 10,000. It was, Greville discovered, a popular spectacle in itself, 'like a great rout; all London was there strolling and staring about in the midst of a thousand workmen going on with their business all the same, and all the fine ladies scrambling over vast masses of timber, or ducking to avoid the great beams that were constantly sweeping along'. It was not much better the next day when Gladstone embarked upon his own 'exploratory expedition' for the same purpose. 'All the west', he wrote, 'and in our part seems one vast beehive: the stir immeasurable.'[31] It was, he judged, nevertheless safe for Mrs Gladstone and their daughter Mary to attend.

Forebodings persisted, none more so than in the mind of Charles Dickens. 'I am quite vexed about the state funeral', he declared. 'I think it altogether wrong as regards the memory of the Duke ... a vulgar holiday, with a good deal of business for the thieves, will be the chief result.'[32] Nevertheless, the authorities were sufficiently confident that the aura of the occasion would guarantee order — if not deter all Dickens's perpetrators of petty crime — that they chose to deploy just over 5,000 police rather than troops for funeral day itself, Thursday 18 November. The previous evening, just before midnight, Wellington's body had been transferred from Chelsea to the Horse Guards, the Wellesley family having declined an offer that it should pass its final night at Apsley

House. Thus it was from the Horse Guards that the grand funeral procession set out at 7.15 a.m., many of those processing having been in position for over an hour previously. In weather conditions that remained unsettled, some 10,000 marched, headed by Prince Albert, government ministers, judges, 83 Chelsea pensioners and representatives of Wellington's many offices. The greatest part numerically, however, comprised soldiers from every regiment in the British army, including over 3,000 infantrymen, eight squadrons of cavalry and three artillery batteries. Lord Anglesey carried Wellington's field marshal's baton. Part way along the procession came the Duke's body. Behind it walked his immediate family, relatives and closest friends; behind them, what many, including Peter Hawker, considered the most poignant image of the day, John Mears leading Wellington's horse with the eponymous boots reversed in the stirrups.[33]

Hawker had risen before 4 a.m. ('our retired part of town already in a roar with carriages'), and had secured a good vantage point at his club by 6.30 a.m. For those less well-connected, those best able to witness the proceedings were the estimated 300,000 or so who had secured seats in hastily erected stands amid the many public buildings draped in black. Enterprising shopkeepers were said to be letting space in their shop fronts for at least a guinea a time. The *Observer* reckoned that perhaps £80,000 changed hands in this way. This may well be an under-estimate: one man, whose house fronted St Paul's, was reputedly asking £1,000 to let it for the day.[34] Such stories merely served to confirm Charles Dickens in his earlier apprehensions. He gave vent to his feelings against such 'ghouls', those dealing in Wellington memorabilia as well as seats, in an article entitled 'Trading in Death' in *Household Words*. Even so, he had happily roused his son at 3 a.m. in order to secure the vantage point offered to him and a dozen friends and family by the Duke of Devonshire at Devonshire House.[35]

To facilitate public viewing of the two-hour long procession, its route was deliberately circuitous. From the Horse Guards, it passed through St James's Park, along the Mall past Buckingham Palace and Constitution Hill, then past Apsley House and along Piccadilly and St James's Street, to return to the Mall. Only then did it head, via Charing Cross and The Strand, towards the City. The Lord Mayor met and joined it at Temple Bar, leading it thence along Fleet Street and Ludgate Hill to St Paul's.[36] For those so inclined there was thus ample opportunity to view the spectacle more than once. Thomas Cooper, for example, watched from the south side of Green Park as the procession came down the Mall for the first time, then crossed the park to see it wend its way down Piccadilly. Queen Victoria, though protocol forbade her from attending the funeral in person, did personal homage to her most faithful subject in similar manner, first watching from the balcony of Buckingham Palace and then crossing to St James's Palace. The Duke's passing seems to have personally affected her more than most have allowed, it being 'the first funeral of anyone I had known and who was dear to me that I had ever seen'.[37]

It was shortly after noon by the time the procession finally reached St Paul's. Then, because of mechanical failure on the funeral car, another hour elapsed before the Duke's coffin could be conveyed inside the cathedral. Up to 20,000 had gathered inside. Dickens, who may well have been unique in refusing Dean Milman's personal invitation to attend the funeral, on the grounds that 'I could not contemplate the waiting in St Paul's', doubtless felt vindicated.[38] The ensuing two-hour service included Psalms 9 and 39, sung to chants composed by the Duke's father, an anthem and dirge composed specially for the occasion, and more familiar works by Handel and Mendelssohn. Gladstone, who had managed to watch 'the whole solemn and magnificent procession' from Jane Wortley's house before returning to the House of Commons and then travelling to St Paul's by boat, considered the Mendelssohn 'sublime in effect almost beyond anything I ever heard ...' The solemnities, he recorded, were finally concluded at 2.40 p.m., with a recitation of the Duke's seemingly innumerable titles prefiguring 'the most nobly and touchingly conceived part of all ... the slow lowering of the coffin, surmounted by the Duke's coronet and baton, his military hat and sword, while the organ played the dead march'.[39]

The main source of controversy arising from the day was undoubtedly the huge funeral car which had transported Wellington on his final journey. Prince Albert, who oversaw the project, instructed that it should be 'a symbol of English military strength and statesmanship'. Six foundries contributed to its casting and over 100 men had worked on it over 18 days to finish it on time. When complete, it measured 27 feet long, 10 feet wide and 17 feet high, and weighed in excess of 10 tons. Evocative for some of a Roman victory chariot, and cast in bronze from cannon captured at Waterloo, it was surmounted by a silk and silver canopy suspended from four halberds. Twelve horses were required to pull it, and 60 policemen were needed to free it when one of its six wheels stuck in The Mall, even before its final ignominious delay near St Paul's.[40] The *Annual Register* described it diplomatically as having aroused 'unexampled interest'. In truth, opinion varied wildly. The Queen, predictably, loved it whilst Hawker's 'feelings were excited at ... such a car as eyes never yet beheld'. Lord Hardinge was even moved to call it a 'beautiful specimen of art'. But those who presumed to be the arbiters of good taste were more inclined to condemn it. Thomas Carlyle dismissed it as 'an incoherent huddle of expensive palls, flags, sheets and gilt emblems and cross poles', whilst John Millais thought it more 'like a palsied locomotive'. Dickens reflected that 'for forms of ugliness, horrible combination so of colour, hideous motion and general failure, there never was such a look achieved as the car.' He consummated his disgust in fiction the following year in *Bleak House* where the car unmistakably provided the inspiration for his description of the funeral of the murdered lawyer, Tulkinghorn.[41]

At least all agreed that Wellington's funeral car was memorable. But it did not mark the end of the funeral proceedings.

On 25 November, the indefatigable Hawker went to a private viewing of Wellington's batons and other insignia. The following day, not having been to St Paul's before the funeral, he obtained a ticket to view the cathedral's interior before the funerary trappings were finally taken down. Only then, in an echo of the great gathering of the previous year could he at last write that 'Here ends what may be considered the last "lion" of the grand and mournful exhibition of 1852.'[42]

Some of those present at the events of 18 November 1852 harboured reservations over what they had witnessed. Sir John Colborne, for example, found the recitation of Wellington's many titles at his funeral 'inapplicable to the present age', whilst Dickens disliked the 'frippery' of the Lord Chamberlain and the College of Arms for 'choreographing' the funeral in a way he thought irrelevant to the age. Clearly, neither fully appreciated just how far events had been dictated by precedent.[43] A separate tack was taken by a few parliamentary Radicals who questioned whether the expense of such a state occasion was justified. More fundamentally, given whose funeral it was, Count Walewski, the French ambassador, was reluctant to attend at all, only to be told by Baron Brunnow that 'If this ceremony were intended to bring the Duke to life again, I can conceive your reluctance to appear at it; but as it is only to bury him, I don't see you have anything to complain of.'[44]

The most common general criticism, however, was that the Duke's funeral had been too secular and martial in character, in the process losing sight of the mortal being that had been Wellington. Dickens thought it 'a grievous thing — a relapse into semi-barbarous practices ... a pernicious corruption of the popular mind, just beginning to awaken from the long dream of inconsistencies, monstrosities, horrors and ruinous expences [sic], that has beset all classes in connexion with death — and a folly sure to miss its object and to be soon attended by a strong reaction on the memory of the illustrious man so *mis*represented'. Carlyle, in keeping with his rubbishing of the car, found it 'all hypocrisy, noise, and expensive upholstery ... a big bag of wind and nothingness ... a painful, miserable kind of thing to me and others of a serious turn of mind'. But it was the evangelical Lord Shaftesbury who was most vexed and who put it best in judging that the day had been 'fine, very fine, but hardly impressive; signs of mortality but none of resurrection; much of a great man in his generation, but nothing of a great spirit in another; not a trace of religion, not a shadow of eternity ...'[45]

The choice of words used by critics with reference to Wellington's funeral is itself instructive. Hawker called it an 'exhibition', Lady Palmerston a 'festival', Gladstone a 'spectacle' and Dickens a 'show'. Shaftesbury, significantly, used the same word in writing that the funeral procession had been 'a show, an eye-tickler to 999 out of every 1,000 — a mere amusement'.[46] The collective objection from those who had had at least a nodding acquaintance with Wellington in life was that his funeral had been turned into theatre for the masses. Whilst one can understand their disquiet, one also needs to remember that this, even if it was not expressed in quite those terms, had very much been the intention, certainly of the Queen, her consort and her prime minister.[47]

Seen in those terms, that is to say as a public celebration of a great man's passing that was meant to impress the popular mind, Wellington's funeral must be judged a great success. Its impact upon those who witnessed it was both profound and long lasting. Cooper recalled it as 'the most impressive grand spectacle I ever beheld'. Hawker considered it 'the most glorious of all funerals ever before heard of in the world'. Even more lofty individuals such as Gladstone confessed that 'The spectacle was magnificent in the highest degree.' Hence, too, the proliferation and success of coins and commemorative medallions, at least 46 by 1853, the retention of orders of service or tickets, and even such ephemera as resident passes issued by the police.[48]

The Queen and prime minister shared the belief that the funeral had been a great success and could thus reflect on a job well done in a round of mutual self-congratulation in the days that followed it. In a much-praised speech in the House of Lords on 19 November, Derby chose to dwell particularly upon the respectful and orderly manner of the vast crowds which had assembled. It was a sentiment prompted in part perhaps by relief that no major accident or more premeditated incident of public order had occurred, but seems genuine enough for all that.[49] The same point was acknowledged by Dickens in the columns of *Household Words*: he lauded 'the sincere and deep expression ... of reverence' shown by ordinary artisans on London's streets on 18 November, however much he continued to deplore the whole event as wrong-headed in its execution. Queen Victoria was surely a better placed judge, however, both literally and metaphorically, in feeling compelled to write to her prime minister congratulating him on his speech, that 'What the Queen however saw (which Lord Derby from being in the procession could not witness) was touching and impressive in the highest degree and will ever remain engraved in her memory and she is sure in that of the countless thousands assembled to do honour to England's greatest hero!'[50]

IV

Historians and biographers, like the great mass of Britons in 1852, have also been impressed by Wellington's funeral. Gash, for example, describes it as 'probably the most ornate and spectacular funeral ever seen in England', Hibbert as 'perhaps unparalleled in its grandeur'.[51] Neither contemporaries, nor subsequent writers, however, have shown sufficient awareness of the wider context of what might be called 'great deaths'. State (as opposed to public) funerals for non-royals can be said to have begun with that of Oliver Cromwell in 1658, followed by those of Monk in 1670 and Marlborough in 1722. Thereafter, there was none until Chatham's funeral in 1778, the funerals of Nelson and Pitt the Younger in 1806 (both of which Wellington attended), the Duke's own, that of

Gladstone in 1898, and of Churchill in 1965.[52] A cursory consideration of some of them, for all their admitted differences of detail, does in fact reveal some striking similarities with Wellington's. If nothing else, the exercise should at least caution us against Tennyson's claim in his *Ode* that 'the last great Englishman is low'.

The grand lying-in-state, whether it be in the Painted Chamber of Westminster Palace as for both Pitts, Westminster Hall as for Gladstone and Churchill, and Greenwich Hospital for Nelson, were as apposite in their location as Wellington's at Chelsea.[53] More mundanely, the popular penchant for souvenirs of sorts, which so annoyed Dickens in 1852, is another salient feature. So too, before Gladstone, was the substantial delay between the subject's death and funeral. Some 54 days elapsed in the case of Marlborough, 29 in the case of Chatham, and 30 for his son. Wellington's 'interim' period of 64 days, was thus not so very exceptional as Wolffe presumes, and significantly shorter than Nelson's understandably more protracted 80 days.[54]

All the funerals were sanctioned by Parliament with more or less general acclamation. The relative exceptions were those of the Pitts. Although the Commons voted unanimously for Chatham's state funeral, as also to pay his debts, the House of Lords defeated a motion that they attend the funeral — George III, too, had reservations about Chatham's 'general conduct' — leading the *Morning Post* to judge that it turned out to be a 'very pitiful pageant'. A generation later, with the outcome of the French war far from certain, Charles James Fox and William Windham mustered 89 votes against the motion for his son's state funeral in 1806.[55] Against this, the parliamentary objections to Wellington's state funeral can be dismissed as insignificant. They came from a handful of Radicals headed by Joseph Hume, and should be seen in the context of their more general campaign for retrenchment — they repeated wildly exaggerated rumours that Wellington's funeral would cost £250,000 — than an explicit denial of Wellington's entitlement to the honour as such. The most vociferous of their number, Samuel Carter, in declaring 'a national funeral a national folly' and that it would 'foster in the minds of the poorer classes the love for expensive funerals, a folly to which they were already too prone', would appear to have been disowned by his allies for his eccentricity.[56]

Neither was Wellington's funeral car perhaps as unique (or, as its detractors might have it, as disturbing), as contemporaries deemed it. Nelson had had one that resembled HMS *Victory*, which the *Annual Register* considered to be less well suited for purpose. Monk's and Marlborough's were both probably more martial and grandiose still. Bedecked in heraldic emblems, Marlborough's bore not only a full suit of armour but a life-sized effigy. The Wellesley family was at least spared that. But Wellington's, largely at Prince Albert's insistence, was very much the last state funeral which harked back to sixteenth-century precedents, with the concomitant emphasis on heraldic display. Greater involvement by the Lord Chamberlain's Office, the crown's ability to vary precedent and the Gladstone's family's dislike of show meant that the Grand Old Man's funeral was a far simpler affair in 1898.[57]

Gladstone's state funeral also stands as an exception, of course, as an honour conferred upon one who did not in some way lead the nation in war. The sense of national loss in the others, however, is common: Hague writes that there was 'undoubtedly a sense of national loss' on Pitt's passing in 1806, though this phenomenon, given the timing and circumstances, was understandably most pronounced in the case of Nelson.[58] Neither was the feeling that an age was closing unique to Wellington's passing. *The Times* had said the same when Sir Robert Peel died in 1850; for the Queen and others, Wellington's death merely seemed to confirm them in their perception. But was the perception any less true in 1965 for, as David Cannadine has written, 'As long as Churchill lived, Britain seemed to be a great power. But after he died, the illusion could no longer be sustained. It was not just a man who was mourned in January 1965: it was a nation's sense of its past and its purpose and its power.' Even the emphasis on duty, the absolute *sina qua non* with Wellington's obituarists, was far from unique: commemorative medallions struck in honour of the Younger Pitt bore the legend 'He lived not for himself but for his country.'[59] England, after all, as Nelson signalled, expected duty from all its sons.

Nelson's is also the state funeral which most obviously invites comparison with the Duke's. Hibbert describes the former as 'the finest public ceremonial laid on in England since Elizabethan times, and the most magnificent funeral ever staged'. Some more explicit comparisons with Wellington's funeral were ventured by Andrew Lambert in his Wellington lecture of 2005.[60] His contention, understandable from a fellow son of Norfolk, is that Nelson's funeral represented the nation's homage to a greater hero. Thus his observation that when the home secretary, Spencer Walpole, suggested that Nelson's tomb be moved so that Wellington might share centre stage beneath the dome of St Paul's, 'The Dean [Henry Hart Milman] very properly rejected this blasphemous suggestion … Nelson was divine, Wellington was an outstanding soldier.'[61] Nelson's funeral was on the grand scale. His body lay in state at Greenwich Hospital from 23 December, before being taken by river to the Admiralty in Whitehall on 8 January. On 9 January it made its final journey to St Paul's on its mock *Victory* funeral car, in a two-hour procession, the ensuing funeral service itself lasting nearly four hours. Nelson does, undeniably, figure more prominently in the modern British psyche as the 2005 celebration of the bi-centenary of Trafalgar bears testimony. But this owes not a little to the ways in which Nelson was remembered by posterity, typically Benjamin West's absurdly stylised painting, *Death of Nelson*, which first went on sale in 1811, and which contributed much to his deification; and the creation of Trafalgar Square in the decade after 1835, to which Wellington subscribed £200.[62] In 1852, however, contemporaries did not see Wellington as a lesser hero: rather, the early Victorian public, including explicitly the Queen, prime minister and home secretary, saw Wellington and Nelson as being on a par. It seems literally to have been the case that only the unco-operative Dean Milman prevented their juxtaposition in death. At almost £30,000, nearly twice the cost of Nelson's, Thompson is surely correct in describing Wellington's funeral 'at least as magnificent as Nelson's'.[63]

In many ways, perhaps, Wellington's funeral is better compared with Churchill's. Both were examples, albeit in different measure, of that rarity in British public life, the soldier-statesman. Both experienced, but outlived, long periods of political unpopularity. Both were revered in old age. Both consequently survived long enough to see for themselves something of how they would be commemorated by posterity, though it would be fair to admit that the Duke thought far more of Matthew Cope Wyatt's statue of him erected at Hyde Park corner in September 1846 than Churchill did of Graham Sutherland's portrait, which was presented to him by the House of Commons in 1954 and which Lady Churchill subsequently destroyed.[64] More significantly, both survived by a generation their defining moment in the national drama. Thus many at the funerals of Wellington and Churchill must have shared memories of the common struggle and the human symbols of national survival to whom they were paying homage. Sir Winston, like Wellington, expressed little interest in the details for his funeral beyond a desire for plenty of bands, but he must have had a fair idea of what lay in store.[65] Like Wellington he suffered a stroke; like him, a young and grateful Queen ordered a state funeral, in attending which she made a major break with precedent. After three days lying-in-state in Westminster Hall, during which 300,000 viewed the coffin draped in the Union Flag, Churchill's remains made their way to St Paul's. Mercifully, they travelled on a simple gun-carriage in a one-hour procession. During the funeral, the same six candlesticks that were used at Wellington's funeral stood around the coffin. The service over, the body was taken by river, the defining moment for many being the quayside cranes dipping their masts in salute as the funeral barge passed between Tower Bridge and London Bridge. The final journey to Bladon for burial set off from Waterloo station.

V

Churchill's funeral was a global event; an estimated 350,000,000 watched it on television. Those of the Pitts, even Nelson's, were essentially London affairs.[66] What made Wellington's funeral particularly distinctive was the sense of a nation participating, something which has been insufficiently acknowledged. Estimates before the event projected that somewhere between 1 million and 1.5 million people would attend. Reports afterwards confirmed this, some even going so far as to claim that 2 million had watched Wellington's funeral procession. These are extraordinary numbers. If we go by the latter estimate, they equate to nearly three quarters of London's population or nearly 10% of Britain's mainland population as a whole.[67] It was a phenomenon made possible by a dual revolution in communications; the first, in the press which made people want to attend, the second in railways which allowed them to.

As has rightly been observed, excepting perhaps only the monarch, Wellington's was the most portrayed image in his own lifetime through a plethora of prints, portraits and other memorials. Even at the time of his premiership there were seven London morning papers. During the 1840s, moreover, new organs were appearing, including *Lloyd's Weekly Newspaper* (1842), the *News of the World* (1843) and *Reynolds's Weekly Newspaper* (1850). *Punch* (1841) also prospered and could boast sales of 6,000–8,000 by mid-century. In Wellington it found a wonderful figure, and contributed materially to making the Duke known through both his caricatured image and the parodies of his terse written style. His passing led to the first of *Punch's* obituary cartoons: out went the caricature of the hooked nose, to be replaced by the benign elder statesman and a sorrowful British lion.[68] More influential and respectable still was the *Illustrated London News*, published from 1842. Its meticulous funeral coverage ran to over 100 pages of prints and engravings between September and November 1852. It repaid the effort: the numbers for 20 and 27 November were to sell 2 million copies and are still relatively easy to obtain. At provincial level too, editors sensed an opportunity. The *Hampshire Chronicle* devoted extensive coverage to events over the same period: from its own and other papers' obituaries, to, successively, details for the lying-in-state, details for the funeral procession and the order of service — each weekly edition interlaced with recollections of the Duke. For the first time in its 80 year history, it produced a special illustrated supplement to accompany its reporting of the funeral itself.[69]

But no editor was as perspicuous as John Delane of *The Times*. One of the innovations of his editorship was to expand that newspaper's obituary coverage. In September 1852 he told his deputy that the Duke's death 'will be the only topic'. Wellington's obituary, written by Henry Reeve was, at 47,000 words, well over twice the length of Gladstone's, itself considerably longer than any other of the Victorian period. Appearing first on 15 September, it was, Greville informed its author, 'a prodigious success'. Indeed, it proved so popular that it was republished as a pamphlet. Public interest in Wellington created by the print media also found a market in poetic form: the first print run of 10,000 of Tennyson's *Ode* quickly sold out, even at a shilling apiece. In his Carlisle speech, Sir James Graham for one, drew attention to how, in his view, the press had performed a beneficial service in having conveyed the Duke's essence to the nation, even though he was quick to add that they were no absolute substitute for reading the Duke's published despatches.[70]

The print media thus created a Wellington that people could know and wanted to honour. For most this had to be satisfied by attendance at one of the numerous memorial services up and down the country, a phenomenon which had become fashionable with the death in childbirth of Princess Charlotte in 1817.[71] For others, however, an even closer participation was possible: to view the funeral procession in London in person. This was thanks chiefly to the railways, what John Ruskin vividly described in 1849 as 'the iron veins that traverse the frame of our country'. In 1832 there had been only 166 miles of track in Britain. Between 1830 and 1853, however, some 27 new lines opened. In 1848 alone, at the peak of 'railway mania', 1,253 miles of track were completed; some 6,000 miles of track had been laid in total by 1850. By 1852 just about every major town had a rail terminus and London was connected with places as far flung as Plymouth, Norwich, Cardiff, Birmingham, Manchester, Hull, Newcastle, Edinburgh and Glasgow. Speeds on the main routes averaged 30 to 40 miles per hour and the journey from London to Manchester could be accomplished in just over eight hours. Arguably the most important changes were introduced by Gladstone's Railway Act of 1844. This created a Railways Board and required rail companies to run at least one passenger service a day at the fixed rate of a penny a mile, the famous 'parliamentary trains'. Parliamentary returns record over 7.7 million rail passengers in 1851–2, nearly 4 million of whom travelled in third class. Many of the 6 million who flocked to the Great Exhibition in just five months during 1851 did so by train, facilitated by the likes of Thomas Cook who was offering a return fare of only five shillings between Leeds and London on his Midland Railway. 'Never before in any one year', as Norman Gash observed, 'had the British population moved about so much'. There was thus much truth in the Duke's less than enthusiastic comment that railways would 'encourage the lower classes to travel about'.[72]

Whilst one cannot with any precision gauge how many people used railways to get to London for Wellington's funeral procession, the numbers were surely significant. By mid-October, the *Hampshire Chronicle* was observing that 'The interest felt throughout the country in the matter is already beginning to manifest itself, and excursion trains are advertised to run daily

during the ceremonial from all the important towns in the kingdom.'
For the funeral itself, the paper noted that 'The trains, coaches and
other conveyances brought continuous shoals of people from all
parts of the country on Wednesday and Thursday.' The procession
route was said to be busy from at least midday on the Wednesday;
with fresh arrivals from 2 a.m. on the Thursday, most advantageous
spaces were filled by 4 a.m. Whilst rail companies were clearly right
to sense a commercial opportunity — thus advertising special trains
— ample provision probably already existed. From Southampton
to Waterloo, for example, there were seven trains daily at three
shillings return fare in open carriages for the three hour journey.[73]
It is more than a little revealing of contemporary preoccupations
that the first series of external examination papers set by the
University of Cambridge in December 1858 (the precursor of our
modern public exams), should invite its junior candidates to
'Discuss the change produced in the habits of the people by
railways', whilst simultaneously its senior candidates were
being asked to provide 'a sketch of the character of the Duke
of Wellington'. A few of those first candidates, perhaps, cited
travelling to Wellington's funeral as evidence in support of their
answer to the former. The more poetically-inclined, in answer to
the latter, may even have closed using words similar in sentiment to
those that appeared in *Punch*:[74]

> Peace to him! Let him sleep near him who fell
> Victor at Trafalgar; by Nelson's side
> Wellington's ashes fitly may abide.
> Great Captain — noble heart! Hail to thee, and farewell!

References
[1] Dickens to Messrs Macmillans, 10–15 Dec 1852: *The letters of Charles Dickens*. Vol. 6, *1850–1852* eds. G.Story, K.Tillotson and N.Burgis (Oxford, 1988) p. 821 (hereafter *Dickens*). Dickens' recurring criticisms of the funeral are explained by his connections with the Wellesley family. Wellington had befriended Lt. Col. Robert Thomson, formerly of the Royal Engineers, an uncle of Mrs Dickens.

[2] C.C.F.Greville *A journal of the reign of Queen Victoria from 1837–1852* (3 vols., London, 1885) iii, p. 474; Greville to Reeve, 20 Sep 1852: *The letters of Charles Greville and Henry Reeve 1836–1865* ed. A.H.Johnson (London, 1924) p. 213.

[3] *Annual register* (London, 1853) pp. 188–95, 482–96.

[4] J.McCarthy *A history of our own times* (London, 1889) ii, p. 108; G.R.Gleig *The life of Arthur Duke of Wellington* (London, 1909) pp. 390–4.

[5] E.Longford *Wellington. Pillar of state* (London, 1972) pp. 398–404; N.Thompson *Wellington after Waterloo* (London, 1986) pp. 257–65; C.Hibbert, *Wellington. A personal history* (London, 1997) pp. 396–404; R.Holmes *Wellington. The Iron Duke* (London, 2002) pp. 293–9; Gerald Wellesley, seventh Duke of Wellington, 'The great Duke's funeral', *History Today* 2 (1952) pp. 778–84. See also M.Greenhalgh, 'The funeral of the Duke of Wellington' *Apollo* (1973) pp. 220–6.

[6] N.Thompson, 'Immortal Wellington: literary tributes to the hero' *Wellington studies III* ed. C.M.Woolgar (Southampton, 1999) pp. 257–80; J.Wolffe *Great deaths. Grieving, religion, and nationhood in Victorian and Edwardian England* (Oxford, 2002) chapter 2; P.W.Sinnema *The wake of Wellington. Englishness in 1852* (Ohio, 2006).

[7] *Hampshire Chronicle*, 14 Aug and 25 Sep 1852; 16 Sep 1852: P.Hawker *The diary of Colonel Peter Hawker 1802–1853* (2 vols., Bath, 1988) ii, pp. 346–7. Hawker (1786–1853) had served in the Fourteenth Light Dragoons before being invalided out after Talavera in 1809. He is best remembered today for his 1814 *Advice to Young Sportsmen*; R.E.Foster *The Duke of Wellington in Hampshire 1817–1852* (Winchester: Hampshire Papers, 30; 2010) pp. 5–6.

[8] Longford, *Pillar of* State, pp. 398–400.

[9] *Illustrated London News*, 13 Nov 1852; Greville to Reeve, 20 Sep 1852: *Letters of Charles Greville and Henry Reeve*, ed. Johnson, p. 213.

[10] 16 Sep 1852: *Hawker Diary*, ii, pp. 346–7; Dickens to Angela Burdett-Coutts, 14 Sep 1852: *Dickens*, pp. 762–3; 16 Sep 1852: *The Gladstone diaries.* Vol. IV: *1848–54* ed. M.R.D.Foot and H.C.G.Matthew (Oxford, 1974) p. 455; A.Hawkins *The forgotten prime minister. The 14th Earl of Derby* (2 vols., Oxford, 2007–8) ii, p. 43.

[11] Hawkins, *Derby*, ii, pp. 43–46.

[12] *Hampshire Chronicle*, 18 Sep 1852; Gleig, *Wellington*, pp. 391–2.

[13] Hawkins, *Derby*, ii, p. 44; letter of 15 Nov 1852: Wellington, 'Great Duke's funeral', p. 784; Wolffe, *Great deaths*, pp. 29–33; *Salisbury and Winchester Journal*, 25 Sep 1852, for Derby's letter.

[14] Wolffe, *Great deaths*, p. 33; Wellington, 'Great Duke's funeral', pp. 779–81; *Annual register*, p. 194.

[15] Wolffe, *Great deaths*, pp. 33–6; Hawkins, *Derby*, pp. 44–6.

[16] Greville, *Journal of the reign of Queen Victoria, 1837–1852*, iii, p. 474; *Hampshire Chronicle*, 25 Sep 1852.

[17] McCarthy, *History of our own times*, ii, pp. 109–10; Thomas Cooper *The life of Thomas Cooper* (London, 1872) pp. 329–30; Greville, *Journal of the reign of Queen Victoria, 1837–1852*, iii, p. 478.

[18] Cooper, *Life of Thomas Cooper*, pp. 330, 333.

[19] *Parliamentary Debates*, 3rd series, cxxiii, cols. 149–54; *Salisbury and Winchester Journal*, 18 Sep 1852; Thompson, *Wellington*, p. 265.

[20] *Salisbury and Winchester Journal*, 18 Sep 1852.

[21] *Hampshire Chronicle*, 25 Sep 1852; *Salisbury and Winchester Journal*, 18 Sep 1852; Palmerston to William Temple, 17 Sep 1852: A.E.Ashley *The life and correspondence of Henry John Temple Viscount Palmerston* (3 vols., London, 1879) ii, pp. 249–50.

[22] *The Times*, 14 Sep 1852; *Salisbury and Winchester Journal*, 18 and 25 Sep 1852.

[23] W.F.Monypenny and G.E.Buckle *The life of Benjamin Disraeli Earl of Beaconsfield* (2 vols., London, 1929) I, pp. 1208–11 and appendix C; R.Blake *Disraeli* (London, 1966) p. 335; *Parliamentary Debates*, 3rd series, cxxiii, cols. 149–54.

[24] Wolffe, *Great deaths*, pp. 38–9 and appendix.

[25] Wolffe, *Great deaths*, p. 278; Sinnema, *Wake of Wellington*, p. 35; *Parliamentary Debates*, 3rd series, cxxiii, cols. 211–14; J.Ridley *Lord Palmerston* (London, 1970) p. 395.

[26] *Hampshire Chronicle*, 25 Sep 1852, for Derby's letter of 20 Sep.

[27] Wellington, 'Great Duke's funeral', p. 778; Longford, *Wellington: pillar of state*, p. 401.

[28] Wellington, 'Great Duke's funeral', pp. 778–81; *Parliamentary Debates*, 3rd series, cxxiii, cols. 211–14.

[29] 10–12 Nov 1852: Hawker, *Hawker diary*, ii, pp. 348–9.

[30] Hibbert, *Wellington*, p. 400; *Annual register*, p. 189; Wolffe, *Great deaths*, p. 36.

[31] C.C.F.Greville *A journal of the reign of Queen Victoria 1852–1860* (3 vols., London, 1887) i, p. 7, 16 Nov 1852; 17 Nov 1852: *Gladstone diaries*, ed. Foot and Mathew, p. 469 and note.

[32] Dickens to Angela Burdett-Coutts, 3 Nov 1852: *Dickens*, pp. 794–95.

[33] 18 Nov 1852: Hawker, *Hawker diary*, ii, p. 349; *Annual register*, pp. 482–96.

[34] 18 Nov 1852: Hawker, *Hawker Diary*, ii, p. 349; *Hampshire Chronicle*, 30 Oct 1852; *Annual register*, p. 192.

[35] *Household Words*, 6 (27 Nov 1852) p. 241; Dickens to the Duke of Devonshire, 11 Nov 1852: *Dickens*, pp. 801–2.

[36] *Annual register*, pp. 482–96.

[37] Cooper, *Life of Thomas Cooper*, pp. 332–33; Hibbert, *Wellington*, p. 402; E.Longford *Victoria RI* (London, 1964) pp. 230–1.

[38] *Annual register* p. 492; Dickens to the Duke of Devonshire, 11 Nov 1852: *Dickens*, pp. 801–2; Dickens to Dean Milman, 4 Nov 1852: *Dickens*, pp. 796–7.

[39] 18 Nov 1852: *Gladstone diaries*, ed. Foot and Mathew, p. 469; Wellington, 'Great Duke's funeral', p. 782.

[40] *Gladstone diaries*, ed. Foot and Mathew, p. 381; Sinnema, *Wake of Wellington*, pp. 75–9.

[41] *Annual register*, p. 191; 18 Nov 1852: Hawker, *Hawker diary*, ii, p. 369; Longford, *Wellington: pillar of state*, pp. 403–4; J.A.Froude *Thomas Carlyle. A history of his life in London, 1834–1881* (2 vols., London, 1884) i, p. 125; Dickens to Angela Burdett-Coutts, 19 Nov 1852: *Dickens*, pp. 803–5; Charles Dickens *Bleak House* (London: Everyman edition, 1907) chapter 53; M.Slater *Charles Dickens* (London, 2009) p. 350.

[42] 25–6 Nov 1852: Hawker, *Hawker Diary*, ii, p. 349.

[43] Longford, *Wellington: pillar of state*, p. 404; *Dickens*, pp. 794–5, note 6; Wolffe, *Great deaths*, pp. 287–93.

[44] *Parliamentary Debates*, 3rd series, cxxiii, cols. 211–14; Greville, *Journal of the reign of Queen Victoria 1852–1860*, i, pp. 9–10 and note.

[45] Dickens to Angela Burdett-Coutts, 23 Sep 1852: *Dickens* pp. 764–5; Froude, *Thomas Carlyle*, i, p. 125; P.Guedalla *The duke* (London, 1974 reprint) p. 476.

[46] Guedalla, *The duke*, p. 476; Longford *Wellington: pillar of state*, p. 402; *Gladstone diaries*, ed. Foot and Matthew, p. 469; *Dickens*, pp. 803–5.

[47] Wolffe, *Great deaths*, pp. 29–31; Longford, *Wellington: pillar of state*, p. 404.

[48] Cooper, *Life of Thomas Cooper*, p. 332; 18 Nov 1852: Hawker, *Hawker diary*, ii, p. 349; 18 Nov 1852: *Gladstone diaries*, p. 469; Foster, *Wellington in Hampshire*, p. 16.

[49] *Parliamentary Debates*, 3rd series, cxxiii, cols. 239–43.

[50] *Dickens*, p. 805, note 1; Liverpool City Record Office, Derby Papers, 920 DER (14) 101/2, Queen Victoria to Derby, 20 Nov 1852.

[51] N. Gash, 'Arthur Wellesley, first Duke of Wellington' *ODNB*, lviii, p. 26; Hibbert, *Wellington*, p. 400.

[52] P.H.Stanhope, fifth Earl Stanhope *Notes of Conversations with the Duke of Wellington 1831–1851* (New York, 1973 reprint) p. 169; Wolffe, *Great deaths*, pp. 287–9 for the ambiguities which surround what precisely constitutes a state funeral.

[53] R.Holmes *Marlborough. England's fragile genius* (London, 2008) p. 475; J.Black *Pitt the Elder* (Cambridge, 1992) pp. 298–300; R.Reilly *Pitt the Younger* (London, 1978) chapter 30; A.Lambert *Nelson: Britannia's god of war* (London, 2004) chapter 16; P.Magnus *Gladstone. A biography* (London, 1954) pp. 435–40; G.Best *Churchill. A study in greatness* (London, 2001) pp. 325–7.

[54] Gladstone died on 19 May and was buried on 28 May 1898. Churchill died on 24 Jan and was buried on 30 Jan 1965.

[55] W.Hague *William Pitt the Younger* (London, 2004) pp. xxi–xxiv; Reilly, *Pitt the Younger*, p. 346.

[56] *Parliamentary Debates*, 3rd series, cxxiii, cols. 211–14.

[57] *Annual register*, p. 193; Lambert, *Nelson*, p. 315; Wolffe, *Great deaths*, pp. 54–5.

[58] Hague, *Pitt the Younger*, p. 579; Lambert, *Nelson*, chapter 16.

[59] R.Gaunt *Sir Robert Peel. The life and legacy* (London, 2010) chapter 7; D.Cannadine *History in our time* (London, 1998) p. 232; Hague, *Pitt the Younger*, p. 579.

[60] C.Hibbert *Nelson. A personal history* (London, 1994) chapter 35; A.Lambert, *The immortal and the hero. Nelson and Wellington* (Southampton, 2005).

[61] Lambert, *The immortal and the hero*, p. 18.

[62] Lambert, *Nelson*, chapters 16–17.

[63] Thompson, 'Immortal Wellington', p. 261; Wolffe, *Great deaths*, pp. 33–4.

[64] R.Gaunt, 'Wellington in petticoats: the Duke as caricature' in *Wellington Studies IV* ed. C.M.Woolgar (Southampton, 2008) pp. 163–6; R.Jenkins *Churchill* (London, 2001) pp. 889–90.

[65] Jenkins, *Churchill*, pp. 911–12; Best, *Churchill*, pp. 325–7; P.Addison *Churchill. The unexpected hero* (Oxford, 2005) pp. 244–5.

[66] Best, *Churchill*, p. 326; Hague, *Pitt the Younger*, pp. xxi–xxv; Hibbert, *Nelson*, chapters 34–5.

[67] *Annual register*, p. 192 for the 1.5 million estimate; *Hampshire Chronicle*, 13 and 20 Nov 1852, for claims of 2 million. Mainland Britain's population in 1851 was 20,942,000. See E.J.Evans *The forging of the modern state. Early industrial Britain 1783–1870* (London, 1983) p. 404.

[68] K.T.Hoppen *The mid-Victorian generation 1846–1886* (Oxford, 1998) pp. 215–17; C.M.Woolgar *Wellington, his papers and the nineteenth-century revolution in communication* (Southampton, 2009); Gaunt, 'Wellington in petticoats', pp. 142, 144, 163; R.E.Foster, 'Mr Punch and the Iron Duke' *History Today* 34 (1984) pp. 36–42.

[69] *Hampshire Chronicle*, 23 and 30 Oct 1852; 6, 13 and 20 Nov 1852.

[70] *Great Victorian lives. An era in obituaries* ed. I.Brunskill and A.Sanders (London, 2007) pp. vii–xiii; Greville to Reeve 20 Sep 1852: *Letters of Charles Greville and Henry Reeve*, ed., Johnson, p. 213; Thompson 'Immortal Wellington', p. 264; *Hampshire Chronicle*, 25 Sep 1852.

[71] Wolffe, *Great deaths*, pp. 17–20; Foster, *Wellington in Hampshire*, pp. 15–17.

[72] P.Mathias *The first industrial nation. An economic history of Britain 1700–1914* (second edition, London, 1983) chapter 10; Evans, *Forging of the modern state*, pp. 117–19, 397–8; N.Gash *Aristocracy and people. Britain 1815–1865*

(London, 1979) p. 333; B.Hilton *A mad, bad, and dangerous people? England 1783–1846* (Oxford, 2006) p. 15, for Wellington's comment.

[73] *Hampshire Chronicle*, 25 Sep, 23 Oct and 20 Nov 1852.

[74] *1858 Question Papers* (Cambridge, 2008 reprint) pp. 31, 68. Lines from *Punch*, cited in *Hampshire Chronicle*, 25 Sep 1852.